# DEMOCRATS AND REPUBLICANS — RHETORIC AND REALITY

# Democrats and Republicans — Rhetoric and Reality

## Comparing the Voters in Statistics and Anecdotes

Joseph Fried

Algora Publishing
New York

Library of Congress Cataloging-in-Publication Data —

Fried, Joseph.
  Democrats and Republicans : rhetoric and reality / Joseph Fried.
    p. cm.
  Includes bibliographical references and index.
  ISBN 978-0-87586-603-1 (trade paper: alk. paper) — ISBN 978-0-87586-604-8 (hard
cover: alk. paper) — ISBN 978-0-87586-605-5 (ebook) 1. Party affiliation—United States.
2. Democratic Party (U.S.) 3. Republican Party (U.S. : 1854- ) I. Title.

  JK2271.F75 2008
  324.273—dc22
                        2007050042

Front Cover: The cover illustration is the political cartoon, "They're Off, Again!" by
Clifford K. Berryman. It was first published on September 8, 1949 in the Washington
Star newspaper, and is now part of the Clifford K. Berryman Collection in the United
States Senate Collection of the Center for Legislative Archives of the National Archives,
in Washington, D.C.

Printed in the United States

For
Nina,
My wife, advisor, and best friend for nearly 40 years

*

For
My son, David,
Who has taught me more than he will ever realize

*

And for
My mother, Concetta Fried,
To whom I owe life, confidence, and common sense

# TABLE OF CONTENTS

PREFACE

Getting tired of books filled with political bombast and hot air? Here's an alternative. Within these pages you will find no unsupported views, only comprehensive and objective information. Questions about the constituents of America's two major political parties are answered in a straightforward, thorough, and easy-to-understand manner. Much of the information is presented graphically.

Most chapters have a theme, examining, for example, who pays more taxes, who is smarter, or who is the better citizen. The themes were not selected with the intent of making one political group look better than the other. Rather, they were chosen because they involve verifiable distinctions, distinctions which have two essential attributes:

- They relate to a person's actions, achievements, or specific preferences — not just general thoughts or wishes.
- They can be supported with credible evidence.

This concept can be illustrated with the following example: A verifiable distinction would exist if we had credible survey evidence showing that, during the last three months, Democrats were more likely than Republicans to give money to charity. A verifiable distinction would not exist if the evidence merely showed that Democrats were more likely to say that society should help the poor. In the former case we have a record of personal actions or achievements; in the latter case we simply have words.

The evidence in this book came from the survey results of large and well-respected nonpartisan organizations. Where possible, I used data from the General Social Survey (GSS) and the American National Election Studies (NES). GSS has been accumulating data since the early 1970s, and NES has been conducting its surveys since the early 1950s. Where more support was needed, I looked to surveys conducted by the Pew Research Center for the People and the Press (Pew), the Gallup Organization, the Institute for Public Policy and

1

Social Research, Harris Interactive, and other well-established research entities. In some instances, conclusions are supported by non-survey evidence. This is particularly true with regard to the chapters on taxes and Social Security. In all cases, however, credible sources are used, identified, explained, and referenced.[1]

In addition to comparison data, you will find lots of rhetoric in this book. There are numerous quotations from Democrats, Republicans, philosophers, comedians, pundits, actors, statesmen, and garden-variety fruitcakes. Some of this rhetoric will make you think, some will make you laugh, some will make you mad, and some will make you wince. There was no particular method (or objectivity) used in the selection of rhetoric; I simply chose the quotations that felt right to me.

No doubt some people will hate the book and feel it is mean-spirited, biased, or both. In anticipation of this reaction, let me give a brief defense. No matter how careful we try to be, comparisons are never completely fair, and one side (or both) will probably be slighted. Nevertheless, it would be a dull world if we did not make comparisons. More importantly, comparisons are needed to promote greater understanding and to facilitate progress in our lives. How else do we learn how the other guy thinks, and how else do we identify shortcomings so that solutions can be achieved? Speaking of solutions, Chapter 12 is filled with constructive lessons that, in my opinion, can be learned from the comparisons made throughout the book.

Have I been biased in selecting and presenting the comparison data? I hope not. I am not a political pundit; I am a CPA who has strived to present quantified information in a clear and balanced manner. This is a very transparent work, with sources and methods described in detail. Almost all source information is publicly available and, in nearly every case, relevant statistical information is provided. If a reader believes that I have erred, I hope he will contact me via the publisher so that the appropriate correction can be made.

Finally, I'd like to discuss a matter of potential controversy: the use of the Democrat-Republican paradigm. Some may wonder why this book makes comparisons based on party identification rather than political ideology (e.g., liberal versus conservative). I compare Democrats and Republicans because party identification is where the "rubber hits the road." In America, most of us support a candidate — with time, effort, money, or votes — based on his identification with one of the major political parties. In this manner, our political feelings are connected to tangible action of some sort. This is not true with regard to our ideological identifications such as "liberal" or "conservative."

In addition, the term "conservative" can be very misleading because it is not well understood. How many people realize that, during the last 35 years, 25 to 50 percent of all self-identified "conservatives" have been Democrats? And, how many realize that Democratic conservatives and Republican conservatives are as

---

1 The *General Social Survey* is conducted by the National Opinion Research Center (NORC), and the *National Election Studies* are produced by Stanford University and the University of Michigan. Please see Appendix F on page 364 for more information regarding survey sources used.

different as "night and day"? More discussion of these matters is found in Chapter 11 and in Appendix E.

I believe this is an informative, fair, and constructive book that can broaden your understanding of Democrats and Republicans. Also, it's pretty good if you just need some ammo for that next encounter with your brother-in-law.

## Chapter 1: Lifestyle Differences

### Introduction

Do Republicans live on the edge?

> Live this day as if it will be your last. Remember that you will only find "tomorrow" on the calendars of fools. Forget yesterday's defeats and ignore the problems of tomorrow. This is it. Doomsday.
>
> — Og Mandino, American essayist and psychologist[2]

Now that you have been inspired by Mandino, prepare yourself for oodles of information about Democratic and Republican lifestyles — possibly more than you want. This is my everything-but-the-kitchen-sink chapter, and it contains trivia in addition to matters of consequence. It is a smorgasbord of the particulars that distinguish Democratic and Republican lifestyles.

Before getting to those details, however, consider the "bottom line:" Who leads the more exciting life? Surprisingly, it is Republicans. At least, that is what they think.

### General excitement

When asked, "Do you find life exciting, pretty routine, or dull?" Republicans are consistently more likely to say that life is exciting. As seen in Figure 1, below, this tendency has existed for at least 30 years.

---

2 Og Mandino (attributed), "Thinkexist.Com."

*Figure 1. "In general, do you find life exciting, pretty routine, or dull?" (General Social Surveys (GSS) conducted in 1975 through 2006, based on, left to right, 1946, 3026, 3650, 3233, 2319, and 3355 cases, with a confidence level of 99+% for all differences, and with relative proportions of, left to right, .85, .87, .82, .83, .82, and .88)*[3][4]

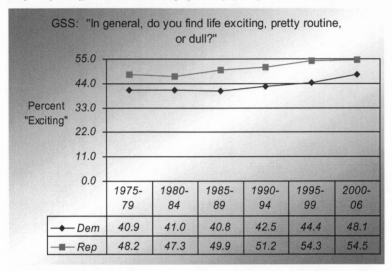

*Figure 2. "How often would you say you have time on your hands that you don't know what to do with...?" (combined results of GSS surveys conducted in 1982 and 2004, based on, left to right, 575, 794, and 1369 cases, with a confidence level of 99+% for all columns, and with relative proportions of, left to right, .74, .78, and .77)*

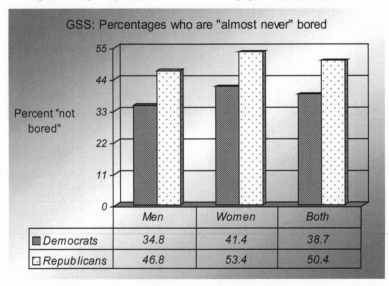

---

3 For the complete citation to the *General Social Survey*, and for appropriate acknowledgements and statements of limitations, please see Appendix F on page 364.

4 As explained in Appendix D, the relative proportion (RP) is simply the percentage of Democrats divided by the percentage of Republicans. For example, for the first column of Figure 1 it is 40.9% divided by 48.2%.

---

In addition, Republicans are less likely to be bored. Although equal percent-ages (about 26%) of Democrats and Republicans say they "always feel rushed even to do things [they] have to do," there seems to be a boredom gap for the other 74 percent. Republican men and women are more likely to say that they rarely have extra time they "don't know what to do with." See Figure 2, above.

Thus, Republicans are more apt to find life exciting, and less likely to be bored. With that matter settled, let's look deeper into the lifestyles microscope.

## DETAILS

*Family, relationships, and sex*

### Sex

#### Multiple Partners

Republicans tend to keep their shades drawn, although there is sel-dom any reason why they should. Democrats ought to, but don't.

— Anonymous (from a document published in the Congressional Record on October 1, 1974)

*Figure 3. Percentage with 2 or more sex partners during the last 12 months (combined results of 6 GSS surveys conducted from 1996 through 2006, based on, left to right, 3662, 4910, and 8572 cases, with confidence level of 99+% for all columns, and with relative proportions of, left to right, 1.52, 1.63, and 1.41)*

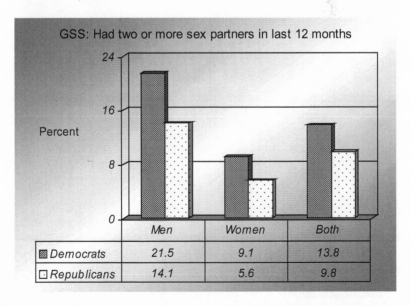

| GSS: Had two or more sex partners in last 12 months | | |
|---|---|---|
| | Men | Women | Both |
| Democrats | 21.5 | 9.1 | 13.8 |
| Republicans | 14.1 | 5.6 | 9.8 |

If Republicans lead more exciting lives, it is not in the area of sexual relations. The results of several GSS surveys, shown in Figure 3, tell us that Democrats are more likely to have multiple sexual partners.

### Condoms

The multiple partners may explain the next statistic: Democrats are more likely to use condoms.

*Figure 4. "The last time you had sex, was a condom used?" (combined results of 6 GSS surveys taken from 1996 through 2006, based on, left to right, 3557, 4636, and 8193 cases, with confidence level of 99+% for all three columns, and with relative proportions of, left to right, 1.40, 1.59, and 1.46)*

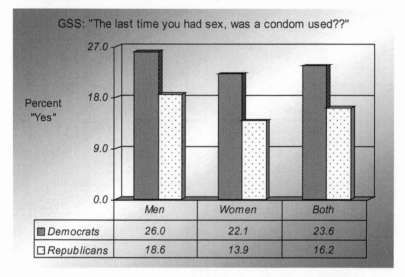

GSS: "The last time you had sex, was a condom used??"

| | Men | Women | Both |
|---|---|---|---|
| ▨ Democrats | 26.0 | 22.1 | 23.6 |
| ☐ Republicans | 18.6 | 13.9 | 16.2 |

### No Sex at All

> Soon after the president and the president's defenders were claiming nightly that oral sex is not sex, the Washington Post reported on oral sex parties being held by local teenagers. The kids explained that the president said oral sex didn't count.

— Author and political activist Ann Coulter[5]

Although Democrats are more likely to have multiple partners, they are also a little more likely to have no sex at all (at least, nothing they consider to be sex).

The results shown in Figure 5 may explain why Democrats are less happy. (See Chapter 9.)

*Figure 5. "How many sex partners have you had in the last 12 months?" (combined results of 6 GSS surveys conducted from 1996 through 2006, based on, left to right, 3662, 4910, and 8572 cases, with confidence level of 98% for men, 98% for women, and 99+% for both, and with relative proportions of, left to right, 1.19, 1.12, and 1.21)*

---

5 Ann Coulter, "Toot in the Bush," in *Uexpress.com* (August 25, 1999), Retrieved September 1, 2006, from: http://www.uexpress.com/anncoulter/index.html?uc_full_date=19990825.

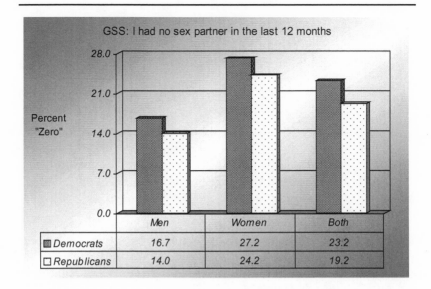

*One Partner Only*

At just about every stage of their lives, Republicans are more likely to have one, and only one, sexual partner.

*Figure 6. Percentages who had exactly one sex partner during last 12 months (combined results of 6 GSS surveys conducted between 1996 and 2006, based on, left to right, 1333, 1829, 1865, 1376, 966, and 740 cases, with confidence level of, left to right, zero (i.e., no significance), 99+%, 99%, 99+%, 99+%, and 91% (marginal), with relative proportions of, left to right, n/a, .88, .94, .88, .83, and .86)*

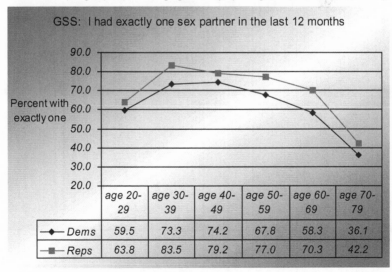

### Gay Sex

One of the biggest un-kept secrets in Washington, DC is that closeted gay Republicans are everywhere — the White House, Republican Party organizations, the halls of Congress, the most influential law offices, and the most powerful lobbying firms in our nation's capitol.

— Columnist Brian van de Mark (4 weeks before the Mark Foley intern scandal became public, and a full year before the toe-tapping exploits of Senator Larry Craig)[6]

Among male Democrats and Republicans, there is a marked difference in the acknowledged rate of homosexual activity. This is evident from a review of Figure 7, which shows that a "gay gap" began to develop after the 1980s. The disparity might be attributable to gays leaving the GOP, or to an increased willingness on the part of Democrats to acknowledge gay sexual orientation.

*Figure 7. (Asked of men) "Have your sex partners in the last 12 months been men?" (combined results of several GSS surveys conducted from 1988 through 2006, based on, left to right, 1147, 1941, and 1957 cases, with confidence level of, left to right, zero (i.e., no significance), 99+%, and 99+%, and with relative proportions of, left to right, n/a, 2.64, and 3.14)*

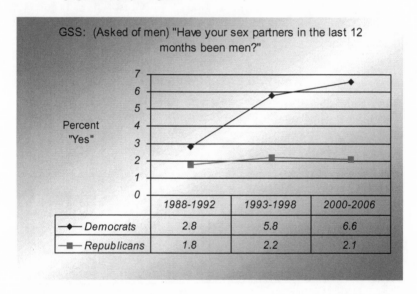

| GSS: (Asked of men) "Have your sex partners in the last 12 months been men?" | | | |
|---|---|---|---|
| | 1988-1992 | 1993-1998 | 2000-2006 |
| Democrats | 2.8 | 5.8 | 6.6 |
| Republicans | 1.8 | 2.2 | 2.1 |

For women, there also is a statistically significant gay gap, albeit very tiny. By 2.6 to 1.7 percent, Democratic women are slightly more likely to have had sex with a female in the last year (6038 cases from 1988 through 2006, with 99% confidence level, and with a relative proportion of 1.53).

---

6 Brian van De Mark, "Gay Republicans - an Oxymoron?," in *Gay & Lesbian Times* (www.gaylesbiantimes.com, August 31, 2006), Retrieved September 1, 2006, from: http://www.gaylesbiantimes.com/?id=6206.

*Sex Sundries*

How did sex come to be thought of as dirty in the first place? God must have been a Republican.

— Will Durst, Political satirist[7]

Democratic males are a bit more likely than Republican males to engage in sex for money. See Table 1. For females there is no statistically significant difference. Less than 2 percent of women state that they have engaged in such conduct.

*Table 1. Other surveys involving sex*

| Issue | Survey | Dem % "yes" | Rep % "yes" | No. of cases | Conf % | *RP |
|---|---|---|---|---|---|---|
| "Have you ever had sex with a person you paid or who paid you for sex? — males | 8 GSS surveys from 1991 through 2006 | 17.8 | 13.9 | 5018 | +99 | 1.28 |
| "Do you or did you ... feel sexually attracted to someone of the same sex?" | 2006 Harris Interactive survey | 11.0 | 5.0 | 634 | 99 | 2.20 |

*RP is relative proportion, which is the Democratic % divided by the Republican %.

## Marriage

If variety is the spice of life, marriage is the big can of leftover Spam.

— The late Johnny Carson, Comedian[8]

*Marriage Rates*

Republicans are now far more likely to be married, with a 9-point gap for men and a 20-point gap for women. This marriage disparity developed during the last 30 to 40 years, prior to which, marriage rates were similar. Male marriage rates are shown in Figure 8, below.

*Figure 8. Are you married? (Men) (various surveys of the American National Election Studies (NES) conducted in 1952 through 2004, based on, left to right, 592, 2386, 2357, 2507, 2841, and 2047 cases, with no statistical significance for the 1952 through 1974 years, with 99% or more confidence level for the 1975 through 2004 years, and with relative proportions of, left to right, n/a, n/a, n/a, .94, .92, .86)[9]*

7 Will Durst (attributed), "Brainyquote.Com."

8 Johnny Carson (attributed), "Quotationz.Com."

9 For the complete citation to the American National Election Studies (NES), and for appropriate acknowledgements and statements of limitations, please see Appendix F on page 364.

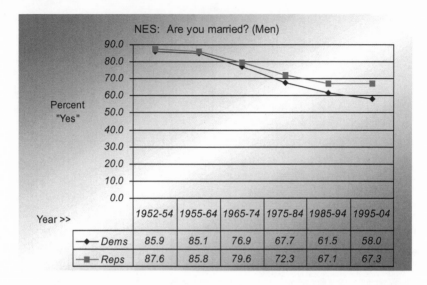

| Year >> | 1952-54 | 1955-64 | 1965-74 | 1975-84 | 1985-94 | 1995-04 |
|---|---|---|---|---|---|---|
| ◆ Dems | 85.9 | 85.1 | 76.9 | 67.7 | 61.5 | 58.0 |
| ■ Reps | 87.6 | 85.8 | 79.6 | 72.3 | 67.1 | 67.3 |

There has been a "rebound" in marriage rates among women — particularly Republican women. (See Figure 9, below.) Is this due to welfare reform (which was enacted in the mid-90s), to disenchantment with feminism, or to general frustration with the single life scene?

*Figure 9. Are you married? (Women) (various NES surveys conducted in 1952 through 2004, based on, left to right, 735, 3035, 3344, 3694, 3751, and 2677 cases, with no statistical significance for the 1952 through 1954 years, and with 99% or more confidence level for the 1975 through 2004 years, and with relative proportions of, left to right, n/a, 1.10, .92, .86, .80, and .72)*

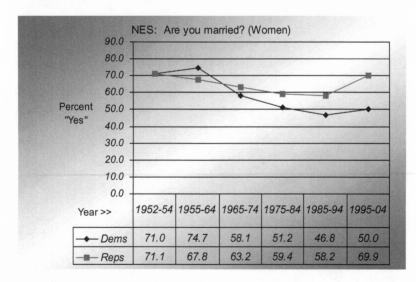

| Year >> | 1952-54 | 1955-64 | 1965-74 | 1975-84 | 1985-94 | 1995-04 |
|---|---|---|---|---|---|---|
| ◆ Dems | 71.0 | 74.7 | 58.1 | 51.2 | 46.8 | 50.0 |
| ■ Reps | 71.1 | 67.8 | 63.2 | 59.4 | 58.2 | 69.9 |

## Reasons Not Married

Don't marry for money; you can borrow it cheaper.

— Scottish proverb

There are three reasons Democrats are less likely than Republicans to be married, and each reason applies to both genders and to people in different age groups. First, they are more likely to have never married. This is particularly true for Democratic females.

*Figure 10. People who never married (combined results of 5 NES surveys conducted from 1996 through 2004, based on, left to right, 2044, 1519, 2665, and 1915 cases, with confidence level of, left to right, 96%, 99+%, 99+%, and 99+%, and with relative proportions of, left to right, 1.18, 1.37, 1.94, and 2.32)*

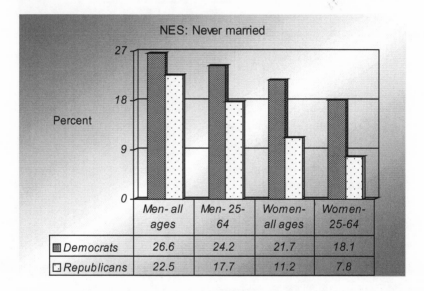

| | Men- all ages | Men- 25-64 | Women- all ages | Women- 25-64 |
|---|---|---|---|---|
| Democrats | 26.6 | 24.2 | 21.7 | 18.1 |
| Republicans | 22.5 | 17.7 | 11.2 | 7.8 |

Democrats are also less likely to be married because of divorce or separation.

> We think there's a war that hasn't been discussed, and that's the Republican war on the American family.
>
> — Howard Dean, Former governor of Vermont, and Chairman of the Democratic National Committee[10]

The divorce divide is particularly pronounced among women.

---

10 Howard Dean interviewed on, "Face the Nation," (Transcript: CBS News, October 29, 2006).

*Figure 11. People who are divorced or separated (combined results of 5 NES surveys conducted from 1996 through 2004, based on, left to right, 2044, 1519, 2665, and 1915 cases, with confidence level of 95%, 91% (marginal), 99+%, and 99+%, and with relative proportions of, left to right, 1.35, 1.33, 1.47, and 1.54)*

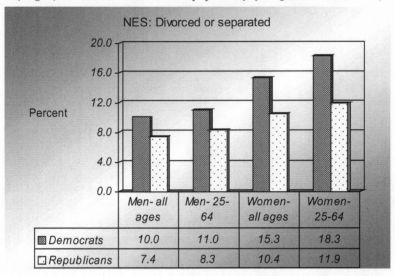

Finally, Democrats are more likely to be unmarried because of the death of a spouse. This is the case even when we restrict the analysis to people aged 25 to 64 years. (See Figure 12, below.)

*Figure 12. People who are widows/widowers (combined results of 5 NES surveys conducted from 1996 through 2004, based on, left to right, 2044, 1519, 2665, and 1915 cases, with confidence level of, left to right, 99+%, 98%, 99+%, and 98%, and with relative proportions of, left to right, of 2.04, 4.50, 1.53, and 2.00)*

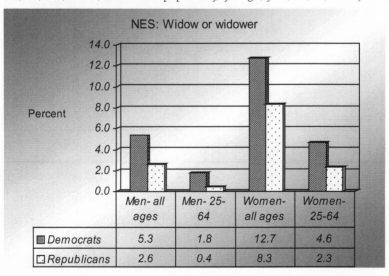

## Premarital Sex

It isn't premarital sex if you have no intention of getting married.
— George Burns, Comedian[11]

Democrats are less likely to view premarital sex negatively. When asked if premarital sex is always wrong, GSS obtained the following results:

*Figure 13. "If a man and woman have sex relations before marriage, do you think it is always wrong...?" (various GSS surveys conducted in 1986 through 2006, based on, left to right, 2848, 2542, 3283, and 2237 cases, with confidence level of at least 99% for all points, and with relative proportions of, left to right, .84, .81, .71, and .70)*

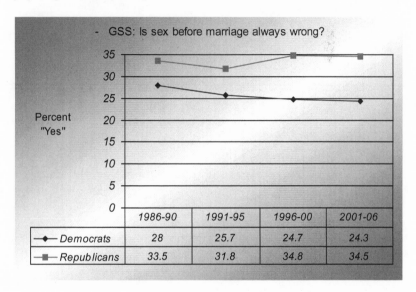

GSS: Is sex before marriage always wrong?

| | 1986-90 | 1991-95 | 1996-00 | 2001-06 |
|---|---|---|---|---|
| Democrats | 28 | 25.7 | 24.7 | 24.3 |
| Republicans | 33.5 | 31.8 | 34.8 | 34.5 |

## Adultery

The best thing to do with the best things in life is to give them up.
— Movie star Doris Day[12]

Democrats are more likely to acknowledge having sex with others while married. Are they simply being more truthful than Republicans, or are they really more adulterous? If the latter is the case, this might explain the higher divorce rate.

*Figure 14. Had sex with others while married? (9 GSS surveys conducted from 1991 through 2006, based on 3821 cases for men, 5584 cases for women, and 9405 for both, with confidence level of 99+% for all 3 columns, and with relative proportions of, left to right, 1.24, 1.44, and 1.26)*

---

11 George Burns (attributed), "Lifestyles News," Retrieved April 3, 2007, from: http://www.life-stylesnews.com.
12 Doris Day cited in, "Columbia World of Quotations," (Columbia University Press, 1996).

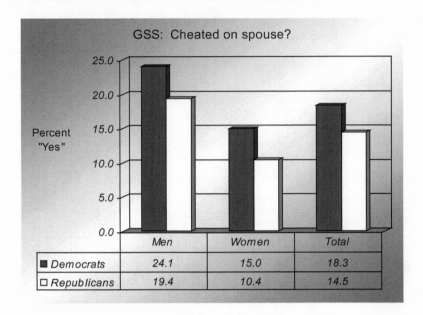

| GSS: Cheated on spouse? | Men | Women | Total |
| --- | --- | --- | --- |
| ■ Democrats | 24.1 | 15.0 | 18.3 |
| □ Republicans | 19.4 | 10.4 | 14.5 |

### Children

#### *Who Is More Likely To Have Children?*

Democrats and Republicans are equally likely to have children. GSS surveys of 11,092 Democrats and Republicans, conducted from 1996 through 2006, show that the average Democrat has 1.94 children and the average Republican has 1.91 — a difference that is not statistically significant. If we limit the survey to Democrats and Republicans aged 30 years or less, the average Democrat has .57 children and the average Republican has .59, a difference that is still not significant.

#### *Reality check — What about the so-called "fertility gap"?*

In a much-discussed Op-Ed in the Wall Street Journal, Arthur C. Brooks (Professor at Syracuse University) noted that liberals are in danger of becoming politically disadvantaged due to the higher reproductive rate of conservatives.[13] Indeed, liberals do reproduce at a much lower rate than conservatives. However, as stressed in Chapter 11, the liberal-conservative paradigm must not be confused with the Democrat-Republican paradigm. For Democrats and Republicans there is procreation parity.

Although the likelihood of Democrats and Republicans having children is roughly equal, there is a large difference in the reproduction rate when we limit the analysis to unmarried Democrats and Republicans.

> Illegitimacy is something we should talk about in terms of not having it.
> — Vice President Dan Quayle[14]

---

13 Arthur C. Brooks, "The Fertility Gap," *Wall Street Journal*, August 22, 2006.
14 Vice President Dan Quayle (attributed), "The Quotations Page."

Unmarried Democrats are far more likely than unmarried Republicans to have children in the home, and this trend has existed since the 1950s.

*Figure 15. Do you have a child under age 18 living in the household? (unmarried men and women) (various NES surveys conducted in 1955 through 2004, based on, left to right, 1170, 585, 1872, 2011, and 910 cases, with confidence level of 90% (marginal) for the far left difference and 99+% for all other differences, and with relative proportions of, left to right, 1.20, 2.01, 1.53, 1.35, and 1.77)*

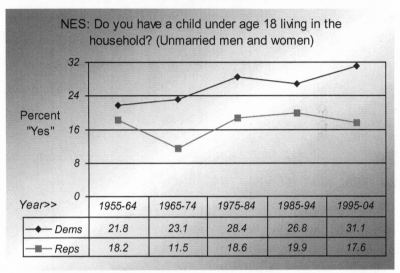

| NES: Do you have a child under age 18 living in the household? (Unmarried men and women) | | | | | |
|---|---|---|---|---|---|
| Year>> | 1955-64 | 1965-74 | 1975-84 | 1985-94 | 1995-04 |
| ◆ Dems | 21.8 | 23.1 | 28.4 | 26.8 | 31.1 |
| ■ Reps | 18.2 | 11.5 | 18.6 | 19.9 | 17.6 |

Just about all of the difference shown in Figure 15 is attributable to women. Unmarried Democratic and Republican men are about equally likely to have a child under age 18 in the home.

### Children at What Age?

> The children of adolescents are more likely to be born prematurely and 50 percent more likely to be low-birth weight babies ... suffer poorer health ... child abuse or neglect ... [perform] more poorly on tests of cognitive ability ... drop out of high school. ... [T]he sons of young teen mothers are nearly three times more likely to be incarcerated than those born to adult mothers.

> — "Fact Sheet" on the web site of the FSU Center for Prevention & Early Intervention Policy[15]

It is widely acknowledged that babies born to teen parents are at greater risk with regard to a variety of health, social, and educational problems. Figure 16, below, shows the percentage of Democratic and Republican men, under the age of 50, who were aged 19 years or less when their first child was born. From this graphic, it is clear that Democratic males are almost twice as likely to have a

---

15 "The Children of Teen Parents - Fact Sheet," April 15, 2005, FSU Center for Prevention & Early Intervention Policy, Retrieved April 3, 2007, from http://www.cpeip.fsu.edu/resourceFiles/resourceFile_78.pdf.

child by the age of 19. The average difference in age, when the first child is born, is about 13 months.[16]

*Figure 16. What was your age when your first child was born? (Men aged up to 50 years) (6 GSS surveys conducted from 1996 through 2006, based on 1543 cases, with overall confidence level of 99+%, and with a relative proportion of 1.97)*

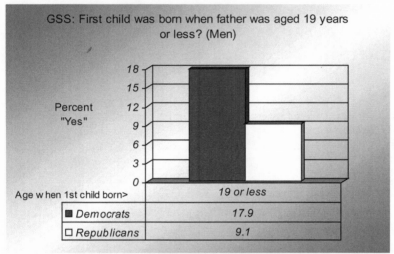

In Figure 17, below, we see a similar pattern for women. Democratic women are much more likely to procreate in their teenage years.

*Figure 17. What was your age when your first child was born? (Women aged up to 50 years) (6 GSS surveys conducted between 1996 and 2006, based on 2412 cases, with overall confidence level of 99+%, and with a relative proportion of 1.64)*

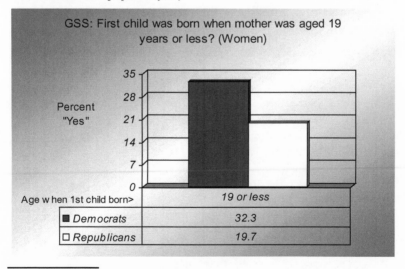

---

16 The analysis is limited to Democratic and Republicans aged
   50 years or less at the time of the surveys.

Democratic women are about 60 percent more likely to have children while still teenagers.[17] For women (under the age of 50), the average difference in the age of procreation is about 12.7 months.

*Figure 18. Do you agree that it is sometimes necessary to discipline a child with a "good, hard spanking"? (5 GSS surveys conducted in 1998 through 2006, based on, left to right, 1837, 2582, and 4419 cases, with confidence level of 99+% for all columns, and with relative proportions of, left to right, .91, .93, and .91)*

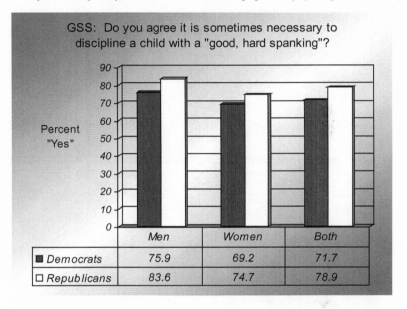

*Spanking*

A Democratic assemblywoman from Mountain View says she will submit a bill next week ... proposing that California become the first state in the nation to make spanking of children 3 years old and under a misdemeanor. Penalties could include child-rearing classes for offenders to one year in jail.

— Jennifer Steinhauer, January 21, 2007, the New York Times

Since 1986 the General Social Survey has been asking people if they believe in spanking. In most of those years the views of Democrats and Republicans were almost the same. However, a small divide has developed.

*Computer Filters*

Republicans are more likely to have use computer filters to prevent their children from viewing pornography on the Internet. The results in Figure 19 pertain to parents with computers in the home.

---

17 The analysis is limited to Democratic and Republicans aged 50 years or less at the time of the surveys.

*Figure 19. "Does your home computer have a filter installed to prevent access to pornography ..." (Limited to parents) (2005 Pew News Interest Index, based on 242 cases, with confidence level of 96%, and with a relative proportion of .78)*[18]

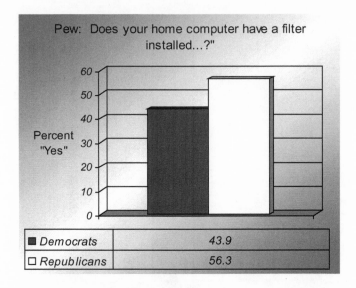

| Pew: Does your home computer have a filter installed...?" | |
| --- | --- |
| ■ Democrats | 43.9 |
| □ Republicans | 56.3 |

*Figure 20. "Is this a religious or church affiliated school ...?" (2005 Pew Religion and Public Life Survey, based on 53 cases, with confidence level of 94% (marginal), and with a relative proportion of .79)*

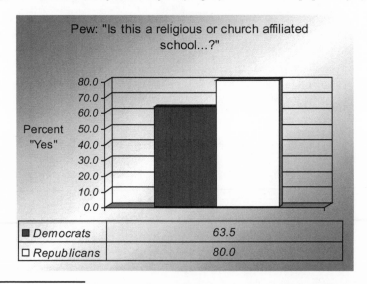

| Pew: "Is this a religious or church affiliated school...?" | |
| --- | --- |
| ■ Democrats | 63.5 |
| □ Republicans | 80.0 |

---

18 The Pew News Interest Index survey, and all "Pew" surveys in this book, was conducted and released to the public by the Pew Center for Research Center for the People & the Press, which is sponsored by the Pew Charitable Trusts. For appropriate acknowledgements and statements of limitations, please see Appendix F on page 364.

## Private Schools

President-elect Bill Clinton, who has made improving public education a priority throughout his political career, announced today that he was sending his daughter, Chelsea, to an expensive private school attended by many children of Washington's power elite....

— Columnist Thomas L. Friedman[19]

Constituents of the two parties are equally likely to send their kids to private schools according to a Pew 2005 Religion and Public Life Survey of 352 Democrats and Republicans. However, Republicans are significantly more likely to send their kids to religiously-affiliated schools. See Figure 20, above.

### Family, Friends, Thugs and Activities

Miscellaneous matters related to social activities and acquaintances are noted in Table 2, below.

*Table 2. Miscellaneous issues related to family friends and activities*

| Issue | Survey | Dem % "yes" | Rep % "yes" | No. of cases | Conf % | *RP |
|---|---|---|---|---|---|---|
| Are you "acquainted with" one or more people in prison? | GSS 2006 survey | 23.8 | 13.4 | 375 | 99 | 1.78 |
| Have any of your close friends or relatives given their life while serving in the military? | Rasmussen November 2007 | 34.0 | 41.0 | **1000 | 95 | .83 |
| Are you "acquainted with" one or more people in the military? | GSS 2006 survey | 52.6 | 64.9 | 421 | 99 | .81 |
| Are you "acquainted with" one or more women "in a romantic relationship with a man to whom they are not married"? | GSS 2006 survey | 69.6 | 54.9 | 361 | +99 | 1.27 |
| Are one or more of the women in your extended family "in a romantic relationship with a man to whom they are not married"? | GSS 2006 survey | 45.6 | 34.0 | 300 | 96 | 1.34 |

---

19 Thomas Friedman, "The New Presidency," *The New York Times*, January 6, 2003, 1.

| On a typical week day, do you contact 10 or more individuals (people you know) in person, on the telephone, via email, etc.? | GSS 2006 survey | 58.6 | **69.1** | 823 | +99 | .85 |
|---|---|---|---|---|---|---|
| Do you have a friend, colleague, or family member who is gay? | Pew Late March 2005 Political Typology Callback | **48.7** | 39.0 | 708 | +99 | 1.25 |
| Do you have home schooling friends or family members? | Rasmussen August 2004 | 36.0 | **50.0** | **1000 | 95 | .72 |
| Yesterday, did your family have a meal together? | Pew 2002 Biennial Media Consumption Survey | 60.9 | **67.7** | 966 | 99 | .90 |
| Does your family discuss politics with a passion on holidays? | Rasmussen December 2007 | 13.0 | **22.0** | **1000 | 95 | .59 |
| Do you discuss politics with family and friends? | Combined results of NES surveys from 1984 through 2004 | 64.0 | **69.5** | 12642 | +99 | .92 |

*RP is relative proportion, which is the Democratic % divided by the Republican %.

**Case numbers include independents and others in addition to Democrats and Republicans.

*Health and fitness*

### Who Is Healthier?

The best activities for your health are pumping and humping.

— Arnold Schwarzenegger, Actor and Republican Governor of California[20]

### General Health

Republicans seem to be healthier — or at least they think they are. As shown in Figure 21, below, this is true for both males and females.

*Figure 21. "Would you say that your own health, in general, is excellent?" (24 GSS surveys conducted in 1972 through 2006, based on, left to right, 10278, 13974, and 24252 cases, with confidence level of 99+% for all columns and with relative proportions of, left to right, .84, .78, and .80)*

20 Arnold Schwarzenegger (attributed), "Brainyquote.Com."

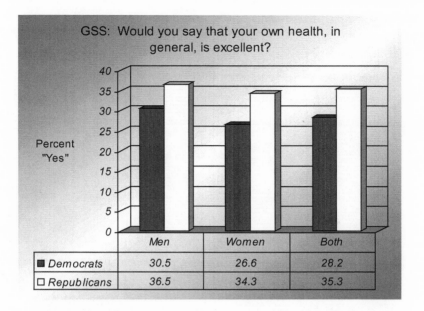

GSS: Would you say that your own health, in general, is excellent?

Percent "Yes"

| | Men | Women | Both |
|---|---|---|---|
| ■ Democrats | 30.5 | 26.6 | 28.2 |
| □ Republicans | 36.5 | 34.3 | 35.3 |

A recent Gallup analysis shows a similar disparity, with Democrats being less likely to claim "excellent" health, by 27 to 35 percent.[21] In addition, Democrats are less likely to say that, during the prior 4 weeks, they had "a lot of energy" all or most of the time (62% to 71%),[22] and Democrats are more likely to state that poor health is a limiting factor in regard to "moderate activities, such as moving a table, pushing a vacuum cleaner, bowling, or playing golf" (15% to 5%).[23] Another survey found that Democrats were more likely to state they had a "condition that substantially limits one or more basic physical activities such as walking, climbing stairs, reaching, lifting, or carrying" (21% to 12%).[24] Among Democrats and Republicans who are not gainfully employed, Democrats are about twice as likely to say they are disabled (25% to 12%).[25]

21 Joseph Carroll, "Strong Majority of Americans in Good Physical and Mental Health," *The Gallup News Service* (December 8, 2006), Retrieved January 2, 2007, from Http://brain.gallup.com.

22 GSS 2000, based on 817 cases, with statistical significance of 99% and relative proportion of .87.

23 GSS 2000, based on 811 cases, with statistical significance of 99+% and relative proportion of 3.00.

24 GSS 2006, based on 1612 cases, with statistical significance of 99+% and relative proportion of 1.75.

25 GSS 2006 and 1998, based on 450 cases, with statistical significance of 99+% and relative proportion of 2.08.

## The Long-Term Trends

*Figure 22. "Would you say your own health, in general, is excellent ...?" (Combined results of 18 GSS surveys taken from 1977 through 2006, based on, left to right, 5069, 7316, and 6988 cases, with confidence level of 99+% for all categories, and with relative proportions of, left to right, .80, .82, and .79)*

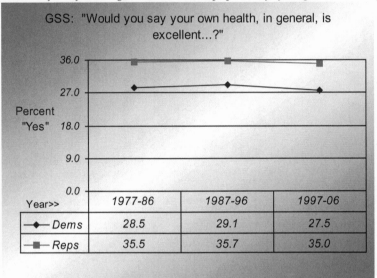

| Year>> | 1977-86 | 1987-96 | 1997-06 |
|---|---|---|---|
| Dems | 28.5 | 29.1 | 27.5 |
| Reps | 35.5 | 35.7 | 35.0 |

The differences in reported health status have been consistent for at least 30 years, and could be due to several causes. Democrats might become less healthy because of lifestyle choices. For example, survey evidence (discussed elsewhere in this chapter) shows that Democrats are more likely to smoke and (possibly) to be overweight. Age, gender, and lack of health insurance coverage could be other factors. On the other hand, people may gravitate towards programs of the Democratic Party once they become ill. Yet again, Republicans may simply feel healthier due to a general sense of optimism (a trait discussed in Chapter 9).

### General Health by Income Bracket

The first wealth is health.

— Ralph Waldo Emerson, 19th century American essayist[26]

When Democrats and Republicans are grouped by income bracket (in constant dollars), significant differences remain, but are diminished. For constituents of both parties, excellent health appears to increase significantly with income.

---

26 Ralph Waldo Emerson, "Columbia World of Quotations," (Columbia University Press, 1996).

*Figure 23. "Would you say your own health, in general, is excellent ...?" (Combined results of 24 GSS surveys taken from 1972 through 2006, based on, left to right, 6377, 3267, 2782, 2879, 2377, and 6570 cases, with confidence level, left to right, of 99+%, zero, 99%, 99+%, 98% and 99%, and with relative proportions of, left to right, .70, n/a, .85, .80, .88, and .93)*

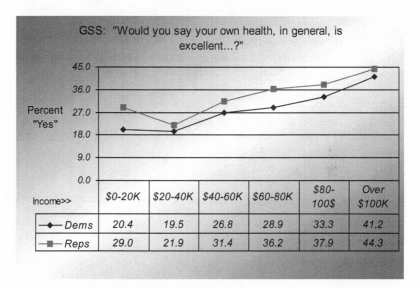

GSS: "Would you say your own health, in general, is excellent...?"

| Income>> | $0-20K | $20-40K | $40-60K | $60-80K | $80-100$ | Over $100K |
|---|---|---|---|---|---|---|
| Dems | 20.4 | 19.5 | 26.8 | 28.9 | 33.3 | 41.2 |
| Reps | 29.0 | 21.9 | 31.4 | 36.2 | 37.9 | 44.3 |

*Figure 24. Percentages of Democrats and Republicans with excellent mental health, based on self-assessments (4 consecutive Gallup surveys conducted in 2004 through 2007, based on 4014 total cases including independents, who are not shown, and with confidence level of at least 95% and a relative proportion of .64)*

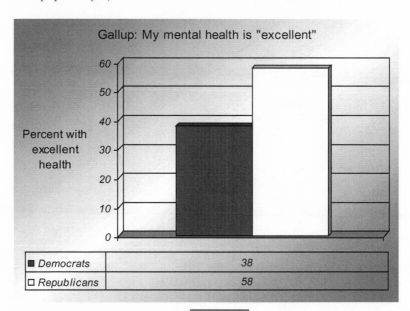

Gallup: My mental health is "excellent"

| | |
|---|---|
| ■ Democrats | 38 |
| □ Republicans | 58 |

## Mental Health

In November, 2007, Gallup reported that it had found a large disparity between the self-described mental health of Republicans versus Democrats and independents. The aggregate results of 4 consecutive surveys conducted in 2004 through 2007 showed that Republicans were far more likely to claim "excellent" mental health. The results are summarized in Figure 24, above.

Gallup also used multiple regression analysis in an effort to gauge the relationship between mental health and several variables, including party identification. Interestingly, the analysis showed that Republicans were more likely to report good mental health, even after controlling for the other variables, which included income, education, age, gender, race, marriage, and children.[27]

In addition, a 2006 GSS survey found that, by 17 to 11 percent, Democrats were more likely to say that they had "received treatment for a mental health problem."[28] And, by 9.8 to 6.4 percent, Democrats are more likely to have taken Prozac as treatment for depression and other disorders.[29]

### Healthy Habits

#### Who Is More Overweight?

I'm not overweight. I'm just nine inches too short.

— The late Shelley Winters, Actress[30]

The available evidence is pretty slender, but it appears that weight control is more of a problem for Democrats than Republicans. At least, this was true for respondents of recent Michigan-based surveys. In a 2004 survey, Democrats were more likely to say they were overweight. See Figure 25, below.

Are Democrats really more overweight, or are they just more truthful and/or realistic about their weight? The results from another survey suggest that Democrats truly are more overweight. In a 2002 survey, respondents were asked for their individual heights and weights. The average results for men, by political party, are shown in Table 3, below. In addition, body mass calculations have been added. (Body mass is simply weight divided by height, using metric measures.) Generally, body mass numbers over 25 are considered potentially unhealthy. Using this standard, males of both political parties are overweight, but Democratic males are about 10 percent more so than Republican males.[31]

---

27 Frank Newport, "Republicans Report Much Better Mental Health Than Others," *The Gallup News Service* (November 30, 2007), Retrieved November 30, 2007, from Http://brain.gallup.com.

28 The results are based on 799 cases, with statistical significance of 98% and a relative proportion of 1.55.

29 The results are from the aggregate results of GSS surveys conducted in 1998 and 2006, based on 1478 cases, with 98% statistical significance and a relative proportion of 1.53.

30 Shelley Winters (attributed), "Brainyquote.Com."

31 If the survey population is adjusted to exclude minorities, Democratic male body mass drops slightly, to 28.5. This lowers the differential between Democrats and Republicans from

*Figure 25. Are you overweight? (Michigan State of the State survey conducted in 2004, based on 242 cases for males, 341 cases for females, and 583 cases for both, with confidence level, left to right, of 94% (marginal), 99%, and 99+%, and with relative proportions of, left to right, 1.38, 1.45, and 1.42)* [32]

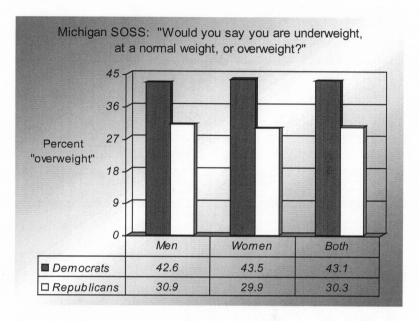

Michigan SOSS: "Would you say you are underweight, at a normal weight, or overweight?"

Percent "overweight"

| | Men | Women | Both |
|---|---|---|---|
| ■ Democrats | 42.6 | 43.5 | 43.1 |
| □ Republicans | 30.9 | 29.9 | 30.3 |

*Table 3. What is your height and weight? (Men) (Michigan SOSS No. 26 conducted in summer, 2002, based on 194 cases, with confidence level of 95%)*

| Men | Height | Weight in lbs. | Body Mass Index* |
|---|---|---|---|
| Democrats | 5' 9.9" | 202.6 | 29.2 |
| Republicans | 5' 11.1" | 189.8 | 26.4 |
| Difference | –1.2" | 12.8 | 2.8 |
| Percentage excess | | 10.6% | |

*25-30 is overweight; over 30 is obese.

The body mass of Republican women averages just below the "normal" limit of 25; however, Democratic women are about 12% heavier.[33]

10.6 percent to 8 percent, suggesting that weight control may be a little more of a problem among minority populations.

32 Michigan *State of the State* surveys are conducted by the Institute for Public Policy and Social Research (IPPSR), a nonprofit entity located within the Michigan State University. Please see Appendix F on page 364 for acknowledgements and limitations.

33 If the survey population is adjusted to exclude minorities, Democratic female body mass drops very slightly, to 27.5. This changes the body weight differential between Democrats and Republicans from 12% to 11% (essentially, no change).

*Table 4. What is your height and weight? (Women) (Michigan SOSS No. 26 conducted in summer, 2002, based on 296 cases, with confidence level of 99+%)*

| Women | Height | Weight in lbs. | Body Mass Index* |
|-------|--------|----------------|-------------------|
| Democrats | 5' 4.4" | 163.4 | 27.8 |
| Republicans | 5' 4.9" | 148.0 | 24.8 |
| Difference | –.5" | 15.4 | 3.0 |
| Percentage excess | 12.1% | | |

*25-30 is overweight; over 30 is obese.

National Harris polls conducted in 2006 and 2007 also show that Democrats are slightly more likely to be overweight (by 58.6 to 53.6 percent); however, in the Harris surveys all of the statistically significant difference is attributable to women. The results, which are based on height and weight figures, are shown in Table 5, below.

*Table 5. The percentages of women who are overweight or obese, based on height and weight measurements reported by respondents to Harris interviewers. For men, there was no statistically significant difference.*

| Surveys of women | % Overweight | | No. of Cases | Conf % | *RP |
|------------------|--------------|------|--------------|--------|------|
| | Dems | Reps | | | |
| Harris Feb. 2007 | 52.4 | 40.2 | 342 | 96 | 1.30 |
| Harris Feb. 2006 | 54.0 | 40.4 | 354 | 98 | 1.34 |
| Harris Jan. 2006 | 51.7 | 35.5 | 415 | +99 | 1.46 |
| Overall | 52.7 | 38.4 | 1111 | +99 | 1.37 |

*RP is relative proportion, which is the Democratic % divided by the Republican %.

The reason Democratic women are more likely to be overweight may be that they lack the time or inclination to cut back on eating. In a recent Harris survey, Democratic women were much less likely (by 51 to 72 percent) to report that they had reduced their food intake during the previous 30 days in an effort to shed pounds.[34] Here is another possibility: By 44 to 62 percent, Democratic women are less likely to drink caffeine beverages every day, according to a Georgia state survey conducted in 2007. Could this be linked to lower weight?[35]

It seems logical that Democrats might be slightly heavier, given the fact that, on average, they have less income than Republicans. Today's "fat cats" are more likely to be poorer people, as noted in an article published by a senior fellow with the National Center for Policy analysis (2003):

---

34 The results are from a Harris Interactive survey conducted in 2006, based on 216 cases, with a +99% confidence level and a relative proportion of .71.

35 The results are from a 2007 Georgia "Peach State" poll, based on 280 cases, with a 99% confidence level and a relative proportion of .71.

One of the more curious consequences of these trends is that the poor are now more likely to be obese than the wealthy. Indeed, obesity is now a problem in developing countries where starvation was the norm not too many years ago, according to the World Health Organization.[36]

Being overweight or obese diminishes the quality and length of life and has enormous implications for the cost of health care. In a recent research report, the Milken Institute estimated that America could eventually save over $300 billion annually, if it could get its obesity rate back to the level that existed just a few years ago, in 1998.[37] Some employers, struggling with rising health insurance costs, are now charging overweight employees an extra percentage of health insurance premiums. This is sure to be controversial, especially if obesity is more prevalent among the constituents of one major political party than the other.

### Who Is to Blame for the Thick Thighs?

[M]organ Spurlock has invaded the [movie] theaters with his widely praised "Super Size Me," a wild jihadist tilt against the golden arches.... By gorging himself on vast quantities of the worst sludge on the McMenu — guess what? Spurlock gains 25 pounds ...
— Alex Beam, Boston Globe, May 11, 2004[38]

It is widely acknowledged that many poor people suffer from obesity; however, the causes are more controversial. Some people subscribe to a radical notion: Poor people, like most of us, don't use enough self-control with regard to the quantities they eat. Others attribute the bulging waistlines to a lack of nutritional information, a lack of money to buy healthy foods, a lack of playgrounds for poor children to play on, and/or the prevalence of enticing fast food restaurants. The truth may lie in between.

A Michigan survey asked respondents if they thought eating in fast food restaurants contributes to people becoming overweight. A majority of both constituencies answered, "Yes." However, Democrats were more likely to do so (Figure 26).

### Who Exercises More?

Here, the evidence is conflicting. In a Pew Research Center poll conducted in 2002, respondents were asked if, during the prior day, they engaged in "some kind of vigorous exercise such as jogging, working out in a gym, or playing a racquet sport." By 38.8 to 34.3 percent Democrats were more likely than Republicans to respond in the affirmative (966 cases, with confidence level 96% and with a relative proportion of 1.13). However, a more recent Pew survey (conducted in 2004) found no statistically significant difference in the answers of Democrats and Republicans to this same question.

36 Bruce Bartlett, "Gaining Weight," in *Commentary* (National Center for Policy Analysis, April 23, 2003), Retrieved September 2, 2006, from: http://www.ncpa.org/edo/bb/2003/bb042303.html.

37 Ross DeVol and Armen Bedroussian, "An Unhealthy America: The Economic Burden of Chronic Disease," (October, 2007), Retrieved October 21, 2007, from: www.milkeninstitute.org.

38 Alex Beam, "A Super-Size Portion of Half Truths," in *Boston.com* (May 11, 2004), Retrieved September 2, 2006, from: http://www.boston.com/ae/food/articles/2004/05/11/a_super_size_portion_of_half_truths/.

*Figure 26. "How much do you think eating in fast food restaurants contributes to people becoming overweight?" (Michigan State of the State survey conducted in 2003, based on, left to right, 208 and 320 cases, with confidence level of 99% for both differences, and with relative proportions of, left to right, 1.21 and 1.23)*

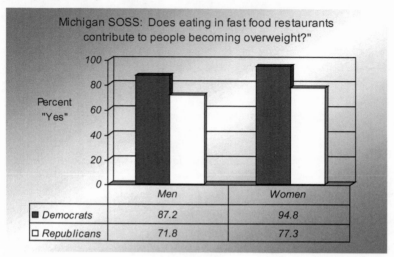

| Michigan SOSS: Does eating in fast food restaurants contribute to people becoming overweight?" | | |
| --- | --- | --- |
| | Men | Women |
| ■ Democrats | 87.2 | 94.8 |
| ☐ Republicans | 71.8 | 77.3 |

### Who Is More Likely to Smoke Tobacco?

They're talking about banning cigarette smoking now in any place that's used by ten or more people in a week, which I guess means that Madonna can't even smoke in bed.

— Comedian Bill Maher[39]

All surveys suggest that Democrats are more likely to smoke. See Table 6, below.

*Table 6. Surveys regarding smoking*

| Survey and Issue | Dem % "yes" | Rep % "yes" | No. of cases | Conf % | *RP |
| --- | --- | --- | --- | --- | --- |
| Pew survey 2005: "Do you smoke cigarettes on a regular basis?" | 20.9 | 14.7 | 708 | +99 | 1.42 |
| Michigan SOSS 2004: "Have you smoked at least 100 cigarettes in your entire life?" | 53.1 | 40.9 | 749 | +99 | 1.30 |
| Michigan SOSS 2003: "Do you now use any form of tobacco?" | 32.8 | 25.6 | 712 | 96 | 1.28 |
| GSS surveys conducted between 1977 and 1994: Do you smoke? | 36.0 | 28.4 | 10695 | +99 | 1.27 |

*RP is relative proportion, which is the Democratic % divided by the Republican %.

39 Bill Mahler (attributed), "Brainyquote.Com."

## Who Wants to Ban Smoking?

It may surprise you to learn that Republicans are the activists when it comes to smoking bans, according to a survey released in July, 2005. Gallup reported: "Republicans are more likely than Democrats or independents to show increased support for smoking bans in restaurants, hotels and motels, and the workplace." The survey found that Republicans were more likely than Democrats to support restaurant smoking bans by 62 to 53 percent, hotel and motel smoking bans by 41 to 33 percent, and workplace bans by 47 to 37 percent. Perhaps Republicans support these restrictions because they are less likely to smoke.[40]

## Who Is More Likely to Use Illegal Drugs?

> The historical record is that 19 years ago, I used marijuana once at a party ... in New Orleans .... It didn't have any effect on me. As a matter of fact, I never went back and revisited it.

— Former Republican Speaker of the House Newt Gingrich[41]

Only tiny percentages of Democrats and Republicans state that they have tried crack cocaine. However, Democrats comprise the majority of those who have tried the drug, according to the GSS surveys depicted in Figure 27, below.

*Figure 27. "Have you ever used 'crack' cocaine?" (combined results of 4 GSS surveys conducted in 2000 through 2006, based on 2398 cases for men, 3158 cases for women, and 5556 cases for both, with confidence level of 97% for men, 99% for women, and 99+% for both, and with relative proportions of, left to right, 1.45, 1.74, and 1.50)*

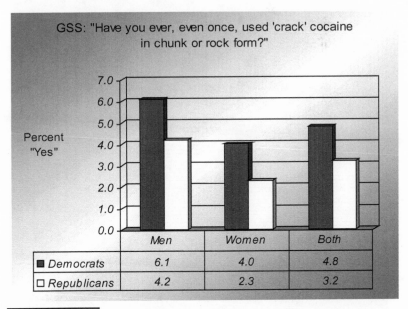

GSS: "Have you ever, even once, used 'crack' cocaine in chunk or rock form?"

| | Men | Women | Both |
|---|---|---|---|
| ■ Democrats | 6.1 | 4.0 | 4.8 |
| □ Republicans | 4.2 | 2.3 | 3.2 |

---

40 David Moore, "Increased Support for Smoking Bans in Public Places," *The Gallup News Service* (July 20, 2005), Retrieved January 31, 2007, from http://www.secondhandsmokesyou.com/ resources/one_news_article.php?id=98.

41 Jill Lawrence, "Speaker Gingrich," *AP*, November 28, 1994.

Even smaller percentages have taken illegal drugs by means of injection; however, Democrats again are slightly more likely to say they have done so.

*Figure 28. [Not including doctor's prescriptions] "Have you ever, even once, taken any drugs by injection with a needle (like heroin, cocaine, amphetamines, or steroids)?" (combined results of 4 GSS surveys conducted in 2000 through 2006, based on 2401 cases for men, 3159 cases for women, and 5560 cases for both, with no statistical significance for men, 99% for women, and 90% (marginal) for both, and with relative proportions of, left to right, n/a, 2.08, and 1.29)*

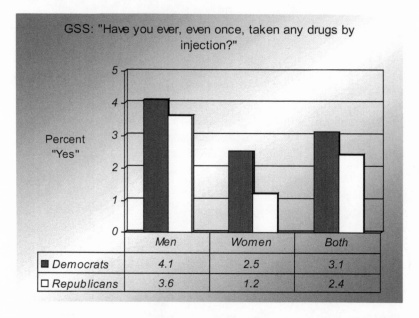

Republicans are just as likely as Democrats to have tried marijuana, according to a 1999 Gallup poll where 33 percent of Republicans and 31 percent of Democrats reported having experimented with the drug (statistically a tie).[42]

> Whenever a conservative is exposed as a "hypocrite" the behavior — Limbaugh's drug use, Bennett's gambling, whatever — <u>never</u> offends the Left as much as the fact that they were telling other people how to live. This, I think, is in part because of the general hostility the Left has to the idea that we should live in any way that doesn't "feel" natural.
>
> — Columnist Jonah Goldberg[43]

42 Jennifer Robison, "Who Smoked Pot? You May Be Surprised," *The Gallup News Service* (July 16, 2002), Retrieved August 21, 2004, from Http://brain.gallup.com. The results are based on a survey of 1000 adults aged 18 years or more (sampling error at 95% = plus or minus 3%).

43 Jonah Goldberg, "What Is a 'Conservative'?," in *National Review Online* (May 11, 2005), Retrieved August 14, 2006, from: http://www.nationalreview.com/goldberg/goldberg200505111449.asp.

## Other Health Issues

### Health Insurance

Democrats are less likely than Republicans to have health insurance, and this could explain why they seem particularly motivated to expand governmental programs in this area. See Figure 29, below.

*Figure 29. Percentage without health insurance (NES 2004 Pre-election survey, based on 729 cases, with confidence level of 97%, and with relative proportion of 1.55)*

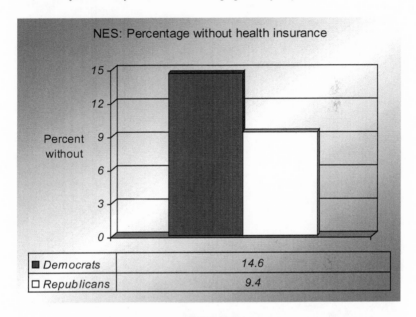

### HIV Testing

By 40.5 to 33.8 percent, Democrats are more likely to have been tested for HIV, based on a 2006 GSS survey of 1433 men and women.[44]

### Cleaner teeth and other important health matters

According to a 2001 ABC News poll:

> Republicans divide evenly on whether genetically modified foods are safe or unsafe. Independents rate them unsafe by a 20-point margin; Democrats by a 26-point margin.[45]

Other health-related issues are shown in Table 7, below.

---

44 The statistical significance is 99% and the relative proportion is 1.20.
45 The results are based on a sample of 1024 adults, with statistical significance of 95%.

*Table 7. Miscellaneous health*

| Survey | Issue | Dem % "yes" | Rep % "yes" | No. of cases | Conf % | *RP |
|---|---|---|---|---|---|---|
| Harris 2006 Interactive survey | During the last 30 days have you cleaned your teeth 3 or more times in a single day? | 40.0 | 61.0 | 334 | +99 | .66 |
| Rasmussen 2006 survey | Do you belong to a health club? | 13.0 | 22.0 | **1000 | 95 | .59 |
| GSS surveys from 1998 through 2004 | Are you a member of a sports group? | 14.9 | 20.2 | 931 | 97 | .74 |
| 1996 NBC, Wall St. Journal, via Roper | Do you use vitamins or supplements, or try to eat mostly organic foods? | 48 | 55 | 1116 | 97 | .87 |

*RP is relative proportion, which is the Democratic % divided by the Republican %.

**Case numbers include independents and others in addition to Democrats and Republicans.

*Figure 30. "Aside from weddings and funerals, how often do you attend religious services ...? (February, 2007 Pew Survey, based on 910 cases, with confidence level of 99+%, and Phi of .25 for the series)*

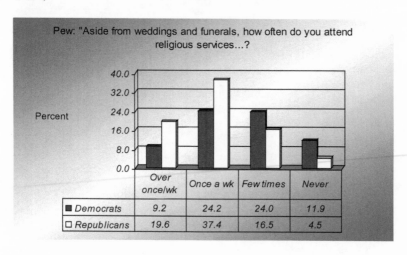

Pew: "Aside from weddings and funerals, how often do you attend religious services...?

| | Over once/wk | Once a wk | Few times | Never |
|---|---|---|---|---|
| ■ Democrats | 9.2 | 24.2 | 24.0 | 11.9 |
| □ Republicans | 19.6 | 37.4 | 16.5 | 4.5 |

*Religion*

> My generation, faced as it grew with a choice between religious belief and existential despair, chose marijuana. Now we are in our Cabernet stage.
>
> — Peggy Noonan, Republican political analyst and author[46]

## Frequency of Attendance and Strength of Convictions

It appears that Republicans are more likely to attend religious services on a frequent basis. See Figure 30, above.

Other surveys addressing the issue of religious attendance are shown in Table 8, below.

*Table 8. Other relevant surveys*

| Survey | Specific Issue | Dem % "yes" | Rep % "yes" | No. of cases | Conf % | *RP |
|--------|----------------|-------------|-------------|--------------|--------|-----|
| Rasmussen March 2007 | Do you attend a religious service every week or more frequently? | 23.0 | **47.0** | **1000 | 95 | .49 |
| Pew July 2005 Religion and Public Life Survey | Do you attend services once per week or more? | 37.5 | **55.0** | 1288 | +99 | .68 |
| Pew 1987-2003 Combined Values Surveys | Do you attend services once per month or more? | 55.6 | 62.9 | 9475 | +99 | .88 |

*RP is relative proportion, which is the Democratic % divided by the Republican %.

**Case numbers include independents and others in addition to Democrats and Republicans.

Gallup surveys show that, by 66 to 57 percent, Republicans are more likely than Democrats to describe religion as being very important in their lives.[47] And, by 44.6 to 39.4 percent, Republicans are more likely to describe their religious convictions as "strong," according to several GSS surveys conducted during the last 10 years.[48] A 2006 Harris poll shows that Republicans are far more likely (by 92 to 73 percent) to say that, during the previous 30 days, they "felt the presence of God" in their lives.[49]

---

46 Peggy Noonan (attributed), "Brainyquote.Com."

47 Frank Newport, "An Abiding Relationship: Republicans and Religion," *The Gallup News Service* (June 14, 2007), Retrieved September 29, 2007, from Http://brain.gallup.com. The results are based on surveys conducted in 2004 through 2007, with statistical significance of at least 95%.

48 The GSS results are based on 8227 cases in surveys conducted from 1995 through 2004, with statistical significance of 99+% and a relative proportion of .88.

49 The Harris results are based on 370 cases, with a confidence level of 99+%, and with a relative proportion of .79.

According to a 2007 Rasmussen survey of 1000 adults (including all political parties), Republicans are more likely to believe that Jesus Christ actually walked the earth (by 91 to 76 percent), that Jesus Christ was the Son of God and died for our sins (by 89 to 71 percent), and that Jesus Christ rose from the dead (by 89 to 69 percent). A Rasmussen survey conducted in 2005 found that 77 percent of Republicans believed the literal truth of the Bible, versus just 59 percent of Democrats. Another Survey conducted by Rasmussen in 2005 found that 63 percent of Republicans claimed to pray "every day or nearly every day." Only 52 percent of Democrats made that same claim.[50]

### Religion and Politics

> Jihad Jesus Republicans need to understand that the separation of church and state has kept this country from getting into religious wars.
>
> — Phillip Paulson, who (with the ACLU) has sued to remove the Mt. Soledad memorial cross[51]

Republicans are often accused of mixing religion and politics, however, the link between religion and politics may be stronger for Democrats.

*Figure 31. Did your clergy encourage you to vote for a candidate or party? (NES post-election survey conducted in 2000, based on 803 cases, with confidence level of 99+%, and relative proportion of 2.94)*

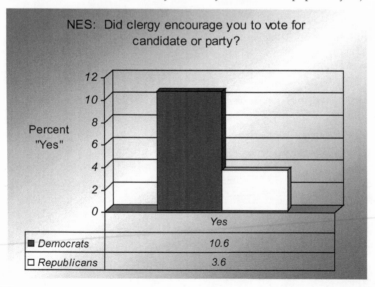

| | Yes |
|---|---|
| ■ Democrats | 10.6 |
| □ Republicans | 3.6 |

---

50 All Rasmussen survey responses have a confidence level of 95 percent or higher.
51 "Congress Gets into ACLU Cross Brouhaha," *WorldNetDaily*, Retrieved September 3, 2006, from http://www.worldnetdaily.com/news/article.asp?ARTICLE_ID=41617.

## Religious Denominations
See Appendix A: Demographic Trends over 50 Years.

*Entertainment and leisure*

> We aren't in an information age; we are in an entertainment age.
>
> — Anthony Robbins, Motivational speaker and writer[52]

## The Couch Potato Award

### Time Spent Watching TV

Democrats consistently watch more television, as evident from Figure 32, below. They watch TV for an extra half hour (about) each day, or 3.5 extra hours per week. This disparity has been fairly steady for at least 25 years, and is true for both genders.

*Figure 32. "On the average day, about how many hours do you personally watch TV?" (16 GSS surveys conducted between 1982 and 2006, based on 15064 cases, with confidence level of 99+%)*

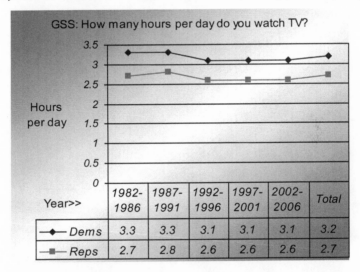

GSS: How many hours per day do you watch TV?

| Year>> | 1982-1986 | 1987-1991 | 1992-1996 | 1997-2001 | 2002-2006 | Total |
|---|---|---|---|---|---|---|
| Dems | 3.3 | 3.3 | 3.1 | 3.1 | 3.1 | 3.2 |
| Reps | 2.7 | 2.8 | 2.6 | 2.6 | 2.6 | 2.7 |

*Table 9. Other relevant surveys*

| Survey and issue | Dem % | Rep % | No. of cases | Conf % | *RP |
|---|---|---|---|---|---|
| Rasmussen November 2007: Percentage watching more than 2 hours of TV in a typical day | 34.0 | 24.0 | **1000 | 95 | 1.42 |
| Rasmussen November 2007: Percentage for whom Hollywood writers' strike has an impact on life | 44.0 | 29.0 | **1000 | 95 | 1.52 |

---

52 Anthony Robbins (attributed), "Brainyquote.Com."

| | | | | | |
|---|---|---|---|---|---|
| Pew 2006 Biennial Media Consumption survey: Percentage watching TV for 4 hours or more per day (not counting news shows) | 22.2 | 11.8 | 839 | +99 | 1.88 |
| Pew 2004 Biennial Media Consumption survey: Percentage watching TV for 4 hours or more per day (not counting news shows) | 21.8 | 11.8 | 598 | +99 | 1.85 |

*RP is relative proportion, which is the Democratic % divided by the Republican %.

**Case numbers include independents and others in addition to Democrats and Republicans.

## TV Sex and Violence

The Republican-controlled FCC has, in the Bush years, already been heavy-handed in targeting what it deems broadcast speech too impure for you to hear.... From the ACLU to libertarian conservatives, predictions ... are dire.

— Doug Ireland, LA Weekly, March 24, 2005[53]

Republicans are more bothered than Democrats by adult language and sexual content on TV shows.

*Figure 33. Does seeing adult language and sexual content on TV shows "bother you, personally"? (Pew News Interest Index survey conducted in March, 2005, based on, left to right, 484 and 979 cases, with confidence level of, left to right, 99+% and 97%, and with relative proportions of, left to right, .73 and .83)*

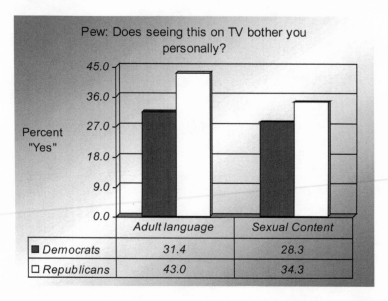

Pew: Does seeing this on TV bother you personally?

Percent "Yes"

| | Adult language | Sexual Content |
|---|---|---|
| ■ Democrats | 31.4 | 28.3 |
| □ Republicans | 43.0 | 34.3 |

---

53 Doug Ireland, "Censor Alert," *LA Weekly*, March 24, 2005.

The following pair of Rasmussen surveys show that, while Republicans are more bothered by inappropriate sexual content on television shows, Democrats are much more concerned with TV violence.

| Survey | Issue | Dem % | Rep % | No. of cases | Conf % | *RP |
|---|---|---|---|---|---|---|
| Rasmussen, June 2007 | Sexual content is the biggest problem with TV | 27.0 | **47.0** | **1000 | 95 | .57 |
| Rasmussen, June 2007 | Violence is the biggest problem with TV | **55.0** | 32.0 | **1000 | 95 | 1.72 |

*RP is relative proportion, which is the Democratic % divided by the Republican %.

**Case numbers include independents and others in addition to Democrats and Republicans.

### Who Is More Likely to Watch an X-Rated Movie?

Both Democratic men and women outpace Republicans in regard to X-rated movies.

*Figure 34. "Have you seen an X-rated movie in the last year?" (GSS surveys conducted between 1987 and 2006, based on, left to right, 4692, 6425, and 11117 cases, with confidence level of 99+% for all columns, and with relative proportions of, left to right, 1.26, 1.20, and 1.17)*

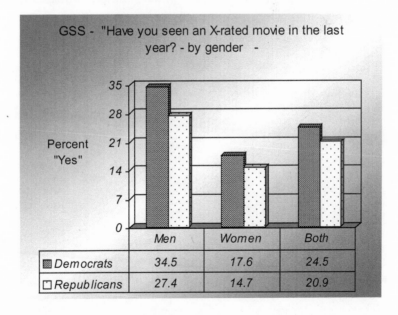

| | Men | Women | Both |
|---|---|---|---|
| Democrats | 34.5 | 17.6 | 24.5 |
| Republicans | 27.4 | 14.7 | 20.9 |

The X-rated movie gap extends to constituents in various age groups. See Figure 35, below.

*Figure 35. "Have you seen an X-rated movie in the last year?" (GSS surveys conducted between 1987 and 2006, based on, left to right, 2117, 4566, and 4409 cases, with confidence level of 99+% for all columns, and with relative proportions of, left to right, 1.17, 1.18, and 1.42)*

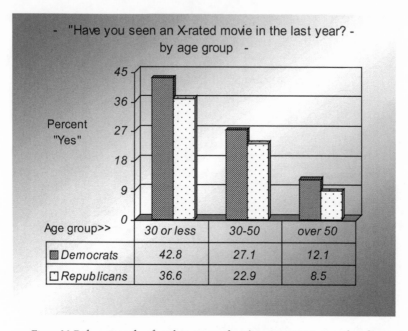

*Figure 36. Did you "go online from home" yesterday? (Pew 2006 BMC survey, based on 1285 cases, with confidence level of 99+%, and with a relative proportion of .73)*

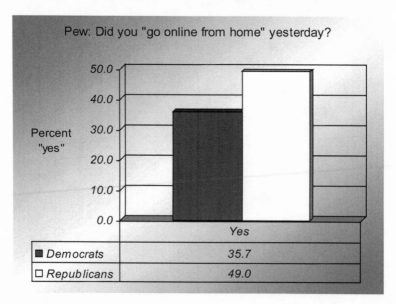

## Net surfing

> The Internet is not something you just dump something on. It's not a truck. It's a series of tubes. And if you don't understand, those tubes can be filled. And if they are filled, when you put your message in, it gets in line and it's going to be delayed by anyone that puts into that tube enormous amounts of material...
>
> — Republican Senator Ted Stevens, giving a "technical" explanation of the Internet[54]

Republicans are more likely to use the Internet. (For what we can only speculate.) According to a 2006 Pew survey, 47 percent of Republicans had, on the prior day, used a computer to access the Internet from their homes. This was true for only 36 percent of Democrats. See Figure 36.

Privacy concerns are probably one reason Democrats use the Internet less frequently. A 2006 Michigan survey shows that, by 61.5 to 44.1 percent, Democrats worry more than Republicans about online privacy (included in Table 10, below).

*Table 10. Various questions about computer and Internet usage*

| Survey | Issue | Dem % | Rep % | No. of cases | Conf % | *RP |
|---|---|---|---|---|---|---|
| Michigan 2006 SOSS | "... ever purchase anything online...?" | 59.6 | 80.5 | 606 | +99 | .74 |
| Michigan 2006 SOSS | "How concerned are you about privacy when you shop on-line?" (Percentage "Very concerned") | 61.9 | 44.0 | 351 | +99 | 1.41 |
| Pew News Interest Index, June, 2005 | Do you ever search the WWW, or send or receive e-mails? | 62.6 | 73.9 | 938 | +99 | .84 |
| Pew 2004 Political Typology | "Do you use a computer at your workplace, at school, at home, or anywhere else on at least an occasional basis?" | 77.5 | 82.6 | 1303 | +99 | .94 |

*RP is relative proportion, which is the Democratic % divided by the Republican %.

## Reading Fine Books

> No entertainment is so cheap as reading, nor is any pleasure so lasting.
>
> — Lady Mary Wortley Montagu, 18th century English aristocrat and writer[55]

---

54 Senator Ted Stevens cited in, "Internet 'Tubes' Speech Turns Spotlight, Ridicule onto Sen. Stevens," in *McClatchy Newspapers*, ed. Liz Ruskin (July 14, 2006).

55 Lady Mary Wortley Montagu cited in, "Columbia World of Quotations," (Columbia University Press, 1996).

Surveys conducted by Pew in 2006 and 2004 asked: "Not including school or work related books, did you spend any time reading a book yesterday?" In each case, around 37 percent of Democrats and Republicans answered affirmatively.[56] This may surprise some readers because a recent poll conducted by AP-Ipsos found that 34 percent of "conservatives" had not read a book in the last year, versus just 22 percent of "liberals."[57] However, as indicated in Chapter 11, we must not confuse Democrats and Republicans with liberals and conservatives. Historically, 25 to 50 percent of self-described conservatives are Democrats, and they tend to be at the lower end of the education scale. On the other hand, Republican conservatives are generally at the upper end of the education scale. For more information about these tendencies, please see page 291.

### Holidays

In general, Republicans seem to value and enjoy holidays more than do Democrats. This is apparent from some of the survey results shown in Table 11.

*Table 11. Surveys related to holidays*

| Issue | Survey | Dem % | Rep % | No. of cases | Conf % | *RP |
|---|---|---|---|---|---|---|
| Considers the holiday season (Christmas/ Hanukkah) to be joyous (versus stressful) | Rasmussen December 2007 | 39.0 | 61.0 | **1000 | 95 | .64 |
| Considers the holiday season (Christmas/ Hanukkah) to be joyous (versus stressful) | Rasmussen December 2006 | 41.0 | 67.0 | **1000 | 95 | .61 |
| Started holiday shopping as of the first week in December 2007 | Rasmussen December 2007 | 44.0 | 63.0 | **1000 | 95 | .70 |
| Started holiday shopping as of the first week in December 2006 | Rasmussen December 2006 | 41.0 | 67.0 | **1000 | 95 | .61 |
| Will decorate the house for the holidays | Rasmussen November 2007 | 62.0 | 77.0 | **1000 | 95 | .81 |
| Will go Christmas caroling | Rasmussen November 2007 | 6.0 | 22.0 | **1000 | 95 | .27 |

56 For 2006 and 2004 the survey populations were 1285 and 973, respectively.

57 The AP-Ipsos poll was conducted between August 6 and 8th, 2007, and comprised 1003 cases with a marginal of error or plus or minus 3 percentage points.

| | | | | | | |
|---|---|---|---|---|---|---|
| Will attend religious service during the holidays | Rasmussen November 2007 | 54.0 | **74.0** | **1000 | 95 | .73 |
| Will travel out of town for the holidays | Rasmussen November 2007 | 20.0 | **34.0** | **1000 | 95 | .59 |
| Prefers saying "Merry Christmas" rather than "Happy Holidays" | Rasmussen December 2007 | 57.0 | **88.0** | **1000 | 95 | .65 |
| Will have a Christmas tree | Rasmussen November 2006 | 59.0 | **69.0** | **1000 | 95 | .86 |
| Will attend a Christmas party | Rasmussen November 2006 | 52.0 | **73.0** | **1000 | 95 | .71 |
| Considers New Year's Day to be important holiday | Rasmussen December 2006 | 9.0 | **15.0** | **1000 | 95 | .60 |
| Will attend a New Year's party | Rasmussen December 2006 | 23.0 | **32.0** | **1000 | 95 | .72 |
| Believes that New Year's resolution will be kept | Rasmussen December 2006 | 44.0 | **58.0** | **1000 | 95 | .76 |
| Considers July 4th to be important holiday | Rasmussen July 2006 | 53.0 | **66.0** | **1000 | 95 | .80 |
| Will eat too much on Thanksgiving | Rasmussen November 2006 | 40.0 | **57.0** | **1000 | 95 | .70 |
| Prefers turkey at Thanksgiving meal | Gallup, 2000 | 41.0 | **50.0** | **1028 | 95 | .82 |
| Prefers stuffing at Thanksgiving meal | Gallup, 2000 | **21.0** | 15.0 | **1028 | 95 | 1.4 |
| Considers Veteran's Day to be one of the most important holidays | Rasmussen November 2007 | 39.0 | **52.0** | **1000 | 95 | .75 |
| Will celebrate Veteran's Day | Rasmussen November 2007 | 35.0 | **50.0** | **1000 | 95 | .70 |

*RP is relative proportion, which is the Democratic % divided by the Republican %.

**Case numbers include independents and others in addition to Democrats and Republicans.

> The Supreme Court has ruled that they cannot have a nativity scene in Washington, D.C. This wasn't for any religious reasons. They couldn't find three wise men and a virgin.

— TV host Jay Leno[58]

*Family finances*

### Income and Spending

Of course, lifestyles are heavily influenced by the availability of money. In each of its surveys, American National Election Studies (NES) asks respondents to estimate total family income, before taxes, including salaries, wages, pensions, dividends, interest, etc. The NES survey results, over a 50-year time span, are presented on page 341, et seq. Those results, which are not repeated here, confirm the widely-held belief that Republicans have more total family income. Another survey indicates that the income differential results in a purchasing differential.

*Figure 37. "Have there been times during the last year when you did not have enough money to buy... food, clothing, medical care, or gasoline? (Pew survey conducted in May, 2005, based on 969 cases for each column, with confidence level of 99+% for each column, and relative proportions of, left to right, 2.07, 1.94, 1.88, and 2.19)*

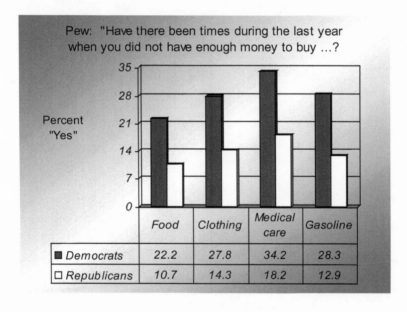

| | Food | Clothing | Medical care | Gasoline |
|---|---|---|---|---|
| ■ Democrats | 22.2 | 27.8 | 34.2 | 28.3 |
| □ Republicans | 10.7 | 14.3 | 18.2 | 12.9 |

Indeed, Democrats are far less likely to indicate that they earn the money they need to live the kind of life they want. See Figure 38, below.

---

58 Jay Leno, "Brainyquote.Com."

*Figure 38. "Do you now earn enough money to lead the kind of life you want, or not? (Pew survey conducted in May, 2005, based on 556 cases, with confidence level of 99+%, and relative proportion of .58)*

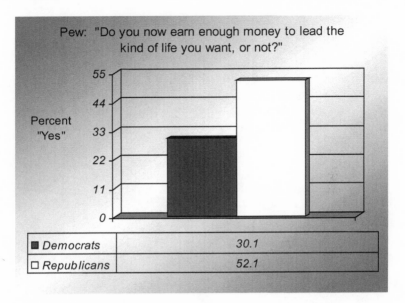

*Figure 39. "Over the past 12 months, has there been a time when you or someone in your household has been without a job and looking for work, or not? (Pew survey conducted in May, 2005, based on 969 cases, with confidence level of 99+%, and relative proportion of 1.85)*

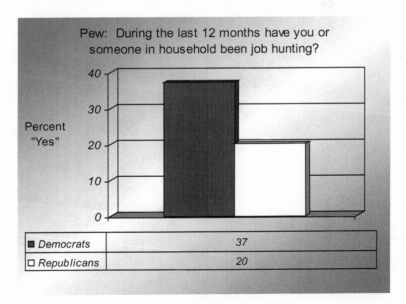

The root cause of the Democratic financial problem is probably unemployment (or underemployment). Democrats are significantly more likely to be out of work, as indicated in the same Pew survey, shown in Figure 39, above.

> I don't want to be a Republican. I just want to live like one.
> — Eugene Cervi, Newspaper publisher [59]

(Note: Extensive information about employment can be found in Chapter 3 and in Appendix A.)

Given these results, it is not surprising that Democrats are more likely to list lack of money and unemployment as their top financial problems. In a report issued in 2005, the Gallup Organization noted:

> The data show some slight variations by partisanship, with Democrats more likely than Republicans to say lack of money and unemployment are the top financial problems and Republicans more likely to not name any financial problems. These differences may result from Republicans being generally more likely to live in higher-income households than Democrats.[60]

The differences identified by Gallup are graphically displayed in Figure 40.

*Figure 40. Most important financial problems by party affiliation (Gallup survey conducted in January-February, 2005, based on 2008 cases, with confidence level of 95% for each column).*

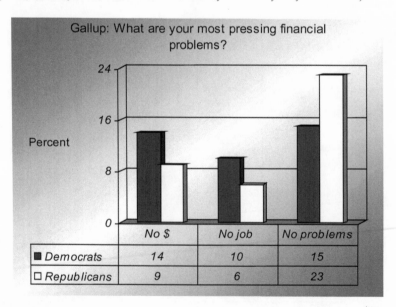

| | No $ | No job | No problems |
|---|---|---|---|
| ■ Democrats | 14 | 10 | 15 |
| □ Republicans | 9 | 6 | 23 |

---

59 Eugene Cervi (attributed), "Hearts & Minds," Retrieved August 17, 2004, from: http://www. heartsandminds.org/humor/fundemrep.htm

60 Joseph Carroll, "Americans' Financial Woes," The Gallup News Service (March 8, 2005), Retrieved August 5, 2006 from http://brain.gallup.com.

*Investments*

### Stocks and Bonds

Republicans study the financial pages of the newspaper. Democrats put them in the bottom of the bird cage.

— Will Stanton, Unknown[61]

Republicans are more apt to trade stocks and bonds. This is reflected in a 2004 Pew Political Typology survey, the results of which are shown in Figure 41, below.

*Figure 41. "Do you trade stocks or bonds in the stock markets?" (Pew survey conducted in July, 2004, based on 1303 cases, with confidence level of 99+%, and relative proportion of .72)*

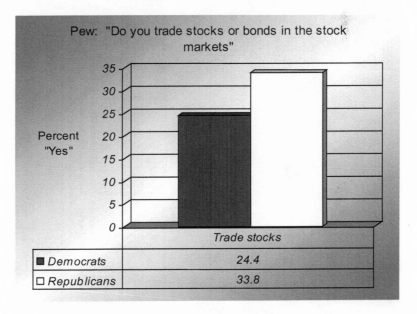

In a 2003 Pew survey, similar results were found, with 25.6 percent of Democrats and 39.4 percent of Republicans reporting that they trade stocks or bonds in the market. Republicans also invest larger sums. This can be deduced by their higher dividend and capital gain income. (See page 226.)

### Retirement Planning

He gave a speech, then Kerry introduced his retirement plan — his wife, Teresa.

— TV host Jay Leno[62]

61 Will Stanton (attributed), "Quotationz.Com."

62 Jay Leno, "Tonight Show," in *About Political Humor*, Retrieved September 2, 2006, from: http://politicalhumor.about.com/library/jokes/blkerryjoke7.htm.

About 66 percent of Democrats and 77 percent of Republicans say that they have "a retirement plan or ... savings set aside for retirement...."[63] Over 80 percent of those amounts (for both Democrats and Republicans) are "in the stock market through stocks, mutual funds or a 401k plan."[64]

Democrats are much more likely to worry that they will not have enough retirement income. (See Figure 42, below.) Presumably, this concern has an impact on the average Democrat's lifestyle.

*Figure 42. "How concerned are you, if at all, about not having enough money for your retirement?" (Pew survey conducted in May, 2005, based on 969 cases, with confidence level of 99+%, and relative proportion of 1.59)*

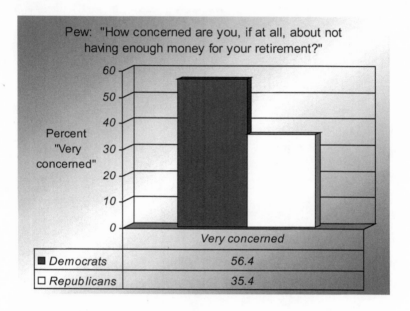

| | Very concerned |
|---|---|
| ■ Democrats | 56.4 |
| ☐ Republicans | 35.4 |

*Habitat*

### Home Ownership

A man builds a fine house; and now he has a master, and a task for life: He is to furnish, watch, show it, and keep it in repair, the rest of his days.

— Ralph Waldo Emerson, 19th century American essayist[65]

Republicans are more likely to own their homes, and have been for at least 50 years.

---

63 2005 Pew News Interest Index survey, based on 737 cases, with statistical significance of 99+%, and with a relative proportion of .86.

64 2005 Pew News Interest Index survey, based on 549 cases.

65 Ralph Waldo Emerson, *Society and Solitude* (New York: Cosimo, 2005).

---

*Figure 43. Do you own your home? (various NES surveys conducted in 1952 through 2004, based on, left to right, 1323, 1176, 4711, 6169, 6465, and 4699 cases, with confidence level of 99+% for all differences, and with relative proportions of, left to right, .88, .84, .85, .86, .89, and .89)*

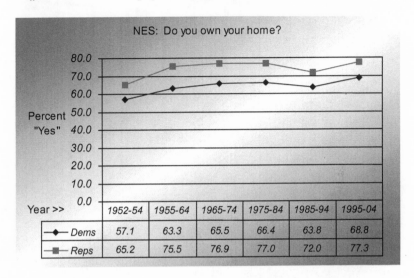

*Miscellaneous*

## Who Is More Likely To Gamble?

Did you hear what [Bill] Bennett's lawyers said today? They said it wasn't gambling, but part of his Indian outreach program.

— TV host Jay Leno[66]

It appears that Democrats are a little more likely to gamble, but an exception might be sports-related betting.

*Table 12. Surveys related to gambling*

| Survey | Issue | Dem % "yes" | Rep % "yes" | No. of cases | Conf % | *RP |
|--------|-------|-------------|-------------|--------------|--------|-----|
| Rasmussen September 2006 | Have you ever bought a lot-tery ticket? | 76.0 | 64.0 | **1000 | 95 | 1.19 |
| Rasmussen September 2006 | Have you ever bet on a sports event or partici-pated in a sports betting pool? | 30.0 | 37.0 | **1000 | 95 | .81 |

66 Jay Leno, "Tonight Show," (About: Political Humor), Retrieved July 28, 2006, from: http://politicalhumor.about.com/library/blrepublicanjokes.htm.

| | | | | | | |
|---|---|---|---|---|---|---|
| Gallup Poll December 2003 | Did you gamble (in any one of several ways, including office pools, sports, and bingo) in last 12 months? | **68.0** | 63.0 | **1011 | 95 | 1.08 |
| Time/CNN 1998 | "Do you consider yourself a regular lottery player?" | **23.0** | 15.0 | 474 | 97 | 1.53 |
| Gallup/ CNN 1996 | "During the last 12 months did you purchase a lottery ticket?" | **60.0** | 49.0 | 633 | 99 | 1.22 |

*RP is relative proportion, which is the Democratic % divided by the Republican %.

**Case numbers include independents and others in addition to Democrats and Republicans.

### Gun Ownership

A large gun gap has developed in recent years. Starting in the 1980s, ownership dropped sharply among Democratic males, while holding steady among Republican males.

*Figure 44. "Do you happen to have in your home (or garage) any guns or revolvers?" (Men) (GSS surveys conducted between 1973 and 2006, grouped by decade, based on, left to right, 1664, 2693, 2312, and 1483 cases. The differences depicted by the graph points on the left side of the chart have no statistical significance. The differences depicted on the right side have a 99+% confidence level, with relative proportions of, left to right, .84 and .65)*

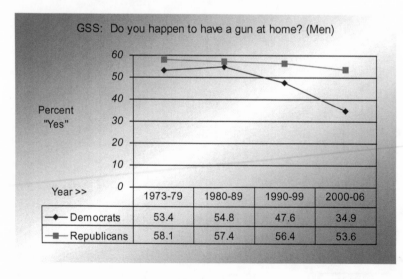

GSS: Do you happen to have a gun at home? (Men)

| Year >> | 1973-79 | 1980-89 | 1990-99 | 2000-06 |
|---|---|---|---|---|
| Democrats | 53.4 | 54.8 | 47.6 | 34.9 |
| Republicans | 58.1 | 57.4 | 56.4 | 53.6 |

> Dick Cheney said he felt terrible about shooting a 78-year-old man, but on the bright side, it did give him a great idea about how to fix Social Security.
>
> — Bill Maher, Comedian[67]

For women, there has always been a statistically significant difference, with Republicans being more likely to own a gun. During the last 30 years, ownership has dropped sharply for women of both political parties, but the drop has been greater for Democrats.

*Figure 45. "Do you happen to have in your home (or garage) any guns or revolvers?" (Women) (GSS surveys conducted between 1973 and 2006, grouped by decade, based on, left to right, 2162, 3955, 3225, and 1867 cases, with 99+% confidence level for all depicted differences, and with relative proportions of, left to right, .83, .76, .72, and .65)*

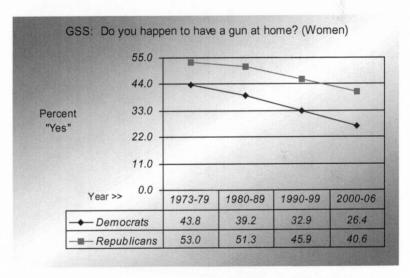

*Table 13. A recent survey regarding gun ownership*

| Survey | Issue | Dem % "yes" | Rep % "yes" | No. of cases | Conf % | *RP |
|--------|-------|-------------|-------------|--------------|--------|-----|
| Rasmussen December 13, 2007 | Does anyone in your house own a gun? | 45.0 | **59.0** | **800 | 95 | .76 |

*RP is relative proportion, which is the Democratic % divided by the Republican %.

---

67 Bill Maher, in *About Political Humor*, Retrieved October 18, 2006, from: http://politicalhumor.about.com/od/cheneyshooting/a/cheneyshooting.htm.

**Case numbers include independents and others in addition to Democrats and Republicans.

### Hunting

Surveys show that only about 2 percent of Democratic women and 4 percent of Republican women go hunting. On the other hand, sizeable percentages of men hunt — particularly Republican men. The trends for men are shown in Figure 46.

*Figure 46. "Do you go hunting?" (Men) (18 GSS surveys conducted in 1977 through 2006, based on, left to right, 2071, 2902, and 1945 cases, with no statistical significance for the left column, and 99+% for the middle and right-side differences, and with relative proportions of, left to right, n/a, .88, and .64)*

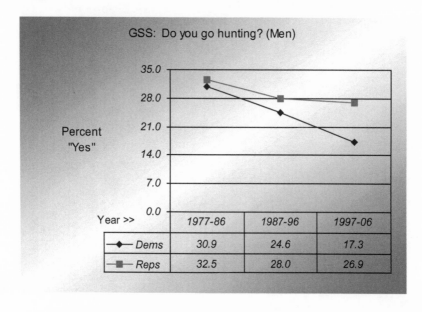

### Violence

An interesting question was posed by a 1999 Michigan survey. Respondents were asked: "Has something ever happened that scared you so much that you thought about it for a long time?" Although there was not a clear difference in the responses of females, Democratic males were much more likely than Republican males to have been seriously scared. This is evident from a review of Figure 47.

Figure 48 may provide insights regarding the nature of those "scary" incidents. It appears that Democratic males (at least, those in Michigan) are much more likely to have been victims of serious physical attacks. This may simply reflect the fact that Democrats are more likely to live in high-crime urban communities.

*Figure 47. Were you "scared so much you thought about it for a long time"? (Men) (1999 Michigan survey, based on 248 cases, with confidence level of 99+%, and with a relative proportion of 1.85)*

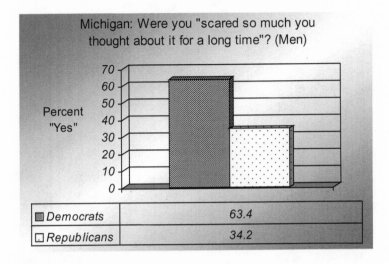

*Figure 48. "Have you ever been the victim of a serious physical attack ... [other than sexual]?" (Men) (1999 Michigan survey, based on 248 cases, with confidence level of 99+%, and with a relative proportion of 2.44)*

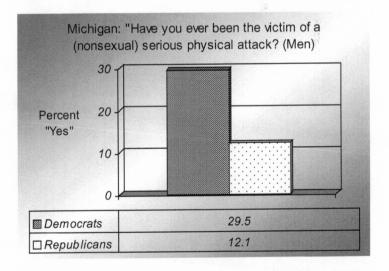

In addition, Democrats are a little more likely to have been threatened with a gun, or shot at. This is true for both genders. In general, the percentage of Democrats and Republicans threatened or shot at is astonishingly high — about 16 percent for Republicans and about 18 percent for Democrats.

*Figure 49. "Have you ever been threatened with a gun, or shot at? (15 GSS surveys conducted between 1973 and 1994, based on 12498 cases, with confidence level of 99+% for each column, and with relative proportions of, left to right, 1.15, 1.34, and 1.16)*

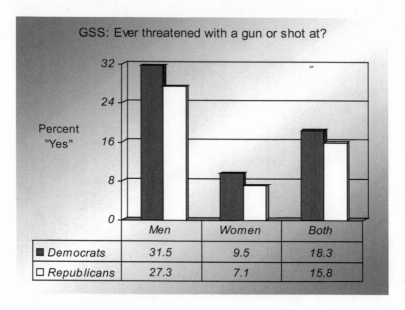

| | Men | Women | Both |
|---|---|---|---|
| ■ Democrats | 31.5 | 9.5 | 18.3 |
| □ Republicans | 27.3 | 7.1 | 15.8 |

## Arrest Rates

Did you hear about the dyslexic cop from Utah that got arrested?
He was handing out IUDs.
— Anonymous[68]

In 1991 and 2004, GSS asked respondents if they had been arrested at any time since 1990. In those surveys (combined), Republicans were more likely than Democrats to state that they had been arrested, by 2 to .7 percent — a small but statistically significant difference. All of the difference in the arrest rates pertained to men.[69]

*Trivia*

*Table 14. Miscellaneous trivia*

| Issue | Survey | Dem % | Rep % | No. of cases | Conf % | *RP |
|---|---|---|---|---|---|---|
| Owns a dog or cat | Eagleton Center for Public Interest NJ Poll 2003 | 44.7 | 61.3 | 238 | 98 | .73 |

---

68 "Police Jokes", Retrieved April 19, 2007, from Aha Jokes: http://www.ajokes.com/jokes/2214. html.

69 1991 and 2004 GSS surveys, based on a total of 1528 cases, with statistical significance of 97%, and with a relative proportion of .35.

| | | | | | | |
|---|---|---|---|---|---|---|
| Displays the flag at home, work, or on car? | Pew 2005 Political Typology Callback | 58.2 | **76.2** | 708 | 99 | .76 |
| Football is favorite sport | Penn, Schoen & Berland 2003 | 22.0 | **31.0** | 590 | 98 | .71 |
| Will watch football on New Year's Day | Rusmussen , December 2006 | 44.0 | **55.0** | **1000 | 95 | .80 |
| Will watch football on Thanksgiving | Rusmussen , November 2006 | 48.0 | **58.0** | **1000 | 95 | .83 |
| "Country" is favorite radio format | Penn, Schoen & Berland 2003 | 14.0 | **21.0** | 590 | 96 | .67 |
| Likes to travel abroad | Penn, Schoen & Berland 2003 | **52.0** | 40.0 | 590 | 99 | 1.3 |
| First child is a female | GSS 1994 | 42.6 | **52.5** | 738 | 99 | .81 |
| Felt "in touch with someone who had died" | 4 GSS surveys from 1984 through 1991 | **42.5** | 36.7 | 3325 | +99 | 1.16 |

*RP is relative proportion, which is the Democratic % divided by the Republican %.
**Case numbers include independents and others.

Last, and least, an Eagleton New Jersey survey found that Democrats were more likely to exclusively drink bottled water by 61 to 50 percent. The significance of this fact is left for the reader to ponder.[70]

## Conclusions

This chapter compares Democrats and Republicans with regard to various aspects of lifestyle. A few conclusions are listed below:

*Sex, Marriage, and Family*

• Democrats are more likely to have multiple sex partners, but are also more likely to have no sex partners.

• Since the 1980s a "gay gap" has developed among men, with Democrats more likely to say they have engaged in gay sex.

• There has been a growing "marriage gap" since the 1960s. Democrats are less likely to be married because they never married, married and became divorced, or married and became widowed.

• Democrats are more likely to engage in adultery.

• On average, Democrats have their first child at a significantly younger age.

70 Ibid, Poll No. 143c, questions qen7 and qd2, May, 2003, based on 555 cases, with 98 percent confidence and a relative proportion of 1.22.

• Democrats and Republicans are about equally likely to have minor children in the household, even though Democrats are less likely to be married when they have those children.

*Health*

• Republicans report that they are healthier, and this has been true for decades. It is particularly true with respect to mental health.

• Republicans are less likely to smoke tobacco, and more likely to want to ban smoking in public places.

• On the whole, it appears that Democrats are a little more likely to be overweight.

• Democrats are less likely to have health insurance.

*Religion*

• Although Republicans attend religious services more frequently, survey evidence suggests that Democrats are more likely to be told how to vote by their clergy.

• Republicans are more likely to believe the Bible, literally, and to believe that Jesus Christ was the son of God, and died for our sins.

*Entertainment and Leisure*

• Democrats watch about 3.5 hours more TV per week than do Republicans.

• Republicans spend more time going "online" from home.

• Republicans are far more likely to perceive that holidays are important and joyous occasions.

*Other*

• Democrats are more likely to get news from the major networks, while Republicans get it from radio and online sources. They are equally likely to read books.

• A shortage of money is of much more concern to Democrats, and more likely to affect purchase decisions with regard to food, clothing, medical care, and gasoline.

• Republicans are more apt to own their homes, and to keep guns in those homes.

## Chapter 2: Who Is More Intelligent, Knowledgeable, and Educated?

### Introduction

#### George Bush, The Chimp

George Bush resembles a chimp in various ways which I will now enumerate: the size of his ears, his intelligence, the look of confusion on his face. Further, democrats are smarter than republicans, and would perform more ably in high positions of governmental power ... [G]iven the facts, I draw the conclusion that Kerry will win the election.

— Blogger named Hildago[1]

Partisans from each side hurl insults; a favorite target for Democrats is the mental acuity of Republicans. In the run-up to the 2004 presidential election, the Internet was filled with proclamations that people in the Democratic "blue states" have higher IQs than those living in the Republican "red states." Many touted a Gallup poll showing that Republicans and less educated people supported the war in Iraq, while Democrats and well-educated people opposed it.[2]

Another survey, conducted in late 2004, showed that nearly half of Bush supporters theorized that Saddam Hussein had weapons of mass destruction and

---

1 Hildago (pseudonym), "Bush & Kerry Round Three: Doin' Damage in Gammage," October 13, 2004, MetaFilter Community Weblog, Retrieved March 11, 2007, from http://www.meta-filter.com/36234/Gammage-Auditorium-ASU-that-is.

2 David W. Moore, "War Support and the Education Gap," *The Gallup News Service* (February 11, 2003), Retrieved November 11, 2004, from Http://brain.gallup.com.

provided support to al Qaeda, prior to the U.S. invasion.[3] To most Democrats, these Republican beliefs were irrefutably wrong and were evidence of ignorance, or worse. After the 2004 election, ABC News correspondent Carole Simpson seemed to imply that those voting for Bush lacked basic intelligence: "I look at the election, and I'm going, 'Well, of course our kids are not bright about these things because their parents aren't'"[4]

Simpson's point was suggested by others, albeit in gentler terms. One columnist wrote:

> It has been said that Democrats tend to be too complex and wordy, but they establish realistic and principled platforms. Republicans, on the other hand, generally are said to be superior at conducting campaigns and coming into power.[5]

A psychology professor said it this way:

> Democrats tend to be more intellectual than Republicans, and to focus more on giving good arguments. ... I see Republican candidates making bad arguments and short-sighted policies, but they skillfully press people's moral buttons and they win elections.[6]

Even Republicans may feel intellectually inferior, given that the college crowd leans sharply leftward. It is certainly the case with faculty members. A 1999 survey of 1,643 teachers at 183 four-year colleges found a 5 to 1 ratio of Democrats to Republicans. A 2005 study found an 8 to 1 ratio of Democrats to Republicans at Stanford and a 10 to 1 ratio at Berkeley. And, after studying the political orientation of Ivy League professors, pollster Frank Luntz reported: "Just 6 percent of Ivy League professors would describe themselves as either conservative or somewhat conservative, and only 3 percent consider themselves to be Republicans. So much for diversity."[7]

> Leftists own higher education. At the University of Colorado, 94 percent of the liberal arts faculty are registered Democrats. Of the 85 English professors, zero are registered Republicans. ... Ensconcing their own in our institutions of higher learning has given the left's "Conservatives are stupid" theory a self-created syl-

3 Program on International Policy Attitudes of the University of Maryland cited by Alan Wirzbicki, "Divide Seen in Voter Knowledge," in *Boston Globe* (Boston: October 22, 2004), Retrieved January 11, 2005, from: http://www.boston.com/news/nation/washington/articles/2004/10/22/divide_seen_in_voter.

4 "National Press Club Forum," (C-span, November 22, 2004), Retrieved January 13, 2005, from: http://www.mrc.org/notablequotables/2004/nq20041122.asp.

5 Tim Botkin, "Lessons from Our Mud-Slinging Election Season," *Sun Newspaper Online* (November 1, 2004), Retrieved November 10, 2004, from http://www.thesunlink.com.

6 Jonathan Haidt, "Intuitive Ethics: Advice for Democratic Candidates," 2004, Faculty Web Page, Retrieved November 10, 2004, from http://faculty.virginia.edu/haidtlab/articles/haidt.advice-for-democrats.doc.

7 Frank Luntz, "Inside the Mind of an Ivy League Professor," in *FrontPageMagazine.com* (August 30, 2002), Retrieved December 22, 2007, from: http://www.frontpagemag.com/articles/Read.aspx?GUID={08DE7057-EA18-4775-B58A-D7A361431936}.

logism. Professors are smart. Professors are leftists. Ergo, leftists are smart.

— Marianne M. Jennings, Professor at Arizona State University[8]

Are Republicans less educated and more ignorant than Democrats? To the contrary, the opposite is the case, and the supporting evidence is substantial and consistent. In addition, there is some evidence suggesting that, as a group, Republicans may have a bit more "apparent intelligence" than Democrats.[9]

## DETAILS

*Who has more civic and political knowledge?*

### Direct Testing

In a Cato Policy Analysis, general political knowledge was assessed on the basis of responses to a survey conducted by the American National Election Studies (NES). In total, 31 questions and responses were considered. They didn't require Einstein-like reasoning skills; rather, the questions were "basic in nature." For example, people were asked to name candidates for the House of Representatives from their congressional districts, and to identify the political offices of prominent people in government. They were also asked who controlled the Senate and the House of Representatives, who was more likely to support gun control (Gore or Bush), and whether U.S. crime rates had increased or decreased between 1992 and 2000. The average respondent answered only 14.4 of the 31 questions correctly.[10]

> The arrogance of this C student!
>
> — Actress Barbara Streisand (referring to President George W. Bush in a blog posting replete with her own misspellings)[11]

Although the Cato Policy Analysis did not include a breakdown of scores based on political party alignments, the author of the study, Professor Ilya Somin

---

8 Marianne M. Jennings, "Are Conservatives Dumb?," in *Jewish World Review* (June 17, 2004), Retrieved October 17, 2007, from: http://www.jewishworldreview.com/cols/jennings061704.asp.

9 Is it possible that Republicans are poorly represented in academia because they have fewer professional accomplishments? After studying 1643 faculty members from 183 colleges and universities, researchers concluded: "[E]ven after taking into account the effects of professional accomplishment, along with many other individual characteristics, conservatives and Republicans teach at lower quality schools than do liberals and Democrats. This suggests that complaints of ideologically-based discrimination in academic advancement deserve serious consideration and further study." (Rothman, Lichter, and Nevitte, "Politics and Professional Advancement Among College Professors," *The Forum* 3, no. 1 (2005).

10 Ilya Somin, "When Ignorance Isn't Bliss - How Political Ignorance Threatens Democracy," *Policy Analysis of the Cato Institute* no. 525 (September 22, 2004).

11 Mike Baron, "Barbra Streisand: Man-Eater Who Can't Spell," in *Post Chronicle* (March 27, 2006), Retrieved March 14, 2007, from: http://www.postchroncile.com/news/entertainment/tittletattle/printer.

of the George Mason School of Law, was kind enough to provide one to me.[12] The breakout he prepared is shown in Figure 50, below.

*Figure 50. Number of correct answers out of a potential of 31 (Ilya Somin's analysis of NES 2000 political knowledge questions. Case numbers vary with questions asked.)*

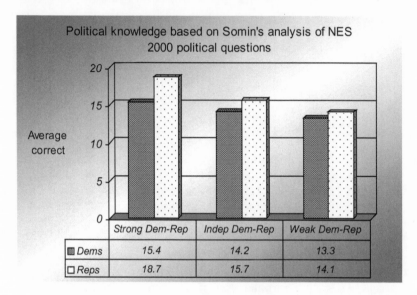

| | Strong Dem-Rep | Indep Dem-Rep | Weak Dem-Rep |
|---|---|---|---|
| Dems | 15.4 | 14.2 | 13.3 |
| Reps | 18.7 | 15.7 | 14.1 |

Two observations can be made based on Somin's results: First, people with stronger convictions, regardless of party affiliation, tend to have more knowledge of basic, political facts. For example, a "strong" Democrat tends to have more political knowledge than does a "weak" Democrat. This makes sense, since people with strong convictions probably follow political news stories more closely.

The second observation is that the average Republican seems to have more political knowledge than does the average Democrat. On average, Democrats answered 14.4 questions correctly, while Republicans answered 16.3 correctly (weighted averages of the 3 columns). These results suggest that Democrats may only have 88 percent of the general political knowledge possessed by Republicans.[13]

> I don't want to lay the blame on the Republicans for the Depression. They're not smart enough to think up all those things that have happened.
>
> — Humorist and author Will Rogers[14]

That is only one test, so it must be taken with a grain of salt. However, similar questions have been asked in multiple NES studies, involving numerous cases

---

12 Ilya Somin, e-mail letter to author, November 29, 2004.
13 The calculation is 14.4/16.3 = 88.3%.
14 Arthur Power Dudden, "The Record of Political Humor," *American Quarterly* 37, no. 1 (1985).

---

and spanning several years. The results are consistent: Democrats are significantly less likely to give correct answers. A summary of the results is presented in Table 15, below.

*Table 15. Political questions asked in several NES surveys*

| Question | No. of cases | Range of test years | Percent correct | | Conf % | RP |
|---|---|---|---|---|---|---|
| | | | Dems | Reps | | |
| Which party had the most Congressmen in Washington before the election this/last month? | 22843 | 21 surveys from 1958 to 2004 | 55.6 | 64.8 | +99 | .86 |
| Which party elected the most Congressmen in the election this/ last month? | 12252 | 12 surveys from 1958 to 1984 | 52.5 | 58.4 | +99 | .90 |
| Which party had the most members in the U.S. Senate before the election? | 11896 | 11 surveys from 1982 to 2004 | 48.6 | 58.2 | +99 | .84 |
| Can you name the candidate who ran in this state for U.S. Senate? | 5323 | 7 surveys from 1978 to 1992 | 39.9 | 47.9 | +99 | .83 |
| Name a candidate in the November elections from this district for the House of Representatives? | 13544 | 12 surveys from 1978 to 2000 | 25.2 | 30.6 | +99 | .82 |
| Average percentage correct | | | 44.4 | 52.0 | | |
| Overall proportion (Dem % divided by Rep %) | | | 85.4% | | | |

On average, Democrats were about 85 percent as likely to correctly answer these questions. (See bottom line of Table 15, above.)

> Ignorance is no excuse, it's the real thing.
> — Epigrammatist Irene Peter[15]

Very similar results can be gleaned from the results of a "Multi Investigator Study" conducted in 1998 and 1999.[16] (See Table 16, below.)

---

15 Irene Peter (attributed), "Womens Media.Com," Retrieved March 14, 2007, from: http://www.womensmedia.com/new/quote-theme-ignorance.shtml.

16 The Multi Investigator Study was a national telephone survey conducted by the Survey Research Center of the University of California at Berkeley, and funded by the National

*Table 16 – Political knowledge questions asked in the 1998-1999 Multi Investigator Study*

| Question | No. cases | Survey years | Percent correct | | Conf % | *RP |
|---|---|---|---|---|---|---|
| | | | Dems | Reps | | |
| Which party has the most members in House of Representatives? | 544 | 1998–1999 | 72.0 | 79.6 | 96 | .90 |
| What majority is required for an override of a presidential veto? | 578 | 1998–1999 | 51.0 | 64.3 | +99 | .79 |
| Average percentage with correct answers | | | 61.5 | 72.0 | | |
| Overall proportion (Dem % divided by Rep %) | | | 85.4% | | | |

*RP is relative proportion, which is the Democratic % divided by the Republican %.

Other data also suggest that Republicans have, on the whole, more political knowledge than Democrats. In March, 2000, the Gallup Organization surveyed 1024 Democrats, independents, and Republicans to see how many could identify the two presidential candidates (Bush and Gore). The results of this survey, with respect to Democrats and Republicans, are depicted in Figure 51, below.[17]

*Figure 51. Who are the presidential candidates? (Gallup poll taken in March, 2000, based on total sample of 1024, including independents, with confidence level of at least 95% and with a relative proportion of .85)*

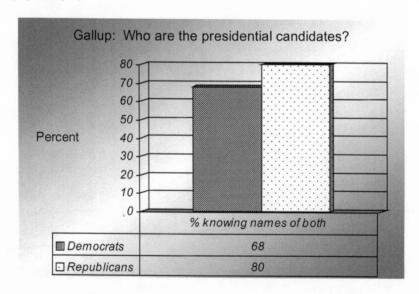

Science Foundation.

17 David W. Moore, "One in Five Americans Unaware That Either Bush or Gore Is a Likely Presidential Nominee," *The Gallup News Service* (March 22, 2000), Retrieved November 11, 2004, from Http://brain.gallup.com.

The percentage of Democrats who answered correctly (68%) was only 85 percent as great as the percentage of Republicans answering correctly (80%).

> The myth of the "dumb" Republican is no more rational than a cultural belief in voodoo or rain dances. It keeps not raining, but the people still believe in it.
>
> — Author and political pundit Ann Coulter[18]

In September, 2003, a "history test" was administered to Democrats and Republicans (and others) by the Gallup Organization. Some of the questions included:

How many senators does each state have?

What is the name of the National Anthem?

Who was the first president of the United States?

Who gave the Gettysburg Address?

Who wrote the "Letter from Birmingham Jail"? (Martin Luther King, Jr.)

Who is the Chief Justice of the Supreme Court?

The results were summarized by the Gallup Organization:

> In general, Republicans outscored Democrats on most of the 10 questions asked. However, this difference likely results from the fact that Republicans tend to be better-educated than Democrats are.[19]

A total of 681 Democrats and Republicans took the 10-question Gallup quiz. On average, Democrats were only 87.5 percent as likely to get the correct answer.

> If liberals were prevented from ever again calling Republicans dumb, they would be robbed of half their arguments. To be sure, they would still have "racist," "fascist," "homophobe," "ugly," and a few other highly nuanced arguments in the quiver. But the loss of "dumb" would nearly cripple them."
>
> – Author and political pundit Ann Coulter[20]

In a 2004 NES survey, respondents were also asked to identify four prominent political figures. The percentage of Democrats and Republicans correctly identifying the people is depicted in Figure 52, below. On average, Democrats were correct 43.2 percent of the time, while Republicans were correct 53.4 percent of the time. In other words, Democrats answered correctly about 81 percent as often as did Republicans.[21]

---

18 Ann Coulter, *Slander* (New York: Crown, 2002), 123.

19 George H. Gallup Jr., "How Many Americans Know U.S. History? Part I," *The Gallup News Service* (October 21, 2003), Retrieved November 11, 2004, from Http://brain.gallup.com.

20 Coulter, *Slander*, 127.

21 The calculation is 43.2/53.4 = 81%.

*Figure 52. Can you identify this person? (2004 NES survey, based on 740 cases for all columns, with confidence level of 97% for the left-side column and 99+% for all other columns, and with relative proportions of, left to right, .62, .92, .76, .71, and .81)*

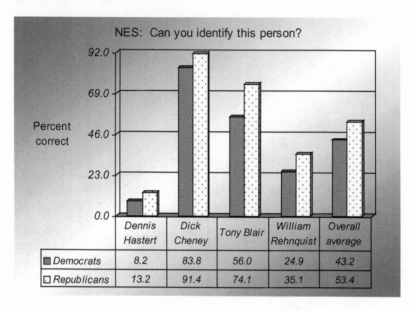

| | Dennis Hastert | Dick Cheney | Tony Blair | William Rehnquist | Overall average |
|---|---|---|---|---|---|
| Democrats | 8.2 | 83.8 | 56.0 | 24.9 | 43.2 |
| Republicans | 13.2 | 91.4 | 74.1 | 35.1 | 53.4 |

> When I listen to the Republicans in Congress on foreign policy, there's such an "I'm stupid and proud of it" attitude.
>
> — Thomas L. Friedman, Columnist, speaking on Face the Nation in 1999[22]

Democrats may now be closing the political knowledge gap, according to Pew surveys conducted in 2000 through 2007. The Pew surveys included many questions directly related to political knowledge, and these are shown in Table 17, below. Although Democrats were only about 88 percent as likely to give correct answers (see bottom-line results), a careful review of the table reveals an interesting pattern. In the Pew surveys conducted in 2000 through 2006 Democrats were only about 82 percent as likely to give correct answers, but that percentage increased to about 96 percent for questions asked in early 2007. This 96 percent rate is far higher than for any other series of political questions I came across, and may reflect the political interest and enthusiasm Democrats had in the wake of the 2006 congressional elections. Democrats did particularly well with regard to questions about Iraq and the new Democratic leadership. Note that Table 17 does not include a few questions for which there was no statistical difference, and if those questions were added, the gap would probably narrow slightly. [23]

---

22 Thomas L. Friedman quoted by Ben Stein and Phil DeMuth, "Can America Survive?," (Carlsbad:New Beginnings Press, 2004), 124.

23 Please see Appendix F on page 364 for more information regarding this survey source.

*Table 17. Political questions asked in recent Pew surveys*

| Pew Survey | Question | Percent correct | | Conf % | *RP |
|---|---|---|---|---|---|
| | | Dems | Reps | | |
| Feb 2007 922 cases | Who is Arnold Schwarzenegger? (Governor of California or actor) | 91.5 | **97.5** | +99 | .94 |
| Feb 2007 922 cases | Who is Barack Obama? (presidential candidate or Democratic leader) | **68.6** | 60.7 | +99 | 1.13 |
| Feb 2007 922 cases | Who is Nancy Pelosi? (Speaker, San Francisco politician, Democratic leader) | 49.6 | **54.9** | 98 | .90 |
| Feb 2007 922 cases | Who is Harry Reid? (Senate majority leader, senator, or Democratic leader) | 13.7 | **16.7** | **93 | .82 |
| Feb 2007 922 cases | Who is the United States Vice President? (Dick Cheney or Richard Cheney) | 70.9 | **79.2** | +99 | .90 |
| Feb 2007 922 cases | Who is your state governor? | 66.8 | **72.5** | 99 | .92 |
| Feb 2007 922 cases | Who is the President of Russia? (Putin or Vladimir Putin) | 35.2 | **40.1** | 97 | .88 |
| Feb 2007 922 cases | Does the Iraq "surge" strategy call for an increase or decrease in troops? (increase) | **90.7** | 88.3 | **91 | 1.03 |
| Feb 2007 922 cases | Which party has a majority in the U.S. House of Reps? (Democratic Party) | 79.4 | **82.8** | **94 | .96 |
| Feb 2007 922 cases | In Iraq, have there been more civilian deaths or more troop deaths? (more civilian) | 71.8 | **75.3** | **92 | .95 |
| Feb 2007 922 cases | Who is the former mayor of NYC who may run for president? (Rudolph Giuliani) | 61.5 | **68.1** | 99 | .90 |
| Feb 2007 922 cases | Bush's surge plan calls for an increase of about how many troops? (20,000, at the time) | **72.6** | 67.0 | 99 | 1.08 |
| June 2006 1285 cases | Who is the current Secretary of State? (Condi or Condoleeza Rice) | 42.5 | **46.1** | **93 | .92 |
| June 2006 1285 cases | Who is the president of Russia (Putin or Vladimir Putin) | 30.3 | **36.5** | +99 | .83 |
| Dec 2004 1303 cases | When is Iraq scheduled to hold its first election? (this winter) | 53.5 | **61.5** | +99 | .87 |

| | | | | | |
|---|---|---|---|---|---|
| June 2004<br>1964 cases | What terrorist group struck the U.S.A. on September 11, 2001? (al Qaeda) | 61.9 | **73.7** | +99 | .84 |
| June 2004<br>1964 cases | Which political party has a majority in the House of Representatives?"<br>(Republicans) | 57.7 | **65.5** | +99 | .88 |
| Jan 2003 –<br>759 cases | What Senate majority leader resigned due to his controversial comments? (Lott) | 46.2 | **50.9** | **92 | .91 |
| June 2002<br>643 cases | Who is the current Secretary of State? (Powell or Colin Powell) | 47.3 | **58.2** | +99 | .81 |
| June 2002<br>1910 cases | Do you happen to know the name of the new European currency? (Euro) | 38.7 | **53.5** | +99 | .72 |
| June 2002<br>1910 cases | When was the state of Israel was created? (1852, 1948, or 1960?" (1948) | 36.3 | **49.4** | +99 | .73 |
| June 2002<br>641 cases | Who is the current Secretary of Defense? (Rumsfeld or Donald Rumsfeld) | 27.8 | **35.2** | +99 | .79 |
| June 2002<br>626 cases | Who is the current vice president of the United States?"<br>(Dick/Richard Cheney) | 58.8 | **70.7** | +99 | .83 |
| Jan 2002<br>738 cases | Which Latin America country has been in a political/economic crisis lately? (Argentina) | 22.7 | **29.2** | +99 | .78 |
| June 2001<br>419 cases | What political party has a majority in the U.S. Senate? (Democrats) | 52.5 | **68.6** | +99 | .77 |
| April 2001<br>381 cases | Did Senate vote for a larger or smaller tax cut than proposed by Pres. Bush? (smaller) | 40.0 | **55.0** | +99 | .73 |
| April 2001<br>381 cases | Did the Senate pass the McCain-Feingold campaign finance reform bill? (yes) | 18.9 | **26.6** | 97 | .71 |
| April 2001<br>381 cases | Was Slobodan Milosevic (former Yugoslavian president) arrested? (yes) | 44.7 | **52.8** | 95 | .85 |
| April 2001<br>381 cases | Did President Bush propose to increase or decrease the education budget? (increase) | 55.6 | **65.2** | 98 | .85 |
| July 2000<br>1243 cases | Which candidate proposed Social Security private investment accounts? (Bush) | 25.5 | **35.3** | +99 | .72 |

| | | | | | |
|---|---|---|---|---|---|
| July 2000 1243 cases | Which candidate proposed reducing U.S. nukes unilateral, if necessary? (Bush) | 14.6 | **22.1** | +99 | .66 |
| July 2000 1243 cases | Which candidate proposed using Medicare surplus to protect the program? (Gore) | 31.3 | 27.6 | 95 | 1.13 |
| June 2000 1897 cases | Who is Alan Greenspan? (Federal Reserve Chairman) | 41.3 | **55.7** | +99 | .74 |
| June 2000 1897 cases | Did the Federal Reserve recently cut interest rates? (raised rates) | 52.6 | **64.9** | +99 | .81 |
| Average percentage with correct answers | | 49.2 | **56.1** | | |
| Overall proportion (Dem % divided by Rep %) | | 87.7% | | | |

*RP is relative proportion, which is the Democratic % divided by the Republican %.
**Marginally significant

> Eighty percent of Republicans are just Democrats who don't know what's going on.
>
> — Robert Kennedy, Jr., Environmental lawyer and political pundit[24]

### Reality check — Neither constituency does well

Although Republicans have the edge with regard to basic political knowledge, there is plenty of ignorance in both constituencies. Apparently, the American educational system is not preparing us to assume our citizenship responsibilities. The dismal state of civics education was addressed in a forum held by the Center for Public& Nonprofit Leadership. One participant noted:

> The schools no longer teach civics, and if you have kids yourself, you probably understand that. Only about 10 percent of public schools teach civics. ... How do you teach people what they should know about being engaged in civic life, about how they can, in fact, change the policy framework? Many do not understand how the city council works, and do not understand how the state legislature works and, in fact, do not even know how to vote.[25]

### Interviewer Impressions

> Better to remain silent and be thought a fool, than to speak and remove all doubt.
>
> — President Abraham Lincoln[26]

24 Greg Esposito, "RFK Jr. Rips President Bush for Environmental Policy," *The Roanoke Times* (2007), Retrieved February 28, 2007, from http://www.roanoke.com/news/nrv/wb/106349.

25 Geri Mannion, "Nonprofit Voter Engagement Initiatives: Expanding the Electorate, Inspiring Participation," in *Issues Forum*, ed. Center for Public & Nonprofit Leadership (Georgetown University, May 1, 2006), Retrieved April 19, 2007, from: http://cpnl.georgetown.edu/doc_pool/NonprofitVoterEngagement%20InitiativesTranscript.pdf.

26 Abraham Lincoln as cited by Daniel E. Cummins, "Lincoln Logs of Wisdom," (Lawjobs.com, 2006), Retrieved March 24, 2007, from: http://www.law.com/jsp/law/careercenter/lawAr-

In several surveys, NES asked its interviewers to assess each respondent's "general level of information about politics and public affairs." This was done by categorizing the level of knowledge as "very high ... fairly high ... average ... fairly low [or] very low." Figure 53, below, shows the percentages of Democrats and Republicans who were categorized as having a "very high" or "fairly high" level of knowledge in the 5 NES surveys conducted in 1996 through 2004. On average, 40.4 percent of Democrats and 54.3 percent of Republicans received these ratings for the 5 year period, in aggregate. This means that Democrats were about 74 percent as likely as Republicans to be judged as having a very or fairly high level of knowledge.[27]

*Figure 53. Interviewer's assessment of respondents' "general level of information about politics and public affairs" (assessments made in 5 consecutive NES pre-election surveys conducted in 1996 through 2004, based on, left to right, 1101, 814, 1068, 970, and 707 cases, with confidence level of 99+% for all differences, and with relative proportions of, left to right, .70, .73, .67, .85, and .73)*

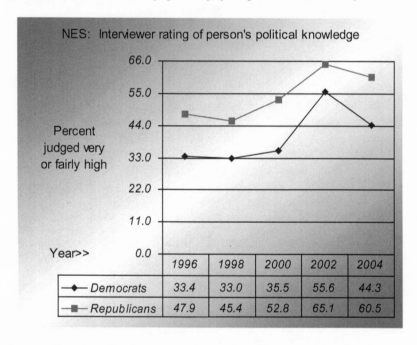

**NES: Interviewer rating of person's political knowledge**

Percent judged very or fairly high

| Year>> | 1996 | 1998 | 2000 | 2002 | 2004 |
|---|---|---|---|---|---|
| Democrats | 33.4 | 33.0 | 35.5 | 55.6 | 44.3 |
| Republicans | 47.9 | 45.4 | 52.8 | 65.1 | 60.5 |

## Time Spent Reading Or Watching Political News

Half the American people never read a newspaper. Half never vote for President — the same half?

— Novelist Gore Vidal[28]

ticleCareerCenter.jsp?id=1171015369928.

27 The calculation is 40.4/54.3 = 74.4%.

28 Gore Vidal quoted by Herbert Mitgang, "Books of the Times: One Affair with Movies and One of Sacrifice," in *New York Times* (NY: September 23, 1992).

By analyzing the cumulative results of numerous surveys of the American National Election Studies, we can determine that Republicans, over the long haul, have been slightly more likely to read about or watch programs about specific political candidates and campaigns.

*Table 18. NES cumulative surveys: Questions reflecting on one's diligence in following political activities*

| Question | No. of cases | Range of test years | Percent "Yes" | | Conf % | *RP |
|---|---|---|---|---|---|---|
| | | | Dems | Reps | | |
| Did you watch the campaign on TV? | 20139 | 19 surveys from 1952 to 2004 | 78.1 | 80.6 | +99 | .97 |
| Did you hear about campaign on the radio? | 18363 | 17 surveys from 1952 to 2004 | 43.9 | 47.4 | +99 | .93 |
| Did you read about campaign in magazines? | 16027 | 15 surveys from 1952 to 2004 | 30.3 | 39.2 | +99 | .77 |
| Did you read about the campaign in newspapers? | 19608 | 19 surveys from 1952 to 2004 | 69.2 | 74.8 | +99 | .93 |
| Average percentages | | | 55.4 | 60.5 | | |
| Overall proportion (Dem % divided by Rep %) | | | 91.6% | | | |

*RP is relative proportion, which is the Democratic % divided by the Republican %.

Based upon the NES survey results (Table 18, above) we might conclude that, on average, Democrats are about 92 percent as likely as Republicans to pay attention to political campaigns and candidates. However, recent survey information suggests that Republican interest in political news has waned since 2004, and there is now a rough parity in the political news appetites of Democrats and Republicans. In a Biennial News Consumption survey, released in July 2006, Pew found that Democrats and Republicans are equally likely to have "high interest" in "hard news," defined as political, international, and business news. Perhaps the drop in Republican news interest between 2004 and 2006 was caused by the GOP's loss of control of Congress, or by the discouraging news from Iraq, prior to the security improvement resulting from the military "surge."

It is also important to realize that, with the exception of Fox News, certain radio political talk shows (such as Rush Limbaugh), and Internet news, Democrats are more likely to watch and listen to most general news programming, including National Public Radio, CNN, PBS, the broadcast evening news shows, and local news shows.

## Reality check — The impact of perceived media bias

So you look at what's happened to the liberal media in the last few months and years, Jayson Blair, the New York Times, lying about circulation at Newsday and all these other newspapers, CBS running with bogus [Bush's National Guard] documents. The list is expanding. The old media is losing credibility and audience by refusing to acknowledge that and clean up its act.

— Author and radio talk show host Rush Limbaugh[29]

Media preferences, discussed above, may be driven by concerns about media bias. Republicans are much more skeptical regarding the accuracy and fairness of reporting by major news organizations. This phenomenon was described by Pew in one of its 2006 reports:

> Republicans express less confidence than Democrats in the credibility of nearly every major news outlet, with the exception of Fox News Channel. Among TV and radio sources, the partisan gap is particularly evident for the NewsHour with Jim Lehrer and NPR — Democrats are twice as likely as Republicans to say they believe all or most of what these outlets report, placing them among the *most* credible sources for Democrats, and among the *least* credible for Republicans.[30]

However, Republicans don't always want objective news coverage. When it comes to the "War on Terror," Republicans are more likely to want pro-American news coverage rather than neutral news coverage. This was the expressed view of 33.5 percent of surveyed Republicans, versus 19.5 percent of surveyed Democrats.[31]

### Who has more scientific knowledge?

> The Bush administration has declared war on science. In the Orwellian world of 21st century America, two plus two no longer equals four where public policy is concerned, and science is no exception. When a right-wing theory is contradicted by an inconvenient scientific fact, the science is not refuted; it is simply discarded or ignored.

> — Howard Dean, Chairman of the Democratic National Committee[32]

In 2006, GSS asked several questions designed to assess scientific knowledge. With regard to very simple questions (i.e., idiot level), there was no significant difference in the likelihood that Democrats and Republicans would answer

29 Rush Limbaugh, "Final Days of Elite Media Empire," (Radio show transcript:Rushlimbaugh. com, September 10, 2004).

30 "Online Papers Modestly Boost Newspaper Readership," *Pew Research Center Survey Reports* (July 30, 2007), Retrieved December 19, 2007, from http://people-press.org/reports/pdf/282. pdf.

31 Pew News Interest Index survey dated June 26, 2005, based on 938 cases, with 99+% significance, and relative proportion of .58.

32 Howard Dean, "Bush's War on Science," *Common Dreams News Center* (July 5, 2004), Retrieved August 3, 2007, from http://www.commondreams.org/views04/0705-04.htm.

correctly. For example, both groups were about equally likely to know that elec-
trons are smaller than atoms (73% correct), the earth goes around the sun (81%
correct), and the center of the earth is very hot (94% correct).

There were a few tougher questions, however, and on those Republicans
were more likely to answer correctly. These are shown in Table 19, below.

*Table 19. GSS 2006 survey: Basic science questions*

| Question | No. of cases | Percent correct | | Conf % | *RP |
| --- | --- | --- | --- | --- | --- |
| | | Dems | Reps | | |
| Is it true that "all radioac-tivity is man-made? | 920 | 80.6 | **88.1** | +99 | .91 |
| Do "antibiotics kill viruses as well as bacteria"? | 996 | 56.4 | **69.3** | +99 | .81 |
| Do "lasers work by focus-ing sound waves"? | 685 | 64.1 | **74.9** | +99 | .86 |
| Is astrology scientific? | 1058 | 63.0 | **77.9** | +99 | .81 |
| Average percentages | | 66.0 | 77.6 | | |
| Overall proportion (Dem % divided by Rep %) | | 85.1% | | | |

*RP is relative proportion, which is the Democratic % divided by the Republican %.

*Figure 54. Is it true that...? (GSS survey conducted in 2006, based on, left to right, 940 and 741 cases, with confidence level of 99+% for each column, and relative proportions of .134 and 1.40)*

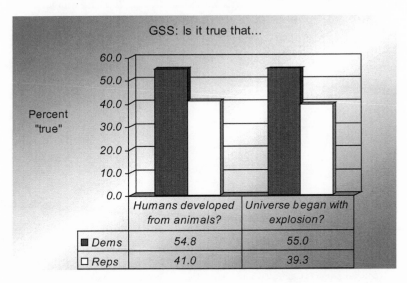

## What Happens When Science Collides With Religion?

> Republicans don't believe in the imagination, partly because so few of them have one, but mostly because it gets in the way of their chosen work, which is to destroy the human race and the planet.

— Columnist Michael Feingold[33]

Republicans are sometimes accused of being anti-science, and there may be some truth to that charge with regard to certain questions that force a choice between science and religion. Responses to two such questions, involving evolution and the "big bang" theory of the universe, are shown in Figure 54. In each case we see that Republicans are more likely to reject the consensus position of the scientific community.

A Gallup survey, conducted in June, 2007, confirms the results pertaining to evolution. By 57 to 30 percent, Democrats were more likely to state that they believed in evolution. Most of the Republicans who rejected the theory cited religious beliefs as the reason.[34]

*Figure 55. Do you have (at least) a high school diploma? (Men) (NES surveys conducted in 1956 through 2004, based on, left to right, 2371, 2343, 2490, 2786, and 2042 cases, with confidence level of 99+% for all differences, and with relative proportions of, left to right, .78, .79, .78, .84, and .90)*

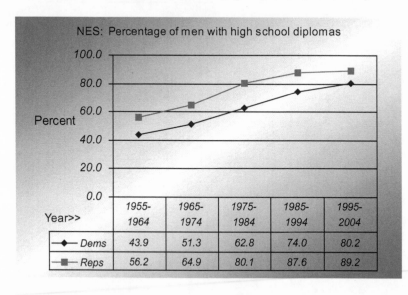

| Year>> | 1955-1964 | 1965-1974 | 1975-1984 | 1985-1994 | 1995-2004 |
|---|---|---|---|---|---|
| ◆ Dems | 43.9 | 51.3 | 62.8 | 74.0 | 80.2 |
| ■ Reps | 56.2 | 64.9 | 80.1 | 87.6 | 89.2 |

33 Michael Feingold, "Foreman's Wake-up Call," *Village Voice* (January 21-27, 2004), Retrieved December 8, 2006, from http://www.villagevoice.com.

34 Frank Newport, "Majority of Republicans Doubt Theory of Evolution," *The Gallup News Service* (June 11, 2007), Retrieved July 30, 2007, from Http://brain.gallup.com. The results were based upon a survey of 1,007 adults.

*Who has more formal education?*

> Education's purpose is to replace an empty mind with an open one.
>
> — Publisher Malcolm S. Forbes[35]

### High School Diplomas

NES has been collecting data regarding diploma and degree attainment for more than 5 decades, and during that time Republicans have been more likely than Democrats to earn high school diplomas. Figure 55 shows the 50-year trend lines for men.

As shown in Figure 56, below, there has been a similar diploma disparity for women.

*Figure 56. Do you have (at least) a high school diploma? (Women) (NES surveys conducted in 1956 through 2004, based on, left to right, 3017, 3332, 3682, 3690, and 2667 cases, with confidence level of 99+% for all differences, and with relative proportions of, left to right, .82, .79, .84, .88, and .90)*

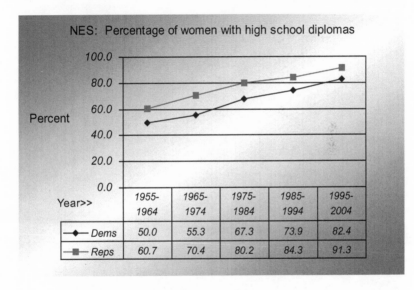

| Year>> | 1955-1964 | 1965-1974 | 1975-1984 | 1985-1994 | 1995-2004 |
|---|---|---|---|---|---|
| Dems | 50.0 | 55.3 | 67.3 | 73.9 | 82.4 |
| Reps | 60.7 | 70.4 | 80.2 | 84.3 | 91.3 |

> Brains, you know, are suspect in the Republican Party.
>
> — Author and journalist Walter Lippmann[36]

By the way, contrary to popular perceptions, women are not less likely than men to have a high school diploma, and this has been true for at least 50 years.

---

35 Malcolm Forbes (attributed), "Quotations on Teaching, Learning, and Education," (National Teaching & Learning Forum), Retrieved March 27, 2007, from: http://www.ntlf.com/html/lib/quotes.htm.

36 Walter Lippman (attributed), *Simpson's Contemporary Quotations* (1988).

Compare the high school graduation rates for men (Figure 55) to the percentages for women (Figure 56).

Surveys conducted by other organizations also show a Republican high school diploma advantage. For example, GSS surveys are show this tendency. (See Appendix B 1.) And, in a report entitled, "Who are the Democrats," Gallup notes:

> Although both Democrats and Republicans have equal numbers of Americans at the upper end of the educational spectrum — that is, with post graduate degrees — Democrats are more likely than Republicans to be in the category of those with only high school educations or less.[37]

Thus, there is agreement by all major survey entities: Republicans are more likely to have, at the least, a high school diploma.[38]

### Four-Year College Degrees

> College-bred is a four-year loaf, using dad's dough, coming out half-baked, with a lot of crust.

— Anonymous[39]

Although the Gallup Organization explicitly commented on the disparity in high school diplomas, it did not address the significant gap in 4-year college degrees. Republican males have dominated at this level (Figure 57).

*Figure 57. Do you have a 4-year college diploma (at the least)? (Men) (NES surveys conducted in 1955 through 2004, based on, left to right, 2371, 2343, 2490, 2786, and 2042 cases, with confidence level of 99+% for all differences, and with relative proportions of, left to right, .45, .48, .51, .60, and .63)*

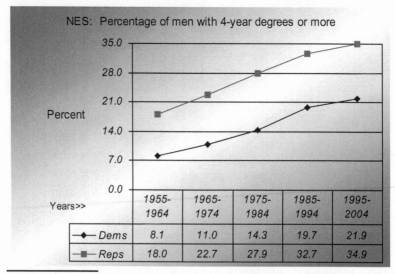

| Years>> | 1955-1964 | 1965-1974 | 1975-1984 | 1985-1994 | 1995-2004 |
|---|---|---|---|---|---|
| Dems | 8.1 | 11.0 | 14.3 | 19.7 | 21.9 |
| Reps | 18.0 | 22.7 | 27.9 | 32.7 | 34.9 |

---

37 Frank Newport, "Who Are the Democrats?," *The Gallup News Service* (August 11, 2000), Retrieved March 13, 2006, from Http://brain.gallup.com.

38 . For GSS surveys pertaining to high school graduation rates, see Appendix B 1.

39 "Quotationz.Com."

The 4-year college degree gap is smaller for women, but still significant, according to NES (Figure 58). Important note: GSS surveys show a much smaller disparity in the attainment of 4-year degrees by Democratic and Republican women. In fact, GSS shows virtually no gap in recent years. Please see Figure 284 on page 347.

*Figure 58. Do you have a 4-year college diploma (or higher degree)? (Women) (NES surveys conducted in 1955 through 2004, based on, left to right, 3017, 3332, 3682, 3690, and 2667 cases, with confidence level of 99+% for all differences, and with relative proportions of, left to right, .66, .49, .66, .74, and .74)*

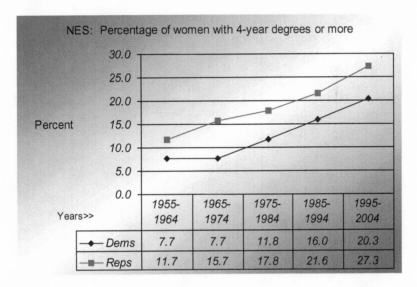

What a waste it is to lose one's mind. Or not to have a mind is being very wasteful. How true that is.

— Vice President Dan Quayle[40]

It is interesting to note (by comparing Figure 57 with Figure 58) that Republican males have earned 4-year college degrees at a significantly higher rate than Republican females. On the other hand, Democratic men and women have earned college degrees at approximately the same rate. GSS and Pew surveys on 4-year college degrees attainment rates can be found in Appendix B 2.

*Reality check — Are college campuses infested with Republicans?*

You may be wondering why more Republicans have college degrees, yet the student bodies of colleges seem to lean to the political left. It is truly not a mystery. Although college students tend to be Democrats (or liberals of some sort), many eventually become Republicans (or conservatives of some type) after they graduate, get jobs, and start their families. This explanation is supported

---

40 Elizabeth Knowles, ed., *Oxford Dictionary of Twentieth Century Quotations* (Oxford: Oxford University Press, 1998), 258.

by survey evidence, discussed on page 266, suggesting that Democrats are more likely to become Republicans, than vice versa. Also, when it comes to earning advanced (graduate school) degrees, there is a rough parity between Democrats and Republicans.

### Graduate School Degrees

A university is what a college becomes when the faculty loses interest in students.

— Poet John Ciardi[41]

NES also shows a small but significant difference between Democratic and Republican men with regard to advanced university degrees, with Republican males having the edge.

*Figure 59. Do you have a graduate college degree? (Men) (NES surveys conducted in 1955 through 2004, based on, left to right, 2371, 2343, 2490, 2786, and 2042 cases, with confidence level of, left to right, 99+%, 99+%, 97%, zero (not significant), and 99+% for all differences, and with relative proportions of, left to right, .29, .55, .73, n/a, and .89)*

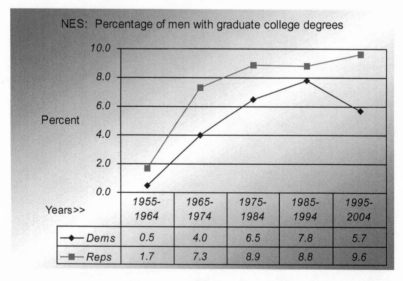

With regard to women, however, NES shows no difference in the rate of attainment of advanced degrees. None of the differences in Figure 60, below, is significant.

*Figure 60. Do you have a graduate college degree? (Women) (NES surveys conducted in 1955 through 2004, based on, left to right, 3017, 3332, 3682, 3690, and 2667 cases, with no statistical significance for any of the differences depicted)*

---

41 John Ciardi cited by W.W. Betts. Jr. in, "Hermes and Apollo," *Peabody Journal of Education* 48, no. 1 (1970): 49.

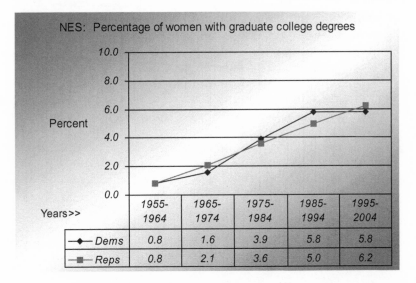

NES: Percentage of women with graduate college degrees

| Years>> | 1955-1964 | 1965-1974 | 1975-1984 | 1985-1994 | 1995-2004 |
|---|---|---|---|---|---|
| Dems | 0.8 | 1.6 | 3.9 | 5.8 | 5.8 |
| Reps | 0.8 | 2.1 | 3.6 | 5.0 | 6.2 |

I never meant to say that the Conservatives are generally stupid. I meant to say that stupid people are generally Conservative. I believe that is so obviously and universally admitted a principle that I hardly think any gentleman will deny it.

— John Stuart Mill, English philosopher and economist[42]

*Figure 61. Do you have a graduate school degree? (Women) (GSS surveys conducted in 1977 through 2006, based on, left to right, 3017, 3332, and 3682 cases, with confidence level of, left to right, zero, 99% and 99+%, and with relative proportions of, left to right, n/a, 1.37, and 1.42)*

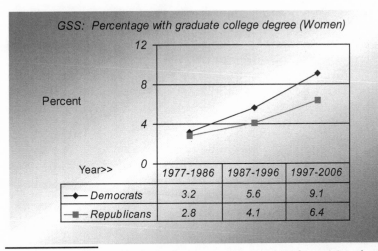

GSS: Percentage with graduate college degree (Women)

| Year>> | 1977-1986 | 1987-1996 | 1997-2006 |
|---|---|---|---|
| Democrats | 3.2 | 5.6 | 9.1 |
| Republicans | 2.8 | 4.1 | 6.4 |

---

42 John Stuart Mill in, "Letter to the Conservative MP, Sir John Pakington (March, 1866)," (Spartacus Educational), Retrieved April 8, 2007, from: http://www.spartacus.schoolnet.co.uk/PRmill.htm.

In most cases, GSS survey results are similar to NES results; however, that is not the case with regard to the attainment of graduate school degrees by women. GSS surveys show that, during the last 30 years, Democratic women have pulled ahead of Republican women, and now are more likely to earn an advanced degree. These results are shown in Figure 61, above.

Thus, we can conclude that Republicans have had a small but consistent advantage with regard to formal education for several decades, with one exception: the attainment of graduate school degrees by women. NES surveys show that Democratic and Republican females have been equally likely to earn advanced college degrees during the last 50 years. And, in conflict with the NES results, GSS surveys show that Democratic women have already overtaken their Republican complements with regard to the attainment of advanced degrees.

*Who is more intelligent?*

> Intelligence recognizes what has happened. Genius recognizes what will happen.

— Poet John Ciardi[43]

### Interviewer Impressions

We noted that NES interviewers are asked to give an overall ranking to the political knowledge of each respondent. Likewise, they are asked to give an assessment of the "apparent intelligence" of each survey participant. Of course, the interviewers are not trained psychologists administering IQ tests, so we must add a large grain of salt when utilizing this information. Nevertheless, it is entirely possible that an interviewer would have a feel for the alertness and mental quickness of a participant, after asking him/her many questions over an extended period of time.[44]

The assessments made during each pre-election survey conducted in 1996 through 2004 are summarized in Figure 62, below, and the percentages of Democrats and Republicans judged to have "fairly" or "very high" intelligence are shown. The differences are quite large. On average (for the 5 surveys in aggregate), 48.8 percent of Democrats were rated fairly or very high in intelligence, whereas 64.4 percent of Republicans were given that assessment. Expressed another way, Democrats were about 76 percent as likely to be judged to have fairly or very high intelligence.[45]

*Figure 62. Interviewer's concluding assessment of "apparent intelligence" (consecutive NES pre-election surveys conducted in 1996 through 2004, based on, left to right, 1099, 814, 927, 970, and 707 cases, with confidence level of 99+% for all 5 differences, and relative proportions of, left to right, .71, .71, .74, .83, and .78)*

---

43 John Ciardi (attributed), "Simpson's Contemporary Quotations," (Houghlin Mifflin Company, 1988).

44 NES conducts "face-to-face" survey interviews in all presidential election years. Often these sessions last for more than an hour.

45 The calculation is 48.8/64.4 = 75.8%.

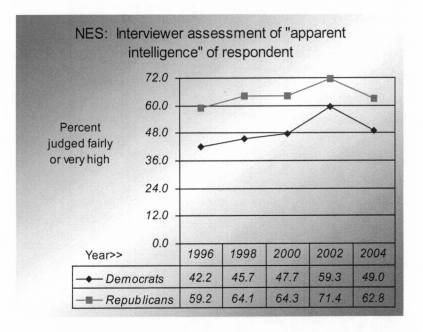

| Year>> | 1996 | 1998 | 2000 | 2002 | 2004 |
|---|---|---|---|---|---|
| Democrats | 42.2 | 45.7 | 47.7 | 59.3 | 49.0 |
| Republicans | 59.2 | 64.1 | 64.3 | 71.4 | 62.8 |

## Tests of Reasoning Ability (Or What's Your "Fruit IQ"?)

I had a lot of experience with people smarter than I am.
— President Gerald Ford[46]

*Figure 63. "In what way are an orange and a banana alike?" (GSS survey conducted in 1994, based on 1872 cases, with confidence level of 99+%, and with a relative proportion of .92)*

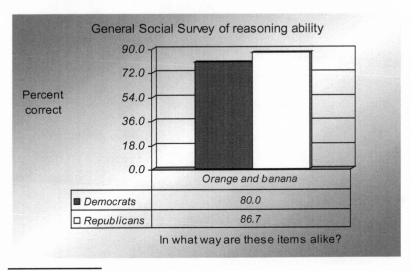

| | Orange and banana |
|---|---|
| Democrats | 80.0 |
| Republicans | 86.7 |

46 President Gerald Ford (attributed), "Brainyquote.Com."

Do Democrats and Republicans differ in their ability to reason? I could not find an abundance of information addressing that subject but, in 1994, the General Social Survey asked respondents 8 questions that could be used to test reasoning ability. Statistically significant differences were found with regard to 6 of the 8 questions, and in each of those cases the Republican respondents were slightly more likely to answer correctly. The results for the six questions are shown in charts below. Unfortunately, the answer options were not published by GSS.

> I won't insult your intelligence by suggesting that you really believe what you just said.
>
> — William F. Buckley, Author and political commentator[47]

Most people had no difficulty with the question about fruit (Figure 63). The question about an egg and seed (Figure 64) was more difficult — especially for Democrats.

*Figure 64. "In what way are an egg and seed alike?" (GSS survey conducted in 1994, based on 1745 cases, with confidence level of 99+%, and with a relative proportion of .73)*

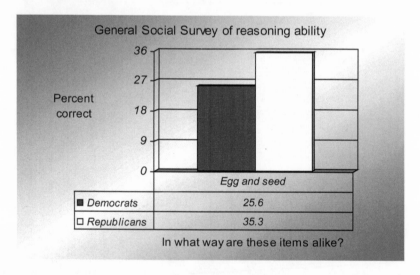

Almost everyone had difficulty with regard to "work and play." The correct answer rate was in single digits for constituents of either party (Figure 65).

> "Weird" may have been okay during my upbringing, but "stupid" most emphatically was not. And Republican affiliation seemed to my parents to represent the most glaring and appalling example of stupidity.
>
> — Michael Medved, Author and radio talk show host[48]

---

47 William F. Buckley (attributed), "Thinkexist.Com."
48 Michael Medved, *Right Turns*, 1st ed. (New York: Random House, 2004), 41.

*Figure 65. "In what way are work and play alike?" (GSS survey conducted in 1994, based on 1782 cases, with confidence level of 96%), and with a relative proportion of .69)*

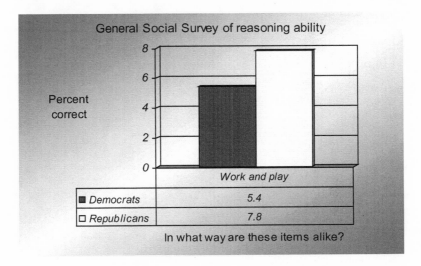

A majority correctly answered a question about animals.

*Figure 66. "In what way are a dog and a lion alike?" (GSS survey conducted in 1994, based on 1865 cases, with confidence level of 98%, and with a relative proportion of .93)*

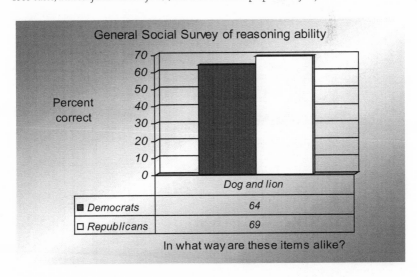

Only half of Republicans and even fewer Democrats correctly answered the following question about anatomy.

*Figure 67. "In what way are an eye and ear alike?" (GSS survey conducted in 1994, based on 1840 cases, with confidence level of 96%, and with a relative proportion of .91)*

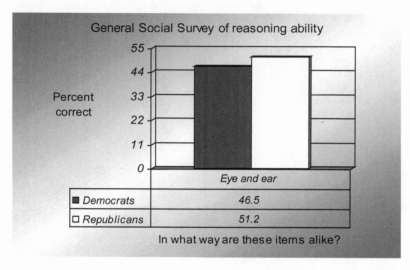

Finally, almost everyone struck out with respect to "praise and punishment."

*Figure 68. "In what way are praise and punishment alike?" (GSS survey conducted in 1994, based on 1689 cases, with confidence level of 91% (marginal), and with a relative proportion of .79)*

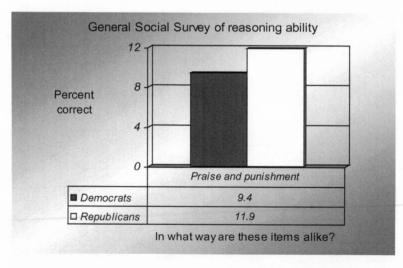

If we combine the results for these 6 questions, we find that, on average, Democrats answered correctly only about 88 percent as often as Republicans. More appropriately, however, we should use the results of all 8 questions, including the 2 for which there was no statistically significant difference. In that case, the Democrats were about 90 percent as likely to correctly answer the questions.

### Word Tests

> Ideas improve. The meaning of words participates in the improvement.
>
> — French writer and film maker Guy Debord[49]

The General Social Survey also tested the word comprehension of participants in several surveys conducted during the last 30 years. Respondents were asked to guess the correct (or most nearly correct) meaning of 10 words, by associated each of them with another listed word with a similar meaning. The results of those tests, for males, are depicted in Figure 69, below. Republican males have consistently scored higher on this test; however, the gap is closing quickly.

*Figure 69. What is the meaning of these 10 commonly-used words? Results equal the percentage of correct answers for men. (GSS surveys conducted in 1977 through 2006, based on, left to right, 2916, 6596, and 3258 cases, with confidence level of at least 99% for each column.)*

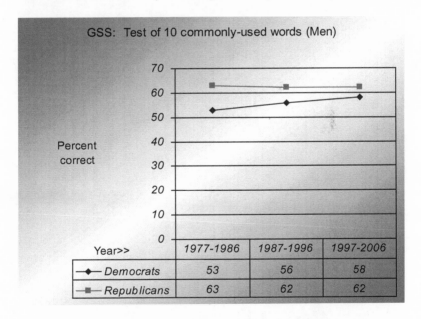

With regard to women, we see similar results. Although Republican women have consistently outscored Democratic women, the differential is getting smaller.

---

49 Guy Debord (attributed), "Columbia World of Quotations," (Columbia University Press, 1996).

*Figure 70. What is the meaning of these 10 commonly-used words? Results equal the percentage of correct answers for women. (GSS surveys conducted in 1977 through 2006, based on, left to right, 1774, 3906, and 1895 cases, with confidence level of at least 99% for each column.)*

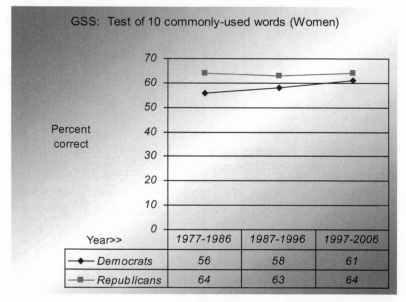

GSS: Test of 10 commonly-used words (Women)

| Year>> | 1977-1986 | 1987-1996 | 1997-2006 |
|---|---|---|---|
| Democrats | 56 | 58 | 61 |
| Republicans | 64 | 63 | 64 |

I think this last year has just proven how stupid Republicans are.

— Comedian Margaret Cho[50]

## ANALYSIS: WHY IS THERE A DISPARITY?

*What Factors Correlate With Education?*

The average Republican has had a discernable education and knowledge advantage, and may have the edge with regard to reasoning and vocabulary skills.[51] Why is this? In the remainder of the chapter, we consider one of the above factors (the number of years of schooling), and determine if it correlates with traits commonly thought to distinguish Republicans from Democrats. Specifically, we consider the relationship between the average years of education and each of the variables in Table 20, below.

### The Thirty-Year Analysis

Using basic statistics and 30 years of GSS survey data it is possible to test the relationship between each factor and the number of years of schooling. Details of

---

50 Margaret Cho as quoted in, "Hollywood Vs. America: Moveon Stays on Bush-Hitler Theme," *WorldNetDaily*, Retrieved March 14, 2007, from http://worldnetdaily.com/news/.

51 With regard to education and political knowledge, numerous and large surveys allow us to reach firm conclusions. However, with regard to reasoning and vocabulary skills relevant survey results are limited, and firm conclusions should be avoided.

the underlying multiple regression analysis are shown in Appendix B 3. We find that education is strongly correlated with income, health, and, to a lesser extent, race. Specifically, having higher income, having good health, and being white are factors that correlate positively with more years of schooling. Surprisingly, there is a moderate and *negative* correlation between years of education and marriage. That is, being married correlates with less education.

*Table 20. Variables commonly thought to distinguish Republicans from Democrats*

| Variable | Specific question used in this analysis |
|---|---|
| Income | Is family income at least $50,000 (in 2006 dollars)? |
| Health | Is respondent's health good or excellent? |
| Race | Is respondent white? |
| Marital status | Is respondent married? |
| Political views | Is respondent a conservative (moderate to strong)? |
| Religiosity | Does respondent claim to have strong religious convictions? |
| Gender | Is the respondent a man? |

The top row of Table 21, below, shows the 30-year Democrat-Republican education gap, if no other variables are considered. The next 3 rows show the gap if we control each of the factors found to significantly and positively correlate with education.

*Table 21. Democratic and Republican years of education, in light of various correlating factors — 30 year analysis*

| Thirty year analysis<br><br>Survey population limited to: | Ave. yrs. of school Dems | Ave. yrs. of school Reps | Gap in years | No. of cases | Conf % |
|---|---|---|---|---|---|
| All respondents (no limitation) | 12.57 | 13.39 | −.82 | 27188 | +99 |
| Just those earning over $50000/year | 13.83 | 14.22 | −.39 | 10725 | +99 |
| Just those in good or excellent health | 13.11 | 13.69 | −.58 | 14747 | +99 |
| Just those who are white | 12.70 | 13.46 | −.76 | 21759 | +99 |
| All of the 3 factors, above | 14.09 | 14.30 | −.21 | 5746 | +99 |

As we would expect, the education gap between Democrats and Republicans (.82 years), shown on the top line, decreases when we control for income, health, or race. When we control for all 3 factors in combination, the Democratic educational deficit is cut from .82 years to just .21 years. That remaining amount (.21 years) could be called the unidentified "Republican educational factor" that existed during the last 30 years.

My guess is more reporters probably vote Democrat than Republican — just because I think reporters are smart.

— TV personality Jerry Springer[52]

## A Nine Year Analysis Produces Different Results

I prepared an alternative analysis that is limited to more recent years, from 1998 through 2006. Details of the underlying multiple regression analysis are shown in Appendix B 4 on page 348. Again, education was found to positively correlate with higher income, good health, and race; and was found to negatively correlate with marriage. The impact of each significant and positively-correlating factor is shown in Table 22, below.

*Table 22. Democratic and Republican years of education, in light of various correlating factors — 9-year analysis*

| Nine-year analysis<br><br>Survey population limited to: | Ave. yrs. of school Dems | Ave. yrs. of school Reps | Gap in years | No. of cases | Conf % |
|---|---|---|---|---|---|
| All respondents (no limitation) | 13.37 | **13.88** | -.51 | 9305 | +99 |
| Just those earning over $50000/ year | 14.63 | 14.57 | .06 | 3878 | * |
| Just those in good or excellent health | 13.72 | **14.12** | -.40 | 5420 | +99 |
| Just those who are white | 13.55 | **13.96** | -.41 | 7197 | +99 |
| All of the 3 factors, above | 14.73 | 14.64 | .09 | 2144 | * |

In the 9-year analysis we find that controlling for the income difference is, by itself, sufficient to eliminate the Republican advantage. The advantage is also eliminated when all 3 correlating factors are combined. In other words, there is no longer a "Republican educational factor."

## The Peculiar Relationship Between Party Identity and Political Ideology

### Too Dumb To Know Which Party Is Which?

I'm a meathead. I can't help it, man. You've got smart people and you've got dumb people.

— Actor Keanu Reeves[53]

---

52 Jerry Springer (attributed), "Brainyquote.Com."

53 Keanu Reeves cited in, "Dumb Beau," in *Guardian Unlimited*, ed. John Patterson (U.K.), Retrieved April 1, 2007, from: http://film.guardian.co.uk/features/featurepages/0,,957479,00.html#article_continue.

---

If we analyze the educational achievements of "conservatives," grouped together without regard to political party, we find only small correlation between years of education and conservatism (generally a positive correlation). However, when we break-out conservatives by political party, the results are quite different: Conservative Republicans tend to be the most educated, while conservative Democrats are likely to be the least educated. A similar pattern is evident for liberals: Democratic liberals tend to have more education than the Republican liberals. This peculiar pattern is depicted in Figure 71, which shows educational attainment for a 30-year period extending from 1975 through 2006. Are liberal Republicans and conservative Democrats so uneducated that they don't realize they are in the wrong party?

*Figure 71. What is your "highest year of school completed"? (GSS surveys conducted in 1977 through 2006 of, left to right, 599, 2845, 2998, 8644, 4023, 4095, and 875 cases, with confidence level of at least 99+% for all differences except the one designated "Slightly liberal," for which there is 95% confidence level)*

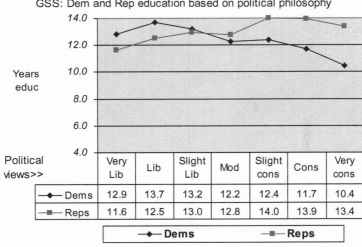

GSS: Dem and Rep education based on political philosophy

| Political views>> | Very Lib | Lib | Slight Lib | Mod | Slight cons | Cons | Very cons |
|---|---|---|---|---|---|---|---|
| Dems | 12.9 | 13.7 | 13.2 | 12.2 | 12.4 | 11.7 | 10.4 |
| Reps | 11.6 | 12.5 | 13.0 | 12.8 | 14.0 | 13.9 | 13.4 |

The difference in educational achievement between conservative Democrats and Republicans is particularly great, and can be quantified by comparing the educational achievements of Democrats and Republicans while controlling for their degree of "conservatism." This is done in Table 23, below.

The second row of Table 23 is illuminating. It shows that Democrats who are conservative have, on average, much less education than other Democrats (11.96 years versus 12.57 years). On the other hand, Republicans who are conservatives have much more education than other Republicans (13.92 years versus 13.39 years). Putting these two tendencies together, there is a difference of nearly 2 years between the educational achievements of conservative Democrats and conservative Republicans (11.96 years versus 13.92 years). I found no demographic variable, or combination of variables, that produces an educational gap this large. If political scientists fail to take heed of this fact, the generalizations they make about conservatives or liberals are apt to be misleading. This is particularly important with regard to conservatives because 25 to 50 percent of all self-identified "conservatives" in the United States are Democrats. Please see Chapter 11 for additional discussion of this phenomenon.

*Table 23. A quantification of the large educational difference between conservative Democrats and conservative Republicans*

| 30-year analysis<br><br>Survey population limited to: | Ave. yrs. of school Dems | Ave. yrs. of school Reps | Gap in years | No. of cases | Conf % |
|---|---|---|---|---|---|
| All respondents (no limitation) | 12.57 | 13.39 | −0.82 | 27188 | +99 |
| All respondents who are conservative | 11.96 | 13.92 | −1.96 | 8982 | +99 |

> Human beings only use ten percent of their brains. Ten percent! Can you imagine how much we could accomplish if we used the other sixty percent?
>
> — Comedian Ellen Degeneres[54]

## CONCLUSIONS

Republicans are more likely to correctly answer questions related to basic political knowledge and, in some cases, scientific knowledge. However, where the scientific knowledge conflicts with religious beliefs, Republicans are less likely to give the answers that most scientists would provide.

There is some information suggesting that Republicans are more likely to correctly identify analogous relationships and the meanings of words. Also, survey interviewers are much more likely to give high marks to Republicans for political knowledge and "apparent intelligence."

During the last 50 years, Republicans have been more likely to earn high school diplomas, 4-year college degrees, and, with regard to men, graduate school (advanced) degrees. Depending upon the survey source, Democratic women have recently equaled or significantly exceeded Republican women with regard to the attainment of advanced college degrees.

Higher family income, good health, and being (racially) white are factors which correlate positively with educational achievement (measured by years of schooling). In fact, they seem to explain most or all of the Republican educational advantage. On the other hand, marriage correlates negatively with educational achievement.

---

54 "Ellen Degeneres: The Beginning" (2000), Retrieved March 14, 2007, from IMdb: http://imdb.com.

There is only a small correlation between political orientation (conservative versus liberal) and education. However, a more meaningful analysis requires that we distinguish conservatives and liberals by political party. Republican conservatives and Democratic liberals are far more educated than Democratic conservatives and Republican liberals. They are at opposite ends of the educational spectrum.

Finally, the ability of someone to make sound judgments depends upon more than college diplomas and hours spent reading the newspaper. People learn valuable lessons in the home and from their personal and economic successes and failures. And, even when they have complete command of the facts, people can fail to reach the proper conclusions, due to their own lack of objectivity.

At the beginning of this chapter, it was noted that, shortly before the 2004 Presidential election, nearly half of surveyed Republicans believed that Saddam Hussein had weapons of mass destruction before the U.S. invasion. In addition, more than half of these Republicans thought that Hussein provided support to al Qaeda. Is this an indication of Republican ignorance or stupidity? Perhaps, it is. However, it could also be evidence of party constituents faithfully supporting their candidate in the heat of a political campaign. Or, it could be evidence that many Republicans thought weapons were removed just prior to the invasion, and that ties to al Qaeda were concealed. (And, neither belief can be proven false.)[55] The point is that a fair analysis of education and intelligence cannot be made on the basis of controversial questions raised in the midst of a political campaign. As shown in this chapter, however, it is possible to make a sound assessment, if it is based upon comprehensive and non-controversial survey data.[56]

---

55 After the Iraq Survey Group's "final" report (dated September 30, 2004), an Addendum was issued, in March 2005, to report findings related to the possible movement of weapons to Syria. The Addendum stated: "There was evidence of a discussion of possible WMD collaboration initiated by a Syrian security officer, and ISG [the Iraq Study Group] received information about movement of material out of Iraq, including the possibility that WMD was involved. In the judgment of the working group [formed by ISG to investigate], these reports were sufficiently credible to merit further investigation. ISG was unable to complete its investigation [due to violence] and is unable to rule out the possibility that WMD was evacuated to Syria before the war." In the subsequent year (2006), a former Iraq Air Force officer, George Sada, publicly declared (without providing evidence) that WMD were transported to Syria via trucks and modified commercial passenger planes during 2002. This allegation has not been confirmed or disproven, but it is compatible with testimony reported by the Iraq Survey Group indicating that, until December, 2002, Sadam Hussein told his military generals that he had WMD. According to Sada, the WMD were shipped to Syria only because of the imminence to the U.S. invasion. This is also the conclusion of some members of Israeli Intelligence. We may never have definitive proof that resolves this controversy. (See Iraq Survey Group Final Report, the Group's Addendum, and Georges Sada, *Sadam's Secrets* (Brentwood (TN): Integrity Publishers, 2006), 250-61.)

56 Another controversial political question has to do with Iraq casualty estimates. When asked (in 2005) how many U.S. soldiers have been killed in Iraq, Democrats were less likely to give the "correct" number because they tended to overestimate the amount. Perhaps they did this out of ignorance, perhaps they did it because they thought the government understated casualty figures, or maybe they did it because they were angry at President Bush. In any event, the failure of Democrats to answer the question accurately does not necessarily reflect simple ignorance. For this reason, the Iraq casualty question was omitted from this chapter.

# Chapter 3: Who Is the Better "Working Man"?

## Introduction

> At the Bush White House, the working man is the forgotten man.
>
> — Senator Robert Byrd, Democrat of West Virginia[1]

> In Congress, the battles were fierce because Republicans tried to leave working people behind.
>
> — David Bonior, former Democratic Rep. of Michigan[2]

> A working person who votes for Bush is like a chicken who votes for Colonel Sanders.
>
> — Robert Reich, former U.S. Secretary of Labor[3]

For some people references to the "working man" or "working people" are part of the daily vernacular, and their words often imply that Democrats believe in helping working people while Republicans oppose them. This may lead some

---

1 Senator Robert Byrd as quoted by Nick Anderson, "Race for the White House," *Los Angeles Times*, October 12 2004.

2 David Bonior as cited in, "Democrats: GOP Forsaking Working Class," (CNN.com, December 29, 2001), Retrieved December 6, 2004, from: http://archives.cnn.com/2001/ALLPOLITICS/12/29/democrats.radio/index.html.

3 Robert Reich as quoted by Candice Rainey, "Do Celebrity Plugs Translate to Votes?," (2004), Retrieved December 7, 2004, from http://us.gq.com/culture/general/articles/040928plc0_02.

to assume that Democrats are working people, and Republicans are not. But, is this true?

To answer the question, we must make two determinations: Who is more likely to work for a living and, among those working, who is the more valuable worker, and why? Given the historical differences in the nature of work done by men versus women, this analysis is best done one gender at a time.

After the separate male and female analyses, this chapter contains some general information on occupational types and job "prestige." Yes, it is possible to estimate, in an objective and quantified manner, the relative cachet of the work we do.

## THE BETTER WORKING MAN

*Who is more likely to work for a living?*

> The Democrats were "the party of the working man" decades ago, but now the Republicans are.
>
> — Peggy Noonan, Republican political analyst and author[4]

Republican men are more likely than Democratic men to work outside of the home, and those who do are likely to work longer hours. In Figure 72, below, employment rates of Democratic and Republican men are shown for 6 time periods in years 1952 through 2004. The source is the American National Election Studies (NES).

*Figure 72. Are you currently employed (Men of all ages)? (NES surveys conducted in 1952 through 2004, based on, left to right, 592, 1955, 1964, 2507, 2841, and 2047 cases, with no statistical significance for the 3 differences on the left side of the chart, and a 99+% confidence level for the remaining differences. For the right-side differences the relative proportions are, left to right, .90, .87, and .87.)*

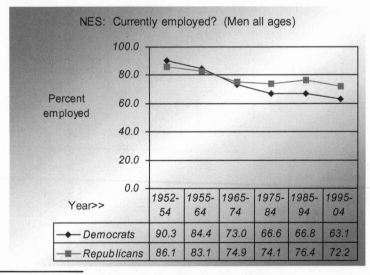

NES: Currently employed? (Men all ages)

| Year>> | 1952-54 | 1955-64 | 1965-74 | 1975-84 | 1985-94 | 1995-04 |
|---|---|---|---|---|---|---|
| Democrats | 90.3 | 84.4 | 73.0 | 66.6 | 66.8 | 63.1 |
| Republicans | 86.1 | 83.1 | 74.9 | 74.1 | 76.4 | 72.2 |

---

4 Peggy Noonan as quoted by Chuck Noe, "Noonan: Why Democrats Become Republicans," in *NewsMax.com* (October 7, 2004), from: http://www.newsmax.com.

An interesting trend is displayed: Forty or fifty years ago, Democratic men were at least as likely as Republican men to be employed. Now, Democratic men are much less likely to be in paid employment (just 88 % as likely during the last 30 years).

> A recession is when your neighbor loses his job. A depression is when you lose yours. A recovery is when Jimmy Carter loses his.
>
> — President Ronald Reagan[5]

If we limit our analysis to men aged 22 to 65 years — the traditional working age — we see a disparity that is similar, but slightly smaller. Among men of this age range the Democratic employment rate has been about 91 percent of the Republican rate during the last 30 years. See Figure 73, below.

*Figure 73. Are you currently employed (Men aged 22 to 65 years)? (NES surveys conducted in 1952 through 2004, based on, left to right, 515, 1648, 1536, 1930, 2231, and 1628 cases, with no statistically significant difference for the left-side differences, and with a 99+% confidence level for the remaining differences. For the statistically significant differences the relative proportions are, left to right, .91, .92, and .91.)*

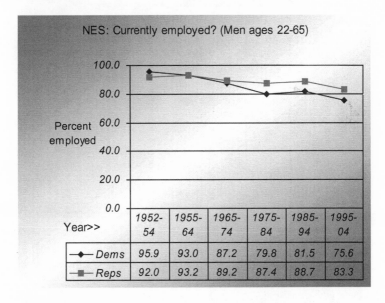

| Year>> | 1952-54 | 1955-64 | 1965-74 | 1975-84 | 1985-94 | 1995-04 |
|---|---|---|---|---|---|---|
| Dems | 95.9 | 93.0 | 87.2 | 79.8 | 81.5 | 75.6 |
| Reps | 92.0 | 93.2 | 89.2 | 87.4 | 88.7 | 83.3 |

The General Social Survey (GSS) also shows an employment gap — but in a different way. It asks men and women how many weeks they worked in the prior year, including paid vacations and sick leave. It appears that Republicans men, aged 22 to 65 years, worked about 3.3 more weeks each year than their Democratic counterparts, between 1994 and 2006.

---

5 Ronald Reagan cited by Brendan Miniter, "The Western Front: Senator No-Show," in *Wall Street Journal* (New York: 2004), Retrieved August 18, from: http://www.opinionjournal.com/columnists/bminiter/?id=110005490.

Figure 74. *"How many weeks did you work either full-time or part-time not counting work around the house? (Include paid vacation and sick time.)" (GSS surveys conducted from 1994 through 2006, limited to men aged 22 to 65 years, based on 4103 cases, with confidence level of 99+%)*

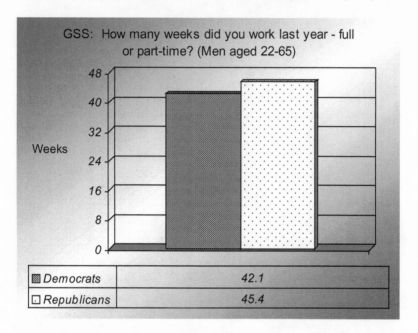

| | |
|---|---|
| ▨ Democrats | 42.1 |
| ☐ Republicans | 45.4 |

The employment gap does not necessarily indicate a difference in work ethics, as there are legitimate reasons why an individual might be unemployed. He could be retired after many years of hard work, he could be disabled, he could be a student too young to work, or he could be laid off from employment — through no fault of his own.

*Why Democratic males are less likely to be employed*

> I have never worked a f---ing day in my life.
> — Democratic Congressman Patrick Kennedy[6]

The General Social Survey (GSS) tracks work status using the 7 categories that are shown in Table 24, below. We see that the employment rate differential is generally linked to factors that are (presumably) unavoidable, such as being unemployed (row 3) or being disabled (row 7). On the other hand, there are a few "lifestyle" choices that also contribute to the employment disparity. These could be characterized as avoidable but legitimate reasons for not being employed. They are found in row 2 (vacation, sick time or strike time), row 4 (retirement by age 65), and row 6 ("keeping house").

6 Lloyd Grove, "Rep. Patrick Kennedy: I've Never Worked a (Bleeping) Day in My Life," in *Jewish World Review* (June 30, 2003), Retrieved August 29, 2006, from: http://www.jewishworldreview.com/0703/grove063003.asp.

*Table 24. Employment status of Democratic and Republican males, aged 22 to 65 years, during the period 1977 through 2006. The differences on the individual rows are not necessarily significant; however the confidence level of the overall cross tabulation (Democratic vs. Republican) is 99+%, and the overall strength of association (Phi) is .11.*

| Row | Work status of Men | Dem % | Rep % | Differ- ence |
|---|---|---|---|---|
| 1 | Working | 78.4 | 85.9 | -7.5 |
| 2 | Vacation, illness, or strike time | 2.9 | 2.6 | 0.3 |
| 3 | Laid off, unemployed | 5.4 | 2.5 | 2.9 |
| 4 | Retired | 6.9 | 4.9 | 2.0 |
| 5 | Student | 1.8 | 1.8 | 0.0 |
| 6 | "Keeping house" | 1.4 | .7 | 0.7 |
| 7 | Other, including disability | 3.2 | 1.6 | 1.6 |
|   | Total | 100 | 100 | 0.0 |

Thus, it is clear that modern Democratic males are less likely than their Republican complements to be in paid employment; however, legitimate reasons may justify all or most of the disparity. Therefore, in our quest to determine the "better working man" we will have to focus on a second criterion: Among those who are employed, who is the more valuable worker?

*Who is the more valuable worker, and why?*

> They say hard work never hurt anybody, but I figure why take the chance.
>
> — President Ronald Reagan[7]

In each of its surveys, the GSS asks respondents to estimate their occupational earnings. Based on the surveys conducted in 1998 through 2004 it is possible to estimate the average earnings for all Democratic and Republican men of working age (assumed to be 22 to 65 years old). These earnings are depicted in Figure 75, below:

As shown in Figure 75, the average working Democratic male (aged 22 to 65 years) earned salary and/or wages that were about $10,400 less per year than his working Republican counterpart (i.e., 18% less.) The median wages (versus average wages) were about $40,200 and $48,500 for Democratic and Republican men, respectively, in 2007 dollars.

> I have ways of making money that you know nothing of.
>
> — John D. Rockefeller, American industrialist[8]

---

7 John C. Hopwood. (2007), "Biography for Ronald Reagan", Retrieved March 16, 2007, from IMdb: http://imdb.com/name/nm0001654/bio.
8 John D. Rockefeller (attributed), "Brainyquote.Com."

*Figure 75. Average earnings reported by Democratic and Republican men aged 22 to 65 years (calculated using wage distributions from GSS surveys in 1998-2004, based on 1862 cases, with confidence level of mean differences of 99+%). The amounts were adjusted by the Consumer Price Index to reflect inflation between the survey years and 2007.*

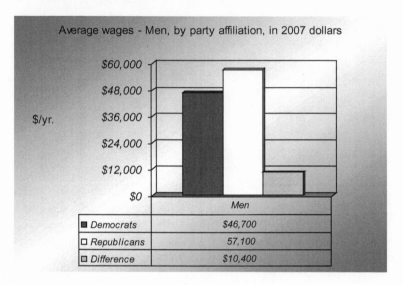

Theoretically, in a free market economy the employees who are paid more are considered (by employers and economists) to be more valuable workers; however, many people distrust decisions made in the market place. They point to "glass ceilings," "silver spoons," "old boys clubs," luck, and outright discrimination as factors that contribute to pay inequities. These skeptics conclude that some people — the working people — truly earn their wages, while others do not. To satisfy such skeptics we must justify the pay differences, and that is what we do in the remainder of this chapter. We compare Democratic and Republican men in the context of 5 assessment criteria: work hours, the amount of education brought to the job, the boss' opinion as manifested by supervisory assignments, expressed work attitudes, and emotional stability. Using that approach, we identify the better "working man."

*Who works longer hours?*

> [T]he Republican's and corporate America's vision ... is that the rich get richer and everyone else fights for the crumbs, everyone else has to work harder, work longer hours....
>
> — Film producer Michael Moore[9]

---

9 Michael Moore as cited in, "Countdown with Keith Olbermann," (In video clip:MSNBC, November 6, 2007), Retrieved November 7, 2007, from: http://www.msnbc.msn.com/id/3036677/.

When the GSS quizzes respondents concerning their employment status, it asks those who are currently working to estimate the hours they worked during the prior week. Figure 76, below, shows the estimated hours worked by male Democrats and Republicans aged 22 to 65 years, who were actively working when surveyed by GSS (at various times in 1993 through 2006). The differences depicted for the separate years are not, in themselves, statistically significant, and are provided merely to show that the Republican work-hour advantage may be fairly constant, over time.

*Figure 76. Average hours/week worked by men aged 22 to 65 years (GSS surveys conducted in 1991 through 2004, based on aggregate sample size of 3927, with overall confidence level of 99+%)*

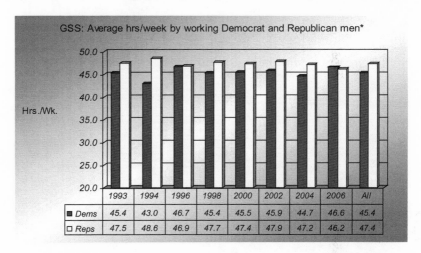

*Differences depicted for individual years are not statistically significant. Confidence level of the "All" column is 99+%.

On the other hand, the difference shown in the "All" column, on the right side of Figure 76, has a confidence level of 99+ percent. It shows that the average employed Democratic male worked about 45.4 hours per week for his paycheck, while the average employed Republican male put in about 47.4 hours — an excess of 2 hours.

> A lot of [Republicans] have never made an honest living in their lives.
>
> — Howard Dean, DNC Chairman[10]

10 Stephen Dinan and Amy Fagan, "Dean Hits GOP on 'Honest Living'," *Washington Times*, June 3, 2005.

*Reality check — NES shows a larger difference*

NES also asked currently-employed respondents to estimate average weekly work hours in surveys conducted in 1996, 1998, 2000, and 2004. In total, 1082 male Democrats and Republicans, aged 22-65 years, were surveyed in those years. Democrats averaged 45.1 hours per week, while Republicans averaged 48.9 hours per week — a statistically significant difference (99+%) of about 3.8 hours. However, in the remainder of this chapter, we use the more conservative difference of 2 hours, reflected in the GSS surveys conducted in 1993 through 2006.[11]

## Being Republican Means Longer Work Hours?

What are the Republican traits that correlate with the tendency to work more hours? I analyzed several variables including income, health, race, marital status, political philosophy, religiosity, and education level. Only one of those variables correlated significantly with hours worked: level of income.[12] In other words, people who earn more work longer hours.

*Figure 77. Average and median hours worked by all men (including Democrats and Republicans), aged 22 to 65 years, by earnings level (GSS surveys conducted in 1991 through 2004, based on, left to right, sample sizes of 1830, 1462, 1442, and 536, and with confidence levels of at least 95%)*

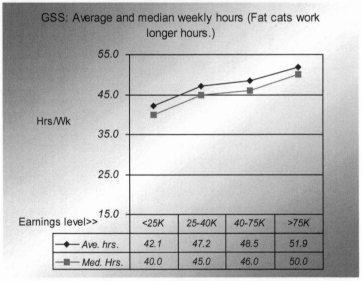

| GSS: Average and median weekly hours (Fat cats work longer hours.) | | | |
|---|---|---|---|
| Earnings level>> | <25K | 25-40K | 40-75K | >75K |
| Ave. hrs. | 42.1 | 47.2 | 48.5 | 51.9 |
| Med. Hrs. | 40.0 | 45.0 | 46.0 | 50.0 |

The link between work hours and income is clearly seen in Figure 77, which shows the average and median hours worked by men of differing wage levels. The "fat cats," earning over $75,000 per year, worked nearly 10 hours more each week

---

11 The NES hours gap may be larger than the GSS gap because NES asks for the work hours of anyone who is "working now/temporarily laid off (in combination with any other status)." In other words, it includes people who may be working while retired, while in school, while disabled, etc.

12 To see the results of a multiple regression analysis, please go to Appendix B 6.

than the men earning under $25,000 per year. This was true for both average and median hours worked, and it was true for Democrats as well as Republicans.

## Two Hours Per Week Can Make A Big Difference

There are no gains, without pains.

— Benjamin Franklin, Author, politician, scientist, philosopher[13]

We know there is a correlation between hours worked and income, and that employed Republican men work about 2 hours per week more than employed Democratic men. The financial implications of this differential are significant. Even if we assume identical pay rates at the U.S. hourly average, a difference of 2 hours per week could let the Republican male safely accumulate an additional $170,000 in his IRA (retirement account), in today's dollars. See Figure 78, below, where the column on the right side depicts the Republican's eventual IRA balance, and the smudge on the left depicts the Democrat's expected balance.[14] For a husband and wife who both work an extra two hours per week, the additional accumulated wealth could easily exceed $300,000.

*Figure 78. Work hours can translate to differences in accumulated wealth! (calculation of present value based on the overall difference in hours shown in Figure 76, times the average male wage rate of $19.57, invested in an IRA for 40 years at after inflation rate of 3%)[15]*

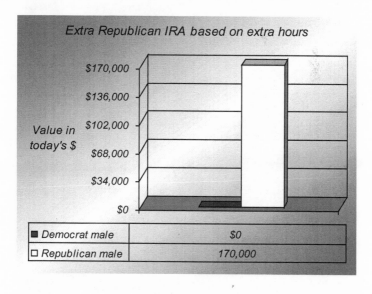

| Democrat male | $0 |
| Republican male | 170,000 |

---

13 Benjamin Franklin, *The Way to Wealth*, 1986 ed. (Bedford, MA: Applewood Books, 1757).
14 If we used the NES 3.8 hour differential, the IRA disparity could be as much as $300,000.
15 See Appendix B 5 for the calculation of the average male hourly rate.

The two-hour-per-week work difference explains much of the Republican wage advantage, and that is good: Work and effort should make a difference. Wealth accumulation should not be based on contacts, "old boys clubs," or luck. However, this hours gap does not explain the entire Democrat-Republican earnings differential. Democratic men work 95.8 percent as many hours as do Republican men;[16] yet they earn only 81.8 percent as much as the Republicans.[17] In other words, there is an 18.2 percent gap in earnings while there is only a 4.2 percent gap in hours worked. There must be other factors in play.

*Who Is the More Educated Worker?*

> An educated workforce is the foundation of every community and the future of every economy.
>
> — Brad Henry, Democratic Governor of Oklahoma[18]

In Chapter 2 we noted that, on the whole, Republicans are a little more educated than Democrats. This is particularly true for males. During the last decade, Republicans males have been 10 percent more likely to have high school diplomas (Figure 55 on page 72), and 60 percent more likely to have 4-year college degrees (Figure 57 on page 74).

One way we can estimate the impact of education on wages is by focusing on the value of these educational diplomas and degrees. Figure 79, below, shows the percentages of working Democratic and Republican males, aged 22 to 65 years, at two ends of the educational spectrum: those without high school diplomas and those with 4-year college degrees.

*Figure 79. Educational differences between working Democratic and Republican men aged 22-65 years (GSS surveys conducted in 2000 through 2004, based on a sample size of 1432, with differences that are at least 99% statistically significant, and with relative proportions of, left to right, 1.96 and .66)*

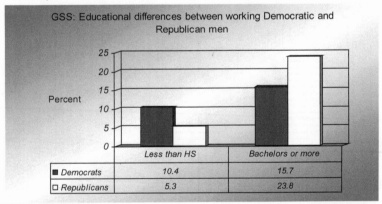

| GSS: Educational differences between working Democratic and Republican men | | |
| --- | --- | --- |
| | Less than HS | Bachelors or more |
| ■ Democrats | 10.4 | 15.7 |
| □ Republicans | 5.3 | 23.8 |

16 The calculation is 45.4/47.4 = 95.8%.
17 The calculation is $46700/$57100 = 81.8%.
18 "State of the State Address," 2005, Office of Governor Brad Henry Web Site, Retrieved March 17, 2007, from http://www.ok.gov/governor/stateofthestate2005.php.

The first column in Figure 79 shows that a Democratic male is about twice as likely to have less than a high school diploma, and the second column shows that a Republican male is far more likely to have a 4-year college degree.

*The Dollar Value of Education*

> Education today, more than ever before, must see clearly the dual objectives: Education for living and education for making a living.
>
> — James Mason Woods (Position unknown)[19]

It is possible to estimate the impact of these educational differences on wages, and this is done in Appendix B 7 on page 350. However, the bottom-line result is that, all other factors being equal (e.g., equal work hours), we'd expect the average Democrat to earn about $51,500 and the average Republican to earn about $56,300. The $4,800 difference equals about 8.5 percent, and that is the amount of the wage gap that may be attributable to educational differences.[20]

The 8.5 percent calculated above is equal to almost half of the total 18.2 percent wage gap (first discussed on page 95). When we add the 8.5 percent to the wage disadvantage attributable to the shortfall in Democratic work hours (4.2%, as calculated on page 95), we find that these two factors — less education and fewer work hours — could explain about 70 percent of the Democrat-Republican wage disparity.

*The Boss' Opinion As Indicated by Supervisory Assignments*

> Suck up to the boss from day one. If he's stupid, tell him he's smart. If she's fat and ugly, tell her she's hot. If he's weak and ineffectual, tell him he's a powerhouse.
>
> — Online tabloid[21]

We have seen that Republican males tend to work more hours and have more education than Democratic males, and those two factors explain a lot of the Republican earnings advantage. However, there is another way to gauge the relative worth of Democratic and Republican male workers: the boss's opinion.

An employer indicates his assessment of a worker's value in two tangible ways: by the amount of compensation and by the amount of responsibility he gives to the worker. As noted, Republicans are generally paid more, and in a free market system economists believe that additional wages usually indicate additional labor value. Likewise, Republicans are more apt to be given supervisory responsibilities — both formal and informal. This is significant because it is generally assumed that employers promote the workers who have superior technical

---

19 James Mason Wood (attributed), "The National Teaching & Learning Forum," Retrieved March 16, 2007, from: http://www.ntlf.com/html/lib/quotes.htm.

20 The calculation is (56300-51500)/56300 = 8.5%.

21 "How to Get the Most out of Your New Job," in *Weekly World News Online* (August 2, 2004), Retrieved March 16, 2007, from: http://unitethecows.com/.

and managerial skills. Thus, by looking at supervision rates, we learn what the boss thinks, so to speak.

> Opportunity is missed by most people because it is dressed in overalls and looks like work.
>
> — Thomas A. Edison, Inventor and businessman[22]

On several occasions in 1972 through 2006, the GSS asked workers if they supervised other employees as part of their job duties. The results (for male employees aged 22 to 65 years) are displayed in Figure 80, below.

*Figure 80. Percentage of Democratic and Republican male supervisors aged 22 to 65 years (GSS surveys conducted in 1972 — 2006, based on 5223 cases, with confidence level of 99+%, and with a relative proportion of .89)*

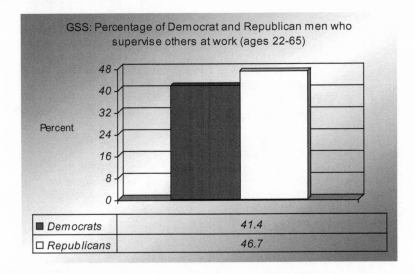

As shown in Figure 80, Republican males are only slightly more likely than Democratic males to supervise other workers on the job. A closer look, however, reveals a more complex pattern with much larger differences.

### With Older Workers The Supervision Gap Is Larger

> To supervise men, you must either excel them in their accomplishments, or despise them.
>
> — Benjamin Disraeli, 19th century British Prime Minister and novelist[23]

---

22 Gerald Beals, "Thomas Edison 'Quotes'," Retrieved April 1, 2007,
 from: http://www.thomasedison.com/edquote.htm.
23 Paul Elmer More, "Disraeli and Conservatism," in *Shelburne Essays*, Retrieved April 1, 2007,
 from: http://jkalb.freeshell.org/more/disraeli.html.

If we just consider the younger workers, aged 25 to 45 years, there is no statistical difference in the supervision rates. As workers get older, however, a significant gap develops. As shown in Figure 81, below, 50.9 percent of Republican males aged 45 to 65 years supervise others in the workplace, whereas only 40.4 percent of their Democratic counterparts are supervisors. Expressed another way, Democratic men in this age range are only about 79 percent as likely to supervise.[24]

*Figure 81. Percentage of Democratic and Republican male supervisors aged 45 to 65 years (various GSS surveys conducted in 1972-2006, based on 1948 cases, with confidence level of 99+%, and of .79)*

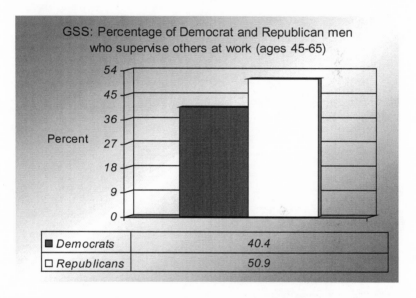

It is important to note that these statistics exclude owner-employees. We are talking about employees who acquire their responsibilities through promotions — not stock purchases.

### With Formal Management Positions The Gap Is Even Larger

Executive ability is deciding quickly and getting somebody else to do the work.

— John G. Pollard, Former Democratic Governor of Virginia[25]

If we look at workers in formal positions requiring managerial duties, we see a more significant difference between male political constituencies. Figure 82, below, shows the percentages of Democratic and Republican men serving

24 The calculation is 40.4/50.9 = 79%.
25 John G. Pollard (attributed), "Quotationz.Com."

as general, production and operating department managers based upon the aggregate results of GSS surveys conducted in years 1988 through 2006. The gap is substantial, even though we are considering men of all ages.

*Figure 82. Percentage of Democratic and Republican men working in formal management positions (GSS surveys conducted in 1988 through 2006, based on 4370 cases, with confidence level of 99+%, and with a relative proportion of .58)*

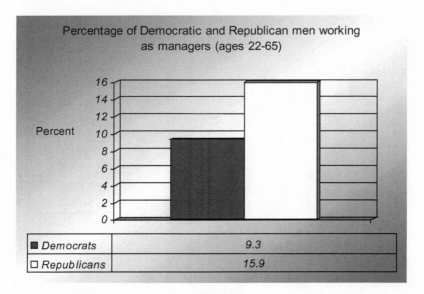

Again, however, a closer look at these numbers reveals a more complicated pattern. For men under age 35, there is no statistically significant difference with regard to the percentages working in formal management positions. However, as men get older, a larger difference develops, as is evident in Figure 83, below.

The chart shows us that the gap between Democratic and Republican men, which is statistically insignificant until age 35, grows until workers are between 61 and 65 years old. At that age, the percentage of men working in management declines for both Democrats and Republicans. Again, it should be noted that these are not business owners — they are employees who (presumably) were promoted to managerial positions.

*Figure 83. Percentage of Democratic and Republican men working in formal management positions, by age ranges (GSS surveys conducted in 1988 through 2006, based on, left to right, 691, 600, 525, 387, 324, 173, and 2700 cases, with confidence level of 99+% for all columns except the age 61-65 column, which is 93% (marginal), and with relative proportions of, left to right, .46, .50, .46, .34, .35, .46, and .44)*

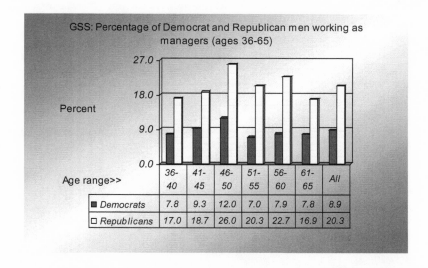

| Age range>> | 36-40 | 41-45 | 46-50 | 51-55 | 56-60 | 61-65 | All |
|---|---|---|---|---|---|---|---|
| ■ Democrats | 7.8 | 9.3 | 12.0 | 7.0 | 7.9 | 7.8 | 8.9 |
| □ Republicans | 17.0 | 18.7 | 26.0 | 20.3 | 22.7 | 16.9 | 20.3 |

> In a hierarchy every employee tends to rise to his level of incompetence.
>
> — Educator and author Lawrence J. Peter[26]

Thus, we can conclude that, among middle-aged and older workers, there is a considerable gap in the percentage of Democrats and Republicans who are given the responsibility of supervising others. Undoubtedly, this is another factor accounting for the earnings gap. It may indicate that "the boss" has a higher opinion of the average Republican than his Democratic counterpart. In addition, it suggests that Republicans have, on average, more important employment responsibilities that justify their earnings advantage.

### *Reality check — Which came first: the chicken or the egg?*

Do Republicans have work or character qualities that increase the likelihood of their becoming managers? Or, is it the other way around? When people become supervisors they change into Republicans because they a) make more money, or b) see things from the perspective of business?

### *Who Has A Better Attitude?*

> Motivation determines what you do. Attitude determines how well you do it.
> — Novelist Raymond Chandler[27]

If you were an employer interviewing candidates for a new job opening, you'd probably ask several questions designed to appraise their general feelings

---

26 Lawrence J. Peter (attributed), "New Dictionary of Cultural Literacy," (Houghton Mifflin Company, 2002).
27 Raymond Chandler (attributed), "Brainyquote.Com."

about work, expectations regarding the new employment, and potential dedication and loyalty as employees. These are also questions that have been asked in some of the surveys conducted by GSS and others. When we sort the questions and answers by the political party of each respondent, we find that there are statistically significant attitudinal differences between Democratic and Republican males.

Republican men are more likely to state that they are "very satisfied" with their jobs. This may indicate that they have more positive attitudes; however, it could also indicate that they have jobs that are truly more satisfying. See Figure 84, below.

*Figure 84. "All in all, how satisfied would you say you are with your job?" (GSS surveys conducted in 2002 and 2006, based on 981 cases, with overall confidence level of +99%, and a relative proportion of .76)*

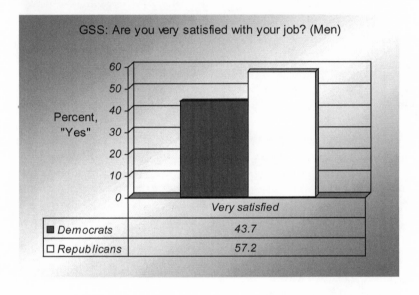

Our environment, the world in which we live and work, is a mirror of our attitudes and expectations.

— Self-improvement author Earl Nightingale[28]

Republican men are also more likely to "strongly agree" that they are "proud to be working for" their employers. That is something any boss loves to hear. See Figure 85.

---

28 Earl Nightingale (attributed), "Quotationz.Com."

*Figure 85. Do you strongly agree with the statement, "I am proud to be working for my employer"? (GSS surveys conducted in 2002 and 2006, based on 974 cases, with confidence level of 99+%, and with a relative proportion of .76)*

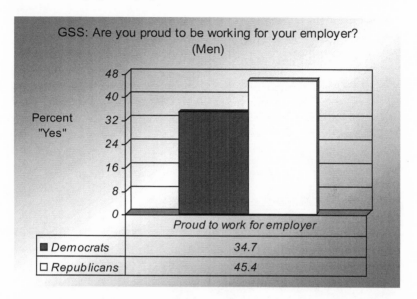

Surveys spanning a 30-year period indicate that Democratic men would be more likely to quit working if they could swing it, financially. Does this reflect an inherent difference in work ethic, or simply a tendency for Democrats to work in less rewarding jobs?

*Figure 86. If you were rich would you stop working? (GSS surveys conducted in 1975 through 2004, based on, left to right, 1320, 1914, and 1383 cases, with confidence level of , left to right, 99+%, 99%, and 98%, and with relative proportions of, left to right, .1.50, 1.22, and 1.21)*

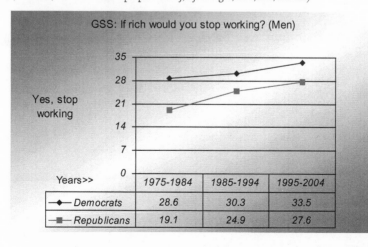

In addition, Democratic men may be a little more likely to leave work early or stay at home because they are dissatisfied with their jobs. This is shown in Figure 87, below, which is based on a 2004 GSS survey.

> Take this job and shove it, I ain't working here no more. ... You better not try to stand in my way as I'm walking out the door.
>
> — Singer Johnny Paycheck[29]

*Figure 87. During the past 3 months did you ever stay home or leave work early because you were unhappy about your job? (GSS 2004 survey, based on 573 cases, with confidence level of 99%, and with a relative proportion of 1.66)*

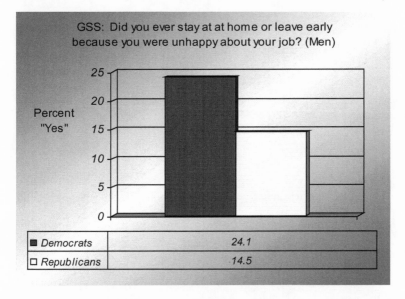

According to a 2006 GSS survey, Democratic men are more likely to reject the proposition that they take a pay cut, or travel greater distances, to avoid unemployment (Figure 88, below). This could be a sign of a poor attitude.

> There is joy in work. There is no happiness except in the realization that we have accomplished something.
>
> — Industrialist Henry Ford[30]

Republican men are more likely to "strongly agree" that they would work harder than required in order to help their employer succeed (Figure 89, below).

---

29 Johnny Paycheck song lyrics cited in, "Lyricskeeper.Com," Retrieved March 17, 2007, from: http://www.lyricskeeper.com.
30 Henry Ford (attributed), "Brainyquote.Com."

*Figure 88. Percentage disagreeing with this statement: "In order to avoid unemployment I would be willing to ..." (GSS survey conducted in 2006, based on 271 cases, with confidence level of, left to right, 99% and 99%, and with relative proportions of 1.69 and 1.76)*

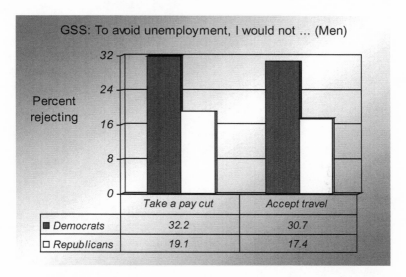

| | Take a pay cut | Accept travel |
|---|---|---|
| ■ Democrats | 32.2 | 30.7 |
| □ Republicans | 19.1 | 17.4 |

*Figure 89. I am willing to work harder than I have to help my employer. (GSS surveys conducted in 1998 and 2006, based on 481 cases, with a confidence level of 99%, and with relative proportion of .70)*

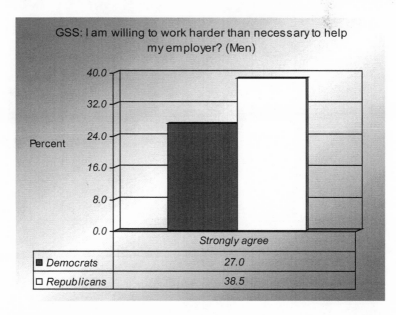

| | Strongly agree |
|---|---|
| ■ Democrats | 27.0 |
| □ Republicans | 38.5 |

> Many Americans suffer from what I call the "union mentality," an eagerness to do everything in their power to shortchange their employer.

— Author and radio talk show host Mike Gallagher[31]

Finally, Democratic men appear to be less proactive in solving problems at work. In a 2006 GSS survey, respondents were asked, "If you were to see a fellow employee not working as hard or well as he or she should..." what actions would you take? Democratic men were more likely than Republican men to indicate that they would not discuss the problem with the co-worker or with the supervisor.

*Figure 90. If I saw an employee who was not working as hard or well as he could, it is "not at all likely" that I would ... (GSS surveys conducted in 2002 and 2006, based on, from left to right, 942 and 854 cases, with a confidence level of 99%, and with relative proportions of, left to right, 1.42 and 1.33)*

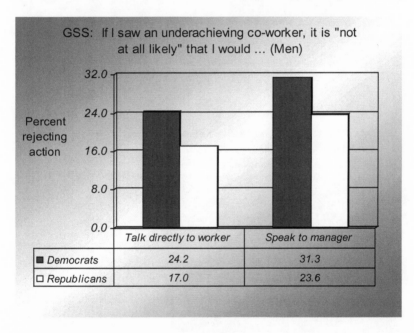

To summarize the issues related to attitude, there are survey data suggesting that Democratic males might be less satisfied with their jobs, less proud of their employers, less willing to help their employers succeed, less willing to take a pay cut to avoid unemployment, and less pro-active in addressing work problems. A higher percentage of Democratic men would quit working if they could afford to, financially, and Democrats are slightly more likely to take time off from work for inappropriate reasons. These results suggest that Republicans might have, on average, attitudes more valued by employers.

---

31 Mike Gallagher, *Surrounded by Idiots* (New York: Thumper Communications, Inc., 2005), 210.

*Emotional Stability*

> Snow was falling as Edmund Muskie spoke, and he claimed that the drops on his cheeks were actually melted snowflakes. That did him no good. The Union Leader declared that crying proved he "lacked stability"...
>
> — Journalist Robert Fulford[32]

In a 2000 GSS survey, respondents were asked whether, during the previous 4 weeks, "emotional problems (such as feeling depressed or anxious)" interfered with work. Democratic males were significantly more likely to state that there was such interference. (See Figure 91.)

*Figure 91. "During the past 4 weeks, have you had ... the following problem ... as a result of any emotional problems (such as feeling depressed or anxious)"? You "didn't do work or other activities as carefully as usual"? — (Men) (GSS survey conducted in 2000, based on 345 cases, with confidence level of 99+%, and a relative proportion of 4.71)*

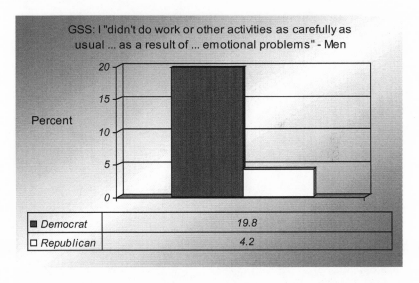

The GSS results are supported by other Gallup and GSS surveys (shown on page 26) that show Democrats are more likely to state that they have poor mental health, and that they have been treated for mental health problems.

> Last week I told my psychiatrist, "I keep thinking about suicide." He told me from now on I have to pay in advance.
>
> — Comedian Rodney Dangerfield[33]

---

32 Robert Fulford, "Male Crying: Now It's Mandatory," *National Post*, May 7, 2002.

33 "Rodney Dangerfield Jokes", Retrieved October 26, 2006, from Ringsurf.com: http://www.ringsurf.com/info/people/celebrities_in_the_news/Rodney_Dangerfield/.

If the mental health of Democrats and Republicans differs, as suggested by these surveys, and the difference has an impact on work performance, we may have identified an additional factor that explains the Democrat-Republican male compensation gap.

## THE BETTER WORKING WOMAN

*Earnings and hours worked*

During the years 1998 through 2006, the likelihood of Democratic and Republican women being in paid employment was about the same (around 69%), as was their average occupational earnings. However, there was a significant difference in the average weekly work hours. As indicated in Figure 92, below, the disparity in work hours developed after the mid-1990s. Democratic women now work about 1.5 hours more per week (in paid employment) than their Republican sisters.

*Figure 92. Percentage of Democratic and Republican women, aged 22-65 years, working at paid jobs (GSS surveys in 1991-2006, based on, left to right, 1737 and 2771 cases, with confidence level of 99% for the right-side difference, and no statistical significance for the left-side difference)*

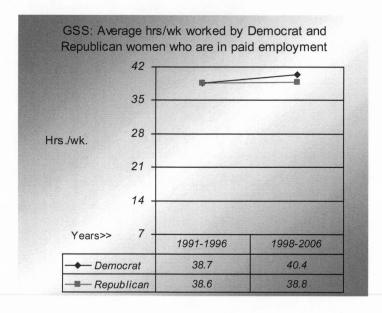

| GSS: Average hrs/wk worked by Democrat and Republican women who are in paid employment | 1991-1996 | 1998-2006 |
|---|---|---|
| Democrat | 38.7 | 40.4 |
| Republican | 38.6 | 38.8 |

... I don't know that [Laura Bush] has ever had a real job — I mean, since she's been grown up.

— Teresa Heinz Kerry, wife of Democratic Senator John Kerry[34]

---

34 "The Real Running Mates," *USAtoday.com* (October 19, 2004), Retrieved March 17, 2007, from http://www.usatoday.com/news/politicselections/2004-10-19-teresa_x.htm.

Why do Democratic women work longer hours than Republican women? There are probably several reasons. First, Democratic women are less likely to be married, and unmarried women — regardless of party — tend to work longer hours outside of the home. The growing "marriage gap" among women of working age is displayed in Figure 93, below:

*Figure 93. Marital status of Democratic and Republican women aged 22 to 65 years (GSS surveys in 1977-2006, based on, left to right, 3566, 4363, and 4065 cases, with confidence level of 99+% for all differences, and with relative proportions of, left to right, .89, .79, and .73)*

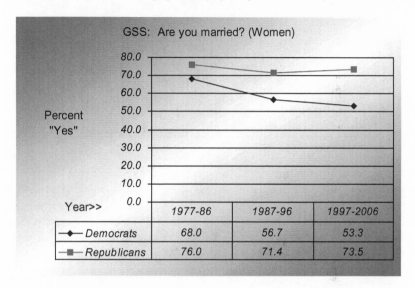

*Reality check — Less married doesn't mean fewer children*

If you're visualizing unmarried Democratic women who are unencumbered by the responsibilities of parenthood, you may want to consult Figure 94, below. It shows that Democratic women are nearly as likely as Republican women to have children in the household — despite their relatively low marriage rate. (The difference shown in the chart is not statistically significant.) This means that Democratic women are probably working more outside of the home, even though they have as many or more responsibilities within the home.

A second factor explaining why Democratic women work more hours might be a different philosophy regarding child rearing.

> Republicans understand the importance of bondage between a mother and child.
>
> — Vice President Dan Quayle[35]

---

35 Dan Quayle (attributed), "Quotationz.Com."

*Figure 94. Percentage of women, aged 22-65 years, with children in the household (GSS surveys in 1991 through 2006, based on 6574 cases. The difference is not statistically significant.)*

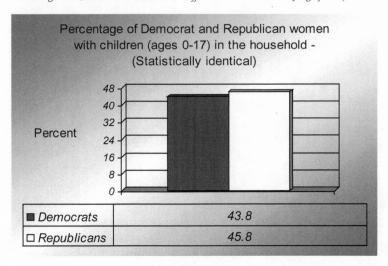

Periodically, the General Social Survey (GSS) asks whether women should work outside the home in various circumstances, and most Democratic and Republican women respond by saying a woman should work if there is no child in the home. However, the views diverge when the hypothetical scenario includes a preschooler in the home. In that case, Republican women are much less likely to agree that the woman should work.

*Figure 95. Should a woman work outside the home "when there is a child under school age"? (GSS surveys in 1988, 1994, and 2002 of women aged 22-65 years, based on 1021 cases, with confidence level of 99+%, and with a relative proportion of .1.40)*

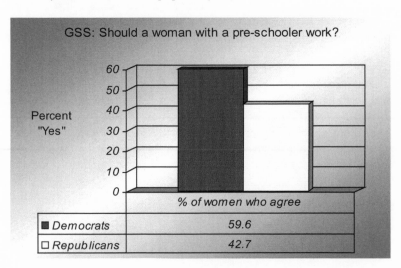

The results shown in Figure 95, above, are not surprising since Democratic women are less inclined to believe that preschool children suffer when the mother works outside of the home. The aggregate results of several GSS surveys, conducted in years 1997 through 2006, show that, by 69.8 to 59.3 percent, Democratic women are more likely than Republican women to disagree that "a preschool child is likely to suffer if his or her mother works."[36]

## Is Housework Fulfilling?

I hate housework! You make the beds, you do the dishes — and six months later you have to start all over again.

— Comedian Joan Rivers[37]

Another possible factor accounting for the difference in female work hours is the attitude of women with regard to housework. In 1988, 1994, and 2002 the GSS asked women: "Do you agree or disagree...being a housewife is just as fulfilling as working for pay?" Republican women were more likely to agree, as evident in Figure 96, below.

*Figure 96. Is housework fulfilling? (GGS surveys conducted in 1994 and 2002 of women aged 22-65 years, based on 769 cases, with confidence level of +99%, and with a relative proportion of .77)*

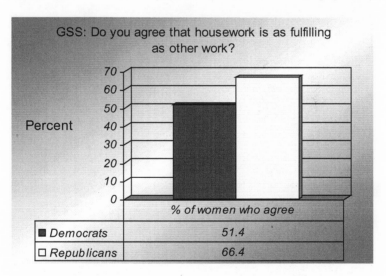

Last, but probably most important, financial need could explain the fact that Democratic women work longer hours outside of the home. We can deduce that the average Democratic woman has a lower pay rate than her Republican coun-

---

36 GSS surveys of 1942 women aged 22-65 years, with statistical significance of 99+% and a relative proportion of 1.82
37 Joan Rivers (attributed), "Quotationz.Com."

terpart, since she works about 1.5 extra hours per week to get (approximately) the same wages. This lower pay rate may be explained by the fact that a Democratic woman is a little less likely to have a 4-year college degree.[38] In addition, Democratic women generally have less family income, even though their own occupational earnings are comparable to those of Republican women. The family income differential is shown in Figure 97, below, and is probably attributable to the fact that Democratic women are less likely to be married.

*Figure 97. Percentage of women, aged 22-65 years, with family incomes over $50,000 per year (GSS surveys conducted in 1998 through 2006, based on 3679 cases, with confidence level of 99+%, and with a relative proportion of .79)*

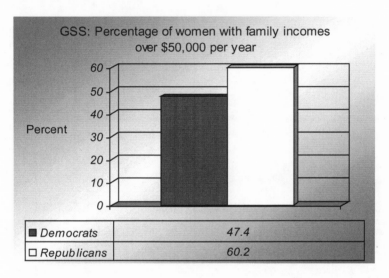

The lower wage rates and the smaller family incomes put Democratic women under greater financial pressure, and this financial pressure increases the need for them to work longer hours.

*Other factors related to women workers*

> To find joy in work is to discover the fountain of youth.
> — Author Pearl S. Buck[39]

In the case of men, there were significant differences with regard to work-attitudes and emotions, and this was also true for women, but to a lesser degree.

---

38 However, Democratic women are as likely, or more likely, to have an advanced (graduate) university degree.

39 Pearl Buck quoted by Frank McDonough, "Another View: You'll Just Know When It's Time to Go," (May 6, 2003), Retrieved March 17, 2007, from http://www.gcn.com/print/22_12/22144-1.html.

Republican women — like Republican men — are a little more likely to say they are "very satisfied" with their jobs.

*Figure 98. "All in all, how satisfied would you say you are with your job?" (Women) (GSS surveys conducted in 2002 and 2006, based on 1106 cases, with overall confidence level of 96%, and a relative proportion of .89)*

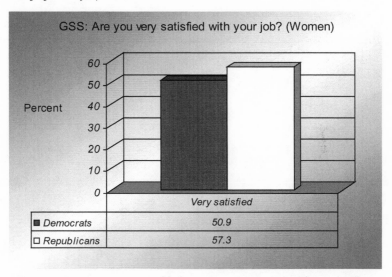

Democratic women are more likely to reject pay cuts in order to avoid unemployment. See Figure 99.

*Figure 99. Percentage disagreeing with this statement: "In order to avoid unemployment I would be willing to accept a position with lower pay." (GSS survey conducted in 2006, based on 265 cases, with confidence level of 95%, and relative proportion of 1.48)*

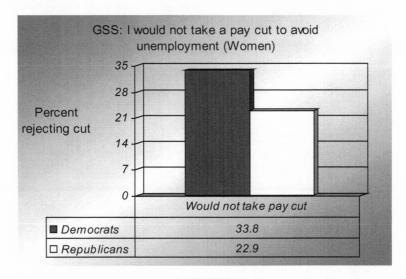

In addition, it appears that a Democratic woman would be less likely than her Republican counterpart to talk to an underachieving employee, or about the underachieving employee to the boss.

*Figure 100. If I saw an employee who was not working as hard or well as he could, it is "not at all likely" that I would ... (GSS surveys conducted in 2002 and 2006, based on, from left to right, 1073 and 1025 cases, with a confidence level of 98% and 93% (marginal), and with relative proportions of 1.23 and 1.19)*

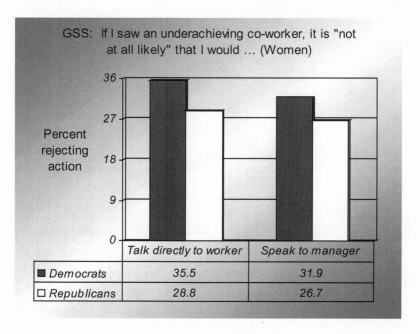

Democratic women are also a bit more likely than Republican women to say that emotions have negatively affected the quality of their work.

Notably, no statistically significant difference was found regarding the attitudes of Democratic and Republican women with respect to their pride in their employers, their willingness to work harder to help their employers, or the likelihood that they would quit their jobs if they could afford to do so, financially.

*Figure 101. "During the past 4 weeks, have you had ... the following problem ... as a result of any emotional problems (such as feeling depressed or anxious)"? You "didn't do work or other activities as carefully as usual"? — (Women) (GSS survey conducted in 2000, based on 471 cases, with confidence level of 97%, and a relative proportion of 1.64)*

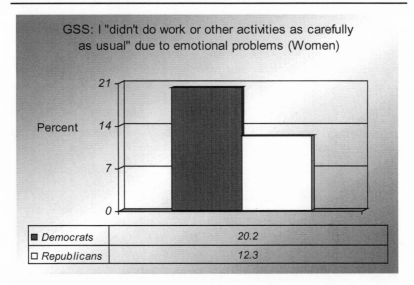

GSS: I "didn't do work or other activities as carefully as usual" due to emotional problems (Women)

| | |
|---|---|
| ■ Democrats | 20.2 |
| □ Republicans | 12.3 |

## MISCELLANEOUS WORK FACTORS FOR MEN AND WOMEN

*Work "prestige"*

> Let's face it, we all have egos. You might not be able to give people huge salary increases, but here is a lot you can do by giving them better titles, access to new perks, etc.
>
> — Bob Rosner, Author and columnist[40]

The National Opinion Research Center (NORC), an organization based at the University of Chicago, developed a system for rating the "prestige" of various occupations. To develop the system, survey respondents were asked to evaluate the prestige of each occupation and assign to it a numerical ranking. Those numerical scores were averaged and summarized in a table of "prestige" scores. A few of the scores are presented in Table 25, below.

GSS uses the NORC system to assign a prestige score to the each of the occupations identified in its surveys. Figure 102, below, shows the mean prestige scores for male Democrats and Republicans. The lowest score possible is 17 and the highest is 86. There has been a small but significant difference between Democratic and Republican men since 1988, when the current index was developed.

> Never make friends with people who are above or below you in status. Such friendships will never give you any happiness.
>
> — Chanakya, Indian politician and writer[41]

---

40 Bob Rosner, "Working Wounded: High Maintenance Help," in *ABC News* (August 25, 2006), Retrieved January 31, 2007, from: http://abcnews.go.com/Business/CareerManagement/story?id=2379097.
41 Chanakya (attributed), "Brainyquote.Com."

*Table 25. NORC/GSS occupational "prestige" scores, as last updated in 1989 (Scores range from a low of 17 to a high of 86.)*

| Occupation | Score | Occupation | Score |
|---|---|---|---|
| Physicians | 86 | Police detectives | 60 |
| Attorneys | 75 | Actors and directors | 58 |
| College professors | 74 | Statisticians | 56 |
| Physicists & astronomers | 73 | Kindergarten teachers | 55 |
| Architects | 73 | Librarians | 54 |
| Aerospace engineers | 72 | Dental hygienists | 52 |
| Judges | 71 | Real estate sales people | 49 |
| CEOs | 70 | Funeral directors | 49 |
| Psychologists | 69 | Musicians | 47 |
| Clergy | 69 | Photographers | 45 |
| Pharmacists | 68 | Receptionists | 39 |
| Registered nurses | 66 | Recreation workers | 38 |
| Athletes | 65 | Artists and performers | 36 |
| Accountants/auditors | 65 | Car sales people | 34 |
| Mechanical engineers | 64 | Hotel clerks | 32 |
| Authors | 63 | Baby sitters | 29 |
| Veterinarians | 62 | Shoe sales people | 28 |
| Sociologists | 61 | Bill collectors | 24 |
| Airplane pilots | 61 | Messengers | 22 |
| Legislators | 61 | Door-to-door sales people | 22 |
| Physicians' assistants | 61 | Newspaper sales people | 19 |

*Figure 102. Average occupational prestige scores for Democratic and Republican men (GSS surveys conducted in 1988 through 2006, based on, left to right, 2000, 2205, and 3198 cases, with confidence level of 99+% for all differences)*

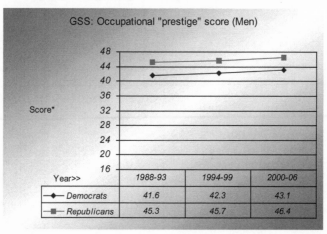

| GSS: Occupational "prestige" score (Men) | | | |
|---|---|---|---|
| Year>> | 1988-93 | 1994-99 | 2000-06 |
| Democrats | 41.6 | 42.3 | 43.1 |
| Republicans | 45.3 | 45.7 | 46.4 |

With regard to women there are a few interesting phenomena. First, women of both parties have increased the prestige of their work substantially, as compared to men. Second, the prestige advantage held by Republican women, just a few years ago, has been cut in half. Finally, Democratic men hold jobs with substantially less prestige than women of either political party. (Compare the most recent prestige rating for Democratic men, shown in Figure 102, with the most recent prestige ratings for women, shown in Figure 103, below.)

*Figure 103. Average occupational prestige scores for Democratic and Republican women (GSS surveys conducted in 1988 through 2006, based on, left to right, 2713, 2931, and 4103 cases, with confidence level of 99+% for all differences)*

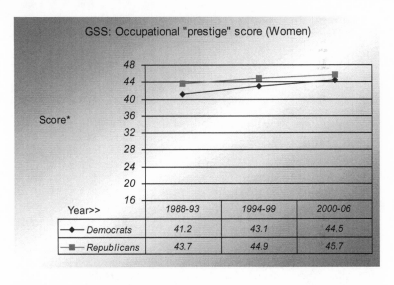

*The lowest score possible is 17, and the highest is 86.

### Reality check – Prestige is in flux

The NORC prestige rankings were produced in 1989, and it is very likely that some professions would now be judged differently. In 2006, a Harris Interactive survey asked respondents to give their prestige rankings for 23 different professions. The five most prestigious fields for Democrats were, in rank order, firefighter, medical doctor, nurse, teacher, and scientist. For Republicans the top spots were firefighter, medical doctor, military officer, scientist, and nurse. The least prestigious occupations, for Democrats, were real estate agent, followed by actor, stockbroker, business executive, and union leader. For Republicans, the least prestigious jobs were actor, real estate agent, union leader, journalist, and stockbroker.

*Type of work*

### Occupations

> At the age of six I wanted to be a cook. At seven I wanted to be Napoleon. And my ambition has been growing steadily ever since.

— Salvador Dali, Spanish artist[42]

Over the years, Republican men have dominated the professional and managerial jobs.

*Figure 104. Are you a professional or managerial worker? (Men) (various NES surveys from 1952 through 2004, based on, left to right, 584, 1938, 1918, 2458, 2773, and 1561 cases, with significance of 99+% for all points on chart, and with relative proportions of, left to right, .56, .64, .64, .60, .70, and .67)*

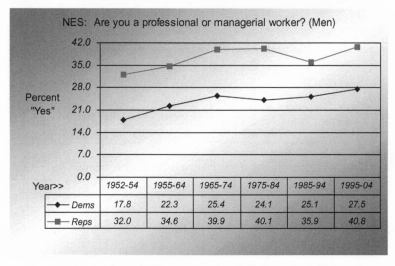

| NES: Are you a professional or managerial worker? (Men) | | | | | | |
|---|---|---|---|---|---|---|
| Year>> | 1952-54 | 1955-64 | 1965-74 | 1975-84 | 1985-94 | 1995-04 |
| Dems | 17.8 | 22.3 | 25.4 | 24.1 | 25.1 | 27.5 |
| Reps | 32.0 | 34.6 | 39.9 | 40.1 | 35.9 | 40.8 |

Democratic men have held sway in the skilled, semi-skilled, and service sectors.

> Ashamed of work! Mechanic, with thy tools? The tree thy axe cut from its native sod, and turns to useful things — go tell to fools — was fashioned in the factory of God.

—From the poem "Labor," by Frank Soule[43]

*Figure 105. Are you a skilled, semi-skilled, or service worker? (Men) (various NES surveys from 1952 through 2004, based on, left to right, 584, 1938, 1918, 2458, 2773, and 1561 cases, with significance of 99+% for all points on chart, and with relative proportions of, left to right, 1.36, 1.35, 1.43, 1.57, 1.40, and 1.58)*

---

42 Salvador Dali (attributed), "Quotationz.Com."

43 Frank Soule, "Labor," in *California Magazine* (San Francisco:Hutchings & Rosenfield, 1858), 521.

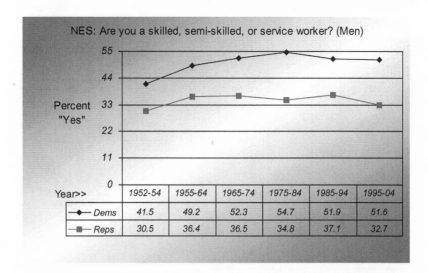

NES: Are you a skilled, semi-skilled, or service worker? (Men)

| Year>> | 1952-54 | 1955-64 | 1965-74 | 1975-84 | 1985-94 | 1995-04 |
|---|---|---|---|---|---|---|
| Dems | 41.5 | 49.2 | 52.3 | 54.7 | 51.9 | 51.6 |
| Reps | 30.5 | 36.4 | 36.5 | 34.8 | 37.1 | 32.7 |

Until recent years, Democratic men have also been more likely to hold un-skilled labor jobs; however, there is no longer a statistically significant differ-ence. In either case, only about 4 percent of men now perform this type of work.

*Figure 106. Are you a laborer (except for farm workers)? (Men) (various NES surveys from 1952 through 2004, based on, left to right, 584, 1938, 1918, 2458, 2773, and 1561 cases, with signifi-cance of 99+% for all points on chart except the "1995-04" column, which is not statistically signifi-cant, and with relative proportions of, left to right, 2.2, 1.77, 2.26, 2.03, 1.6, and n/a)*

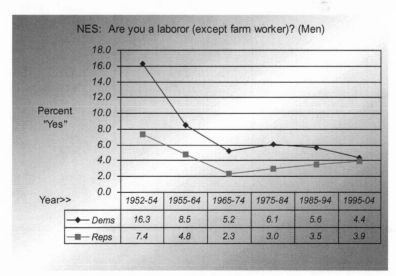

NES: Are you a laboror (except farm worker)? (Men)

| Year>> | 1952-54 | 1955-64 | 1965-74 | 1975-84 | 1985-94 | 1995-04 |
|---|---|---|---|---|---|---|
| Dems | 16.3 | 8.5 | 5.2 | 6.1 | 5.6 | 4.4 |
| Reps | 7.4 | 4.8 | 2.3 | 3.0 | 3.5 | 3.9 |

Since 1952 (or sooner), the percentages of Democrats and Republicans doing clerical, sales and farm-related work have been roughly equal (not shown in any graph).

For women, the job disparities are smaller. In the 10-year span from 1995 through 2004, almost equal percentages of Democratic and Republican women worked as professionals (29.6% of Democrats vs. 30.8% of Republicans). Democratic women were significantly more likely to hold skilled, semi-skilled or service jobs (29.6% vs. 14.9%), and Republican women were slightly more likely to hold clerical and sales jobs (34.2% vs. 29.0%). Less than 1 percent of women from either party were laborers.

### Private vs. Government vs. Self-Employment

A bureaucrat is a Democrat who holds some office that a Republican wants.

— Vice President Alben W. Barclay (1949-1953)[44]

Democrats are more likely to work for the government, rather than a private employer, however, the gap has closed sharply in recent years.

*Figure 107. "Are you employed by the federal, state, or local government?" (combined results of GSS surveys conducted in 1985-1986 and in 2000-2006, based on, left to right, 1888 and 7301 cases, with confidence level of 99+%, and with relative proportions of 1.77 and 1.17)*

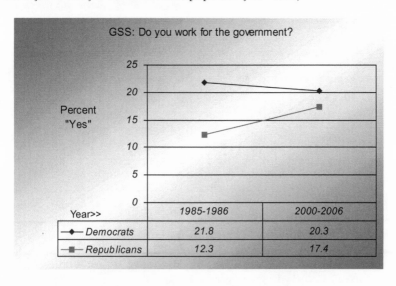

| GSS: Do you work for the government? | | |
|---|---|---|
| Year>> | 1985-1986 | 2000-2006 |
| Democrats | 21.8 | 20.3 |
| Republicans | 12.3 | 17.4 |

Another survey addressing this issue is shown in Table 26, below.

---

44 Vice President Alben W. Barkley (attributed), "The Quotations Page."

*Table 26. Other relevant surveys*

| Survey and Issue | Dems | Reps | No. of cases | Conf % | RP |
|---|---|---|---|---|---|
| NES 2004 survey: "Were you (are you) employed by a federal, state or local government?" | **31.8** | 20.8 | 547 | +99 | 1.53 |

Republicans are more likely to be self-employed. Figure 108, below, shows the trend since 1972.

*Figure 108. "Are you self-employed...?" (various GSS surveys conducted from 1972 through 2004, based on, left to right, 4385, 2629, 4842, 4884, 4477, 3101, and 3354 cases, with significance of 99+% for all points on chart, and with relative proportions of, left to right, .61, .72, .59, .60, .73, .72, and .68)*

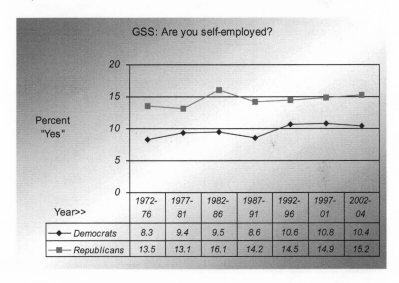

*Other work-related information*

## Union Membership

> No king on earth is as safe in his job as a Trade Union official. There is only one thing that can get him sacked; and that is drink. Not even that, as long as he doesn't actually fall down.
>
> — George Bernard Shaw, Irish playwright[45]

A Democrat of either gender is more likely to have a labor union member in the household; however, the Democrat-Republican gap has narrowed slightly.

---

45 George Bernard Shaw (attributed), "Columbia World of Quotations," (Columbia University Press, 1996).

The trend for more than 50 years is shown in Figure 109, below. Note the sharp decline in membership for constituents of either party.

*Figure 109. Does someone in your household belong to a labor union? (various NES surveys from 1952 through 2004, based on, left to right, 2151, 4439, 5640, 6161, 6563, and 4703 cases, with significance of 99+% for all points on chart, and with relative proportions of, left to right, 1.48, 2.06, 1.77, 1.87, 1.67, and 1.70)*

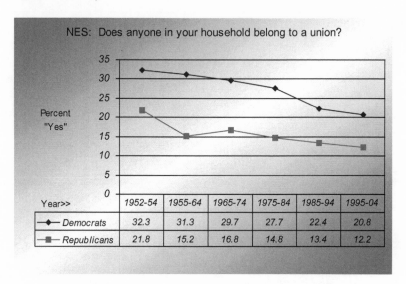

NES: Does anyone in your household belong to a union?

| Year>> | 1952-54 | 1955-64 | 1965-74 | 1975-84 | 1985-94 | 1995-04 |
|---|---|---|---|---|---|---|
| Democrats | 32.3 | 31.3 | 29.7 | 27.7 | 22.4 | 20.8 |
| Republicans | 21.8 | 15.2 | 16.8 | 14.8 | 13.4 | 12.2 |

## Miscellaneous

*Table 27. Other relevant surveys*

| Issue | Survey | Dems | Reps | RP | No. of cases |
|---|---|---|---|---|---|
| Are you a "workaholic"? | Penn, Schoen & Berland 2003 | 10.0 | **20.0** | .50 | 590 |
| "Generally work as a team" | Penn, Schoen & Berland 2003 | **56.0** | 34.0 | 1.65 | 590 |
| "Fax, cell phones, e-mail, internet chang-ing my work" | Penn, Schoen & Berland 2003 | 38.0 | **68.0** | .56 | 590 |

NOTE: Additional employment-related information can be found in Appendix A at pages 325 and 339.

> After many years of trying to find steady work I finally got a job as a historian. Then I realized there was no future in it.
>
> — Anonymous[46]

---

46 "Job Jokes," Retrieved August 8, 2007, from: http://www.analyticalq.com/humor/jobs.htm.

CONCLUSIONS

*The "Working Man" award goes to ...*

Republicans. Prior to 1970, Democratic and Republican men were about equally likely to be employed. Since that time, however, a gap has grown, and Republican men are now significantly more likely to be employed.

Republican males earn more than Democratic males, and there are a few factors that may explain, and even justify, the earnings gap. Employed Republican males:

- Work longer hours than do employed Democrats
- Are more likely to have higher education degrees
- Are more likely to be promoted to supervisory positions, implying that they have greater technical and/or managerial skills and greater job responsibility. This assumes, however, that they didn't become Republicans after their promotions.
- Have work-related attitudes that are, presumably, more valued by employers
- Might be less likely to let emotional problems interfere with work

From all of this, we could conclude that it is the Republican who is the better "Working Man."

*The "Working Woman" award goes to ...*

Democrats. Although there is no statistically-significant difference in the occupational earnings of Democratic and Republican women, Democratic women now average about 1.5 extra hours of work (outside of the home) per week. The extra hours worked may be the result of greater financial need or may simply reflect the fact that Democratic women are more likely to be unmarried (even though they are almost as likely to have children in the household). The longer work-week may also reflect greater Democratic acceptance of the appropriateness or even desirability of working with pre-school children in the home.

The work-related attitudes of Democratic and Republican women vary less than for men. However, Republican women generally express more positive statements regarding their jobs and employers.

*Other Work-Related Information*

Republicans are much more likely to work in professional, managerial, or self-employed positions; and they are more likely to work in "prestige" jobs.

A higher percentage of Democrats are in government jobs, and in unions.

## CHAPTER 4: WHO GIVES MORE TO CHARITY?

### INTRODUCTION

*They Don't F$@#-ing Care!*

> Wake up America! We left-wingers care about people and justice. The Republicans only care about money.
>
> — Blogger named "F--k Bush"[1]

> The Republicans don't care about the working poor — they don't know any.
>
> — James Carville, Democratic consultant and pundit[2]

> [T]he compassionate conservative Republicans DON'T CARE ABOUT YOU OR ME. THEY DON'T F$@#ING CARE.
>
> — Columnist Alan Bisbort[3]

The above-stated views are extreme, but not rare. Many Americans seem to believe that Republicans care mostly about money, while Democrats care more about helping people. However, the evidence does not support those assertions — at least, not with respect to charitable donations.

1 F--k Bush (pseudonym), October 8, 2004, HaloScan.com blog, Retrieved March 17, 2007, from http://www.haloscan.com/comments/.

2 Joan Walsh, "James Carville," *Salon.com* (March 11, 2002), Retrieved March 17, 2007, from http://dir.salon.com/story/people/feature/2002/03/11/carville/index.html?pn=1.

3 Alan Bisbort, "Compassionate Cancer," *AmericanPolitics.com* (May 8, 2003), Retrieved October 28, 2004, from http://www.americanpolitics.com/20030508Bisbort.html.

Republicans are more likely to give both time and money to charities and other nonprofit organizations. The amounts contributed by Republicans tend to be much larger, and this is partly explained by the higher income earned by the average Republican. However, religiosity and political conservatism are two additional factors that seem to correlate significantly with the tendency of Republicans to give more.

DETAILS

*Donations*

### Who Is More Likely To Give?

[W]ealth isn't bad ... and rich Republicans aren't greedy. To the contrary, wealth makes it possible to make a difference in the world.

— Wayne Allyn Root, explaining the thesis of his book, Millionaire Republican.[4]

*Figure 110. Did you donate? (aggregate results of 16 surveys conducted by various entities in 1992 through 2006)*

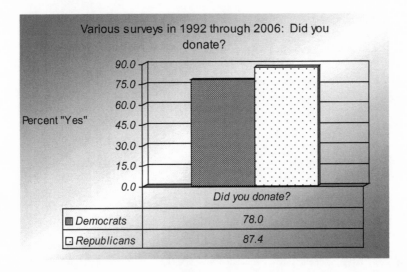

With no apparent exceptions, major surveys indicate that Republicans are more likely than Democrats to contribute both time and money to charities. In addition, the amounts Republicans donate tend to be much larger — even when income levels are held constant. In this chapter we quantify the differ-

4 "Millionaire Republican," Promotional Web site, Retrieved April 19, 2007, from http:// www.millionairerepublican.com/home/charity.php.

ences and try to explain why Republicans appear to give and volunteer more than Democrats.

Figure 110 shows the combined results of 16 surveys taken by various organizations in 1992 through 2006.[5]

The results of the 16 individual surveys, summarized in Figure 110, are itemized in Table 28, below. For a more detailed description of the survey, and the actual question asked, please see Appendix B 8.

*Table 28. Percentage of Democrats and Republicans who reported that they made a donation, or had made one in the prior year*

| Row No. | Survey/Date (Did you donate in prior year?) | Dem % | Rep % | No. of cases | Conf % | *RP |
|---|---|---|---|---|---|---|
| 1 | Michigan SOSS — 2006 | 79.2 | 95.5 | 546 | +99 | .83 |
| 2 | Harris Interactive survey — 2006 | 62.9 | 77.3 | 374 | +99 | .81 |
| 3 | Michigan SOSS — 2005 | 81.1 | 96.1 | 577 | +99 | .84 |
| 4 | NES — 2004 | 75.8 | 81.9 | 649 | 94 (marg) | .93 |
| 5 | GSS — 2004 | 78.7 | 85.7 | 842 | 99 | .92 |
| 6 | Mich. SOSS — 2003 | 80.6 | 87.6 | 555 | 97 | .92 |
| 7 | Community Foundation Trends Survey (CFTS) — 2002/ 2003 | 82.7 | 87.7 | **2404 | 95 | .94 |
| 8 | NES — 2002 | 77.7 | 86.0 | 855 | +99 | .90 |
| 9 | GSS — 2002 | 79.1 | 85.4 | 815 | 98 | .93 |
| 10 | Mich. SOSS — 2001 | 83.8 | 92.4 | 586 | +99 | .91 |
| 11 | Individual Philanthropy Patterns Survey — 2000 | 77.0 | 87.0 | **2545 | 95 | .89 |
| 12 | NES — 2000 | 77.6 | 86.7 | 928 | +99 | .90 |
| 13 | Mich. SOSS — 1999 | 77.2 | 85.4 | 723 | +99 | .90 |
| 14 | GSS — 1996*** | 67.2 | 82.6 | 875 | +99 | .81 |
| 15 | NES — 1996 | 78.8 | 91.0 | 855 | +99 | .87 |
| 16 | Economic Values — 1992 | 73.3 | 80.7 | 1340 | +99 | .91 |
| 17 | Average percentage | 77.0 | 86.8 | | | |
| 18 | Overall proportion (Dem % divided by Rep %) | 88.7% | | | | |

*RP is relative proportion, which is the Democratic % divided by the Republican %.

**Case numbers include independents in addition to Democrats and Republicans.

***Includes work-related entities such as labor unions.

---

5 All survey results available to the author indicate that a higher percentage of Republicans make donations; however, the Republican excess shown by one survey (2002 Michigan SOSS) was not statistically significant. For that reason, those results are not included in Figure 110 or in Table 28.

The bottom line of Table 28 shows that the average Democrat is about 89 percent as likely as a Republican to say he has contributed to charity.

> I don't know what compassionate conservative means. Does it mean cutting kids out of after school programs? Does it mean drilling in the arctic wildlife refuge?
>
> — Democratic Senator John Kerry[6]

### How Much of "Charity" Giving is Church Giving?

Since Republicans are more likely to regularly attend religious services (see page 35), one might assume that church giving accounts for most of the donation disparity. However, this does not appear to be the case. Three of the surveys listed in Table 28 asked respondents to distinguish between their donations to religious versus secular charities. One of these, the 1996 GSS survey shown in the Table on line 14, is depicted in Figure 111, below.

*Figure 111. Did you or your family donate "money or other property for charitable purposes" in the past 12 months? (1996 GSS survey, based on 875 cases, with confidence level of 99+% for all differences, and with relative proportions of, left to right, .81 and .83)*

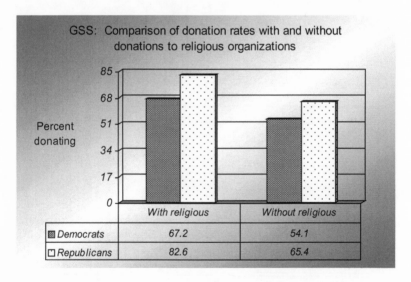

The columns on the left side of Figure 111 show the rate of giving when religious entities are included, and the columns on the right side show the rate of giving when religious entities are excluded. When we exclude the religious organizations the donation percentages drop for both Democrats and Republicans; however, the relative ratio between them is only slightly changed. According to the 1996 GSS survey, Democrats are about 81.4 percent as likely as Republicans

---

6 Anne Q. Hoy, "Kerry Clowns around on 'Daily Show'," *Chicago Tribune*, August 25, 2004.

to donate if religious groups are <u>in</u>cluded,[7] and about 82.7 percent as likely to donate if religious groups are <u>ex</u>cluded.[8]

> The Republicans could care less about these [poor] families. It is the grassroots Democrats who do the fighting for those who can't fight for themselves.

> — Columnist Mark W. Brown[9]

Results from the 2006 and 1999 Michigan surveys (lines 1 and 13 in Table 28) are displayed in Figure 112, below. Again, when religious organizations are excluded the donation percentages drop for both Democrats and Republicans, but the relative ratios between Democrats and Republicans are only slightly changed. The ratio of contributing Democrats to contributing Republicans changes from about 83 percent to 84 percent for 2006, and from about 90 percent to 88 percent for 1999.

*Figure 112. Did you or your family donate "money or other property for charitable purposes" during the past 12 months? (2006 and 1999 Michigan SOSSs, based on, left to right, 546, 551, 722, and 723 cases, with confidence level of 99+% for each comparison, and with relative proportions of, left to right, .83, .84, .90, and .88)*

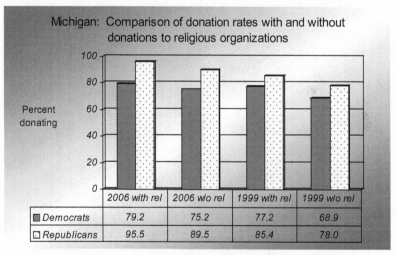

| | 2006 with rel | 2006 w/o rel | 1999 with rel | 1999 w/o rel |
|---|---|---|---|---|
| ▦ Democrats | 79.2 | 75.2 | 77.2 | 68.9 |
| ☐ Republicans | 95.5 | 89.5 | 85.4 | 78.0 |

> Bush Republicans have become the transvestites of the political world. They can put a dress and makeup on, make themselves all pretty, and promise to care about the poor ... but behind the mascara, cheap perfume, and come-hither looks, they're the same guys ...

> — Arianna Huffington, Author and political commentator[10]

---

7 The calculation is 67.2/82.6 = 81.4%.

8 The calculation is 54.1/65.4 = 82.7%.

9 Mark W. Brown, "Finding My Place," in *Democratic Underground.com* (June 3, 2003), Retrieved August 28, 2006, from: http://www.democraticunderground.com/articles/03/06/p/03_place.html.

10 Arianna Huffington, *Fanatics and Fools* (New York: Hyperion, 2004), 153.

The above findings are not surprising in light of the 2000 Social Capital Community Benchmark Survey — a large national survey of 29,233 cases. After analyzing the survey results, Arthur C. Brooks, a professor at Syracuse University, concluded than religious people are more likely to give to secular as well as religious causes:

> Religious people are more generous than secular people with nonreligious causes as well as with religious ones. While 68 percent of the total population gives (and 51 percent volunteers) to nonreligious causes each year, religious people are 10 points more likely to give to these causes than secularists (71 percent to 61 percent) and 21 points more likely to volunteer (60 percent to 39 percent).[11]

If Republicans participate more frequently in religious activities than do Democrats (and the available data suggest that they do), and religious people are more likely to contribute time and money to secular as well as religious causes, we should not be surprised to find (as we do) that Republicans are more likely to donate than Democrats — even with respect to secular causes.

### Who Writes the Larger Check?

> We have things ass-backward here in America.... We constantly hear calls to those who've been the most blessed to "give back something;" that is utter nonsense. It is the thief who should be giving something back because he's produced nothing, whereas the Bill Gates's of the world have already served their fellow man by making life easier for all of us and making jobs in the process.

— Economist Walter Williams[12]

*Figure 113. "[H]ow much do you and/or other family members contribute to charitable organizations each year?" (Michigan SOSS 42 conducted in 2006, based on 384 respondents, with confidence level of 99+%)*

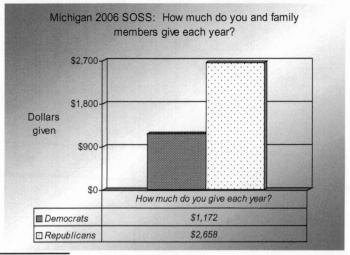

| Michigan 2006 SOSS: How much do you and family members give each year? | |
|---|---|
| **Dollars given** | |
| How much do you give each year? | |
| ■ Democrats | $1,172 |
| ☐ Republicans | $2,658 |

11 Arthur C. Brooks, "Religious Faith and Charitable Giving," *Policy Review* (October and November, 2003): 43.

12 Walter Williams, (Destiny Magazine, July 1995).

With regard to the amount of the donations, the differences between Demo-crats and Republicans are very great. Several surveys suggest that Republicans, on average, contribute significantly larger amounts. One of the more recent dol-lar-quantified surveys is the Michigan State of the State Survey, conducted in 2006. Overall charitable giving averages are shown in Figure 113, above.

The Michigan survey suggests that the average Republican may give more than twice as much to charity as his Democratic counterpart. Similar dispari-ties were found in all other dollar-quantified surveys reviewed. Results of those surveys are shown in Figure 114, below.

*Figure 114. How much do you and/or other family members contribute to charitable organi-zations each year? (Michigan SOSS surveys conducted in 2005 and 2003, Community Foundation Trends Survey conducted in 2002-2003, Individual Philanthropy Patterns Survey conducted in 2000, Michigan SOSS 19 conducted in 1999, and GSS conducted in 1996, based on, left to right, 411, 360, 2404, 2545, 464, and 576 cases, with confidence level of mean differences ranging from 95 to 99%) Note: The case numbers for the Community Foundation Trends Survey and Individual Philan-thropy Patterns Survey include independents as well as Democrats and Republicans.*

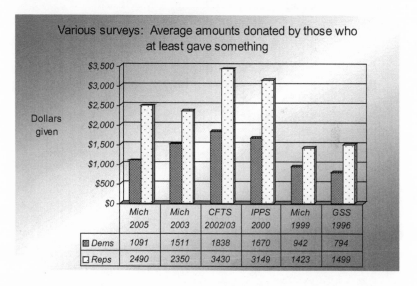

| | Mich 2005 | Mich 2003 | CFTS 2002/03 | IPPS 2000 | Mich 1999 | GSS 1996 |
|---|---|---|---|---|---|---|
| Dems | 1091 | 1511 | 1838 | 1670 | 942 | 794 |
| Reps | 2490 | 2350 | 3430 | 3149 | 1423 | 1499 |

Yet again, President Bush and Republicans in Congress are steal-ing from the poor to give to the rich. Does their shame know no bounds?

— Democratic Congressman Pete Stark[13]

Although the disparities shown in Figure 113 and Figure 114 are large, they are understated because they do not reflect the Democrats and Republicans who

13 "Stark Attacks Republicans for Stealing from the Poor and Giving to the Rich," May 10, 2006, Congressman's Web page, Retrieved March 17, 2007, from http://www.house.gov/stark/news/109th/pressreleases/20060510_Stealing.htm.

gave nothing at all. To get the bottom-line, per capita contribution amounts, we need to multiply the amount given according to each survey by the rate of giving for that survey (found in Table 28, on page 131). Those adjustments slightly increase the donation gap because Democrats tend to give smaller amounts and are more likely to give nothing at all. Adjusted per capita contribution amounts are shown in Figure 115, below.[14]

*Figure 115. Annual donation amounts of those who made contributions (per Figure 113 and Figure 114), multiplied times the percentages who at least gave something (per Table 28)*

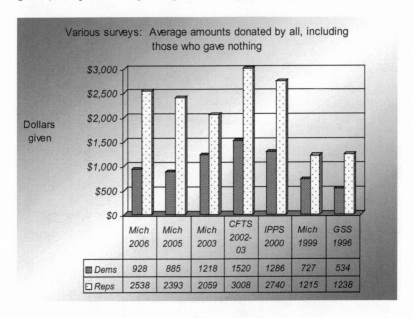

These same results are displayed in Table 29, below. On the bottom line we see the aggregate results of all dollar-quantified surveys. On average, Democrats seem to give less than half as much as Republicans.

*Table 29. Figure 115 results in tabular form. These are average amounts given by all, including those who gave nothing at all.*

| Average amounts donated, including those who gave nothing Survey/Date | Dem Amt. | Rep Amt. | Conf of amt. of giving | Conf of rate of giving |
|---|---|---|---|---|
| Michigan SOSS 2006 | $928 | $2538 | +99 | 99 |
| Michigan SOSS 2005 | 885 | 2393 | +99 | 99 |
| Michigan SOSS 2003 | 1218 | 2059 | +99 | 97 |

14 This was calculated by multiplying frequency of giving times the average amount given.

| | | | | |
|---|---|---|---|---|
| CFTS 2002/03 | 1520 | **3008** | 95 | 95 |
| IPPS 2000 | 1286 | **2740** | 95 | 95 |
| Michigan SOSS 1999 | 727 | **1215** | +99 | +99 |
| GSS 1996 | 534 | **1238** | +99 | +99 |
| Averages | $1014 | **$2170** | | |
| Overall proportion (Dem amt. divided by Rep amt.) | **46.7%** | | | |

In most Democrats' minds, conservative Republicans do not care if children go to bed hungry, and they are racist, intolerant, regard women as inferior, are stingy and mean spirited ...

— Author and radio talk-show host Dennis Prager[15]

## Average Vs. Median

*Figure 116. How much do you and/or other family members contribute to charitable organizations each year? — MEDIAN amounts (Michigan SOSS surveys conducted in 2006, 2005, 2003, and 1999, and GSS conducted in 1996, based on, left to right, 384, 411, 360, 464, and 576 cases)*

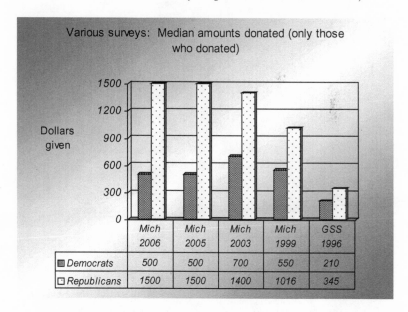

Averages can be misleading, since the large donations of a few can raise the mean to misleading heights. Figure 116 shows some of the same surveys included in Figure 115; however, median contribution amounts are shown instead of aver-

15 Dennis Prager, "Why the Left Fights," in *FrontPageMagazine.com* (July 6, 2005), Retrieved March 17, 2007, from: http://www.frontpagemag.com/Articles/ReadArticle.asp?ID=18665.

age contribution amounts.[16] Of course, the medians represent the midpoints of contribution values. That is, there are equal numbers of contributors who give more and less than these amounts. Republican gifting is still much greater, even when measured by median amounts. This means that the tendency of Republicans to donate larger amounts is probably fairly widespread (involving large percentages of Republicans), and is not attributable to the very large gifts of a few ultra-rich Republicans.

The donations disparity is particularly surprising given that Democrats are much more likely to advocate support for the needy. This is shown in many surveys, one of which is depicted in Figure 117, below.

*Figure 117. How important is it "to help people in America who are worse off than yourself"? (GSS survey conducted in 2004, based on 929 cases, with confidence level of 99+%, and with a relative proportion of 1.31)*

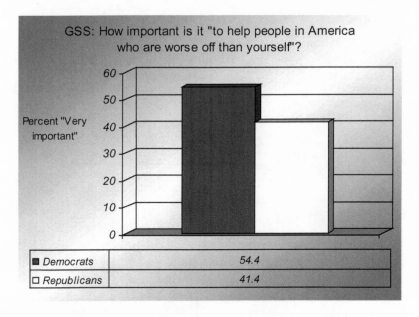

### Do Republicans Diss the Homeless?

A man who sees another man on the street corner with only a stump for an arm will be so shocked the first time he'll give him sixpence. But the second time it'll only be a three penny bit. And if he sees him a third time, he'll have him cold-bloodedly handed over to the police.

— German poet Bertolt Brecht[17]

---

16 The CFTS and IPPS surveys were excluded because median information was not available for those surveys.

17 Bertolt Brecht, "Three Penny Opera," (1928).

Although Republicans generally donate more than their Democratic coun-terparts, they are less likely to give money to people on the street. In a 1996 General Social Survey of 864 Democrats and Republicans, 40 percent of Democrats reported that they gave money, food, or clothing to "homeless or street people," whereas only 33 percent of Republicans reported making such contributions (confidence level = 97%). These results were affirmed in 2004 and 2002 GSS surveys of a total of 1653 Democrats and Republicans, in which 68 percent of Democrats reported giving food or money to the street people, but only 61 percent of Republicans reported making such donations (confidence level = 99+%). It appears that Democrats are more likely to give aid to homeless "street people."

*Volunteerism*

### There Is A Significant Difference

Of course, the general tendency of Republicans to give more, and to give more often, could relate to the fact that they have more money to give. Income level might be what statisticians call an "intervening variable" (the link) in the causal chain between the independent variable (political party) and the dependent variable (level of charitable activity). Income level and other intervening variables are discussed in some detail later in this chapter. However, it is obvious that higher levels of earnings do not entirely explain differences in charitable giving because, even when it comes to volunteering, Republicans still outpace Democrats significantly.

> Behold I do not give lectures or a little charity. When I give I give myself.
>
> — American poet Walt Whitman[18]

Table 30, below, displays the results of several surveys that asked participants whether they recently performed volunteer work. In some cases, the volunteerism was specifically linked to charity work, and in other cases, the respondent might have construed the question to include political or union-related work. Excerpts from the questions are provided. In all cases, Republicans were more likely to have volunteered their time. The table's bottom line shows overall volunteerism rates of 42.5 percent and 53.7 percent for Democrats and Republicans, respectively.

Democrats were only about 79 percent as likely as Republicans to have participated in volunteer causes. The overall results of Table 30 are charted in Figure 118, below, following the table.

---

18 Walt Whitman, "Song of Myself," (1855).

Table 30. *Percentage of Democrats and Republicans who volunteered for charities or other types of organizations (various surveys, as noted)*

| Row No. | Survey/Date*** | Dem % "yes" | Rep % "yes" | No. of cases | Conf % | *RP |
|---|---|---|---|---|---|---|
| 1 | Michigan SOSS #42 — 2006: "Last year ... did you volunteer for any type of organization?" | 40.1 | 64.9 | 551 | +99 | .62 |
| 2 | Michigan SOSS #38 — 2005: "Last year ... did you volunteer for any type of organization?" | 43.7 | 56.6 | 580 | +99 | .77 |
| 3 | NES — 2004: "Were you able to devote time to volunteer work in last 12 months?" | 35.5 | 46.4 | 643 | +99 | .77 |
| 4 | GSS — 2004 and 2002: "During the last 12 months" have you "done volunteer work for a charity"? | 47.8 | 52.0 | 1660 | **92 | .92 |
| 5 | Michigan SOSS #32 — 2003: "This year, have you volunteered for any type of organization?" | 46.0 | 53.2 | 560 | **91 | .86 |
| 6 | NES — 2002: "Were you able to devote time to volunteer work in last 12 months?" | 36.4 | 48.9 | 854 | +99 | .74 |
| 7 | Michigan SOSS #22 — 2001: During the past 12 months, did you volunteer for any type of organization?" | 48.6 | 57.3 | 584 | 96 | .85 |
| 8 | Pew (via Roper) — 2000: In last year, have you "done any volunteer work for any church, charity, or community group"? | 55.0 | 65.0 | 591 | 98 | .85 |

| | | | | | | |
|---|---|---|---|---|---|---|
| 9 | Michigan SOSS #19 — 1999: "During the past 12 months did you volunteer for any type of organization?" | 42.1 | **59.0** | 723 | +99 | .71 |
| 10 | Pew (via Roper) — 1997: In last year, have you In last year, have you "done any volunteer work for any church, charity, or community group"? | 51.0 | **63.0** | 626 | 98 | .81 |
| 11 | General Social Survey (GSS) — 1996: Have you done volunteer work in any of several different types of charities? (Specifically includes labor unions, but not political organizations.) | 52.6 | **65.0** | 876 | +99 | .81 |
| 12 | NES — 1996: "Were you able to devote any time to volunteer work in the last 12 months?" | 38.8 | **50.8** | 859 | +99 | .76 |
| 13 | Economic Values Survey — 1992: "Do you, yourself, happen to be involved in any charity or social service activities...?" | 25.7 | **30.2** | 1340 | +99 | .85 |
| 14 | Economic Values Survey — 1992: "In the past year, have you donated time to a volunteer organization?" | 32.2 | **39.9** | 1340 | +99 | .81 |
| 15 | Average percentages reporting that they volunteered | 42.5 | **53.7** | | | |
| 16 | Overall proportion (Dem % divided by Rep %) | **79.1%** | | | | |

*RP is relative proportion, which is the Democratic % divided by the Republican %.

**Statistical significance is marginal

***See Appendix F for general information regarding survey source.

*Figure 118. Overall percentages of Democrats and Republicans who volunteered for charities or other types of organizations (various surveys, as noted in Table 30, above)*

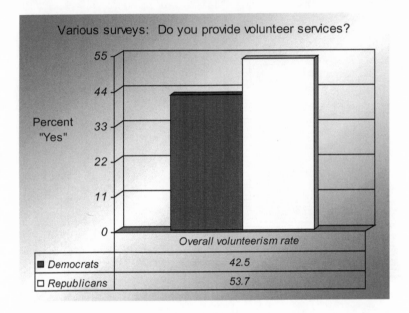

| | Overall volunteerism rate |
|---|---|
| ■ Democrats | 42.5 |
| □ Republicans | 53.7 |

## ANALYSIS: WHY SOME PEOPLE GIVE MORE

> If Democrats are more eager to spend "government" money than Republicans are ... does this mean that Democrats are more "generous? Or does it mean that Republicans are more apt to think of government as spending *their* money, while Democrats think of it as *other people's*?
>
> — Columnist James Taranto[19]

As noted, one might assume that the average Republican donates more to charity simply because he has more income than his Democratic counterpart. However, the disparity in volunteerism raises doubts about that assumption. A careful analysis suggests that, while level of income correlates with the amount of giving, other factors may be just as important.

In the remainder of this chapter, three intervening factors, including income level, are analyzed. The goal is to ascertain why Republicans give more money and time to charity.

It is commonly assumed that Republicans:

- have more income
- are more conservative
- attend religious services more frequently

---

19 James Taranto, "Liberals Are Racist, Study Suggests - 2," *Wall Street Journal*, June 23, 2006.

Each of these 3 factors is reviewed below:

*Income level*

> A check or credit card, a Gucci bag strap, anything of value will do.
> Give as you live.
>
> — Jesse Jackson, Democratic civil rights activist[20]

On average, Republicans earn more than Democrats earn, and their higher incomes give them the ability to donate more. In addition, higher incomes give Republicans a greater tax incentive related to charitable giving. This begs the question: Does the difference in income, between Democrats and Republicans, account for the difference in the amount of charitable giving? Yes, but only to a limited degree.

With regard to 5 of the surveys discussed in this chapter it is possible to break out the amount of donations by the income level of the survey respondents. By so doing, and by using statistical weighting to equalize the number of Democrats and Republicans at each income level, we can determine whether the differences in charitable giving of Democrats and Republicans are caused by income differences.

*Figure 119. "[H]ow much do you and/or other family members contribute to charitable organizations each year?" (Michigan SOSS no. 42 conducted in 2006, based on total of 369 respondents. Only columns marked with an asterisk are individually statistically significant.)*

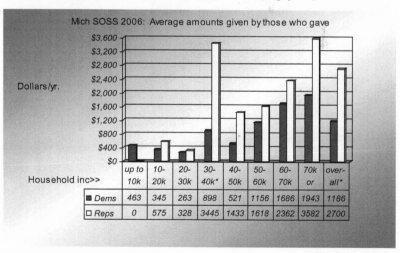

Mich SOSS 2006: Average amounts given by those who gave

| Household inc>> | up to 10k | 10-20k | 20-30k | 30-40k* | 40-50k | 50-60k | 60-70k | 70k or | over-all* |
|---|---|---|---|---|---|---|---|---|---|
| ■ Dems | 463 | 345 | 263 | 898 | 521 | 1156 | 1686 | 1943 | 1186 |
| □ Reps | 0 | 575 | 328 | 3445 | 1433 | 1618 | 2362 | 3582 | 2700 |

*Differences depicted in columns marked with asterisks are statistically significant. The amounts in the "overall" column differ somewhat from those shown in Figure 113, due to fact that a few people represented in Figure 113 did not answer the income question, and thus are excluded from these results.

---

20 Jesse Jackson cited in, "Columbia World of Quotations," (Columbia University Press, 1996).

---

The results for the 2006 Michigan SOSS are shown in Figure 119. We saw the overall results of this survey in an earlier graphic (Figure 113); however, this time the amount of charitable giving is grouped by the total family income of each survey respondent. Although there seems to be a large donations gap within each income range, those differences must be viewed with skepticism due to the relatively small sample sizes and large standard deviations. Only a few columns (marked with asterisks) depict mean differences that are statistically significant. The "overall" column on the far right side of the chart shows a large and statistically significant difference, but it represents all Democrats and Republicans reporting income, without consideration of income level. In other words, part of the overall difference is attributable to the fact that Republicans have higher incomes.

### How Do We Compare the Donations of People with Similar Incomes?

A bone to the dog is not charity. Charity is the bone shared with the dog, when you are just as hungry as the dog.

— Author Jack London[21]

*Figure 120. A comparison of the overall amount of donations shown in Figure 119 to the estimated average amount of donations that would have been made if equal numbers of Democrats and Republicans were represented within each income category. Both differences (unadjusted and adjusted) are 99+% statistically significant. For more information regarding the calculation procedures, see Appendix B 9.*

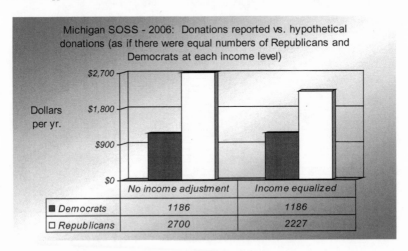

Michigan SOSS - 2006: Donations reported vs. hypothetical donations (as if there were equal numbers of Republicans and Democrats at each income level)

| | No income adjustment | Income equalized |
|---|---|---|
| ■ Democrats | 1186 | 1186 |
| □ Republicans | 2700 | 2227 |

To determine whether Democrats and Republicans at similar income levels donate significantly different amounts, an additional calculation is required. The calculation method is described in Appendix B 9, and the results of that calculation are displayed in Figure 120. The left-side columns of Figure 120 are

---

21 Jack London (attributed), "The Quotations Page."

the same as the "overall" columns shown on the right side of Figure 119. That is, they simply depict the average amounts donated by Democrats and Republicans, without consideration of income level. However, on the right side of Figure 120, the Republican column depicts the hypothetical amount donated by the average Republican — assuming that the number of Republicans within each income range is identical to the number of Democrats in that income range. In other words, the Republican case numbers for each income category have been statistically weighted to make them proportional to the Democratic case numbers for the same income category.

Note that the donation disparity is only partly reduced. According to the unadjusted survey figures (on the left side) Democrats gave about 44 percent as much as Republicans (1186/2700 = 43.9%). The amounts adjusted to equalize income (on the right side) show a disparity that is only partly reduced, with Democrats donating about 53 percent as much as Republicans (1186/2227 = 53.3%). Thus, the gap was lessened, but a very large disparity remains.

> Earn as much as you can. Save as much as you can. Invest as much as you can. Give as much as you can.

> — American Reverend John Wellesly[22]

*Figure 121 "[H]ow much do you and/or other family members contribute to charitable organizations each year?" (Michigan SOSS 38 conducted in 2005, based on total of 386 respondents. Only columns marked with an asterisk are individually statistically significant.)*

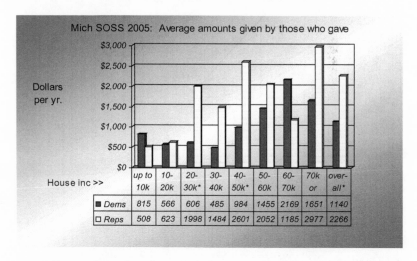

| House inc >> | up to 10k | 10-20k | 20-30k* | 30-40k | 40-50k* | 50-60k | 60-70k | 70k or | over-all* |
|---|---|---|---|---|---|---|---|---|---|
| ■ Dems | 815 | 566 | 606 | 485 | 984 | 1455 | 2169 | 1651 | 1140 |
| □ Reps | 508 | 623 | 1998 | 1484 | 2601 | 2052 | 1185 | 2977 | 2266 |

\* Differences depicted in columns marked with asterisks are statistically significant. The amounts in the "overall" column differ somewhat from those shown in Figure 114 on page 135 due to fact that a few people represented in Figure 114 did not report income, and thus are excluded from these results.

22 Rev. John Wellesly as cited in, "Why Investors Face a Difficult Balancing Act," in *Telegraph.co.uk* (February 24, 2007), Retrieved March 20, 2007, from: http://www. telegraph.co.uk/money/main.jhtml?xml=/money/2007/02/24/cmsave24.xml.

Figure 121, above, shows the results for another survey: the Michigan SOSS conducted in 2005. Each set of columns shows the average donations made by people at a particular income level and, once again, Republicans seem to give more in almost every case. Again, however, we must be skeptical of the results, due to the small samples and large standard deviations associated with each separate column. (Although the "overall" column on the right side of Figure 121 is statistically significant, it doesn't depict Democrats and Republicans at similar income levels.)

> Just because someone's Republican doesn't mean that they don't also, you know, have the capacity to understand or care about children.

— Actress Angelina Jolie[23]

As we did with the 2006 Michigan survey, we can adjust the results so they depict the donations made by people of like income. This is done in Figure 122, where the Republican amounts, depicted on the right side of the chart, are hypothetical amounts that are predicated on the assumption that there are equal numbers of Democrats and Republicans at each level of income.

*Figure 122. A comparison of the overall amount of donations shown in Figure 121 to the estimated average amount of donations that would have been made if equal numbers of Democrats and Republicans were represented within each income category. Both differences (unadjusted and adjusted) are 99+% statistically significant. For more information regarding the calculation procedures, see Appendix B 9.*

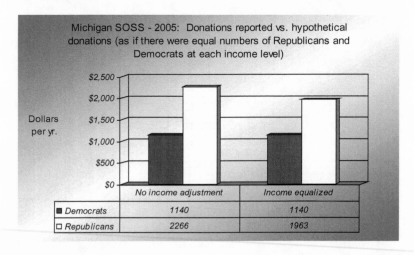

| | No income adjustment | Income equalized |
|---|---|---|
| ■ Democrats | 1140 | 1140 |
| □ Republicans | 2266 | 1963 |

Yet again, we see that equalizing the numbers of Democrats and Republicans within each income range reduces, but does not eliminate, the disparity. For this

23 Angelina Jolie interviewed on, "Anderson Cooper 360 Degrees," (Transcript: CNN, June 20, 2006), Retrieved March 20, 2007, from: http://transcripts.cnn.com/TRANSCRIPTS/0606/20/acd.01.html.

particular survey, the Democratic average donation amount, as a percentage of the average Republican donation amount, changes from 50 to 58 percent.

> The leftist media often portrays conservatives as mean, cruel and insensitive to the plight of the downtrodden. But, as the tax returns of multi-millionaires Dick Cheney and Al Gore prove, the media image is false. The Vice President gives millions to charity, Mr. Gore very little.

— Bill O'Reilly, Author and radio talk show host[24]

There are three other surveys for which we can prepare the same analysis: the Michigan SOSSs conducted in 2003 and 1999, and the GSS conducted in 1996. The results for those surveys, along with those for the 2006 and 2005 Michigan surveys, are shown in Table 31.

*Table 31. Democratic contributions as a percent of Republican contributions, after weighting so that equal numbers of Democrats and Republicans are in each income range*

| Survey | Dem contributions as % of Rep contributions | |
|---|---|---|
| | Not adjusted for income | Adjusted to have equal numbers within income ranges |
| Michigan SOSS 2006 | 43.9 | 53.3 |
| Michigan SOSS 2005 | 50.3 | 58.1 |
| Michigan SOSS 2003 | 61.1 | 69.0 |
| Michigan SOSS 1999 | 66.2 | 76.2 |
| GSS1996 | 52.6 | 57.1 |
| Average percentage | 54.8% | 62.7% |

In Table 31 we see that Democratic contributions increase when an attempt is made to equalize income; however, Democratic contributions remain far below those of Republicans (just 62.7%).[25] This suggests that other factors, in addition to income, must account for the disparity in charitable giving.

### Reality check — Can we really test the impact of income?

As noted, in each instance a significant charity gap remains, even after weighting the case numbers to ensure equal numbers of Democrats and Republicans at each income level. However, if we could reduce the size of the income ranges (e.g., to ranges of just one or two thousand dollars) we would expect the donation gap to get even smaller. That said, it seems very likely that a significant donation gap would remain. This can be demonstrated by the following

---

24 Bill O'Reilly, "Charity: It's the Right Thing to Do," November 30, 2006, Personal Web page, from http://www.billoreilly.com/site/product?printerFriendly=true&pid=20684&said=nul l&satype=null.

25 I have estimated the per-person donations gap to be about $785, on average, stated in 2007 dollars. In aggregate, this charity gap may exceed $50 billion per year. Please see Table 54 on page 307 for the details.

experiment. If we combine the results in the last 5 surveys discussed (Michigan 2006, 2005, 2003, 1999, and GSS 1996) we find that Republicans with total family incomes of $30,000 to $50,000 seem to donate more than Democrats earning $50,000 to $70,000. The average donation amount for the 244 Republicans earning between $30,000 and $50,000 was $1670, while the average donation amount for the 239 Democrats earning between $50,000 and $70,000 was just $1413. It seems that the lower income Republicans give as much or more than the relatively more affluent Democrats.

*Religious beliefs and political ideology*

> Charity is the scope of all God's commands.
>
> — St. John Chrysostom, Christian bishop from the 4th and 5th centuries[26]

Income can only explain part of the difference in the rates of charitable giving by Democrats and Republicans. This begs the question: What other factors relate to the tendency of Republicans to give more?

### The Gianneschi Paper

In a mid-2000 survey conducted by the Social Science Research Center at California State University, Fullerton, 556 randomly-selected residents of Orange County, CA were queried on their charitable activities, income levels, religious activities, political party affiliation, and political ideology (e.g., conservative, liberal, etc.). Based on the results of that survey, the Gianneschi Center for Nonprofit Research issued a comprehensive paper containing several interesting conclusions, some of which are relevant to the central themes of this chapter. For example, it was noted that Republicans tend to give more to charity, and that income level does not seem to be the reason. The report stated:

> There is a significant association ... between [political] party and the value of annual giving" even though "the relationship between party affiliation and total annual household income in Orange County is not statistically significant.[27]

In other words, Democrats and Republicans in Orange County have similar incomes, yet they have significantly different tendencies with regard to charitable contributions.

It was also noted that the biggest gap between Democrats and Republicans pertains to the amount that is given (versus the percentage who give). Specifi-

---

26 St. John Chrysostom as cited in, "Communicating Christ Cross-Culturally," (Church of the Nazarene, 2002).

27 Gregory Robinson and Kathleen Costello, "Patterns of Giving: A Preliminary Study of Ethnic, Political and Religious Differences among Donors in Orange County (Ca)," (Gianneschi Center for Nonprofit Research, 2001), 15, from: http://www.fullerton.edu/gcnr/Patterns. pdf.

cally, the survey found a "high proportion of Republicans (37.9%) compared to Democrats (23.6%) ... that donate $1,000 or more per year." [28]

Why do Republicans give larger amounts to charity? The Gianneschi report concluded:

> Both political party and ideology, and the characterization of religious beliefs and religious activity are significantly associated with giving. The findings indicate that Republicans and political conservatives are the groups most likely to give at the highest levels; as are those defining themselves as religious conservatives/fundamentalists and those most active in the practice of their religious/spiritual development.[29]

These two factors, religiosity and political ideology, are addressed below.

### The Impact Of Religion

> Religion was nearly dead because there was no longer real belief in future life; but something was struggling to take its place —service — social service — the ants' creed, the bees' creed.

> — John Galsworthy, English novelist and playwright[30]

The Gianneschi paper addressed two dimensions of religious practice: the nature of the religious beliefs and the frequency of religious activity. Regarding the nature of religious beliefs, the paper concluded:

> A significantly larger proportion of fundamental/conservatives (31.1%) donate $1,000 or more ... than do [religious] moderates (23.5%) or [religious] liberals (18.4%).... [I]t appears that [religious] conservatives are more likely to donate larger amounts.[31]

Unfortunately, I could not find survey data indicating whether Republicans are religiously more conservative than Democrats. (Although one suspects that they are.) However, there is considerable survey information showing that Republicans, on the whole, attend religious services more frequently. This dimension of religiosity is also addressed by the Gianneschi paper:

> [T]here is a linear <u>decrement</u> in the proportion that gives more than $1,000 annually as one moves from the [religiously] "Very Active" (39.9%) to the [religiously] "Not Very Active" (11.1%). ... Clearly, activity in the pursuit of religious or spiritual practice is strongly related to the value of annual giving.[32]

---

28 Ibid.

29 Ibid., 18.

30 John Galsworthy cited in, "Columbia World of Quotations," (Columbia University Press, 1996).

31 Robinson and Costello, "Patterns of Giving: A Preliminary Study of Ethnic, Political and Religious Differences among Donors in Orange County (Ca)," 16.

32 Ibid., 17.

---

Similar conclusions were reached by Arthur C. Brooks, a professor at the University of Syracuse. In an article in the Oct/Nov 2003 issue of "Policy Review," Mr. Brooks stated his findings with regard to his analysis of the Social Capital Community Benchmark Survey, conducted in 2000:

> The differences in charity between secular and religious people are dramatic. Religious people are 25 percentage points more likely than secularists to donate money (91 percent to 66 percent) and 23 points more likely to volunteer time (67 percent to 44 percent). [33]

The importance of religion is clearly evident in other survey data. The Individual Philanthropy Patterns Survey, conducted in 2000, found that people who attended church at least once per week gave more than twice as much to charity as those who attended on a less-frequent basis ($2,429 versus $1,124). A similar pattern was noted in the Community Foundation Trends Survey, conducted during 2002. Those who attended church at least once per week gave $2,851, while those attending less often gave only $1,331.

### The Impact of Political Ideology

> The conventional wisdom runs like this: Liberals are charitable because they advocate government redistribution of money in the name of social justice; conservatives are uncharitable because they oppose these policies. But note the sleight of hand: Government spending, according to this logic, is a form of charity.
>
> –Author Arthur C. Brooks[34]

Generally, Republicans are more likely than Democrats to classify themselves as "conservative," and, as noted, the Gianneschi paper found that political conservatism positively correlates with charitable giving. The methods used and conclusions reached are described in the paper:

> Respondents characterized their political ideology on a five-point scale ranging from "Very Liberal" to "Very Conservative. ... The clearest effect is that 19.77 percent of those that self-identify as "Very Liberal" or "Somewhat Liberal" report contributing $1,000 or more per year compared to 31.73 percent of respondents that characterize their political ideology as "Somewhat Conservative" or Very Conservative." In other words, political conservatives are more likely to donate larger amounts than are liberals.[35]

The link between charitable giving and political ideology is also evident in the Michigan surveys cited earlier in this chapter. Using data from the 2005 Michigan SOSS, we see a very strong relationship between the average amount of charitable donations and the political ideology of the donor. (See Figure 123, below.) These results are limited to households with total income between $40,000 and $50,000 per year, so income should not be a major factor.

---

33 Brooks, "Religious Faith and Charitable Giving," 41.

34 Arthur C. Brooks, *Who Really Cares: The Surprising Truth About Compassionate Conservatism* (New York: Basic Books, 2006), 20.

35 Robinson and Costello, "Patterns of Giving: A Preliminary Study of Ethnic, Political and Religious Differences among Donors in Orange County (Ca)," 15.

---

*Figure 123. The effect of political ideology on the value of charitable contributions (Michigan SOSS conducted in 2005, based on 55 cases, with confidence level (ANOVA F-statistic) of 99+%)*

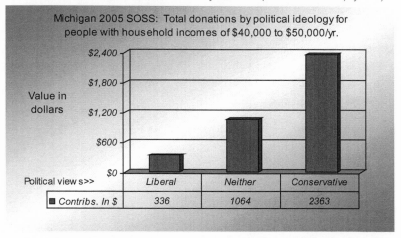

Michigan 2005 SOSS: Total donations by political ideology for people with household incomes of $40,000 to $50,000/yr.

| Political views >> | Liberal | Neither | Conservative |
|---|---|---|---|
| ■ Contribs. In $ | 336 | 1064 | 2363 |

> The modern conservative is engaged in one of man's oldest exercises in moral philosophy; that is, the search for a superior moral justification for selfishness.

— John Kenneth Galbraith, Keynesian economist[36]

We see the very same trend in the 2003 and 2006 Michigan SOSSs, which are combined in Figure 124, below.

*Figure 124. The effect of political ideology on the value of charitable contributions (Michigan SOSSs conducted in 2006 and 2003, based on 129 cases. Confidence level not measured, but presumed to be in excess of 99%, given the much larger sample size than the very significant and similar pattern depicted in Figure 123.)*

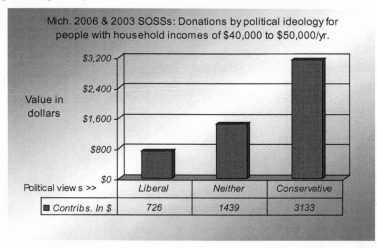

Mich. 2006 & 2003 SOSSs: Donations by political ideology for people with household incomes of $40,000 to $50,000/yr.

| Political views >> | Liberal | Neither | Conservative |
|---|---|---|---|
| ■ Contribs. In $ | 726 | 1439 | 3133 |

36 Amitabh Pal, "Meeting John Kenneth Galbraith," *The Progressive* (May 2, 2006), Retrieved March 21, 2007, from http://progressive.org/.

## *Reality check — How do liberals explain the lack of giving?*

I'd like to offer a personal perspective regarding the liberal lack of giving. My father, Floyd Fried, was a steadfast liberal for all of his life. He was a generous man, and upon his death left significant sums to charities. However, during his life I heard him rail against the general concept of charities. In his mind, they were tools of the rich, designed to forestall needed action by the government. Like many liberals, my father felt that needy people deserved to have guaranteed entitlements.

I believe that my father was, at the least, partially wrong about charities, and he implicitly acknowledged this when he drafted his final will and testament. Why didn't he leave his money to the federal government to reduce the national debt, or to the State of New York to help pay the salaries of its many employees? He left nothing to government, I think, because he felt the charities he selected could use the money more effectively, and with greater focus on the goals that were particularly important to him.

Not all charities are well-conceived or managed. However, many are efficient entities that can adroitly address important needs that are not well handled at the governmental level. For this reason, we need our charities, and we need to support them, regardless of political ideology.

> I would say to myself Democrats care about the poor and Republicans don't, and how can I join the party that doesn't care about the poor. I finally came to the conclusion that we care about the poor more.
>
> — Rudy Giuliani, former Republican Mayor of New York City.[37]

## CONCLUSIONS

Survey data consistently show that Republicans are more likely than their Democratic counterparts to donate time and money to charity. In addition, the average and median amounts given by Republicans tend to be significantly larger. These tendencies can be explained by analyzing the demographic differences between Republicans and Democrats.

Although income level positively correlates with charitable giving, it is not the only important factor. People who frequently attend religious services or who are religiously conservative tend to give more time and money to charitable causes. In addition, people who have politically conservative views are much more likely to donate to charity. All of these traits — higher income, religiosity, and political conservatism — are more prevalent among Republicans than Democrats. Therefore, it is likely that they are the important "intervening variables" that explain the significant difference in charitable giving and volunteerism between Democrats and Republicans.

---

37 "Giuliani Keys on the Economy and Taxes," *Associated Press via MSNBC.com* (February 27, 2007), Retrieved March 21, 2007, from http://www.msnbc.msn.com/id/17360348/.

# Chapter 5: Who Pays More Taxes?

### Red State Welfare Queens

The same red states who voted to reelect the Chimperor are net tax recipients. They get more than they pay. ... In other words — most of the folks who represent the Red States and those in the red states who voted for the chimp are Red State Welfare Queens....

— Anonymous blogger[1]

Every year, the Tax Foundation, a non-partisan tax research organization, compares the federal taxes paid by residents of each of the 50 states to the respective amounts of federal spending in those states. Generally, these comparisons show that the red states (ones that lean Republican) are net beneficiaries, while the blue states (those that generally vote Democratic) get short-changed. For example, the newly-red state of New Mexico receives nearly $2 in federal spending for each $1 dollar in federal taxes paid by its residents. On the other hand, New Jersey receives just 57 cents in federal spending for every dollar of federal taxes paid by its residents.

These comparisons cause some Democrats to believe that the blue states are being cheated by the red states. In other words, Democrats are being cheated by Republicans. However, a spokesman for the Tax Foundation suggests that the differences in federal spending are modest, and understandable:

---

1 "Red State Welfare Queens," June, 2005, Political Web site, Retrieved March 21, 2007, from http://demopedia.democraticunderground.com/.

Spending does lean red, but the reason is demographic, not political. Most federal money is spent on retirees, especially Social Security and Medicare. And of course, the elderly have been moving south and west for years. Every large blue state saw its elderly population depleted during the late 1990s.[2]

In other words, federal spending is higher in the red states primarily because people tend to move to the red states just as they start to collect Social Security and Medicare.

We can't blame Republicans for the disparity in federal spending because they are not responsible for retirees moving to the Sun Belt. However, spending is only half of the story: What about the amount of taxes collected? Does the government collect more from people in the blue states than from people in the red states? The answer is "yes," and the reason is obvious: People in blue states tend to earn more than people in red states. However, this does not mean that Democrats pay more taxes than Republicans. To the contrary, the average Republican pays far more taxes than does the average Democrat — in absolute dollars and as a percentage of income. This is generally true for all types of taxes and at all governmental levels (federal, state, and local).

## DETAILS

*Federal taxes*

### Income Tax

The taxpayer — That's someone who works for the federal government but doesn't have to take the civil service examination.

— President Ronald Reagan[3]

Figure 125, below, shows estimated annual federal income tax amounts paid by men and women in 2003. We see that, on average, Republican men paid about 70 percent ($2,900) more in federal income tax than did Democratic men, Republican women paid about 53 percent ($1,700) more than Democratic women, and, on a gender-neutral basis, Republicans paid about 62 percent ($2,300) more.[4]

*Figure 125. Estimated average federal income tax paid, calculated by multiplying the percentage of Democrats and Republicans in each income quintile (based on General Social Survey results) times the Congressional Budget Office (CBO) 2003 tax rates and income amounts for the respective quintiles*

---

2 William Ahern, "Blue States: Ready for a Less Progressive Tax Code?," in *Commentary* (Tax Foundation, December 15, 2004), Retrieved July 5, 2005, from: http://www.taxfoundation. org/news/show/75.html.

3 President Ronald Reagan, October 27, 1964, Conservativeforum.org, Retrieved March 21, 2007, from http://www.conservativeforum.org/authquot.asp?ID=12.

4 Note: Most of the figures in this chapter are for 2003 amounts. To adjust these amounts for the inflation that took place between 2003 and 2007, add about 15 percent.

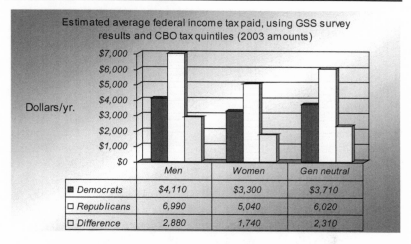

| | Men | Women | Gen neutral |
|---|---|---|---|
| ■ Democrats | $4,110 | $3,300 | $3,710 |
| □ Republicans | 6,990 | 5,040 | 6,020 |
| □ Difference | 2,880 | 1,740 | 2,310 |

[The Republicans] will take food out of the mouths of children in order to give tax cuts to the wealthiest.

— Democratic House Majority Leader Nancy Pelosi[5]

The calculation of these amounts is explained in detail in Appendix B 10, and is extremely exciting if you are an accountant. For other readers, however, the following general overview is more than sufficient. The Congressional Budget Office (CBO) periodically releases a publication entitled, "Historical Effective Federal Tax Rates," and it provides the effective individual federal tax rates for taxpayers in 5 different household income levels (quintiles). The 2003 average tax rates are shown in Figure 126, below.

*Figure 126. Federal individual income tax rates for 2003 by household income quintile, per CBO's Historical Effective Federal Tax Rates, released in December, 2005*

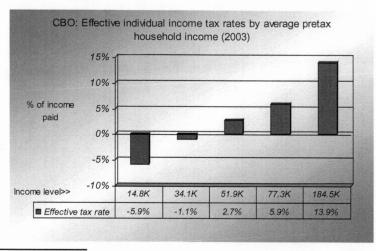

| Income level>> | 14.8K | 34.1K | 51.9K | 77.3K | 184.5K |
|---|---|---|---|---|---|
| ■ Effective tax rate | -5.9% | -1.1% | 2.7% | 5.9% | 13.9% |

---

5 Sue Kirchhoff and Richard Wolf, "Rift Appears in GOP over Cutting Taxes and Spending," *USA Today*, November 13 2005.

> A little history. Congress and the courts repelled the first attempt to impose an income tax, ruling it unconstitutional. Only after state legislatures amended the Constitution, in 1913, did Congress impose the federal income tax. The initial tax rate? One percent.

— Larry Elder, Radio talk show host[6]

The effective average tax rates are negative for the lower 2 quintiles (i.e., people whose household income is in the lower 40%). This is primarily due to the Earned Income Tax Credit (EITC), which is a refundable credit designed to give assistance (a form of welfare) to lower-income working people. When we cite the amount of taxes paid by low-income taxpayers, we are really citing a net number: taxes paid by poor people who don't qualify for the EITC, net of the EITC received by others who do qualify for the credit. It would be preferable to separate the amounts, and to consider the EITC in Chapter 8. However, the available data are not conducive to estimating the EITC component, so net amounts are used in this analysis.

Figure 127, below, shows dollar amounts instead of rates. Obviously, 60 percent of Americans paid little or nothing in 2003; almost all federal income tax was paid by about 40 percent of the population. In fact, people in the lowest 20 percent of the income range "paid" a negative tax in the amount of more than $850 per year. (In other words, they were paid by the government.) Again, this was due to the massive EITC program.

*Figure 127. Federal individual income tax amounts for 2003 by household income quintile, per CBO's Historical Effective Federal Tax Rates, released in December, 2005. Computed by multiplying the CBO rate per quintile times the CBO average household income per quintile.*

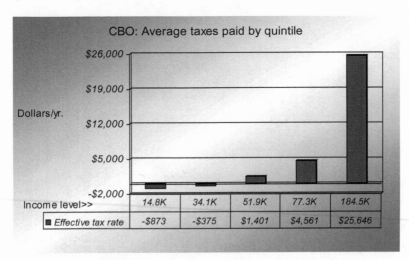

6 Larry Elder, *Ten Things You Can't Say in America* (New York: St. Martin's Press, 2000), 212-13.

> The Government that robs Peter to pay Paul can always depend upon the support of Paul.

— George Bernard Shaw, Irish playwright[7]


*Reality check — By definition, tax cuts are for taxpayers!*

As evident in Figure 127, many Americans pay little or no federal income tax — a point that seems to elude many so-called tax "experts." They seem surprised and incensed by tax reduction plans that give larger tax cuts to high-income than low-income Americans. Yet, simple logic tells us that we can't cut the tax burden of someone who pays no taxes.

For example, after President Bush announced his initial tax cutting proposals (early in his administration), the Center on Budget and Policy Priorities made the following shocking discovery:

> Based on an examination of the most recent Census data, [our analysis] finds that the President's tax-cut proposals would provide no benefit to nearly one in every three U.S. families[8]

What the Center failed to state was that no federal income tax cut plan — Bush's or any other — could possibly provide a reduction in taxes to more than two thirds of Americans. That's because federal income tax is not paid by about a third of the American households that have income. "Tax reductions" for those Americans would be, in reality, a distribution of welfare.

The percentage of non-paying Americans has grown rapidly in recent years. The Tax Foundation reports that, since 1985, the percentage of zero-liability tax returns has nearly doubled. If that trend continues, a potentially tyrannical situation might develop, as noted by the Heritage Foundation:

> Are we close to a tipping point where the non-taxpaying class is larger than the group who pays taxes? Are we nearing the point of government dependency that threatens the American Republic left by our Founding Fathers?[9]

*The Relationship of Federal Income Tax to Household Income*

Of course, we would expect Republicans to pay more income tax because they earn more income. Average 2003 household pretax income for Democrats and Republicans, based on CBO estimates, is shown in Figure 128.

*Figure 128. Estimated 2003 average total pretax household income, calculated by multiplying the percentage of Democrats and Republicans in each income quintile times the CBO income amount for that quintile.*

---

7 George Bernard Shaw cited in, "Columbia World of Quotations," (Columbia University Press, 1996).

8 "Bush Tax Plan Offers No Benefits to One in Three Families," (Center on Budget and Policy Priorities, February 7, 2001), Retrieved July 6, 2005, from: http://www.cb99.org/2-7-01leftoutshort.htm.

9 "The American Political Experiment: What the 2005 Index of Dependency Tells Us," in *Press release advertising tax seminar* (Heritage Foundation, June 13, 2005).

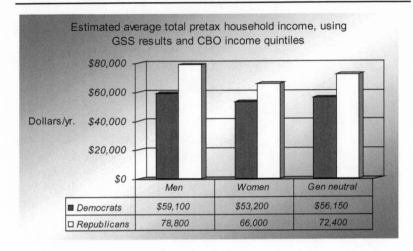

I am in favor of cutting taxes under any circumstances and for any
excuse, for any reason, whenever it's possible.
— Economist Milton Friedman[10]

Although the Republican income advantage is substantial, it is not as large,
percentage-wise, as the tax excess. The excess of taxes paid and income made by
Republicans (in 2003) is shown in Figure 129, below. This chart simply shows
that our progressive tax system is alive and well. It also may explain why Democrats and Republicans often have different perspectives regarding tax rates.

*Figure 129. A comparison of the excess of Republican 2003 federal income taxes paid (Figure
125) to the excess of Republican 2003 pretax household income earned (Figure 128). Both excess
amounts are expressed as percentages.*

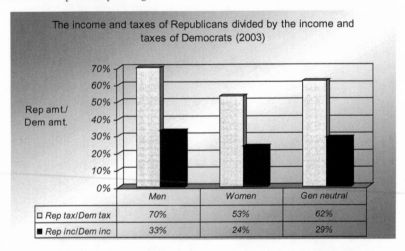

10 Milton Friedman as cited by Gerald Prante, "Economics Community Mourns the Loss of
Milton Friedman," (The Tax Foundation, November 21, 2006), Retrieved March 22, 2007,
from: http://www.taxfoundation.org/news/show/2016.html.

### Average Federal Tax For Median Incomes

Many of you are buckling beneath high-interest debts, insane tax-es, and mortgages.... Islam has no taxes and only limited alms that stand at 2.5 percent.

— Terrorist and flat-tax advocate Osama bin Laden[11]

"Average" can be a poor indication of "typical" when it comes to taxes. Wealthy people (who are more likely to be Republicans) pay a great deal of tax, and this raises the Republican tax average substantially. On the other hand, many people pay no tax whatever. These people tend to be Democrats, and this significantly lowers the Democratic average. For these reasons, a better repre-sentation of "typical" might be the average taxes paid by people with median incomes (incomes above and below which there are equal numbers of people).

*Figure 130. Estimation of 2003 average federal income tax paid by a median-income Democrat and a median-income Republican, by gender (GSS survey results from 1998 through 2004 and CBO quintiles for pretax household income and federal tax, based on 2648 cases for men and 3358 cases for women)*

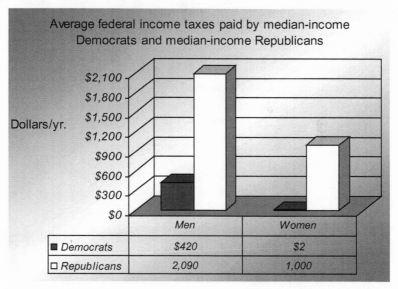

| | Men | Women |
|---|---|---|
| ■ Democrats | $420 | $2 |
| □ Republicans | 2,090 | 1,000 |

Today, under George W. Bush, there are two Americas, not one.... One America that pays the taxes, another America that gets the tax breaks.

— Democratic Senator John Edwards[12]

11 Daniel Kimmage. (September 11, 2007), "Terrorism: Bin Laden Video Represents "Distilled Lunacy" Of Two Cultures", Retrieved September 25, 2007, from Radio Free Europe/ RL, Inc.: http://www.rferl.org/featuresarticle/2007/09/7996EEF9-910C-4E1D-86D2-9E56A1902E8C.html.

12 John Edwards as cited by Michael Duffy, "The Natural," in *Time.com* (July 11, 2004), Retrieved March 21, 2007, from: http://www.time.com/time/printout/0,8816,662792,00.html.

In Figure 130, above, we see that a person with 2003 median Democratic income had a very different tax liability than a person with median Republican income. Federal income tax associated with the Democratic median ranged from about zero to $400, depending on gender. Federal tax related to the Republican median income ranged from around $1,000 to $2,000. Although these gaps are less, dollar-wise, than the average tax differences shown in Figure 125, they may be large enough to account for the attitudinal divergence between Democrats and Republicans with respect to the federal income tax. The estimation of median tax amounts is explained in Appendix B 11 on page 390.

### A very brief history of the United States income tax

In 1895, the Supreme Court ruled that the income tax was unconstitutional under Article I of the Constitution, which barred most taxes that were not apportioned in accordance with the population of each state. The impact of the Supreme Court's decision did not last long. Populists argued that the income tax was needed as a source of revenue and as a tool of social justice. Public demands for the income tax grew very strong "amid a frenzy of 'soak the rich' rhetoric...."[13] By 1913, Congress was given the power to impose an income tax by the 16th Amendment to the Constitution.

Initially, less than 1 percent of the population paid the new income tax, and rates ranged from 1 to 7 percent. Just 5 years later, however, the top rate was pushed to 77 percent, and it grew to 94 percent during World War II. Thereafter, tax rates began to fall, reaching their low points during the Reagan presidency. At that time, the top tax rate was 28 percent. During the Clinton presidency the top rate was increased to about 40 percent, and under the George W. Bush presidency it now stands at about 35 percent.

### Other Federal Taxes

#### Excise Taxes

Most consumers would be shocked to learn how much they ultimately pay in taxes on their beverage of choice. ... If all the taxes levied on the production, distribution and retailing of beer are added up, they amount to an astonishing 44% of the retail price!

— The Beer Institute, an organization representing American breweries[14]

Although the United States constitutional definition of excise tax includes a tax on any "event," including the receipt of income or the purchase of a product, the commonly understood (and IRS) definition of excise tax is limited to those taxes that are paid on the purchase of certain products and services. These in-

---

13 Larry P. Arnn and Grover Norquist. (April 15, 2003), "Repeal of the 16th Amendment", Retrieved September 25, 2007, from The Claremont Institute: http://www.claremont.org/publications/pubid.477/pub_detail.asp.

14 "Beer Tax Facts," (The Beer Institute), from: http://www.beerinstitute.org/BeerInstitute/files/ccLibraryFiles/Filename/000000000275/beertaxfacts.pdf.

clude, among other things, gasoline, cigarettes, tires, certain sports equipment, telecommunication services, and air transportation. We sometimes pay excise taxes directly, but often the taxes are buried in the cost of products and services acquired.

There are two functions served by the use of excise taxes: to raise revenue for the federal government, and to discourage certain behaviors, such as smoking and alcohol consumption. Most excise taxes are proportional to purchases, but regressive to income. To prepare its reports, CBO distributes federal excise taxes to households "according to their consumption of the taxed good or service." As a percentage of income, excise taxes equal about 2.3 percent of income for people in the lowest quintile of household income, but only about .5 percent for those in the highest quintile of household income.

### Federal Corporation Income Tax Attributed To The Owner

> The whole idea of our government is this: If enough people get together and act in concert, they can take something and not pay for it.

— P.J. O'Rourke, American political satirist[15]

*Figure 131. Estimated average 2003 federal income, excise, and imputed corporation taxes paid, calculated by multiplying the percentage of Democrats and Republicans in each quintile times the CBO tax rates and income amounts for the respective quintiles*

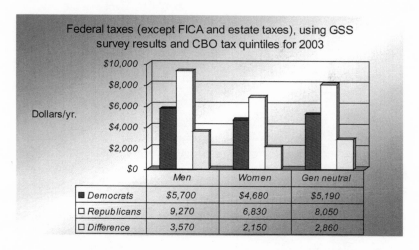

Profitable corporations generally pay a federal income tax, and this tax is indirectly paid by the shareholders of the corporation via lower dividends.[16] When it prepares its individual tax burden reports, CBO distributes corporate income tax to households "according to their share of capital income." It is a progressive

15 P. J. O'Rourke, *Parliament of Whores* (New York: Grove Press, 2003), 232.

16 A profitable corporation does not pay federal income tax if it elects to have each shareholder directly pay tax on his or her share of profits. Also, a profitable corporation may not pay taxes if it qualifies for certain incentive credits, which are intended to promote new energy technologies, the hiring of disadvantaged workers, etc.

tax that ranges from .3 percent of income for people in the lowest income quintile, to 3.4 percent for those in the highest income quintile.

Using the same methods and sources already discussed with regard to federal income taxes (i.e., GSS survey results and CBO quintiles), we can expand our tax estimate to add federal excise taxes and corporation income tax. These taxes, combined with the federal individual income tax, are shown in Figure 131, above.

As indicated in Figure 131, in 2003 the average Republican (on a gender-neutral basis) paid about 55 percent ($2,860) more in federal income, excise, and imputed corporation taxes than did the average Democrat.[17]

### Estate Tax

> When we were at peace, Democrats wanted to raise taxes. Now there's a war, so Democrats want to raise taxes. When there was a surplus, Democrats wanted to raise taxes. Now that there is a mild recession, Democrats want to raise taxes.
>
> — Author and political pundit Ann Coulter[18]

The analysis in this chapter does not include federal estate ("death") tax, which affects a small minority of Americans who are usually fairly wealthy. Intuitively, we might assume that the people who pay estate tax are (or were) more likely to be Republicans. However, I have no factual basis for that hunch.

### My Long-Winded FICA "Tax" Caveat

Before we complete our federal tax estimate by adding FICA (Social Security and Medicare payroll taxes), a lengthy caveat must be given. For the following reasons, FICA "taxes" are not taxes in the normal sense, and are best evaluated separately, net of anticipated benefits:

People who do not contribute to Social Security or Medicare are not eligible to participate.[19] This is normally not the case for a tax, which is defined as "a charge usually of money imposed by authority on persons or property for public purposes."[20] These "public purposes," such as national defense, highway improvements, environmental protection, public schools, and police protection, are available to everybody, whether or not they pay the tax.

About 5 million of America's 145 million workers do not participate in Social Security. Instead of paying payroll "taxes," these state and local government workers make "contributions" to their alternative retirement plans — many of which are like 401k plans. Upon retirement, most of these people get back every nickel of "contributions" — plus earnings. If the Social Security payroll "tax"

---

17 The calculation is $8,050/$5,190 = 155%.

18 Ann Coulter, "Put the Tax Cut in a Lock Box," in *Jewish World Review* (February 21, 2002), Retrieved March 22, 2007, from: http://www.jewishworldreview.com/cols/coulter022102.asp.

19 However, in certain limited circumstances the close relatives of participating workers are also given coverage.

20 The definition is from the Merriam Webster's Collegiate Dictionary — Tenth Edition.

were a tax in the normal sense, the federal government could not allow 5 million government workers to evade that tax by putting their money into these alternative, 401k-type investments.

This is the most important point. Even if we were to classify Social Security and Medicare contributions as "taxes," a balanced analysis would require that we report those taxes net of anticipated individual benefits. In other words, we'd have to reduce the so-called tax by the present value of the expected monthly cash retirement benefits (or, the estimated value of the Medicare insurance). It is intellectually and economically dishonest to credit people with paying Social Security and Medicare "tax," while disregarding the offsetting retirement and health insurance benefits. And, when we count those benefits, there no longer is a tax for many people.

> The principal purpose of the Democratic Party is to use the force of government to take property away from the people who earn it and give it to people who do not.
>
> — Neal Boortz, Author and radio talk show host[21]

In short, the inclusion of Social Security and Medicare contributions in tax calculations makes no sense — especially if there is no offset for the expected monthly cash benefits and medical insurance. For all of these reasons, FICA "taxes" and the offsetting benefits are considered separately, in Chapter 7. However, for those who insist on mixing apples with oranges, FICA is also added to other federal taxes in Figure 132.

*Figure 132 — Estimated average federal income, excise, imputed corporation taxes paid, and FICA tax, calculated by multiplying the percentage of Democrats and Republicans in each quintile times the CBO tax rates and income amounts for the respective quintiles*

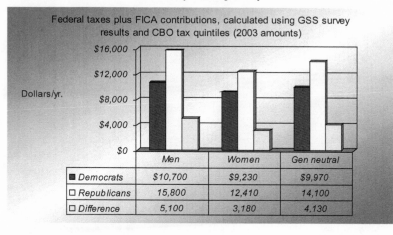

| | Men | Women | Gen neutral |
|---|---|---|---|
| ■ Democrats | $10,700 | $9,230 | $9,970 |
| □ Republicans | 15,800 | 12,410 | 14,100 |
| □ Difference | 5,100 | 3,180 | 4,130 |

21 Neil Boortz (attributed), "Thinkexist.Com."

In Figure 132 we see that, in 2003, the average Republican man paid about 48 percent ($5,100) more than his Democratic counterpart in total federal taxes, including FICA contributions.[22] The average Republican woman paid about 34 percent ($3,200) more than her counterpart. On a gender-neutral basis, the excess paid by Republicans was about 41 percent ($4,100).

### *Reality check — Did FDR think FICA was a "tax"?*

According to Larry DeWitt, a Social Security Administration historian, the Social Security program was designed so that each worker would contribute to the "old age reserve account." There was the "clear idea that this account would then be the source of monies to fund the workers' retirement."

Unlike a tax in the normal sense, "the contributions established an 'earned right' to the eventual benefits." This was extremely important to President Roosevelt, who "strenuously objected to any attempt to introduce general revenue [tax] funding into the program." FDR stated:

> We put those payroll contributions there so as to give the contributors a legal, moral, and political right to collect their pensions and unemployment benefits.[23]

Thus, there is an undeniable connection between an individual's payment of the payroll tax and his moral and political (but not legal) right to collect benefits. This distinguishes the payroll "tax" from other taxes.

*State and local taxes*

> The tax systems of most states already are significantly regressive — that is, they take a larger proportion of the income of lower-income families than the income of more affluent families.
>
> — The Center on Budget and Policy Priorities[24]

### *Average Taxes Paid*

State and local taxes comprise income, sales, excise, and property taxes. Estimating the amount paid by Democrats versus Republicans was no easy task, and required separate calculations for people aged 65 or more years, and for people under the age of 65. These two estimates were then combined into a weighted average by the proportion of people in those two age groups. The details of the sources and calculation methods used are given at Appendix B 12. Figure 133, below, shows the overall results. We see that, the average Republican paid significantly more state and local income, sales, excise, and property taxes than did the average Democrat. However, the disparity was smaller than the federal tax

---

22 This does not include the federal estate ("death") tax.

23 Historian Larry DeWitt, "The 1937 Supreme Court Rulings on the Social Security Act," 1999, Social Security Administration, Retrieved August 13, 2006, from http://www.ssa.gov/history/court.html.

24 "State Tax Systems Are Becoming Increasingly Inequitable," January 15, 2002, Center on Budget and Policy Priorities, Retrieved October 12, 2006, from http://www.cbpp.org/1-15-02sfp-pr.htm.

differential, whether measured in absolute dollars or as a percentage. This is because some state and local taxes are either "proportional" or regressive, rather than progressive.[25] Republican men paid about 33 percent more, Republican women paid about 26 percent more, and, on a gender-neutral basis, Republicans paid about 30 percent more state and local taxes than did their Democratic counterparts.

*Figure 133. Estimate of state and local income, sales, excise, and property tax, based on GSS survey data for 1998 through 2004, 430 separately calculated tax returns, Social Security data, and information published by the Tax Policy Center. A detailed explanation of the calculation is available at Appendix B 12.*

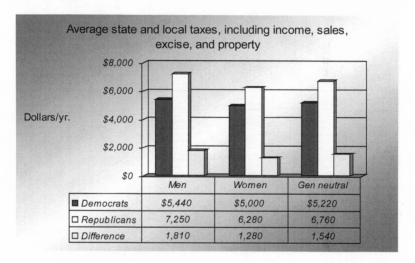

| | Men | Women | Gen neutral |
|---|---|---|---|
| ■ Democrats | $5,440 | $5,000 | $5,220 |
| □ Republicans | 7,250 | 6,280 | 6,760 |
| □ Difference | 1,810 | 1,280 | 1,540 |

Income taxes are progressive.... Other taxes, like sales taxes, property taxes and payroll taxes aren't progressive, that is, everyone pays the same rate regardless of income. We have that mix so that most people pay at least some tax. Otherwise the tax users would pick the taxpayers clean. That's called socialism.

— Mike Rosen, Radio talk show host[26]

## Median Taxes Paid

It is difficult to provide a meaningful estimate of the average state and local taxes paid by a median-income Democrat or a median-income Republican because multiple data sources were used for the different groups of taxpayers (e.g.,

25 "Proportional" taxes are those that increase proportionally to income. For example, a man earning ten times more than his neighbor would pay ten times the income tax. People often mislabel the proportional tax as a "flat" tax — which falsely implies that everyone pays the same amount of tax, regardless of income. Progressive taxes increase at a rate that is faster than the increase in income, and regressive taxes increase at a rate that is slower than the increase in income.

26 Mike Rosen, "Lowdown on Higher Taxes," April 26, 2005, Sean Hannity Web site, Retrieved December 8, 2006, from http://www.hannity.com/forum/showthread.php?t=3981.

for those over age 64 and those under age 65). However, if we limit the results to those under the age of 65, meaningful estimates are possible. These are presented in Figure 134, below.

*Figure 134. Median differences for total state and local taxes for people under age 65, based on GSS survey data for 1998 through 2004, and Tax Policy Center tax amounts by income quintile*

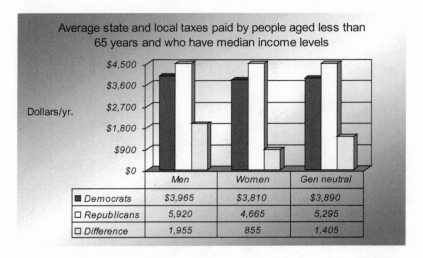

| | Men | Women | Gen neutral |
|---|---|---|---|
| ■ Democrats | $3,965 | $3,810 | $3,890 |
| □ Republicans | 5,920 | 4,665 | 5,295 |
| □ Difference | 1,955 | 855 | 1,405 |

We see that the median ("typical") Republican man paid about 49 percent more than the median Democratic man, and the median Republican women paid about 22 percent more than her Democratic counterpart. On a gender-neutral basis, the difference was about 36 percent.

*Total taxes: federal, state, and local*

> [I]n liberal eyes, the Republican — conservative preference for lowering taxes can only emanate from selfishness and apathy toward the poor.
>
> — Radio talk-show host Dennis Prager[27]

### Total Without FICA Tax

The total taxes paid by Democrats and Republicans are simply all of the amounts presented heretofore, and they are summarized in Figure 135. FICA taxes are not included in this estimate; however, they are added in a subsequent graphic.

Figure 135 shows that the average Republican man paid about 48 percent ($5,380) more in total taxes than did the average Democratic man, while the average Republican woman paid about 35 percent ($3,420) more than her Democratic counterpart. The gender-neutral difference was about 42 percent ($4,400).

27 Prager, "Why the Left Fights."

*Figure 135. Estimate of total average taxes paid. This is simply the combination of federal tax amounts in Figure 131 and the state and local tax amounts in Figure 133.*

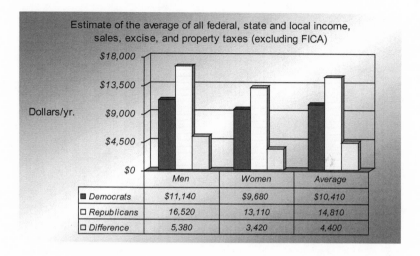

| | Men | Women | Average |
|---|---|---|---|
| ■ Democrats | $11,140 | $9,680 | $10,410 |
| □ Republicans | 16,520 | 13,110 | 14,810 |
| □ Difference | 5,380 | 3,420 | 4,400 |

### Who Pays More Tax In Proportion To Income?

Republicans believe every day is the Fourth of July, but the Democrats believe every day is April 15th.

— President Ronald Reagan[28]

The differences above are almost entirely due to the fact that Republicans, on average, have more per capita income. That is, they are likely to have greater income in proportion to the size of the household. The excess of Republican income, however, is not proportionally as great as the excess of taxes paid, as can be seen in Figure 136, below. Note: This chart is similar to Figure 129; however, it includes state and local, as well as federal taxes.

---

28 President Ronald Reagan (attributed), "Quotationz.Com."

*Figure 136. A comparison of the excess of Republican 2003 federal, state, and local taxes paid (Figure 135) to the excess of Republican 2003 pretax household income earned (Figure 128). Both excess amounts are expressed as percentages.*

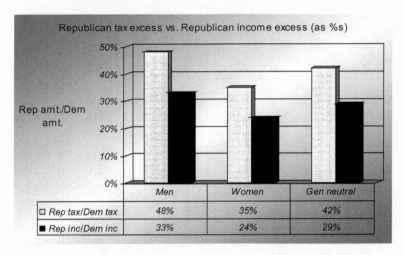

| | Men | Women | Gen neutral |
|---|---|---|---|
| □ Rep tax/Dem tax | 48% | 35% | 42% |
| ■ Rep inc/Dem inc | 33% | 24% | 29% |

Figure 136, above, shows, for example, that the average Republican man paid 48 percent more in taxes, but collected only 33 percent more in household income (than the average Democratic man). For Republican women, a similar, albeit less pronounced, differential is evident.

### Total Taxes Including FICA

> I can remember way back when a liberal was one who was generous with his own money.
>
> — Will Rogers, Humorist and author[29]

In my opinion, Figure 135 displays the most meaningful federal, state, and local tax totals. However, for readers who want to see the impact of FICA tax on this analysis, they are included in Figure 137, below.

As expected, Figure 137 shows that Republicans pay more FICA tax than do Democrats (by virtue of having higher earnings). However, the inclusion of FICA slightly narrows the percentage tax gap between Democrats and Republicans. For example, with the inclusion of FICA tax the percentage of excess taxes paid by Republican men and women (on average) was 37.5 percent — which is a little lower than the amount shown in Figure 136 (42%).

---

29 "Election Wisdom from Will Rogers," in *Virginian-Pilot*, ed. Richard W. Reeks (Landmark Communications, Inc., October 25, 1996).

Figure 137. All taxes shown in Figure 135 plus FICA

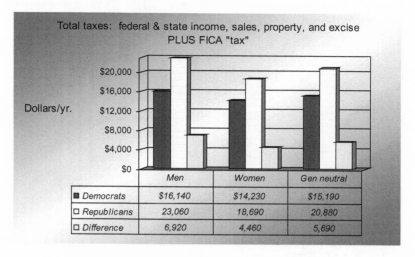

| | Men | Women | Gen neutral |
|---|---|---|---|
| ■ Democrats | $16,140 | $14,230 | $15,190 |
| □ Republicans | 23,060 | 18,690 | 20,880 |
| □ Difference | 6,920 | 4,460 | 5,690 |

Total taxes: federal & state income, sales, property, and excise PLUS FICA "tax"

> This may be all Bush is really good for, for me. I want some money back. I would like a little bit of it.
>
> — Comedian Whoopi Goldberg[30]

## CONCLUSIONS

If we include the effects of the Earned Income Tax Credit (EITC), people in the lowest 2 quintiles (i.e., the lowest 40%) pay, on average, a "negative" federal income tax. Another 20 percent of the income-earning population pays almost nothing. For these reasons, it is never possible to give federal income tax cuts to everyone.

For 2003, the average Republican (on a gender-neutral basis) paid about 62 percent ($2,300) more federal income tax per year than did the average Democrat, and about 42 percent ($4,400) more of all types of federal, state, and local taxes, except for FICA.[31] If we add FICA taxes, the average Republican paid about 37.5 percent ($5,700) more than that paid by the average Democrat.

There is also a significant differential between the tax amounts paid by Republicans and Democrats with median income, and estimates of these amounts are provided in the chapter.

---

30 Whoopi Goldberg speaking on, "Tonight Show " (Transcript: NBC, April 9, 2001), Retrieved March 22, 2007, from: http://www.acmewebpages.com/whoopi/interviews/leno04092001. htm.

31 The gap is nearly $5700 if Social Security and Medicare tax are considered. However, I believe that FICA is not a true "tax," and should be considered separately — net of estimated SS and Medicare benefits.

Although it is no surprise that the average (and median) Republican pays more in taxes (of all types) than does his Democratic counterpart, we rarely or never see these tax differentials quantified. Whether these differentials are the economically or ethically "correct" amounts is beyond the purview of this book.

## Chapter 6: Who Is the Better Citizen?

### Introduction

*What Is "Good Citizenship"?*

> The first requisite of a good citizen in this republic of ours is that he shall be able and willing to pull his own weight.
>
> — President Theodore Roosevelt[1]

> [A radical] is not a bad citizen turning to crime; he is a good citizen driven to despair.
>
> — H. L. Mencken, American journalist and social critic[2]

> The test of good citizenship is loyalty to country.
>
> — Bainbridge Colby, Secretary of State for President Woodrow Wilson[3]

---

1 President Theodore Roosevelt as cited by Richard C. Harwood, "Able, but Willing?," in *The Tampa Tribune* (2000).

2 H.L. Mencken as cited by Mark Lowry in, "Best Way to Defeat Bushite Coup's Attack on America, Democracy and Freedom," in *American Chronicle* (March 11, 2007), Retrieved March 23, 2007, from: http://www.americanchronicle.com/articles/viewArticle. asp?articleID=21946.

3 Colby Bainbridge (Secretary of State under Woodrow Wilson) in his speech, "Loyalty," (The Authentic History Center, 1918), Retrieved March 23, 2007, from: http://www.au-thentichistory.com/audio/wwl/1918_Colby_Bainbridge-Loyalty.html.

Everyone seems to admire good citizenship but we don't necessarily agree on the qualities that define it. Are they hard work, sacrifice, loyalty, political activism, conservation of resources, adherence to the law, or something else? In this book, no attempt is made to define "good citizenship." Rather, Democrats and Republicans are measured against some of the standards that are commonly associated with good citizenship, and for which appropriate survey data are available. It is hoped that the information in this chapter will enable each reader to evaluate and compare Democratic and Republican "citizenship" based on the factors that are most relevant, in his or her judgment.

## DETAILS

*Who supports First Amendment rights?*

> The good citizen always has easy access to a copy of the United States constitution and the Declaration of Independence. ... These documents should be read, studied, learned, understood, and appreciated.

> — "On the Nature of Good Citizenship in a Democratic Society" by Winfield H. Rose[4]

### Tolerance For Controversial Speech

The first amendment to the Constitution states that Congress shall make no law ... abridging the freedom of speech. ..." Which constituency, Democratic or Republican, is more likely to support and respect this important constitutional right? Does it depend on who is doing the speaking?

On several occasions from the mid-1970s through 2006, the General Social Survey (GSS) questioned respondents concerning hypothetical free-speech situations. Some questions involved speech by people associated with the "right" side of politics, while others involved people normally associated with the "left" side of politics. Figure 138, below, summarizes the responses of Democrats and Republicans when asked if a racist should be allowed to speak in their communities. Republicans were more a little more likely to say they would allow the racist speech.

> One of the curious things about censorship is that no one seems to want it for himself. We want censorship to protect someone else; the young, the unstable, the suggestible, the stupid. I have never heard of anyone who wanted a film banned because otherwise he might see it and be harmed.

> — Edgar Dale, Educator[5]

---

4 Winfield H. Rose, "On the Nature of Good Citizenship in a Democratic Society," January, 1999, Personal Web site, Retrieved July 4, 2006, from http://campus.murraystate.edu/academic/faculty/winfield.rose/goodcit.html.

5 Edgar Dale (attributed), "Quotations Site," in *BellaOnline*, ed. Danielle Hollister, Retrieved March 23, 2007, from: http://www.bellaonline.com/articles/art35627.asp.

*Figure 138. If a person wanted to speak in your community, "claiming that Blacks are inferior, should he be allowed to speak, or not?" (GSS surveys conducted from 1976 through 2006, based on, left to right, 6803, 9418, and 16221 cases, with confidence level of, left to right, 99+%, 95%, and 99+%, and with relative proportions of, left to right, .90, .96, and .92)*

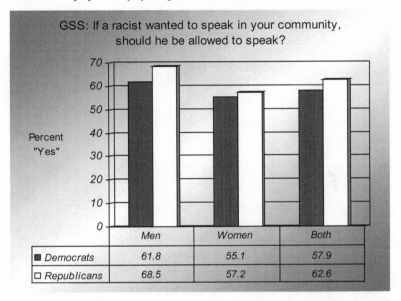

GSS: If a racist wanted to speak in your community, should he be allowed to speak?

Percent "Yes"

| | Men | Women | Both |
|---|---|---|---|
| ■ Democrats | 61.8 | 55.1 | 57.9 |
| □ Republicans | 68.5 | 57.2 | 62.6 |

*Figure 139. Should a person who is "against all churches and religion" be "allowed to speak in your community? (several GSS surveys conducted 1977 through 2006, based on, left to right, 6882, 9515, and 16397 cases, with confidence level of 99+% for all columns, and with relative proportions of, left to right, .88, .94, and .91)*

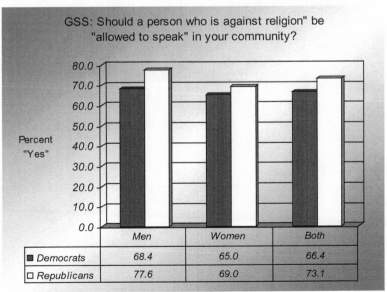

GSS: Should a person who is against religion" be "allowed to speak" in your community?

Percent "Yes"

| | Men | Women | Both |
|---|---|---|---|
| ■ Democrats | 68.4 | 65.0 | 66.4 |
| □ Republicans | 77.6 | 69.0 | 73.1 |

Interestingly, Republicans were also more likely to express tolerant views for speech advocating positions presumed to be contrary to their own values. An example is shown in Figure 139, above, which summarizes views regarding someone who is "against all churches and religion."

These and the results from all similar GSS questions (regarding speech by homosexuals, Communists, and anti-militarists) are summarized in Table 32. Republicans were slightly more likely to express tolerance in each instance.

*Table 32. Views of Democratic and Republican men and women concerning the right to free speech in their communities, based on GSS surveys conducted in 1977 through 2006*

| Allow speech in your community by person who is ... | Dems | Reps | No. of cases | Conf % | *RP |
|---|---|---|---|---|---|
| Racist | 57.9 | 62.6 | 16221 | +99 | .92 |
| Against all churches and religion | 66.4 | 73.1 | 16397 | +99 | .91 |
| Communist | 59.7 | 65.4 | 16150 | +99 | .91 |
| Homosexual | 74.3 | 75.8 | 16090 | 98 | .98 |
| For letting military run country | 56.5 | 62.3 | 16245 | +99 | .91 |

*RP is relative proportion, which is the Democratic % divided by the Republican %.

## What Are The Trends?

> You know it's ironic that we're fighting for democracy in Iraq because we ultimately aren't celebrating democracy here. Because anybody who has anything to say against the war or against the president or whatever — is punished, and that's not democracy — it's people being intolerant.
>
> —Popular singer Madonna Ciccone[6]

The data above comprise the aggregate results from extended time periods, spanning about 30 years. Have these attitudes been changing during that time? The answer can be found in the following four graphics, each of which breaks out the attitudes of Democrats and Republicans into three 10-year periods. Note: There is no trend breakout for views regarding homosexuals because, when reduced to 10-year periods, there is no statistically-significant difference in the expressed views of Democrats and Republicans.

First, we see the views regarding racists, and their right to speak. In each 10-year time span, Republicans have been more likely to express tolerance for having racists speak in their communities. See Figure 140.

*Figure 140. If a person wanted to speak in your community, "claiming that Blacks are inferior, should he be allowed to speak, or not?" — 30-year trend (GSS surveys conducted various times from*

---

6 "Madonna Talks Democracy," in *SFGate.com* (April 15, 2003), Retrieved March 23, 2007, from: http://www.sfgate.com/cgi-bin/article.cgi?file=/gate/archive/2003/04/15/ddish.DTL.

*1977 through 2006, based on, left to right, 4955, 6836, and 4430 cases, with confidence level of 99+%*
*for all differences, and with relative proportions of, left to right, .92, .94, and .93)*

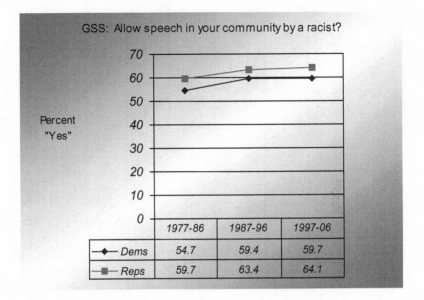

| | 1977-86 | 1987-96 | 1997-06 |
|---|---|---|---|
| Dems | 54.7 | 59.4 | 59.7 |
| Reps | 59.7 | 63.4 | 64.1 |

The atmosphere in my country is poisonous, intolerable for those of
us who are not right-wing....

— Actress Jessica Lange[7]

In the next graphic (Figure 141) we see a general increase, during the 30 years,
in tolerance for speech that is critical of religion. Nevertheless, there remains
a tolerance gap between Democrats and Republicans. Republicans seem to be
more accepting of anti-religious speech, even though they are generally assumed
to be more religious.

Liberals claim to want to give a hearing to other views, but then are
shocked and offended to discover that there are other views.

— William F. Buckley, Jr., American author and journalist[8]

*Figure 141. Should a person who is "against all churches and religion ... be allowed to speak*
*in your community, or not?" — 30-year trend (GSS surveys conducted various times from 1977*
*through 2006, based on, left to right, 5034, 6911, and 4452 cases, with confidence level of 99+% for all*
*differences, and with relative proportions of, left to right, .88, .95, and .91)*

7 Jessica Lange as cited by James H. Hansen, "Radical Road Maps," (Nashville: WND Books, 2006), 197.
8 William F. Buckley (attributed), "Conservativeforum.Org," Retrieved March 23, 2007, from: http://www.conservativeforum.org/quotelist.asp?SearchType=5&Interest=15.

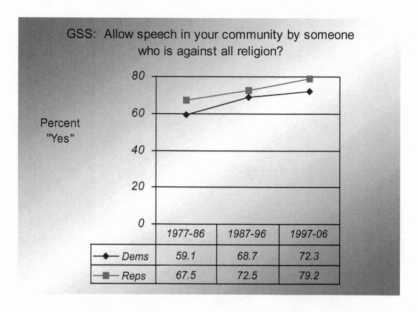

Figure 142. Should a person who is an "admitted Communist ... be allowed to speak in your community, or not? — 30-year trend (GSS surveys conducted from 1977 through 2006; based on, left to right, 4919, 6832, and 4399 cases, with confidence level of 99+% for all differences, and with relative proportions of, left to right, .92, .95, and .90)

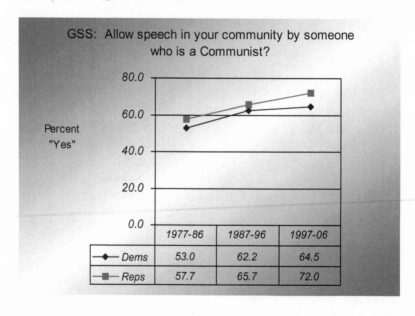

Tolerance for speech by Communists has grown sharply within both constituencies. This may be partly due to the end of the "cold war." Although Republicans have a reputation for being particularly critical of communism, during the last 30 years they have expressed more willingness to allow Communists to speak in their own communities. These trends are reflected in Figure 142, above.

The final trend analysis has to do with militarists. Not surprisingly (given all the other results) Republicans have been more willing than Democrats to allow speech by militarists.

*Figure 143. Should a person "who advocates doing away with elections and letting the military run the country ... be allowed to speak [in your community] or not?" — 30-year trend (GSS surveys conducted various times from 1977 through 2006, based on, left to right, 4968, 6845, and 4432 cases, with confidence level of 99+% for all differences, and with relative proportions of, left to right, .91, .92, and .92)*

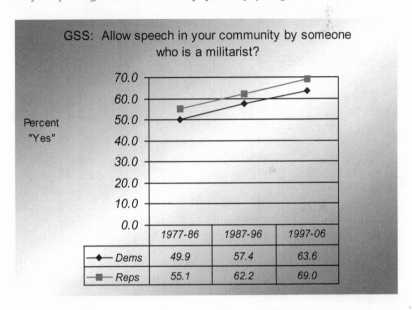

GSS: Allow speech in your community by someone who is a militarist?

Percent "Yes"

| | 1977-86 | 1987-96 | 1997-06 |
|---|---|---|---|
| Dems | 49.9 | 57.4 | 63.6 |
| Reps | 55.1 | 62.2 | 69.0 |

The hypocrisy of it is palpable. The left-wing thought police are forever paying lip service to the ideals of free expression, but they are the first ones in line to place restriction on it for those with whom they disagree.

— Rush Limbaugh, Author and radio talk show host[9]

*Reality check — The real life implications for free speech*

Talk is cheap. Republicans may express more tolerance of controversial speech, but are they truly more tolerant? Do their claims of tolerance have real life implications that are measurable? To test this theory I conducted the fol-

---

9 Rush Limbaugh, *See, I Told You So* (New York: Pocket Books, 1993), 228.

lowing, highly scientific experiment in July 2006: First, I "Googled" the three-word phrase, "prevented from speaking."[10] Then, I scanned the first 100 articles retrieved from that Google search, looking for instances where it was claimed that a person was seriously harassed while speaking (e.g., pie thrown in face, subject to constant loud shouting and/or threats), or "prevented from speaking" (e.g., speech was cut short or cancelled). Finally, I classified the person by his apparent political orientation (Conservative and/or Republican vs. Liberal and/or Democrat). I have not confirmed the veracity of these claims or the motives and political orientation of the parties. The results are listed below, for your own evaluation.

| Harassed or prevented from speaking<br>(per review of the first 100 Google results for "prevented from speaking") | |
| --- | --- |
| Conservative and/or Republican speaker | Liberal and/or Democratic speaker |
| Pat Buchanan, Conservative commentator and author | Ward Churchill, Professor and critic of U.S. foreign policy |
| Ann Coulter, Conservative commentator and author | |
| Dan Flynn, Author of a book critical of Mumia Abu Jamal (convicted cop-killer) | |
| Alexander Haig, Secretary of State under the Reagan Administration | |
| David Horowitz, Conservative commentator and author | |
| William Kristol, Conservative commentator and editor | |
| Henry Kissinger, Secretary of State under Richard Nixon | |
| Jeane Kirkpatrick, Former Ambassador to the U.N. | |
| Michelle Malkin, Conservative commentator and author | |
| Daniel Pipes, Bush appointee to U.S. Institute of Peace | |
| Caspar Weinberger, Secretary of Defense under Ronald Reagan | |

In total, eleven conservatives/Republicans claimed to be "prevented from speaking" or seriously harassed, versus one liberal/Democrat. That same Google search also revealed that the following conservative foreign leaders were allegedly seriously harassed or prevented from speaking at universities in the United States: Nathan Sharansky (Israeli Minister), Benjamin Netanyahu (former Israeli Prime Minister), and Adolfo Calero (Nicaraguan resistance leader during the 1980s).

---

10 I simply made up the phrase. It was the only one I tested.

---

Readers are encouraged to conduct their own "Google test" to see if these results can be replicated.

### Are Democrats Conflicted About Free Speech?

We forbid any course that says we restrict free speech.

— Dr. Kathleen Dixon, Director of Women's Studies, Bowling Green State University[11]

We might conclude from the survey evidence (and from the "scientific" Google search) that Republicans are more likely to tolerate free speech by controversial figures. If true, why is it so? There is an interesting theory advanced by John Leo, a columnist and contributing editor at U.S. News & World Report. He notes that on many college campuses (which generally tilt leftward) free speech has almost become unacceptable behavior.

> A whole vocabulary has sprung up to convert free expression into punishable behavior: hate speech, verbal assault, intellectual harassment, and nontraditional violence, a fancy term for stinging criticism. ...

> Protestors and half the faculty take an impassioned pro-brown shirt stance, arguing that the so-called offense was an understandable reaction to hate speech and great psychic injury. They refer here to the pain of being exposed to ideas they don't agree with.[12]

In the view of Mr. Leo, some college students and faculty feel that conservative ideas are so hateful and so dangerous that it is OK — and even necessary — to prevent those ideas from being expressed.

### Tolerance For Controversial Books And Literature

GSS surveys conducted during the last 30 years show that Democrats are a little more likely to advocate the removal, from their community libraries, of books written by people with controversial perspectives. The hypothetical authors are from the same 5 categories we considered with respect to free speech: racists, atheists, Communists, homosexuals, and militarists. The percentages of Democrats and Republicans who would have books removed are presented in Table 33, below:

> [I]f you're burning a Harry Potter book you need some serious counseling, you don't get it, you're missing the whole point.

— Actor Michael Berryman[13]

---

11 Larry Elder, "The Politically Incorrect Professor," in *Jewish World Review* (September 29, 2000), Retrieved February 18, 2007, from: http://www.jewishworldreview.com/cols/elder092900.asp.

12 John Leo, "Ivy League Therapy," in *Jewish World Review* (March 27, 2001), Retrieved July 8, 2006, from: http://www.jewishworldreview.com/cols/leo032701.asp.

13 Michael Berryman (attributed), "Brainyquote.Com."

*Table 33. Views of Democratic and Republican men and women concerning whether books should be removed from the public library, based on GSS surveys conducted in 1977 through 2006*

| Remove book from your public library if author is a person who ... | Dem % "yes" | Rep % "yes" | No. of cases | Conf % | *RP |
|---|---|---|---|---|---|
| "believes that Blacks are genetically inferior" | 39.0 | 33.7 | 16065 | +99 | 1.16 |
| "is against churches and religion" | 36.1 | 31.3 | 16131 | +99 | 1.15 |
| "admits he is a Communist" | 39.6 | 33.8 | 15977 | +99 | 1.17 |
| "admits that he is a homosexual" | 36.8 | 33.8 | 16061 | +99 | 1.09 |
| "advocates letting ... the military run the country" | 41.5 | 35.4 | 16078 | +99 | 1.17 |

*RP is relative proportion, which is the Democratic % divided by the Republican %.

## What Are The Current Trends?

For the most part, surveys conducted during the last 10 years show a similar pattern, with Republicans being a bit more tolerant of controversial books within their community's public library. However, Democrats and Republicans now have the same outlook with regard to books written by homosexuals.

*Figure 144. Would you favor removing this person's book from the public library? (the aggregate results of GSS surveys conducted from 1997 through 2006, based on, left to right, 4378, 4388, 4364, 4377, and 4378 cases, with confidence level of 99% for all differences except with respect to homosexuals (not significant), and with relative proportions of, left to right, 1.16, 1.16, 1.21, 1.03, and 1.12)*

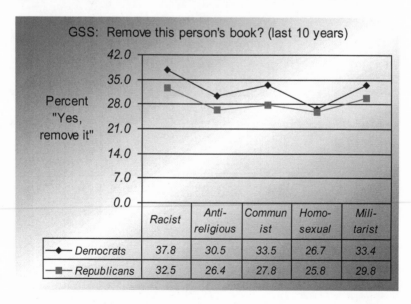

GSS: Remove this person's book? (last 10 years)

| | Racist | Anti-religious | Communist | Homo-sexual | Mili-tarist |
|---|---|---|---|---|---|
| Democrats | 37.8 | 30.5 | 33.5 | 26.7 | 33.4 |
| Republicans | 32.5 | 26.4 | 27.8 | 25.8 | 29.8 |

They have expelled Huck from their library as "trash and only suitable for the slums." That will sell us 25,000 for sure.

— Author Samuel Clemmons ("Mark Twain"), writing to his editor after the Concord Public Library banned his book, Huckleberry Finn.[14]

## Respect For The Right Of Assembly

The "right of people peaceably to assemble" is guaranteed by the first Amendment to the U.S. Constitution. In Figure 145, below, we see that Democrats and Republicans have slightly different views with respect to this constitutional right. Most Republicans would "definitely not" allow the assembly of "people who want to overthrow the government by force...." A slightly smaller percentage of Democrats feel that way. On the other hand, Republicans are a little more willing to allow assembly by racists and religious extremists.

*Figure 145. Should these people "be allowed to hold public meetings"? (GSS surveys conducted in 2004, based on, left to right, 918, 924, and 907 cases, with confidence level of, left to right, 95%, 97%, and 98%, and with relative proportions of, left to right, .87, 1.20, and 1.63)*

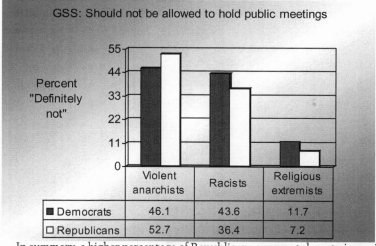

In summary, a higher percentage of Republicans express tolerant viewpoints with regard to controversial speech and books within their communities, and this tendency has existed for at least 30 years. They are slightly more willing to let racists and religious fanatics meet publicly, but most Republicans would bar meetings by those advocating the violent overthrow of the government.

Liberals are stalwart defenders of civil liberties — provided we're only talking about criminals.

— Author and political activist Ann Coulter[15]

14 Samuel Clemens as quoted in, "Twain Classics Have Often Been Banned," (Star-Gazette. com, February 15, 2004), Retrieved October 5, 2007, from: http://www.stargazettenews. com/newsextra/marktwain/021504_2.html.

15 Ann Coulter, "Mothers against Box Cutters Speak Out," in *Jewish World Review* (October 18, 2001), Retrieved March 24, 2007, from: http://www.jewishworldreview.com/cols/ coulter101801.asp.

*Who is more bigoted?*

This section is presented with reticence because negative attitudes about people do not necessarily translate into negative treatment of those people. That concern notwithstanding, Democrats and Republicans seem to have statistically significant differences in their personal feelings towards some groups of people, identified by religion, race and ethnicity, and sexual orientation.

### With Regard To Jews

To some it may be surprising to learn that Republicans are (now) less likely than Democrats to express anti-Semitic views. In a report issued in 2003 (based on a survey of 1013 individuals conducted in 2002), the Institute for Jewish & Community Research stated: "On nearly all variables, Democrats held more anti-Semitic beliefs than Republicans, reversing a historical trend." For example, "Republicans are less likely to view Jews as selfish (12%) than Democrats or independents (20% each)." The report also noted that Republicans are less likely to subscribe to the belief that Jewish control of the media contributes to our failure to get the "whole truth in some stories." Only 16 percent of Republicans expressed this view, versus 28 percent of Democrats and 26 percent of independents.

> A great many people think they are thinking when they are really rearranging their prejudices.

— William James, American philosopher and psychologist[16]

*Figure 146. How do you feel about Jews? (GSS survey conducted in 2004, based on 513 cases, with confidence level of 99+%, and relative proportion of 2.33)*

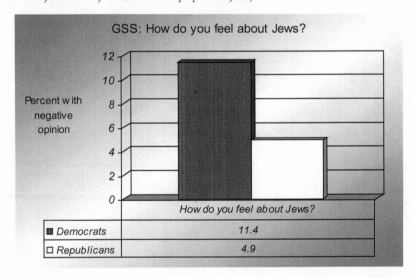

GSS: How do you feel about Jews?

Percent with negative opinion

| | How do you feel about Jews? |
|---|---|
| ■ Democrats | 11.4 |
| □ Republicans | 4.9 |

---

16 William James (attributed), "The Quotations Page."

These findings are not surprising in light of a 2004 General Social Survey (GSS). Respondents were asked if they felt "warm or cold" towards different religious groups, and so indicated by giving a number between zero and 100 on a "feelings thermometer." In Figure 146, above, we see that Democrats were more likely than Republicans to express negative feelings (i.e., "temperatures" below 50 degrees) in regard to Jews.

Note: The disparity in Democratic and Republican feelings regarding Jews is a recent phenomenon. The same thermometer was used by GSS in 1986, 1988, and 1989 and, during those years, statistically significant differences were not found.

### With Regard To Other Religious Groups

GSS also used its "thermometer" to gauge feelings about Protestants, Catholics, and Muslims. There was no significant difference in the likelihood of negative views being expressed regarding Catholics and Muslims, but there was with regard to Protestants. Democrats were more likely to view Protestants in a negative light (by 8.3% to 2.4%).[17]

Bigot — a person who wins an argument with a liberal.

— Rush Limbaugh, Author and radio talk show host[18]

*Figure 147. How do you feel about ...? (NES surveys conducted in years from 2000 through 2004, based on, left to right: 2255, 1664, and 2336 cases, with confidence level of, left to right, 98%, 99%, and 99+%, and with relative proportions of, left to right, 1.53, 1.81, and 1.77.)*

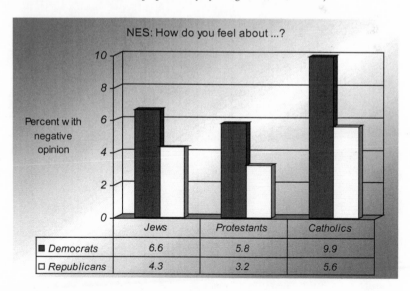

| | Jews | Protestants | Catholics |
|---|---|---|---|
| ■ Democrats | 6.6 | 5.8 | 9.9 |
| □ Republicans | 4.3 | 3.2 | 5.6 |

NES: How do you feel about ...?

Percent with negative opinion

---

17 GSS survey conducted in 2004, based on 514 cases, with statistical significance of 99+%, and with relative proportion of 3.46.

18 Rush Limbaugh (attributed), "Thinkexist.Com."

NES is another organization that uses "thermometers" to assess feelings regarding various groups. Democrats are substantially "colder" with regard to Christian Fundamentalists —by 30.6 to 19.8 percent.[19] In addition, Democrats are slightly more negative regarding Jews, Protestants, and Catholics. The feelings towards those 3 groups are depicted in Figure 147.[20]

> ... I have reluctantly concluded that I was wrong. The far right does not have a monopoly on bigotry and hatred and sanctimony.
>
> — Lanny J. Davis, Special counsel to President Bill Clinton[21]

The Gallup Organization does not use "thermometers" to measure feelings towards members of different groups, but in August 2006 it conducted a survey to measure the degree of *positive* feelings of 1001 Democrats and Republicans towards followers of various religions.[22] The religious groups considered were:

Jews
Catholics
Methodists
Baptists
LDS/Mormons
Muslims
Evangelical Christians
Fundamentalist Christians
Atheists
Scientologists

Gallup concluded:

> Democrats have less positive views towards a number of religious groups in America. ... The gap between the percent of Democrats and Republicans who have a positive image of the religious groups extends across Jews, Catholics, Baptists, Methodists, Mormons, Evangelical Christians, and Fundamentalist Christians.

On the whole, Democrats were only 72 percent as likely as Republicans to have warm feelings for the groups identified by Gallup (above). The only specific category for which Democrats had warmer feelings was atheists.[23]

---

19 NES surveys conducted in 2000, 2002, and 2004, based on 2117 cases, with statistical significance of 99+%, and with a relative proportion of 1.55.

20 The NES results are based on surveys conducted in the years 2000, 2002, and 2004, except for those pertaining to Protestants, which were only asked in 2000 and 2002.

21 Lanny J. Davis, "Liberal Mccarthyism," *Wall Street Journal*, August 8, 2006.

22 The 1001 Democrats and Republicans included independents who "leaned" towards the Democratic or Republican parties.

23 Frank Newport, "Democrats View Religious Groups Less Positively Than Republicans," *The Gallup News Service* (September 7, 2006), Retrieved January 2, 2007, from Http://brain. gallup.com.

## With Regard To Racial And Ethnic Groups

[T]here isn't a day that goes by without Democrats effectively using the race card against their opponents in every political debate
ranging from education to border security to the courts. It's time
for conservatives, Republicans in Washington and minorities with
half a brain to call their bluff.

— Author and columnist Michelle Malkin[24]

Republicans are often accused (by Democrats and people in the media) of
harboring intolerance towards racial and ethnic groups. However, those alleged
tendencies are not evident in the results of the major surveys reviewed by this
author.

NES uses its "feeling thermometers" with respect to four ethnic/racial groups:
whites, blacks, Hispanics, and Asian-Americans. The aggregated results for years
2000 through 2006 did not show a statistically significant difference in attitudes
expressed by Democrats and Republicans.

In 2002, GSS asked respondents "how warm or cool" they felt towards each
of those same four ethnic/racial groups. The proportion of Democrats and Republicans expressing negative views did not differ to a statistically significant
degree, except with respect to whites. Slightly more Democrats had negative
feelings towards whites (8.1% to 3.8%).[25]

### Gays And Lesbians

Figure 148. How do you feel about gays and lesbians? (combined results of NES surveys conducted in
2000, 2002, and 2004, based on 2324 cases, with confidence level of 99+%, and relative proportion of .63)

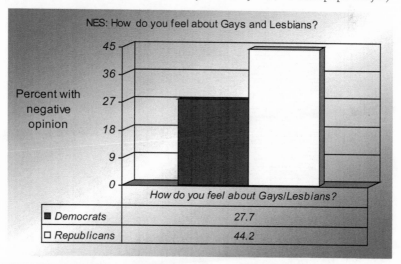

24 Michelle Malkin, "The 'D' Stands for Demagogue," (Jewish World Review, January 18,
2006), Retrieved April 2, 2007, from: http://www.jewishworldreview.com/michelle/mal-
kin011806.php3.

25 GSS survey conducted in 2002, based on 1677 cases, with statistical significance of 99+%,
and with relative proportion of 2.13.

Republicans are far more likely than Democrats to express negative feelings about gays and lesbians, judging by the results of recent NES surveys. See Figure 148, above.

> I was going to have a few comments on the other Democratic presidential candidate, John Edwards, but it turns out you have to go into rehab if you use the word 'faggot.'
>
> — Author and political activist Ann Coulter[26]

*Who contributes more to society?*

### Military Service

In a 2004 GSS survey, Democrats and Republicans were asked:

> There are different opinions as to what it takes to be a good citizen. As far as you are concerned personally ... how important is it to be willing to serve in the military at a time of need?

In response to the questions, Republicans were much more likely to state that it is "very important." The views express, by party and gender, are shown in Figure 149, below.

*Figure 149. How important is it to serve in the military when needed? (2004 GSS survey based on 414 cases for males, 507 cases for females, and 921 cases for both, with confidence level of 99+% for males, females, and both, and with relative proportions of, left to right, .68, .56, and .59)*

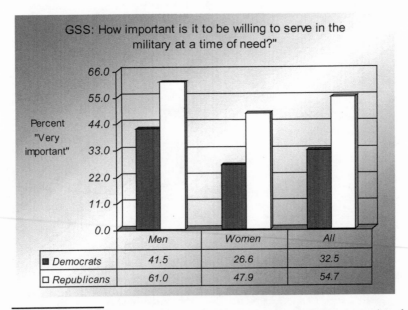

| | Men | Women | All |
|---|---|---|---|
| ■ Democrats | 41.5 | 26.6 | 32.5 |
| □ Republicans | 61.0 | 47.9 | 54.7 |

---

26 Ann Coulter, "John Edwards Breaks Silence on Coulter's 'Faggot' Barb," *Foxnews.com* (March 5, 2007), Retrieved April 2, 2007, from http://www.foxnews.com/story/0,2933,256526,00. html.

Are these Republican beliefs reflected in actual service? Probably, but the record is mixed.

> When it was their turn to serve, where were they? AWOL, that's where they were. The lead chicken hawk against Senator Kerry is the vice president of the United States. What nerve!

— Democratic Senator Frank Lautenberg[27]

A 2004 ABCNEWS poll asked 629 Democrats and Republicans if they were military veterans. Almost identical percentages of Democrats and Republicans responded in the affirmative. However, that result was contradicted by a 2005 Pew Religion and Public Life Survey:

*Figure 150. Are you a veteran of the armed forces?" (2005 Pew survey based on 1288 cases, with confidence level of 99+%, and with a relative proportion of .64)*

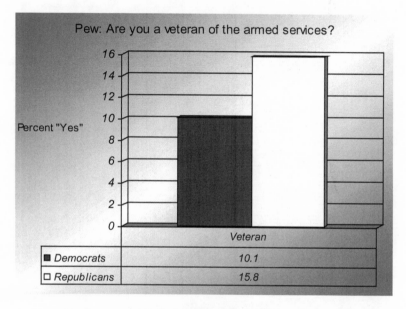

> In Louisiana, President Bush met with over 15,000 National Guard troops. Here's the weird part — nobody remembers seeing him there.

—Comedian Craig Kilborn[28]

Only a tiny percentage of the constituents of either party are serving in the military at any given point in time. However, the results of several NES surveys, conducted in 1990 through 2004, suggest that Republicans are more likely to be

27 James G. Lakely, "Cheney Emerges as Attack Magnet," *Washington Times*, April 29, 2004.

28 Craig Kilborn, "AWOL Bush Jokes," in *ABOUT: Political Humor*, ed. Daniel Kurtzman, Retrieved April 2, 2007, from: http://politicalhumor.about.com/library/blbushawoljokes. htm.

serving as current members of the armed forces. The survey results are depicted in Figure 151, below. None of the surveyed women — Democratic or Republican — was currently serving as a member of the armed forces. The results below are limited to males.

*Figure 151. Are you a "current member of the armed forces"? (Men only) (NES surveys conducted from 1990 through 2004, based on 3280 cases, with confidence level of 99%, and relative proportion of .38)*

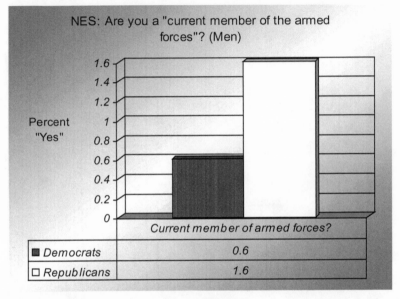

...Cliff May, who now works as the president of the Foundation for the Defense of Democracies ... called the "chicken hawk" theory a "wrong and rather cheap argument. In the United States, we have civilian control of the military and that's probably a good idea."

—Terry M. Neal, Washingtonpost.com[29]

We can also consider this matter from the opposite perspective: the party preference of active members of the military. With respect to a 2004 survey of 655 adults who had served on active duty, the Annenberg Public Policy Center noted:

> Forty-three percent [of respondents] called themselves Republican, 19 percent called themselves Democrats and 28 percent said they were independents.[30]

---

29 Terry M. Neal, "Chickenhawk Vs. Chicken Little," *Washington Post*, September 6, 2002.

30 "Service Men and Women Upbeat on Bush," in *National Annenberg Election Survey Report* (Annenberg Public Policy Center, October 15, 2004), Retrieved March 17, 2006, from: www.naes04.org.

And, the New York Times reported:

> Various studies in the past have found that overall, military personnel and their families vote at least 2 to 1 Republican; in some subsets, like elite officers, the ratio is as high as 9 to 1.[31]

Among the professional military, Republicans clearly dominate. This is evident from the results of surveys performed by *the MilitaryTimes* magazine.

*Figure 152. "In politics today, do you consider yourself a ..." (Military Times survey conducted November 14, 2006, based on 1215 cases randomly selected from the magazine's list of active-duty subscribers, with confidence level of at least 95%)*

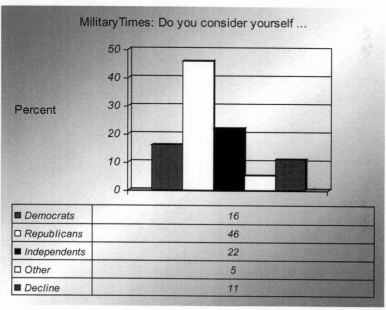

| | |
|---|---|
| ■ Democrats | 16 |
| □ Republicans | 46 |
| ■ Independents | 22 |
| □ Other | 5 |
| ■ Decline | 11 |

Considering all of the survey evidence, it seems that Republicans are more likely than Democrats to be serving, or to have served, in the military.

## Charitable Causes

> Be of service. Whether you make yourself available to a friend or co-worker, or you make time every month to do volunteer work, there is nothing that harvests more of a feeling of empowerment than being of service to someone in need.
>
> — Gillian Anderson, American actress[32]

A detailed discussion of charitable donations and volunteerism is found in Chapter 4. Those results are not replicated here; however, no assessment of

---

31 Elisabeth Rosenthal, "Among Military Families, Questions About Bush," *The New York Times,* April 11 2004.

32 Gillian Anderson (attributed), "Brainyquote.Com."

citizenship would be complete without some reflection on this issue. Survey evidence suggests that Republicans are more likely than Democrats to donate to charities, and to donate larger amounts. This appears to be the case even when income levels between Democrats and Republicans are controlled. In addition, Republicans are more likely to state that they have volunteered for charitable causes.

### Helping The Environment

#### Gas-Guzzling SUVs

"The blame for the world's higher temperature rests on gas guzzling vehicles."

— Democratic Senator Barack Obama, who drove off in an SUV shortly after making the statement at a town hall meeting.[33]

By 53 to 37 percent, Democrats are more likely than Republicans to state that it is "very important" for SUV drivers to switch to more fuel-efficient vehicles. In addition, 39 percent of "liberal Democrats" state that they have purchased a car that gets better mileage. This is only true of 20 percent of "conservative Republicans." These words are backed up by deeds according to a Pew 2003 "Religion and Public Life" survey. It shows that Democrats are much less likely to own a sports utility vehicle.

*Figure 153. Do you own an SUV? (2003 Pew survey, based on 1226 cases, with confidence level of 99+% and relative proportion of .55)*

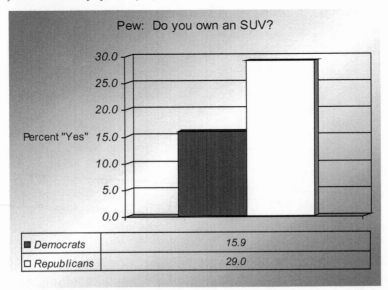

| | |
|---|---|
| ■ Democrats | 15.9 |
| □ Republicans | 29.0 |

---

33 "Obama Preaches Fuel Efficiency from the Back Seat of an Suv," in *The Illinois Review* (LaComb, Dennis, August 16, 2006), Retrieved April 2, 2007, from: http://illinoisreview.typepad.com/illinoisreview/2006/08/obama_preaches_.html.

## Recycling

> What's most curious about recycling is that it seems bulletproof to criticism. A few years ago, The New York Times Magazine ran an article exposing curbside recycling as a sham. Turns out there are much more efficient market systems that would dispose of our trash without all that individual participation.

— Jack Hitt, American author[34]

There is one thing that Democrats and Republicans seem to agree on: the need for recycling waste. A 2006 survey conducted by the Opinion Research Corporation showed that about 70 percent of Democrats and Republicans utilized curbside recycling programs. In addition, about 95 percent of each constituency stated that recycling was, at the least, "somewhat important." In a 2003 Gallup survey, respondents were asked if they had "voluntarily recycled newspapers, glass, aluminum, motor oil or other items." Again, approximately equal percentages of Democrats and Republicans (about 90 percent) said that they had recycled. [35] Questions regarding recycling efforts were also asked in 3 GSS surveys in 1993, 1994, and 2000. The combined results of those surveys also show no statistically significant difference between Democrats and Republicans with regard to recycling.

## Other Environmental Efforts

Although the record is mixed, it appears that Democrats are more likely to volunteer in support of environmental causes. A 2003 Gallup survey showed that Democrats were no more likely to have "been active in a group or organization that works to protect the environment." [36] And, on the basis of a mail survey of 623 residents of central Pennsylvania, it was concluded (in 2002):

> Although Democrats are more likely to support government mitigation programs, party identification accounts for much less variance than either cognitive or economic measures. Partisan identification has almost no impact on voluntary actions.[37]

However, those results are out of sync with surveys conducted by GSS and by the State of Michigan. The results of the GSS surveys, conducted in 1993, 1994, and 2000, and the results of Michigan surveys, conducted in 1999, 2003, and 2005, are shown in Figure 154, below.

*Figure 154. Do you participate in a group dedicated to helping the environment? (GSS surveys conducted in 1993, 1994, and 2000, and Michigan SOSS surveys conducted in 1999, 2003, and 2005, based on, left to right, 2610 and 1060 cases, with confidence level of 99+%, and relative proportions of, left to right, 1.47 and 1.83)*

---

34 Jack Hitt, "A Gospel According to the Earth," *Harpers*, July 2003.

35 "The Environment," in *Gallup Poll Social Series* (Gallup Organization, March, 2003), 363.

36 Ibid., 338.

37 Robert E. O'Connor, Richard J. Bord, and Brent Yarnal, "Who Wants to Reduce Greenhouse Gas Emissions?," *Social Science Quarterly* 83, no. 1 (March, 2002): 10.

---

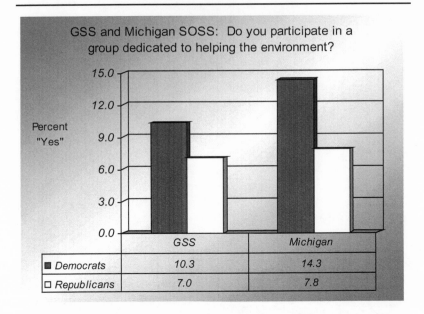

Democrats are also more likely to have reduced their "household use of energy" in an effort to help the environment, according to a 2003 Gallup survey of 323 Democrats and Republicans (82% to 72%).[38]

Thus, with regard to the environment, we might conclude that Democrats are more likely to drive environmentally-friendly vehicles, participate in environmental organizations, and reduce home energy usage. On the other hand, the evidence does not suggest that they are more likely to recycle.

### Other Contributions

#### Blood Donations

A brave man's blood is the best thing in the world when a woman is in trouble.

— Abraham Van Helsing, the fictional character from Dracula.[39]

It seems that the donation of blood might be a good indicator of civic responsibility. After all, wealth is not a requirement for blood donations. I found two surveys addressing this subject, and they suggest that Republicans are a little more likely to contribute to the blood bank. The combined results are shown in Figure 155, below.

*Figure 155. During the last 12 months have you donated blood? (2 GSS surveys conducted in 2002 and 2004, based on 1660 cases, with confidence level of 95% for men, no statistical significance for women, overall significance of 99%, and with relative proportions of, left to right, .77, .79, and .76)*

38 "The Environment," 368.
39 Bram Stoker, *Dracula* (New York: Bantam Books, 1981).

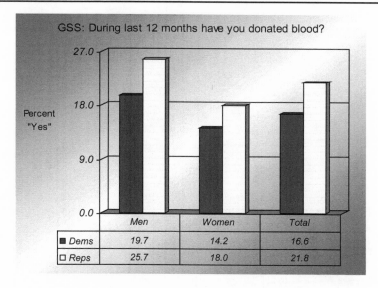

*Jury Duty*

A jury consists of twelve persons chosen to decide who has the better lawyer.

— Robert Frost, American poet[40]

*Figure 156. "If you were selected to serve on a jury, would you be happy to do it or would you rather not serve?" (NES surveys conducted in 1996 and 2000, based on, left to right, 857 and 899 cases, with confidence level of 94% (marginal) for 1996 and 99+% for 2000, and relative proportions of, left to right, .90 and .85)*

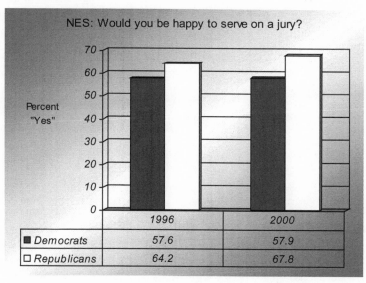

---

40 Robert Frost (attributed), "The Quotations Page."

I was able to find two surveys addressing this issue, conducted by NES in 1996 and 2000. Respondents were asked: "If you were selected to serve on a jury, would you be happy to do it or would you rather not serve?" Republicans were more likely to indicate a willingness to serve. See Figure 156, above.

*Who is more likely to participate in the political process?*

### Voting

Bad officials are the ones elected by good citizens who do not vote.

— George Jean Nathan, American drama critic[41]

As generally assumed, Republicans are more likely to vote in presidential elections. This fact is apparent in the results of 50 years of NES surveys, which are summarized, by decade, in Figure 157.

*Figure 157. Did you vote in the presidential election? (Several NES surveys conducted between 1952 and 2004, based on, left to right, 2605, 3149, 4508, 6098, 5856, and 2776 cases, with confidence levels of 99% for all differences, and with relative proportions of, left to right, .88, .90, .83, .92, .94, and .86)*

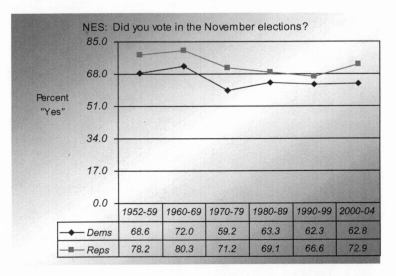

NES: Did you vote in the November elections?

| | 1952-59 | 1960-69 | 1970-79 | 1980-89 | 1990-99 | 2000-04 |
|---|---|---|---|---|---|---|
| Dems | 68.6 | 72.0 | 59.2 | 63.3 | 62.3 | 62.8 |
| Reps | 78.2 | 80.3 | 71.2 | 69.1 | 66.6 | 72.9 |

GSS surveys show a similar pattern, but with slightly smaller disparities. To see the GSS results, go to Appendix B 15 on page 357.

> Well, Republicans, I guess, can do that [vote]. ... But for ordinary working people, who have to work eight hours a day, they have kids, they got to get home to those kids, the idea of making them stand for eight hours to cast their ballot for democracy is wrong.

— Howard Dean, Chairman of the Democratic National Committee[42]

---

41 George Jean Nathan (attributed), "The Quotations Page."
42 Dinan and Fagan, "Dean Hits GOP on 'Honest Living'."

*Reality check — Should we necessarily encourage people to vote?*

Conservative columnist Jonah Goldberg wonders if we have our priorities wrong when we encourage the uninformed (of either political party) to vote:

> Maybe the emphasis on getting more people to vote has dumbed-down our democracy by pushing participation onto people uninterested in such things. Maybe our society would be healthier if politicians aimed higher than the lowest common denominator.... Perhaps cheapening the vote by requiring little more than an active pulse (Chicago famously waives this rule) has turned it into something many people don't value. ...

> Instead of making it easier to vote, maybe we should be making it harder. Why not test people about the basic functions of government? Immigrants have to pass a test to vote; why not all citizens?[43]

According to Goldberg, if we "threaten to take the vote away from the certifiably uninformed," we will send the message that voting is a valued accomplishment. Ironically, that could lead to a boost in voter turnout.

## Political Campaigns, Rallies And Protests

A recent Michigan survey suggests that Democrats are more likely to volunteer for a political organization or campaign. (See Figure 158, below.)

*Figure 158. Last year, did you volunteer for "a political organization or campaign (such as the Democratic or Republican parties)"? (2005 Michigan SOSS, based on 297 cases, with statistical significance of 99+%, and with a relative proportion of 2.23)*

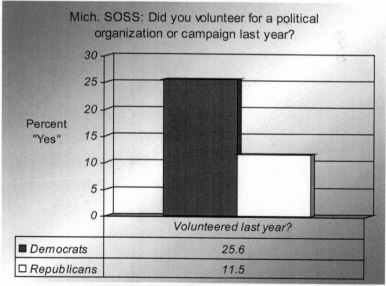

Two questions on the 2004 GSS survey address related subjects. Respondents were asked if they "took part in a demonstration" or "attended a political meeting or rally." Again, Democrats were more likely to answer in the affirmative.

---

43 Jonah Goldberg, "Too Uninformed to Vote?," *Los Angeles Times*, July 31, 2007.

*Figure 159. Last year, did you take part in a demonstration or attend a political meeting or rally? (GSS survey conducted in 2004, based on, left to right, 927 and 929 cases, with confidence level of, left to right, 99% and 99+%, and with relative proportions of, left to right, 2.02 and 1.58)*

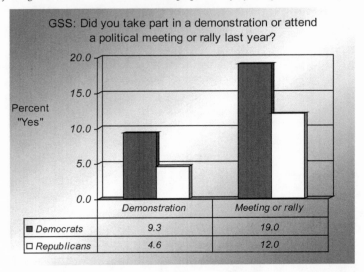

GSS: Did you take part in a demonstration or attend a political meeting or rally last year?

| | Demonstration | Meeting or rally |
|---|---|---|
| ■ Democrats | 9.3 | 19.0 |
| □ Republicans | 4.6 | 12.0 |

Say you want a revolution, we better get on right away. Well you get on your feet, and out on the street, singing Power to the People!

— Popular song-writer John Lennon[44]

Protest rallies and marches were the topic of a 2002 GSS survey. In Figure 160, below, we see that Democrats dominate in this area, regardless of gender.

*Figure 160. Over the past 5 years have you joined a protest, rally or march? (GSS survey conducted in 2002, based on, left to right, 343, 519, and 862 cases, with confidence levels of, left to right, 97%, 95%, and 99+%, and with relative proportions of, left to right, 2.41, 2.22, and 2.24)*

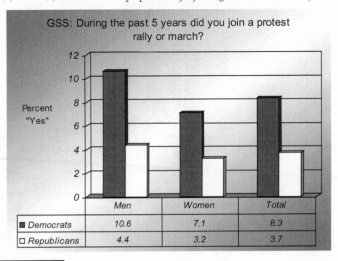

GSS: During the past 5 years did you join a protest rally or march?

| | Men | Women | Total |
|---|---|---|---|
| ■ Democrats | 10.6 | 7.1 | 8.3 |
| □ Republicans | 4.4 | 3.2 | 3.7 |

---

44 John Lennon, "Power to the People (Song)," in *Oldielyrics.com.*

### Directly Contacting Public Officials

> If you think you're too small to have an impact, try going to sleep with a mosquito.

— Philip Elmer-DeWitt, Science and Technology writer[45]

In 2004, NES asked respondents if they had contacted the government to express views regarding a public matter. Republicans were a little more likely to indicate that they had.

*Figure 161. "During the past twelve months, have you telephoned, written a letter to, or visited a government official to express your views on a public issue?" (2004 NES survey, based on 643 cases, with confidence level of 96%, and relative proportion of .73)*

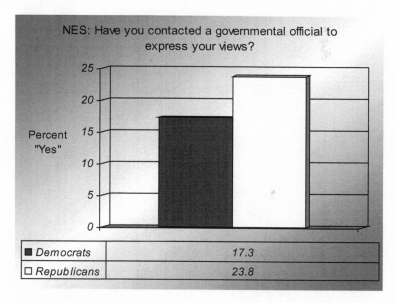

These results are supported by a 2004 GSS survey, where people were asked if they had ever "contacted, or attempted to contact, a politician or a civil servant to express [their] views." By 48.9 to 41.2 percent Republicans were more likely to have done so.

*Reality check — There was no statistically significant difference for:*

- Contacting or appearing in the media to express a view. (About 16% did it.)
- Joining an Internet political forum. (About 9% did it.)
- Boycotting products for political reasons. (About 40% did it.)
- Signing a petition. (About 70% did it.)[46]

---

45 Philip Elmer-DeWitt, "Anita the Agitator," *Time Magazine*, January 25, 1993.
46 Based on GSS surveys conducted in 2004, and involving about 930 cases.

*Who is more likely to avoid negative social behavior?*

The flip side of ethical behavior is the avoidance of negative social behavior, which can include a wide variety of improper conduct, from littering all the way up to murder and mayhem. There are few (if any) surveys that question participants with regard to such matters; however, it was possible to glean some information with respect to felonies and bankruptcy.

### Who Gets The Felon Vote?

> You could abort every black baby in this country, and your crime rate would go down. That would be an impossible, ridiculous and morally reprehensible thing to do, but your crime rate would go down.
>
> — William Bennett, former Secretary of Education under President Reagan[47]

Although social surveys are useless for detecting felony rates among Democrats and Republicans, an academic analysis of this subject has been performed. Two professors of sociology, Christopher Uggen and Jeff Manza, estimated felon voting preferences by analyzing the demographic makeup of felons (e.g., race, gender, and economic background) and applying the voting preferences associated with that demography. Based upon their research and analysis, published in 2002, they concluded:

> [T]he survey data suggest that Democratic candidates would have received about 7 of every 10 votes cast by the felons and ex-felons in 14 of the last 15 U.S. Senate election years.[48]

Assuming they are right, we could conclude that 70 percent of felons were Democrats when they committed their crimes, or we could speculate that there is something about the judicial process and/or incarceration that makes turns criminals into Democrats.

### Who Is More Likely To File For Bankruptcy?

> Capitalism without bankruptcy is like Christianity without hell.
>
> — Former astronaut Frank Borman[49]

Bankruptcy is painful for the debtor, and it is costly for society. The unpaid debts of the bankrupt result in losses to his private and/or public creditors, and those losses get absorbed by society, as a whole. The combined results of 2 GSS

---

47 Brian Faler, "Bennett under Fire for Remark on Crime and Black Abortions," *Washington Post*, September 30, 2005, 5.

48 Christopher Uggen and Jeff Manza, "Democratic Contraction? Political Consequences of Felon Disenfranchisement in the United States," *American Sociological Review* 67, no. 1 (2002): 786.

49 Frank Borman, "The Growing Bankruptcy Brigade," *Time Magazine*, October 18, 1982.

surveys — taken in 1991 and 2004, suggest that Democrats file for bankruptcy at a slightly higher rate than Republicans. Like most of the survey results in this book, these can be viewed from two perspectives: On the one hand, we have to conclude that bankruptcy is a very slim likelihood for either constituency. On the other hand, these results suggest that a large majority of personal bankruptcies involve Democrats.

*Figure 162. During the last year did you declare bankruptcy? (GSS surveys conducted in 1991 and 2004, based on 1528 cases, with confidence level of 97%, and with a relative proportion of 3.2)*

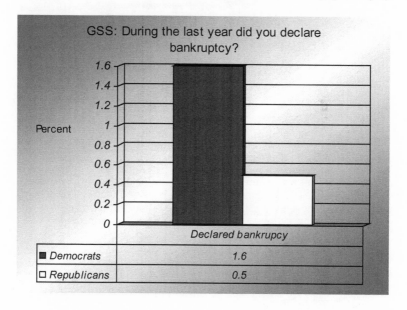

## Who Is More Honest?

Honesty is the best policy — when there is money in it.

— Author and humorist Samuel Clemens ("Mark Twain")[50]

I found only a few surveys quizzing Democrats and Republicans regarding their honesty in certain hypothetical situations. The responses show that a higher percentage of Democrats than Republicans say it is acceptable to cheat with respect to taxes and government benefits. Of course, it could be that Republicans are so dishonest that they won't admit how dishonest they are.

*Figure 163. It is not wrong or only slightly wrong to conceal part of my income to save taxes, or to give the government false information to get benefits (aggregate results of GSS surveys conducted in 1991 and 1998, based on 1598 cases, with confidence level of, left to right, 99+% and 98%, and with a relative proportions of, left to right, 1.34 and 2.13)*

---

50 "Mark Twain Quotations," (March 30, 1901), Retrieved April 2, 2007, from: http://www. twainquotes.com/Honesty.html.

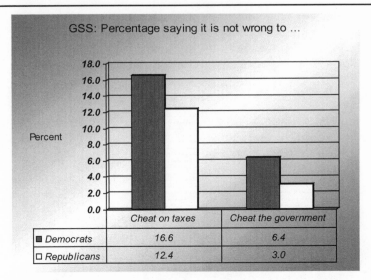

The only other "honesty" question I found was in a 2006 National Cultural Values Survey. Respondents were given this hypothetical moral dilemma:

> You are out to dinner with a group of friends. When the check arrives you notice that several items are missing from the bill. Your friends say you should just pay the bill, and that it's the restaurant's own fault for making the mistake. What would you do?

The responses suggest that Democrats would be more likely to pay the lower (incorrect) bill. See Figure 164.

*Figure 164. I would go along with my friends and cheat the restaurant (National Cultural Values Survey conducted in December, 2006 by the Cultural and Media Institute, based on 2000 cases, with confidence level of 95% and with relative proportion of 1.65)*

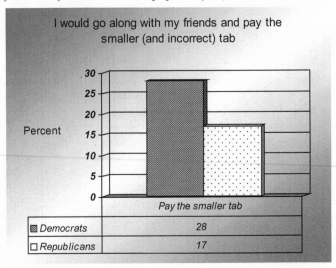

> I like to do my principal research in bars, where people are more
> likely to tell the truth or, at least, lie less convincingly than they do
> in briefings and books.

— P.J. O'Rourke, American political satirist[51]

## *Driving over the speed limit*

Republicans truly live in the fast lane. By 50 to 38 percent they are more
likely to "often drive over the speed limit."[52]

### CONCLUSIONS

This chapter has presented statistical comparisons concerning bigotry, support for first amendment rights, contributions to society, political participation,
and the avoidance of negative social behavior. Survey evidence indicates that
there are statistically significant differences between Democrats and Republicans in each of these areas. Specifically, the survey results indicate:

Democrats have slightly more unfavorable views regarding whites and most
religious groups, and Republicans express much more negativity regarding gays
and lesbians. The unfavorable views regarding racial and ethnic groups do not
differ to a statistically significant degree.

Democrats express less tolerance for controversial speech and books in their
communities, and have done so for decades. They are also more likely to state
that public meetings by racists and religious extremists should not be permit-
ted. Republicans are more likely to bar meetings by those advocating the violent
overthrow of the government.

It appears that Republicans are more likely to participate in the military,
charitable activities, jury duty, and voting. Their statements indicate that they
are more likely to directly contact public officials to express their views.

Surveys indicate that Democrats are more likely to participate in environmental organizations, to participate in political campaigns, protests and boy-
cotts, and to not drive SUVS.

Academic research suggests that a higher percentage of convicted felons are
Democrats, although this constitutes a very tiny percentage of Democrats as
a whole (of course). In addition, survey evidence suggests that Democrats are
slightly more likely to have gone through bankruptcy.

There are a couple of surveys showing that Democrats are more likely to state
that they would engage in dishonest conduct in certain situations.

As noted in the introduction, it is left to the reader to determine the specific
elements that comprise the "good citizen." Some of the items addressed herein
may not be included within your definition, and some of the elements in your
definition may be omitted here. If so, this was due to author oversight or, more
likely, a lack of relevant survey data.

---

51 P. J. O'Rourke, *Holidays in Hell* (London: Picador, 1989), 212.

52 The results are from a 2004 Harris survey, based on 635 cases, with a confidence level of
99+%, and with a relative proportion of 1.32.

# CHAPTER 7: WHO GETS MORE FROM SOCIAL SECURITY AND MEDICARE?

## INTRODUCTION

### Dismantling the New Deal

> Since the days of Barry Goldwater, the Republican right has really wanted to dismantle Social Security. And now they have a degree of political dominance that lets them push it to the top of the agenda....
>
> — Economist Paul Krugman[1]

> With special interests, not seniors, in mind, Republicans designed a [prescription drug] bill that will dismantle Medicare. For the sake of our seniors, we must dismantle this cruel hoax of a bill.
>
> — Democratic Congresswoman Nancy Pelosi[2]

It is not clear that most Republicans want to dismantle Social Security and Medicare (as claimed by some), but many of them criticize the effectiveness and funding of these programs. They do this more than Democrats, so we might assume that Republicans are less likely to derive significant benefits from these entitlements. However, this is not the case. The average Republican, retiring now or during the next 40 years, can expect to get a net benefit (i.e., an investment

---

1 Paul Krugman, "The Fake Crisis," in *Rollingstone* (January 13, 2005), Retrieved January 27, 2006, from: http://www.rollingstone.com/politics/story/6822964/the_fake_crisis/.

2 Congresswoman Nancy Pelosi, "For the Sake of Our Seniors, We Must Dismantle This Cruel Hoax of a Medicare Bill," January, 2004, Pelosis Web site, Retrieved January 28, 2006, from http://www.house.gov/pelosi/press/releases/jan04/Medicare012804.html.

return) on his Social Security and Medicare tax dollars that is at least as high as that of his Democratic counterpart.

## Caveats

### Economics And Demographics May Change

The amounts shown in this chapter are predicated on the assumption that several demographic and economic factors remain constant over an extended time period. The results will change if the presumed real interest rate proves to be unrealistic, or if there are significant changes in the percentage of Democrats and Republicans who are male, female, married and working. In addition, it is assumed that the Social Security and Medicare programs remain solvent, and there is no restructuring of benefit or tax rates. (Of course, there is great public concern about the solvency of these programs, and this is why many Republicans — and Democrats — feel that program reform is required.)

### Average Isn't Typical

In the case of Social Security and Medicare, averages mask huge variations in benefits, attributable to income level, gender, age, marital status, the distribution of wages among members of the household, and the year of retirement. In many cases, the variations seem arbitrary and inequitable. A meaningful analysis of these programs requires awareness of these factors, some of which are described below.

## DETAILS

### Social Security

> A leading Republican said Sunday that President Bush is so worried about Social Security that he is only able to sleep ten hours a night.
>
> — Comedian Tina Fey[3]

## Who Does Relatively Well in the Social Security System?

### Compared To Others, Women And The Poor Do Well

As noted, the value of net benefits varies sharply, depending on certain demographic factors. Indeed, it would be fair to say that the Social Security system has some "winners" and many "losers."

Social Security benefit rates are not adjusted for gender longevity differences so women usually collect far more benefits than do men. In addition, people with lower wage incomes usually get benefits that are much higher in proportion to the FICA taxes they pay.

---

3 Comedian Tina Fey as cited in, "Saturday Night Live," (Transcript: NBC, February 19, 2005), Retrieved March 23, 2007, from: http://snltranscripts.jt.org/04/04mupdate.phtml.

The importance of these two factors — gender and wage level — is clearly evident from an inspection of Figure 165, below, which depicts the net lifetime Social Security benefits of single men and women with varying levels of wage income. Information used in the chart (and subsequent charts) was derived from a Web-based Social Security benefits calculator created by economists C. Eugene Steuerle and Adam Carasso of the Urban Institute.[4]

*Figure 165. The information is from a table of net lifetime transfers (benefits minus taxes) prepared by C. Eugene Steuerle and Adam Carasso of the Urban Institute. These are the average net benefits of single men and women turning 65 in years 2005 through 2045.*

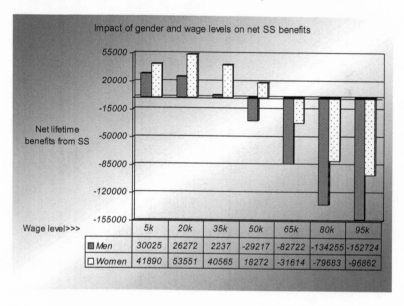

Social Security is not in crisis. It's a crisis the president's created. Period.

— Democratic Senator Harry Reid[5]

The columns represent estimated net lifetime benefits from Social Security (total estimated benefits less total estimated taxes paid, in today's dollars). Both men and women with higher wage levels (towards the right side of the chart) have much lower net lifetime Social Security benefits than those at the lower wage levels. In fact, these columns depict very negative amounts, signifying that

4 C. Eugene Steuerle and Adam Carasso, "The USA Today Lifetime Social Security and Medicare Benefits Calculator," (Urban Institute, October 1, 2004), from: http://www.urban.org/publications/900746.html. NOTE: The calculator does not include the value or cost of the Social Security disability program.

5 Senator Harry Reid as cited in, "Judy Woodruff's inside Politics," (Transcript: CNN, March 3, 2005), Retrieved March 23, 2007, from: http://transcripts.cnn.com/TRANSCRIPTS/0503/03/ip.01.html.

middle and upper-class single workers lose substantial sums by participating in Social Security. It is also evident that matters are even worse for men — no matter what the level of wage income. Because they don't live as long as women (on average) and because there are no significant early payout options provided by Social Security, men generally get lower benefits than women.

We might say that women are Social Security "winners;" however, this is only with respect to the benefits paid by Social Security to men. Comparisons with private retirement accounts, or with state and local government pension plans, could lead to a different conclusion.

> According to a study by researchers at Harvard University, virtually every woman-single, divorced, married, or widowed-would be better off financially under a system of fully private retirement accounts
>
> — Michael Tanner, Director of Health and Welfare studies at the libertarian CATO Institute[6]

### Married Workers With Stay-At-Home Spouses Are Social Security Winners

Based on a review of Figure 165, one would assume that Republicans do very poorly in the Social Security system because the average Republican is more likely to be male, and is more likely to have high wages. However, this is not the case, due to a very important offsetting factor: The Republican worker is more likely to have a stay-at-home spouse.

In 1939, four years after the enactment of Social Security, the program was changed to provide generous spousal and survivor benefits to workers with stay-at-home spouses. The workers get these extra benefits, even if they are wealthy. In fact, the more a worker earns, the greater his extra (spousal and survivor) benefits will be.

Figure 166, below, shows the net benefits of a worker with a stay-at-home spouse, assuming various wage levels (the same wage levels depicted in Figure 165). Two significant factors are evident: First, every column in Figure 166 depicts a net benefit that is higher than any column in Figure 165. In other words, the average married person (with a stay-at-home spouse) gets a greater benefit per FICA tax dollar paid than does the average single person — no matter what the gender or wage level. Second, there is only limited progressivity among married workers with stay-at-home spouses. Review Figure 166 carefully: The net benefits drop as the wage levels increase from $50,000 to $95,000; however, they increase as the wage levels grow from $5,000 to $50,000. In fact, net benefits are lowest for those earning just $5,000 per year. (These people get smaller benefits per FICA tax dollar paid.)

---

6 Michael Tanner and Darcy Olsen, "Increasing Social Security," in *PBS Online Newshour Forum* (December 1998), Retrieved August 30, 2006, from: http://www.pbs.org/newshour/forum/december98/socsec2.html.

*Figure 166. The information is from a table of net lifetime transfers (benefits minus taxes) prepared by C. Eugene Steuerle and Adam Carasso of the Urban Institute. These are the average net benefits of married people (with non-working spouses) turning 65 in years 2005 through 2045.*

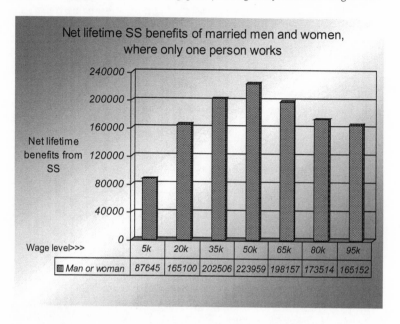

Republicans know that people will get a better return on their [Social Security] money if they are allowed to invest it in things that bring a larger return rather than investing it in the phony promises of government and in the patronage system of politicians. ... Republicans trust the people. Democrats trust the government.

— Alan Keyes, Former diplomat and Republican presidential aspirant[7]

### Bill Gates Is A Social Security Winner?

The current system of spousal and survivor benefits results in huge transfers of wealth from low-income workers to high-income workers. It is likely, for example, that Bill Gates will get a higher rate of return from Social Security (assuming his wife has no wage income) than the two-earner married couple earning just $40,000 per year (together). Some people feel that marital benefits should be "means tested;" however, politics seems to prevent candid public discourse regarding this topic. For an in-depth analysis, refer to my book, *How Social Security Picks Your Pocket* (Algora Publishing, 2003).

Figure 167, below, is simply a combination of Figure 165 and Figure 166. In other words, one graph has been placed on top of the other. Now we see that the "average" masks huge variations in a patch quilt benefit structure. For example,

---

7 Alan Keyes, "The Key to Republican Victory," in *WorldNetDaily* (March 19, 1999), Retrieved March 23, 2007, from: http://www.worldnetdaily.com/news/article. asp?ARTICLE_ID=18658.

a worker making $95,000 per year could be one of the biggest "winners," if he is married to a stay-at-home spouse. His expected net benefit would be more than $160,000. On the other hand, if he remains single he can expect a net benefit of negative $150,000. (In other words, he would end up subsidizing the system.) That should be sobering information for any confirmed bachelor.

*Figure 167. This chart combines the information in Figure 165 and Figure 166. Note the wide variances in net benefits for people at any given level of income — particularly at the upper earnings levels.*

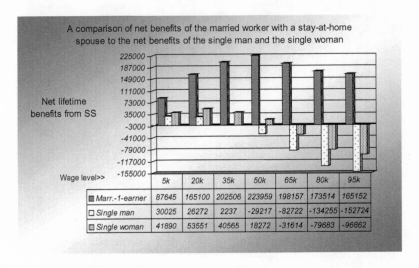

A comparison of net benefits of the married worker with a stay-at-home spouse to the net benefits of the single man and the single woman

| Wage level>> | 5k | 20k | 35k | 50k | 65k | 80k | 95k |
|---|---|---|---|---|---|---|---|
| Marr.-1-earner | 87645 | 165100 | 202506 | 223959 | 198157 | 173514 | 165152 |
| Single man | 30025 | 26272 | 2237 | -29217 | -82722 | -134255 | -152724 |
| Single woman | 41890 | 53551 | 40565 | 18272 | -31614 | -79683 | -96862 |

> The Democrats cannot be bribed, cajoled or threatened into voting for Social Security reform — it can't happen.

—GOP strategist Grover Norquist[8]

## Comparing Democratic Benefits To Republican Benefits

Now that we have reviewed the basic benefit structure of Social Security, we can use these findings to estimate the expected net benefits of Democrats and Republicans. As noted, economists C. Eugene Steuerle and Adam Carasso of the Urban Institute designed a Web-based Social Security benefits calculator that can be used to estimate the total lifetime value of benefits as opposed to the total lifetime cost of payroll taxes.[9]

Using the calculator, net benefits can be estimated separately for single males, single females, one-earner married couples, and two-earner married couples. In addition, separate calculations can be made for people in different wage

---

8 Grover Norquist as quoted by Michael Abramowitz, "President Remains Eager to Cut Entitlement Spending," in *Washington Post* (August 11, 2006), Retrieved March 23, 2007, from: http://www.washingtonpost.com/wp-dyn/content/article/2006/08/10/AR2006081001508_pf.html.

9 Steuerle and Carasso, "The USA Today Lifetime Social Security and Medicare Benefits Calculator."

brackets (by $5,000 increment) and for people in of different age brackets (i.e., people reaching age 65 in years 1975 through 2045, by 5-year intervals). Other parameters and assumptions used in the calculator are noted in Appendix B 13.

To estimate the net benefits of the average Democrat or Republican, we simply determine the percentage of Democrats and Republicans within each of the major parameters used by Steuerle and Carasso. This was done in a two-step process, using demographic information obtained from General Social Survey (GSS) surveys conducted over a 14-year period spanning 1991 through 2004. It's pretty boring, but I feel compelled to provide a brief overview of the calculation process. If you want to skip the calculation overview and get to the results, please advance to the bottom line of Table 35.

### Net Benefits for Each Type of Beneficiary

> The deceptive marketing of Social Security has been deliberate, carefully designed to prevent the American public from realizing that Social Security is simply a pay-as-you-go welfare system. As Arthur Altmeyer, Roosevelt confidante and first Social Security commissioner, said, "Every effort was made to use terminology that would inspire confidence rather than arouse suspicion."

> — Political scientist and author James L. Payne[10]

Lifetime net benefit amounts were determined, by political party, for each major category of benefit recipient. These net benefit amounts are shown in Table 34, below. For this step, the differences between the Democratic and Republican columns are entirely attributable to differences in the average levels of wage income of Democrats and Republicans. The impact of the varying wage levels on each category is explained in the "Comments" column of the table.

*Table 34. Total average net SS benefit amounts for various categories of beneficiaries. The slight differences in the amounts for Democrats and Republicans (in each row) are attributable to differences in wage levels, the impact of which is explained in the "Comments" column.*

| Type of beneficiary | Net benefits ($) | | Comments |
|---|---|---|---|
| | Dems | Reps | |
| Married – spouse works full-time | 41,500 | 37,100 | For two-earner couples, net benefits are progressive. Therefore, Republicans (who generally earn more) get less. (Note: These are the benefits for each man or woman in the couple.) |
| Married man – spouse works part-time or less | 188,500 | 190,700 | For one-earner couples, benefits are regressive up to about $50,000; thereafter they are progressive. It appears that Republicans get slightly more. |

---

10 James Payne, "How America Drifted from Welfare To "Entitlement"," (The American Enterprise March, 2005), 26, Retrieved March 23, 2007, from: http://www.taemag.com/docLib/20050131_Payne.pdf.

| | | | |
|---|---|---|---|
| Married woman –spouse works part-time or less | 186,000 | 192,800 | Same as above. |
| Single man | -2,200 | -7,300 | For single men, benefits are progressive. Therefore, Republican men (who generally earn more than Democratic men) get less. |
| Single woman | 39,600 | 40,700 | Benefits are progressive; however, there is no statistically significant difference in the earnings of Democratic and Republican single women. Therefore, the benefits are essentially the same. In either case, the benefits are much greater than for single men, due to the greater longevity of women. |

The dimensions of the conservative campaign to destroy Social Security — and dismantle the New Deal — are now heaving into view. Determined to achieve the victory that has eluded them for more than 70 years, George W. Bush's aides and allies are building a very big, very ugly propaganda juggernaut.

— Columnist Joe Conason[11]

*Weighted Average Of Net Benefits, By Political Party*

The figures shown in Table 34, above, were multiplied times the percentages of Democrats and Republicans within each category, as shown in Table 35, below.

*Table 35. Average estimated net benefits for Democrats and Republicans turning 65 in years 2005 through 2045, calculated as an average of the net benefits for all categories of beneficiaries, weighted to reflect the percentage of Democrats and Republicans in each category.*

| Type of beneficiary | Democrats | | | | Republicans | | |
|---|---|---|---|---|---|---|---|
| | % in category * | Dollar amount per Table 34 | % times dollar amt. | | % in category * | Dollar amount per Table 34 | % times dollar amt. |
| Married and both work full-time | 0.36 | 41,500 | 14,940 | | 0.43 | 37,100 | 15,953 |
| Married and spouse works part-time or not at all — men | 0.10 | 188,500 | 18,850 | | 0.20 | 190,700 | 38,140 |

11 Joe Conason, "Beware the Coming Propaganda Juggernaut," (Salon.com, February 25, 2005), Retrieved January 27, 2006, from: http://dir.salon.com/story/opinion/conason/2005/02/25/propaganda/index.html.

| | | | | | | |
|---|---|---|---|---|---|---|
| Married and spouse works part-time or not at all— women | 0.02 | 186,000 | 3,720 | 0.02 | 192,800 | 3,856 |
| Single men | 0.19 | -2,200 | - 418 | 0.19 | -7,300 | -1,387 |
| Single women | 0.33 | 39,600 | 13,068 | 0.16 | 40,700 | 6,512 |
| Total | 1.00 | | $50,160 | 1.00 | | $63,074 |

*Confidence level of numbers in this column is 95% or greater.

The bottom line of Table 35 shows us that, during his lifetime, the "average" Republican will get nearly $13,000 more in total net benefits than will the "average" Democrat.[12] Given the many economic and demographic assumptions used, we should take the $13,000 difference with a large grain of salt. However, it is fair to say that, as a group, Republicans are at least as likely to benefit from Social Security as are Democrats.

> In years past ... Democrats and Republicans might have had a reasonable debate over whether to partially privatize Social Security. Today, though, all chance for a civil debate on the merits of the issue is lost, giving way to the politics of fear.
>
> — Sean Hannity, Author and TV talk show host [13]

### A Gender-Neutral Calculation

As noted, Republicans comprise a higher percentage of males than do Democrats. Does this affect the results? Yes, but only to a minor degree, as can be seen in Table 36, below.

*Table 36. Estimated SS net benefits for people turning 65 in years 1975 through 2045 — gender neutral.*

| Gender | Dems | Reps |
|---|---|---|
| Males | $48,500 | $65,000 |
| Females | 47,500 | 53,000 |
| Gender neutral (average) | $48,000 | $59,000 |

The gender neutral amount, shown in the bottom row of Table 36, above, represents the amount of benefits received by the average Democrat and Republican, assuming that each party comprises equal numbers of men and women. These estimated amounts are not much different than the bottom-line amounts in Table 35.

Whether we use the amounts calculated in Table 35, or the gender-neutral amounts shown in Table 36, the average Republican can expect to get net life-

---

12 The calculation is $63,074-$50,160 = $12,914.

13 Sean Hannity, *Let Freedom Ring*, 1st Edition ed. (New York: HarperCollins, 2002), 275.

time Social Security benefits that are as much or more than the average Democrat. This suggests that the overall Social Security benefit structure is not progressive, and that Republicans, on the whole, have as much to lose as Democrats from any "dismantling" of the system.

### One More Critical Factor: Young People of Either Party Get Less

When Social Security began, the payroll tax was just 2 percent of income. Now it's 12.4 percent. ... Twenty-five-year-old workers can expect a return of minus 0.64 percent — they actually lose money.

— Edwin Feulner, President of Heritage Foundation and Doug Wilson, Chairman of Townhall.com[14]

Before leaving the subject of Social Security, a comment is required regarding the impact of a person's retirement date on the amount of his net lifetime benefits. Generally, people who retire sooner get more than those who retire later. For example, a person who retired in 2005 can expect to get significantly greater net lifetime Social Security benefits than a person retiring in 2045. This is due to the fact that payroll taxes were relatively modest until recent years. As a result, younger workers have paid and will pay more in payroll tax to get their benefits than did older workers. This fact is evident from a review of Figure 168, below, which compares expected benefits for men at differing wage levels, assuming two different retirement dates: 2005 and 2045. The man retiring in 2045 gets substantially less than does the man retiring in 2005, no matter what the wage level.

*Figure 168. The information is from a table of net lifetime transfers (benefits minus taxes) prepared by C. Eugene Steuerle and Adam Carasso of the Urban Institute. These are the average net benefits of single men who turn 65 in 2005 and in 2045.*

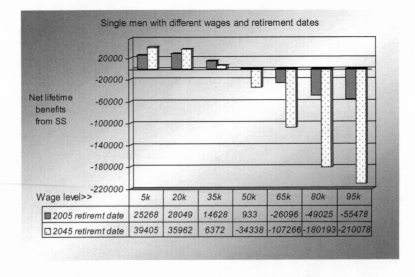

| Wage level>> | 5k | 20k | 35k | 50k | 65k | 80k | 95k |
|---|---|---|---|---|---|---|---|
| ■ 2005 retiremt date | 25268 | 28049 | 14628 | 933 | -26096 | -49025 | -55478 |
| □ 2045 retiremt date | 39405 | 35962 | 6372 | -34338 | -107266 | -180193 | -210078 |

Single men with different wages and retirement dates

Net lifetime benefits from SS

---

14 Edwin Feulner and Doug Wilson, *Getting America Right* (New York: Crown Forum, 2006), 79.

> Seniors tend to be opposed to change, and they don't, for under-
> standable reasons, care about Social Security's dismal rate of return
> for workers who will retire decades from now. Fine. Preserve the
> current system for seniors, but let young workers experiment with
> private accounts
>
> — Rich Lowry, Author and columnist.[15]

Does this factor affect the members of one political party more than another? It probably is not a significant factor because the age distribution of Democrats and Republicans is fairly equal. It does mean, however, that there are two key problems facing future Social Security recipients: a dismal rate of return on their Social Security contributions, and funding problems that may force a reduction in those meager benefits. Add to these the inequitable patch quilt benefit structure (discussed on page 207) and there is plenty to justify reform of this retirement system.

### Who gets the very best deal from Social Security?

How would you like to receive $45,000 for each one dollar you put into your retirement plan? Sound too good to be true? It's not. In 2003 and 2004, 7 tiny Texas school districts ran special programs where thousands of retiring teachers were hired to work for just a single day as "custodians" or "clerks." On average, the one-day workers earned wages of about $40, on which they paid only $2.50 in FICA tax. For many of the teachers, that was the only FICA tax they paid during their entire careers. However, due to a loophole in the law (since closed), these one-day cleaners and clerks could each receive, on average, about $113,000 in retirement benefits (in today's dollars). In total, this could cost the Social Security trust fund over $2 billion dollars.

Although the loophole was considered to be legal, the way the school districts exploited it was not. This author first identified the potentially fraudulent nature of these work programs in his book *How Social Security Picks Your Pocket* (Algora Publishing, 2003). Later, he confirmed that some of the school districts weren't really paying anything to their one-day workers: Effectively, these were sham transactions where the workers paid themselves via special "processing fees" that were given to the school districts in advance of their work days. In addition, many of the districts were violating signed Social Security agreements by extending the Social Security coverage to workers in part-time positions. These allegations were presented to the Inspector General of Social Security, who launched a major audit that concluded in January, 2007. The findings confirmed the author's suspicions:

> We identified 20,248 individuals who were employed as 1-day work-
> ers by the 7 school districts.... Over their lifetimes, they will potentially re-
> ceive about $2.2 billion in spousal benefits.... We found that individuals
> employed as 1-day workers by the seven Texas school districts did not ap-

---

15 Rich Lowry, "Young People Be Damned," in *National Review Online* (December 7, 2004), Retrieved December 8, 2006, from: http://www.nationalreview.com/lowry/lowry200412070848.asp.

pear to meet the requirements to receive a GPO exemption [the loophole]. This occurred because of the questionable nature of these individuals' employment. We also found that five of the school districts did not have the authority to provide these individuals Social Security coverage.[16]

Case closed? Not so fast. Thus far, the Social Security Administration has taken no action to cut off benefits to these 20,248 jani-teachers, and has imposed no penalties on the districts that operated the shady hiring programs. The OIG audit report is at http://www.ssa.gov/oig/ADOBEPDF/A-09-06-26086.pdf.

## Medicare

### Everyone's A "Winner" — Except For Future Generations?

I care about our young people, and I wish them great success, because they are our Hope for the Future, and some day, when my generation retires, they will have to pay us trillions of dollars....

—Dave Barry, American writer and humorist.[17]

Gender and wage levels affect Medicare benefits in the same way they impact Social Security benefits: Woman tend to get higher net benefits than men (because they live longer), and workers with low wages tend to get higher net benefits than those with higher wages (because they get the same benefits even though they pay less payroll tax). Unlike Social Security, however, there are no apparent "losers" (except for future generations who will probably have to pay for these benefits via legislated tax hikes).

Every beneficiary, regardless of gender or wage level, can expect to get a substantial net lifetime Medicare benefit. This is evident by reviewing Figure 169, below. By way of comparison, consider Figure 165. There, many people (at the higher income levels) received sharply negative "benefits."

As was the case with Social Security, one would expect Republicans to get lower net lifetime Medicare benefits because the average Republican is more likely to be male and to have higher wages. Again, however, this is not the case, due to the fact that the Republican worker is more likely to have a stay-at-home spouse.

*Figure 169. Net lifetime Medicare benefits for single men and women at various income levels. The information is from a table of net lifetime transfers (benefits minus taxes) prepared by C. Eugene Steuerle and Adam Carasso of the Urban Institute. These are the average net benefits of single men and women who turn 65 in years 2005 through 2045.*

16 Office of Inspector General, "Government Pension Offset Exemption for Texas School Districts' Employees," ed. Social Security Administration (January 2007), from: http://www.ssa.gov/oig/ADOBEPDF/A-09-06-26086.pdf.

17 Dave Barry, "Kids, Please Be Spank to Your Elders," in *Daily Athenaeum* (West Virginian University, 1998), Retrieved March 23, 2007, from: http://www.da.wvu.edu/archives/000509/news/000509,04,03.html.

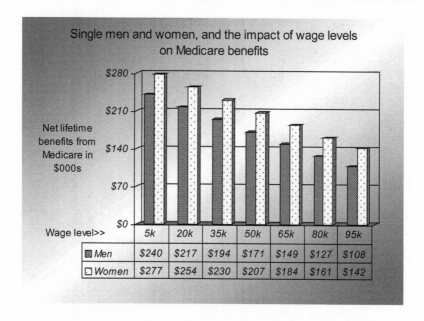

| Wage level>> | 5k | 20k | 35k | 50k | 65k | 80k | 95k |
|---|---|---|---|---|---|---|---|
| ■ Men | $240 | $217 | $194 | $171 | $149 | $127 | $108 |
| □ Women | $277 | $254 | $230 | $207 | $184 | $161 | $142 |

We believe in Medicare; they don't. They brag about voting to kill Medicare or to prevent it from being created 30 years ago. We believe it was an enormously important achievement.

— Mike McCurry, Whitehouse spokesman during the Clinton presidency[18]

With regard to Medicare, a man or woman with a stay-at-home spouse gets benefits that are approximately twice those of the single worker or of the person in a two-earner marriage. This is evident from a review of Figure 170, below, which compares the average benefits that would go to a man or woman with a stay-at-home spouse to those of a single, working woman. The single woman's net benefits never come close to those of the man or woman with the stay-at-home spouse. In fact, the poorest single woman gets far less in net benefits ($277,000) than does the wealthiest person married to a stay-at-home spouse ($393,000). Effectively, the system transfers wealth from poorer workers to wealthier workers.

*Figure 170. The information is from a table of net lifetime transfers (benefits minus taxes) prepared by C. Eugene Steuerle and Adam Carasso of the Urban Institute. These are the average net benefits of single women and a married person with a non-working spouse, who turn 65 in years 2005 through 2045.*

18 Press Secretary Mike McCurry, "White House Press Briefing," October 26, 1995, Retrieved March 23, 2007, from http://www.ibiblio.org/pub/archives/whitehouse-papers/1995/Oct/1995-10-26-Press-Briefing-by-Mike-McCurry.

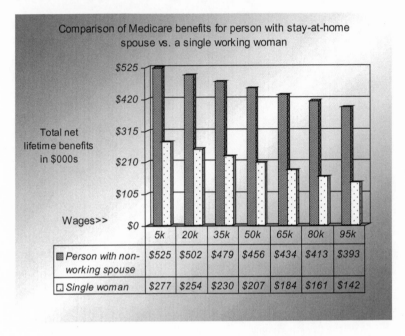

Comparison of Medicare benefits for person with stay-at-home spouse vs. a single working woman

| Wages>> | 5k | 20k | 35k | 50k | 65k | 80k | 95k |
|---|---|---|---|---|---|---|---|
| ■ Person with non-working spouse | $525 | $502 | $479 | $456 | $434 | $413 | $393 |
| ☐ Single woman | $277 | $254 | $230 | $207 | $184 | $161 | $142 |

*Total net lifetime benefits in $000s*

## Estimating Democratic vs. Republican Medicare Benefits

> Republicans have made their intentions clear from the beginning — they want to kill Medicare.
>
> — Democratic Congresswoman Nancy Pelosi[19]

The Medicare benefit estimates in this chapter were derived from tables created by Economists C. Eugene Steuerle and Adam Carasso. As we did with regard to Social Security benefits, we can use the Steuerle/Carasso tables to estimate total lifetime net Medicare benefits for single males, single females, one-earner married couples, and two-earner married couples. In addition, we can use the information to calculate benefits for people with differing wage histories, and with different retirement dates.

By using a two-step estimation process, similar to that used for estimating Social Security net benefits, we find that average Medicare net benefits are about the same for Democrats and Republicans — $231,000 and $245,000, respectively. The calculation of these amounts is shown in Appendix B 14.

## The Future of Medicare Is Scary

> I reject the notion that Republicans are trying to kill Medicare. I think that is ridiculous. I don't think there is any indication that is

---

19 "Pelosi: AARP Letter Confirms That House Republican Medicare Prescription Drug Bill Is Another Empty Promise," July 15, 2003, Retrieved March 23, 2007, from http://www.house. gov/pelosi/press/releases/July03/prAARPletter071503.html.

the cased, never has been, but it is party of the political mantra that we hear over and over again.

— Republican Senator Bob Bennett[20]

Finally, we need to address the issue of retirement date. Do retirees in 2005 get about the same net lifetime Medicare benefits as those retiring in 2045? The answer is no. The man retiring in 2045 will get far *more* net Medicare benefits than the man retiring in 2005, as is evident from a review of Figure 171, below. If you will recall, Figure 168 (on page 212) shows dramatically different results with regard to Social Security benefits. In that case, the person retiring in 2045 would receive far less in net benefits. In fact, he would have a large loss.

*Figure 171. The information is from a table of net lifetime transfers (benefits minus taxes) prepared by C. Eugene Steuerle and Adam Carasso of the Urban Institute. These are the average net Medicare benefits of single men who turn 65 in 2005 and in 2045.*

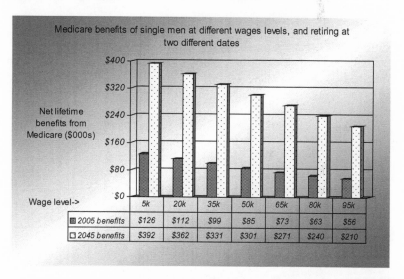

As was true with Social Security, however, retirement dates do not significantly impact our estimations of net benefits because the ages of Democrats and Republicans do not vary significantly. Of course, one day we will have to figure out how to pay for all of these unfunded benefits. One solution would be to means-test Medicare benefits; another would be to raise payroll and/or income taxes. Either solution is more likely to adversely affect Republicans because they tend to have higher earnings, which would make them more susceptible to means testing plans, or tax increases. Perhaps Republicans instinctively suspect this and, consequently, are more eager to reform the system.

---

20 Senator Bob Bennett in debate of, "Medicare Prescription Drug, Improvement, and Modernization Act of 2003," (Transcript: Senator's Web site, November 22, 2003), from: http://bennett.senate.gov/press/record.cfm?id=226106.

I'm too young for Medicare and too old for women to care.

— Kinky Friedman, Humorist, singer, and politician[21]

## Conclusions

Generally, low wage earners and women, two major constituencies of the Democratic Party, get above-average net benefits from Social Security. However, high-earning married people with stay-at-home spouses (prevalent among Republican ranks) get the highest net benefits of all, due to lucrative spousal and survivor benefits. The net result of these factors is a rough parity between the parties, with the "average" Republican getting the same or slightly higher total net benefits than the "average" Democrat. For our purposes, total net benefits are the excess of lifetime benefits received over lifetime payroll taxes paid in today's dollars, assuming a conservative real interest rate of 2 percent.

Like Social Security, Medicare favors low earners and women (two Democratic constituencies) and high-earning married workers with stay at home spouses (a Republican constituency). Medicare total net benefits are roughly the same for the average Democrat and Republican — around $235,000 to $245,000.

Unlike Social Security, Medicare doesn't have benefit winners and losers. Instead, it has winners and huge winners. The Medicare benefit structure is such that everyone can expect to gain from the system — that is, everyone except the future generations that will have to pay for it.

It is important to understand that the averages discussed in this chapter mask the great variances — inequities — built into the benefit formulas. Those inequities, and the looming insolvency issues, should compel Democrats and Republicans, alike, to search for ways to improve the systems. A good starting point would be to eliminate or, at least, "means test," spousal and survivor benefits.

---

21 Kinky Friedman (attributed), "Brainyquote.Com."

# Chapter 8: Who Gets More Welfare?

## Introduction

### Democrats on Strike and Wal-Mart on Medicaid

What would we do without Democrats working? Who would make the $5 coffees at $tarphucks, who would teach the incoming freshmen how to hate the US? Would [a day without Democrats] mean *Democrats on welfare* would strike against welfare so they would get out and work?

— Blogger named Spobot[1]

Wal-Mart gets Medicaid. Lockheed-Martin gets food stamps. Everyone knows that Halliburton is on the dole.... If checks from us didn't arrive in corporate mailboxes at the first of each month, we would immediately see what a joke American "capitalism" is.

— Columnist Jane Stillwater[2]

In this chapter we define "welfare," determine its cost, and roughly estimate who — Democrats or Republicans — collects more welfare dollars. Necessarily, the definitions are subjective and the estimates are crude. Nevertheless, reasonably fair conclusions can be reached. As usual, sources and methods are presented so that the user can assess their validity.

---

1 Spobot (pseudonym), November 3, 2004, Sgt Grit's Marine Forum, Retrieved February 26, 2006, from http://www.grunt.com/forum/topic.asp.

2 Jane Stillwater, "How Come Lockheed Gets Food Stamps and We Don't," *Novakeo.com* (February 15, 2005), Retrieved February 26, 2006, from http://novakeo.com/?p=98.

The average Democrat probably collects about twice as much "traditional (social) welfare" as does the average Republican. On the other hand, Republicans are more likely to benefit from "corporate welfare."

DETAILS

*Traditional (social) welfare*

### What Is It, And How Much Does It Cost?

[W]hen [John] Kerry was running for re-election, he uncorked a priceless rib-ticker about his opponent, Massachusetts Governor Bill Weld. "This guy ... takes more vacations than the people on welfare." Is that a Hoot? And yet, believe it or not, some people didn't think it was funny.

— Columnist Jeff Jacoby[3]

In November, 2003, the Congressional Research Service (CRS) of the Library of Congress issued a report describing our public welfare system:

More than 80 benefit programs provide aid — in cash and non-cash form — that is directed primarily to persons with limited income. Such programs constitute the public "welfare" system, if welfare is defined as income-tested or need-based benefits.[4]

The report described a network of 80 different programs involving total payments (in FY 2002) of $522.2 billion: $373.2 billion in federal funds and $149 billion in state and local funds. The 80 assistance programs are found within the following broad categories:
- Medical aid, such as Medicaid
- Cash aid, such as Supplemental Security Income (SSI)
- Food aid, such as Food Stamps and free school lunch programs
- Housing aid, such as Section 8 low-income housing assistance
- Educational assistance, such as Head Start and Pell Grants
- Services, such as the Emergency Food and Shelter Program
- Job and training programs such as Job Corps and Welfare-to-Work grants
- Energy assistance, such as the Low-Income Home Energy Assistance (HEAP) program

Most women are one man away from welfare.

— Feminist Gloria Steinem[5]

---

3 Jeff Jacoby, "Heard the One About Kerry's Sense of Humor?," *The Boston Globe* (September 12, 2004).

4 Vee Burke, "Cash and Noncash Benefits for Persons with Limited Income: Eligibility Rules, Recipient and Expenditure Data, Fy2000-Fy2002," ed. Congressional Research Service, CRS Report for Congress (The Library of Congress, 2003), from: http://www.opencrs.com/rpts/RL32233_20031125.pdf.

5 "Gloria Steinem Quotes," in *About: Women's History*, ed. Jone Johnson Lewis, Retrieved March 23, 2007, from: http://womenshistory.about.com/cs/quotes/a/qu_g_steinem.htm.

Most of these programs target very needy Americans; however, one suspects that some may also be used by significant numbers of middle-class Americans. For example, Pell Grants are mostly used by families with very low income (under $20,000); however, the grants can be used by families earning substantially more. In addition, certain programs, such as veteran medical benefits, simply do not fit the common perception of "welfare." And, finally, some benefits, such as the Earned Income Tax Credit, are distributed in the form of tax reductions, and in this book, such benefits are considered to be offsets to taxes paid, in Chapter 5. The cost of items such as these must be subtracted from the CRS welfare estimate ($522.2 billion) before we attempt to estimate who gets most of the benefits from programs we typically consider to be "welfare." This is done in Table 37, below.

*Table 37. FY 2002 traditional (social) welfare expenditures*

| Total federal and state/local expenditures for income-tested benefits | $522.2 |
|---|---|
| Less certain education assistance | −20.2 |
| Less tax credits (primarily the Earned Income Tax Credit) | −32.9 |
| Less certain veteran medical and dependent benefits | −5.1 |
| Less other benefits | −4.7 |
| Adjusted amount of welfare expenditures | $459.3 |

In Table 37, above, we see that the $522.2 billion figure has been reduced to $459.3 billion, and this is the amount that can be allocated on the basis of income levels.

## Who Gets More Traditional Welfare?

[C]ompassion is defined not by how many people are on the government dole but by how many people no longer need government assistance.

— Rush Limbaugh, Author and radio talk show host[6]

Table 38, below, presents the results of surveys that asked Democrats and Republicans whether they receive or received "Medicaid," "cash assistance," "Food Stamps," "SSI," or "welfare." When these statistically significant results are averaged, we find that Democrats seem to be about twice as likely to receive welfare assistance.

If total welfare expenditures are about $459 billion (Per Table 37), and Democrats are twice as likely to get welfare, we can roughly guesstimate that, as a group, Democrats get about $150 billion more in welfare than Republicans (using basic math and the simplifying assumption that there are equal numbers of Democrats and Republicans).[7]

---

6 Rush Limbaugh, *The Way Things Ought to Be* (New York: Pocket, 1993), 2.

7 In reality, there are usually more people that identify with the Democratic Party than the Republican Party, and this means that the welfare gap is larger than the estimate presented

Table 38. *Various surveys pertaining to welfare benefits*

| Row | Survey and Issue | % of Dems receiving aid | % of Reps receiving aid | No. of cases | Conf % | *RP |
|---|---|---|---|---|---|---|
| 1 | GSS 2006 and 1998 (If not currently working for pay, "what is your main source of economic support"?) (percentage saying "welfare")* | 10.4 | 5.1 | 492 | 99 | 2.04 |
| 2 | Michigan State of the State Survey #27, 2002 ("ever received cash assistance?") | 24.8 | 10.5 | 577 | +99 | 2.36 |
| 3 | NES PreElection Survey, 2002 (currently receive Medicaid benefits?) | 8.2 | 3.3 | 946 | +99 | 2.48 |
| 4 | Pew Religion & Public Life Survey, 2002 ("ever received welfare?") | 18.3 | 12.1 | 1247 | +99 | 1.51 |
| 5 | NES PreElection Survey, 1992 (currently receive Medicaid benefits?) | 10.8 | 5.3 | 1488 | +99 | 2.04 |
| 6 | 1986 General Social Survey (ever received AFDC, general assistance, SSI, or food stamps?) | 23.0 | 10.0 | 957 | +99 | 2.30 |
| 7 | Average percentages | 15.9 | 7.7 | | | |
| 8 | Overall proportion (Dem % divided by Rep %) | **206.5% | | | | |

*RP is relative proportion, which is the Democratic % divided by the Republican %.

**The disparity is slightly understated since Democrats are a little less likely to be currently employed.

in this chapter. Also note that these are 2002 values, and would be about 16% higher if restated into 2007 dollar values.

222

*Reality check: Has Welfare been a curse or a benefit?*

Bill ... attacked the worst aspects of the Republican Contract, such as the welfare bill, as "weak on work and tough on kids."

— Democratic Senator Hillary Clinton, describing her husband's political strategies with respect to welfare reform[8]

Although Democrats receive more welfare dollars than do Republicans, they are not necessarily receiving more help. After welfare reform was enacted in the mid-1990s, a new understanding emerged: For many, welfare was never help at all — it was a curse.

Ron Haskins, an expert on welfare programs, describes the early predictions regarding reform:

It would be difficult to exaggerate the predictions of doom hurled against the Republican welfare reform bill ... [Critics of welfare reform] claimed that it "attacked," "punished" and "lashed out at" children. Columnist Bob Herbert said the bill conducted a "jihad" against the poor. Sen. Frank Lautenberg said poor children would be reduced to "begging for money, begging for food, and ... engaging in prostitution."

Despite the dire predictions, the results of welfare reform seem to be extremely positive. According to Haskins:

In the decade that has passed since the 1996 reforms, the welfare rolls have plummeted by nearly 60 percent, the first sustained decline since the program was enacted in 1935. Equally important, the employment of single mothers heading families reached the highest level ever.[9]

With that increase in employment, there has been a steady augmentation of earnings and a marked decrease in black-child poverty and poverty among female-headed families.

We can't give welfare reform the credit for all of these improvements but it most likely had a positive impact by motivating people to help themselves. Perhaps this thought was expressed most succinctly by Robert J. Samuelson, a columnist for the Washington Post: "[W]hat people do for themselves often overshadows what government does for them."[10]

*Corporate welfare*

To the Honorable Secretary of Agriculture
Washington, D.C.
Dear Sir:

Our competitor, P. Gish Farm Corporation, received over $1 million from the government for not raising hogs. So, we'd like to go into the "not raising hogs" business next year.

What I want to know is, in your opinion, what is the best kind of farm not to raise hogs on, and what is the best breed of hogs not

---

8 Hillary Clinton, *Living History* (New York: Simon & Shuster, 2003), 288.

9 Ron Haskins, "Welfare Check," *Wall Street Journal*, July 27 2006. Mr. Haskins is the author of the book, *Work OverWelfare* (Brookings Institution Press, 2006).

10 Robert J. Samuelson, "Lessons of Welfare Reform Success," *Washington Post*, August 2, 2006.

to raise? We would prefer not to raise razorbacks, but if that is not a good breed not to raise, then we will just as gladly not raise Yorkshires or Durocs.

Sincerely,

— J. P. Fleecem, CEO, Oink Oink, Inc.[11]

## What Is Corporate Welfare, And How Much Does It Cost?

According to the libertarian think tank, Cato Institute:

> Corporate welfare consists of government programs that provide unique benefits or advantages to specific companies or industries. Corporate welfare includes programs that provide direct grants to businesses, programs that provide indirect commercial support to businesses, and programs that provide subsidized loans and insurance.[12]

The specific agencies distributing these funds are listed in Table 39, below.[13]

*Table 39. Per Cato "Handbook for Congress," based on the Budget of the United States for FY2003.*

| Federal Department | FY 2002 expenditures in billions |
|---|---|
| Agriculture | $35.0 |
| Health & Human Services | 9.1 |
| Transportation | 10.7 |
| Energy | 5.9 |
| Housing and Urban Development | 7.8 |
| Defense | 4.0 |
| Interior | 2.0 |
| Commerce | 2.0 |
| All other agencies | 16.1 |
| Total | $92.6 |

11 Loosely based upon an anonymous letter posted on the Internet

12 *Cato Handbook for Congress: Policy Recommendations for the 108th Congress*, ed. Edward Crane and David Boaz (Washington: Cato Institute, 2003), 338. NOTE: Cato does not include corporation tax credits in its calculation — and it should not for two very good reasons: When we calculate the amount of tax paid by corporations and their shareholders, we use the net amount paid — after any "welfare" credits. (Indeed, we used the net tax amounts in the tax chapter of this book.) Were we to also treat those tax credits as welfare, we'd effectively be double-deducting the same amounts. In addition, to treat corporate tax credits as corporate welfare is inconsistent with how we compute traditional (social) welfare. Millions of Americans get exemptions and credits for children, education, rehabilitation of old houses, etc. Yet, those credits are never added into the traditional welfare tally.

13 Ibid., 339.

As shown in the table, the total 2002 federal corporate welfare expenditures, according to Cato, were about $93 billion.

> All I want to say is that Republicans are always worried about welfare, welfare for poor people. They never talk about *welfare for the rich*, education, that George Bush got into Yale. How did he get into Yale?
>
> — Joy Behar, Co-host of the television talk show, "The View"[14]

*Reality check — Is it real "welfare" or public policy welfare?*

The libertarian Cato Institute has an expansive definition of "corporate welfare." For example, it regards federal agricultural and energy research as "welfare" because the research may ultimately prove useful and profitable to businesses. Of course, that same research may lead to findings that benefit individuals in their homes and in their daily routines. Would it be logical, therefore, to also classify agricultural and energy research as welfare for individuals (similar to food stamps, SSI, or TANF)?

Cato also includes, in its welfare tally, governmental loan guarantees and risk insurance for corporations that invest in third world countries, or in other expensive and risky ventures. In some cases, however, that is not truly welfare, in the normal sense of the word. Rather, it is the compensation we must pay to businesses (or individuals) that incur unusual risks and costs in order to fulfill an important public policy need.

The above concerns notwithstanding, Cato's estimate of $93 billion has been used here without modification, to avoid the introduction of additional subjectivity into this analysis.

To Cato's estimate of federal corporate welfare we need to add the assistance provided by state and local governments. Although this component is very difficult to determine, two independent sources have (roughly) estimated it to be around $50 billion per year. These sources and their estimates are described by Alan Peters and Peter Fisher, two University of Iowa professors, in a report issued in 2004.

> In a recent study, Thomas (2000) estimates conservatively that total state and local expenditures on economic development incentives were around $48.8 billion in 1996. In an ongoing study of incentive expenditures using a variety of methods and using a conservative definition of economic development, we estimate a likely top-end annual state and local number of around $50 billion.[15]

---

14 Joy Behar as cited in, "Real Time with Bill Maher," (Transcript: HBO, September 16, 2005), Retrieved February 26, 2006, from: http://www.safesearching.com/billmaher/print/t_hbo_realtime_091605.html.

15 Alan Peters and Peter Fisher, "The Failures of Economic Development Incentives," *Journal of the American Planning Association* 70, no. 1 (Winter, 2004): 28.

---

By adding the state and local estimate of $50 billion to Cato's federal estimate of $93 billion, we get a total of around $143. This is the estimated corporate welfare distributed by federal, state, and local governments.

### Who Gets More Corporate Welfare?

> Ronald Reagan memorably complained about "welfare queens," but he never told us that the biggest welfare queens are the already wealthy. Their lobbyists fawn over politicians, giving them little bits of money — campaign contributions, plane trips, dinners, golf outings — in exchange for huge chunks of taxpayers' money.
>
> — John Stossel, Author and TV commentator[16]

When a corporation gets "welfare," there are many parties who benefit, including creditors, employees, and investors. However, for the sake of simplicity, we assume here that all of the benefits accrue to the shareholders (an assumption that tends to shift more of the estimated corporate welfare towards Republicans). Therefore, we only need to figure out how much of America's corporate stock is owned by the average Democrat vs. the average Republican. This can be done in the following way: A table published by the Tax Policy Center (TPC) breaks out estimated qualifying dividends and capital gain income by household income level.[17] With the use of GSS survey data (1998-2004) we can determine the percentage of Democrats and Republicans in each of those TPC income ranges and, in turn, determine the amount of dividend and capital gain income earned by the "average" Democrat versus the "average" Republican. Using this procedure, we find that the average Republican earned about $3,500 in dividends and capital gains, while the average Democrat earns only about $2,100.[18]

It seems reasonable to assume that the relationship between these amounts of investment income correlate closely with the relationship between the amounts of stock owned, and in turn with the amount of corporate welfare. This implies a $35 billion corporate welfare differential in favor of Republicans, assuming equal numbers of Democrats and Republicans. (I.e., Democrats get about $54 billion in corporate welfare and Republicans get about $89 billion — a difference of $35 billion.)[19]

> Corporate welfare-the enormous and myriad subsidies, bailouts, giveaways, tax loopholes, debt revocations, loan guarantees, and other benefits conferred by government on business-is a function of political corruption.
>
> — Consumer activist, Ralph Nader[20]

16 John Stossel, "Confessions of a Welfare Queen," (ReasonOnline, March, 2004), Retrieved August 30, 2006, from: http://www.reason.com/0403/fe.js.confessions.shtml.

17 Table T05-0009, published on the TPC Web site in 2005. This table was produced using the Urban-Brookings microsimulation tax model.

18 The GSS survey was based on a total of 6010 men and women. The statistical significance of the overall GSS distribution difference was 99+%, with Phi of .20.

19 These amounts would be about 16% higher if restated into 2007 dollar values.

20 Ralph Nader, *Cutting Corporate Welfare* (New York: Seven Stories Press, 2000), 13.

## CONCLUSIONS

Traditional (or social) welfare is defined as "income-tested or need-based benefits." There are over 80 different traditional welfare programs, which cost the federal, state, and local governments over $520 billion in 2002. Of that amount, I have estimated that about $460 billion was distributed to low-income Americans in the form of direct assistance and another $33 billion was distributed in via the Earned Income Tax Credit (EITC). We considered the EITC in Chapter 5 (as an offset to taxes paid) so it would be redundant to consider it again (as a welfare benefit) in this chapter.

Survey evidence suggests that Democrats are twice as likely as Republicans to be on welfare, or to have been on welfare. By implication, this means that, of the $460 billion in direct welfare assistance distributed in 2002, Democrats probably received about $150 billion more than did Republicans. Here, we are using the simplifying assumption that there are equal numbers of Democrats and Republicans. (The actual amount distributed to Democrats would be larger because there are usually more Democrats than Republicans.).

It is estimated that, in 2002, the federal government spent about $93 billion in corporate direct and indirect subsidies. In addition, state and local governments are estimated to spend about $50 billion each year on corporate assistance. These corporate welfare payments are more likely to benefit Republicans than Democrats because Republicans are more likely to own corporate stock. If we assume that all corporate welfare benefits accrue to the corporate investors (and not to the employees or creditors of the corporation), we would expect Republicans to get $35 billion more corporate welfare than Democrats would get. Again, we assume equal numbers of Democrats and Republicans. (The actual amount distributed to Republicans would be smaller, since there are usually fewer Republicans than Democrats.)

Often, there is a thin line separating real welfare from public policy welfare. This is particularly the case when we compensate an individual or business for undertaking a project that has multiple beneficiaries.

# CHAPTER 9: WHO IS HAPPIER, WHO IS MORE MISERABLE, AND WHY?

## INTRODUCTION

*Do narrow, selfish goals lead to happiness?*

> I hypothesize that Republicans, as a group, may be happier because
> ... compared with Democrats and Independents, their main goals
> are narrower and more selfish, and thus more easily obtained.

— Matt Vidal, Op-Ed, CommonDreams.org, 2006[1]

All surveys suggest that Republicans are happier than Democrats, but the reasons for this tendency are not entirely clear. There are many characteristics associated with happiness, such as being married, wealthy, religious, and better educated; and those traits are more prevalent among Republicans than Democrats. However, even after controlling for all obvious factors, Republicans seem to be happier than Democrats.

At the end of this chapter, I offer my own hypothesis of the factors contributing to the bliss disparity. I argue that Democrats are less happy than Republicans due, in part, to a certain type of Democratic cynicism, identifiable in survey results. This cynicism comprises three distinct elements:
1. A general lack of trust in other people
2. A sense that destiny can not be controlled
3. A belief that capitalism is inherently unjust.

Each element is addressed in detail, and supported by reference to survey evidence.

---

1 Matt Vidal, "Republican Bliss: The Selfish Road to Happiness," *Common Dreams News Center* (April 6, 2006), Retrieved April 20, 2006, from http://www.commondreams.org/views06/0406-30.htm.

DETAILS

*Who is happier?*

### Happiness in General

On the radio show I've hosted since 1996, no subject provokes more anger from callers across the country than my contention that conservatives aren't just more astute and practical than their liberal counterparts, they are also happier, more fulfilled in their lives and their work.

— Michael Medved, Author and radio talk show host[2]

Republicans are more likely than Democrats to state that they are "very happy," a fact that is reflected in several Gallup surveys conducted in 1996 through 2003. The results of those surveys are shown in Figure 172, below. Note that the 2001 survey (depicted in the middle of the graph) was taken 2 months after the attack on the World Trade Center, and may account for that year's sharp dip in happiness, for both Democrats and Republicans.

*Figure 172. Are you "very happy"? (Gallup polls conducted in 1996 through 2003, based on, left to right, total sample sizes (including non-Democrats and non-Republicans) of 979, 1052, 1005, 1001, and 1011, with confidence levels of 95% or more, and with relative proportions of, left to right, .96, .85, .88, .78, and .81)*

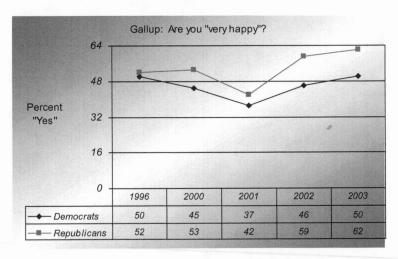

| Gallup: Are you "very happy"? | 1996 | 2000 | 2001 | 2002 | 2003 |
|---|---|---|---|---|---|
| Democrats | 50 | 45 | 37 | 46 | 50 |
| Republicans | 52 | 53 | 42 | 59 | 62 |

The Gallup Organization states that the happiness gap has been fairly consistent:

---

2 Medved, *Right Turns*, 229.

Why Republicans are happier is not clear, but the result has been the same in nearly every asking of this measure since 1996, including one reading under former President Bill Clinton, a Democrat, and three under Republican President George W. Bush. Only in 1996 did Republicans and Democrats express about equal levels of happiness.[3]

Actually, the contentment chasm developed long before 1996. In each of the 25 surveys conducted by the General Social Survey (GSS) since its inception in 1972, Republicans were more likely to state that they were "very happy." The disparity existed in years when Republicans were in and out of control of the federal government, and it has existed for both men and women. For men, see Figure 173.

> Everyone knows that a happy Republican is an annoyed Republican. Being perpetually pissed off about everything is at the very heart of Republicanism today.
>
> — Linwood Barclay, Columnist for the Toronto Star[4]

*Figure 173. Would you say that you are very happy...?" (Men) (25 GSS surveys taken from 1972 through 2006, based on, left to right 2184, 1173, 2061, 2112, 1963, 1381, and 1460 cases, with confidence level of, left to right, 99+%, 95%, 99%, 98%, 99%, 97%, and 99+%, and with relative proportions of, left to right, .82, .86, .83, .86, .84, .84, and .73)*

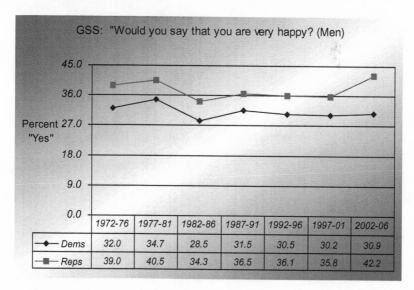

GSS: "Would you say that you are very happy? (Men)

| | 1972-76 | 1977-81 | 1982-86 | 1987-91 | 1992-96 | 1997-01 | 2002-06 |
|---|---|---|---|---|---|---|---|
| Dems | 32.0 | 34.7 | 28.5 | 31.5 | 30.5 | 30.2 | 30.9 |
| Reps | 39.0 | 40.5 | 34.3 | 36.5 | 36.1 | 35.8 | 42.2 |

3 Lydia Saad, "A Nation of Happy People," *The Gallup News Service* (January 5, 2004), Retrieved August 20, 2004, from Http://brain.gallup.com.
4 Linwood Barclay, "An Annoyed Republican Is a Happy Republican," *Toronto Star*, August 30, 2004.

Figure 174 shows an even larger disparity among women. Again, Republicans have claimed to be happier for at least 35 years.

*Figure 174. "Would you say that you are very happy...?" (Women) (25 GSS surveys taken from 1972 through 2006, based on, left to right, 2693, 1681, 3065, 3037, 2737, 1882, and 1948 cases, with confidence level of, left to right, 99+%, 83% (not significant), 99+%, 99%, 99+%, 99+%, and 99+%, and with relative proportions of, left to right, .77, n/a, .74, .73, .69, .83, and .79)*

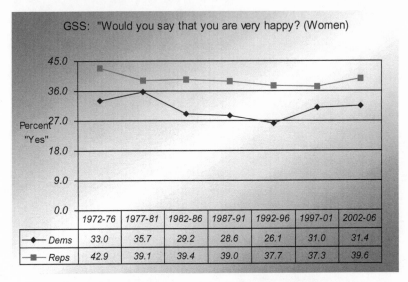

GSS: "Would you say that you are very happy? (Women)

| | 1972-76 | 1977-81 | 1982-86 | 1987-91 | 1992-96 | 1997-01 | 2002-06 |
|---|---|---|---|---|---|---|---|
| Dems | 33.0 | 35.7 | 29.2 | 28.6 | 26.1 | 31.0 | 31.4 |
| Reps | 42.9 | 39.1 | 39.4 | 39.0 | 37.7 | 37.3 | 39.6 |

[Y]ou look around your country today, at the squandered promises, the unfulfilled promises, and you can't sit back and sing "Be Happy," you know, that song, "Be Happy, Don't Worry...."

— Katrina vanden Heuvel, Editor of "The Nation"[5]

A similar glee gulf is apparent from several surveys conducted by the Pew Research Center for the People and the Press (Pew). The results of Pew's November, 2005 survey are shown in Figure 175, below, and those results show that Republicans are more likely than Democrats or independents to state that they are "very happy."

A general summary of various Pew surveys is found in a report entitled, "Are We Happy Yet?" In that report, Pew notes that Republicans were found to be happier in all of its recent surveys:

> Pew surveys since 1991 also show a partisan gap on happiness; the current 16 percentage point gap [for the November, 2005 survey] is among the largest in Pew surveys, rivaled only by a 17 point gap in February 2003."[6]

---

5 Katrina Vanden Heuval, "ABC's This Week," (Transcript: The LIberal Oasis Blog, February 19, 2006), Retrieved April 2, 2007, from: http://www.liberaloasis.com/archives/021906.htm.

6 Pew, "Are We Happy Yet?," in *Social Trends Report* (The Pew Research Center, February 13, 2006), 5.

*Figure 175. Percentage very happy by party identification (Pew survey conducted in October and November, 2005, based on 3014 interviews with people of all political orientations, and with confidence level of 95%)*

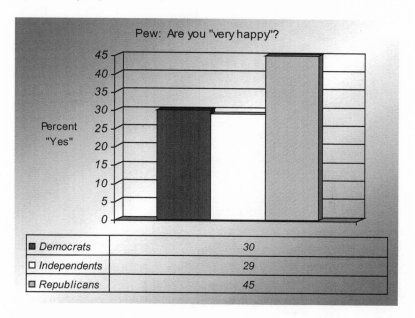

| Pew: Are you "very happy"? | |
|---|---|
| ■ Democrats | 30 |
| □ Independents | 29 |
| □ Republicans | 45 |

Other surveys addressing the subject of happiness are shown in Appendix B 16 on page 358.

## Happiness With Regard To Specific Aspects Of Life

### Marriage

The most happy marriage I can imagine to myself would be the union of a deaf man to a blind woman.

— Samuel Taylor Coleridge, English poet and philosopher[7]

Republicans appear to be happier with regard to certain aspects of their lives, one of which is marriage. As seen in Figure 176, below, this is true for both genders.

*Figure 176. "Would you say that your marriage is very happy?" (combined results of 25 GSS survey taken from 1973 through 2006, based on, left to right, 7343, 8449, and 15792 cases, with confidence level of at least 99% for all three columns, and with relative proportions of, left to right, .94, .88, and .91)*

---

7 *The Times Book of Quotations*, (Glasgow: Harper Collins, 2000), 452.

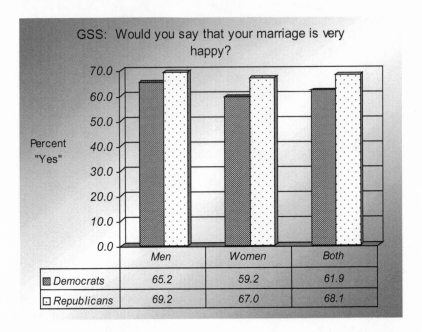

The difference in marital bliss has been fairly constant during the last three decades. See Figure 177.

*Figure 177. "Taking all things together, how would you describe your marriage?" (several GSS surveys taken from 1977 through 2006, based on, left to right, 4714, 5215, and 3271 cases, with confidence level of at least 99% for all three columns, and with relative proportions of, left to right, .93, .88, and .90)*

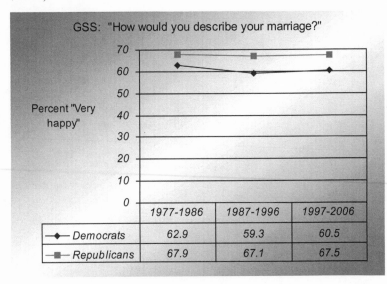

Happiness is having a large, loving, caring, close-knit family —in another city.

— Comedian George Burns[8]

## Finances

They say that money doesn't buy happiness, but don't believe it! Republicans tend to have higher incomes, and they also tend to have warm and fuzzy feelings about financial matters, as shown in Table 40.

*Table 40. Surveys dealing with the satisfaction of Democrats and Republicans regarding aspects of their financial condition*

| Survey | Issue | Dems | Reps | No. cases | Conf % | *RP |
|---|---|---|---|---|---|---|
| GSS surveys conducted 26 times in 1972 through 2006. | Are you satisfied "with financial condition"? (% answering "satisfied") | 27.6 | 38.4 | 29465 | +99 | .72 |
| Pew News Interest Index survey — May, 2005 | "Do you now earn enough money to lead the kind of life you want, or not?" | 30.0 | 52.1 | 556 | +99 | .58 |
| (same as above) | "How concerned are you, if at all, about going too deeply into debt? (Percentage who responded, "very concerned") | 46.7 | 29.5 | 969 | +99 | 1.58 |

*RP is relative proportion, which is the Democratic % divided by the Republican %.

## Work

Busy people are happy people whether they want to admit it or not.

— Terry Paulson, Psychologist and organizational advisor[9]

Democrats are less satisfied with their jobs, and much more worried about losing them. See Table 41, below.

---

8 George Burns (attributed), "Brainyquote.Com."

9 Terry Paulson, "Ten Sure Fire Ways to Fail as a Manager," 2006, from http://terrypaulson. typepad.com/leaderline/difficult_people/index.html.

*Table 41. Surveys dealing with the employment satisfaction of Democrats and Republicans*

| Survey | Issue | Dems | Reps | No. of cases | Conf % | *RP |
|---|---|---|---|---|---|---|
| GSS survey — 2006 | "All in all, how satisfied would you say you are with your job?" (% answering "very satisfied") | 47.8 | **57.1** | 2087 | +99 | .84 |
| Pew News Interest Index survey — May, 2005 | "How concerned are you, if at all, about losing your job or taking a cut in pay? (% responding "very concerned") | 37.5 | 21.9 | 969 | +99 | 1.71 |

*RP is relative proportion, which is the Democratic % divided by the Republican %.

## Age

Thomas Jefferson once said, "We should never judge a president by his age, only by his works." And ever since he told me that I stopped worrying.

— President Ronald Reagan at age 73[10]

Within every 5-year age interval between 18 and 82, Republicans are more likely to say that they are "very happy." This trend even extends beyond age 82; however, at that point the sample sizes get pretty small — for obvious reasons. The figures in Figure 178, below, reflect a 33-year period from 1973 through 2006.

*Figure 178. "Would you say that you are very happy?" (combined results of 25 GSS survey taken from 1973 through 2006, based on, left to right, 1620, 2708, 3029, 3054, 2828, 2567, 2384, 2193, 2133, 1944, 1775, and 1426 cases, with confidence level of at least 99% for all columns except the youngest (96%) and the oldest (95%), and with relative proportions ranging from .66 to .87)*

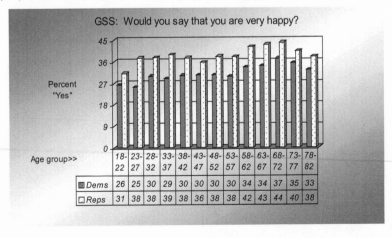

10President Ronald Reagan, *Simpson's Contemporary Quotations* (1984).

*Who is more miserable?*

### Sadness And Depression

There is no greater pain than to remember a happy time when one is in misery.

— Durante Degli Alighieri (Dante), 13th Century Italian poet[11]

Since Democrats are less happy, it is not surprising to learn that they are more likely to be sad and depressed. This is indicated by the results of a 2004 GSS survey, shown in Figure 179, below.

*Figure 179. Are you "a person who often feels sad and blue"? (2004 GSS Survey, based on, left to right, 670, 840, and 1510 cases, with confidence level of, left to right, 99%, 96%, and 99+%, and with relative proportions of, left to right, 1.62, 1.39, and 1.50)*

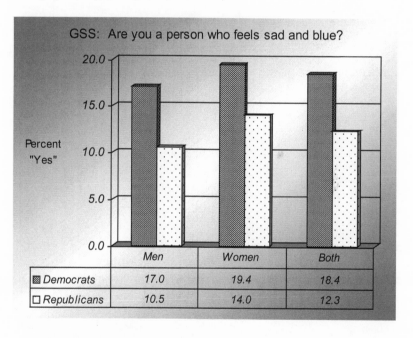

Similar results were indicated in all of the other relevant surveys found, which are shown in Table 42.

11 Elizabeth Knowles, ed., *Oxford Dictionary of Quotations*, 5th ed. (Oxford: Oxford University Press, 1999), 249.

*Table 42. Various surveys regarding "the blues"*

| Surveys and Dates | Dem % "yes" | Rep % "yes" | No. of cases | Conf % | *RP |
|---|---|---|---|---|---|
| Harris Interactive 2006: During the past 30 days have you "felt very sad throughout most of [a] day"? | **32.7** | 14.8 | 371 | +99 | 2.21 |
| GSS 2000: During the last 4 weeks, have you felt "downhearted and blue" some or all of the time? | **30.4** | 23.5 | 817 | 97 | 1.29 |
| Michigan 1999 State of the State: In the past month were you depressed some or all of the time? | **38.1** | 23.6 | 635 | +99 | 1.61 |
| GSS 1996: During the last 7 days have you felt "sad" on some days? | **64.2** | 57.5 | 899 | 96 | 1.12 |
| GSS 1996: During the last 7 days were there times when you "felt that you couldn't shake the blues"? | **49.9** | 37.0 | 901 | +99 | 1.35 |

*RP is relative proportion, which is the Democratic % divided by the Republican %.

### Emotional Problems

> According to the Boca Raton News, Bush's victory has triggered psychological disorders in this tiny South Florida Democratic community.... [W]hen some 20 Kerry voters met for their first therapy session ... the group's rage became uncontrollable.
>
> — NewsMax.com[12]

It's normal to have emotions, but if they go unchecked and interfere with normal, desirable activities, the consequence can be misery. Surveys show that emotions may be more of a problem for Democratic males than Republican males. Respondents were asked if emotions affected the amount they accomplished during the previous 4 weeks (Figure 180, next page, top). Note: For women there was not a significant difference.

Emotions and the quality of work were the subject of another survey question. In this case, Democratic males and females were both more likely to say that "emotional problems ("such as feeling depressed or anxious") affected performance. (See Figure 181, next page, bottom.)

*Figure 180. "During the past 4 weeks ... as a result of any emotional problems (such as feeling depressed or anxious)" have you "accomplished less than you would like"? (GSS survey conducted in 2000, based on, left to right, 346, 471, and 817 cases, with confidence level of, left to right, 94%, 79% (not significant), and 95%, and with relative proportions of, left to right, 1.68, n/a, and 1.33)*

---

12 "Group Therapy 'Screaming Epithets' at Bush," in *NewsMax.com* (December 5, 2004), from: http://www.newsmax.com/archives/ic/2004/12/5/113802.shtml.

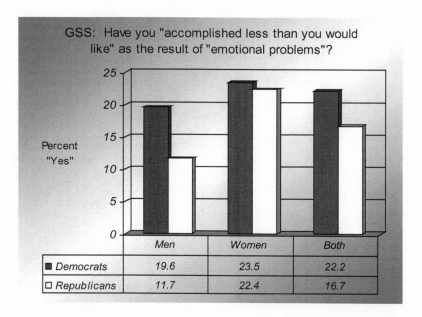

*Figure 181. "During the past 4 weeks ... as a result of any emotional problems (such as feeling depressed or anxious)" have you performed less carefully than usual? (GSS survey conducted in 2000, based on, left to right, 345, 471, and 816 cases, with confidence level of, left to right, 99+%, 97%, and 99+%, and with relative proportions of, left to right, 4.71, 1.64, and 2.56)*

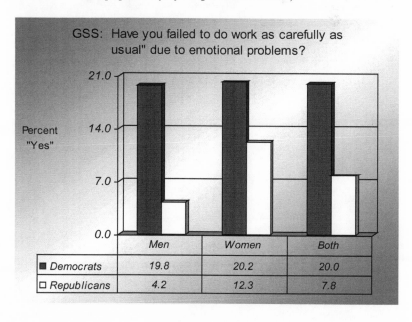

> It's a real conflict for me when I go to a concert and find out somebody in the audience is a Republican or fundamental Christian. It can cloud my enjoyment. I'd rather not know.

— Popular singer Linda Ronstadt[13]

A 1996 GSS survey asked respondents: "On how many days in the past 7 days have you ..." [been anxious, been worried, or been fearful]? In each case, the average number of days was higher for Democrats. (See Figure 182, below.)

*Figure 182. "On how many days in the past 7 days have you ... ?" (GSS survey taken in 1996, based on surveys, left to right, of 894, 900, and 899 Democrats and Republicans, with confidence level, left to right, of 98%, 95%, and 99%)*

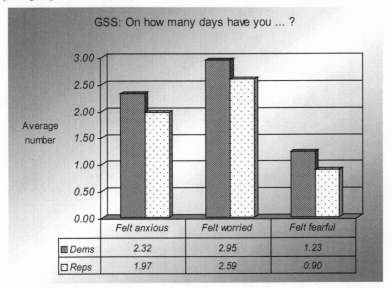

The results of other surveys involving mental health are shown in Table 43.

*Table 43. Miscellaneous surveys regarding mental health*

| Survey | Issue | Dem % "yes" | Rep % "yes" | No. of cases | Conf % | *RP |
|---|---|---|---|---|---|---|
| Harris 2004 | Are you or have you been diagnosed with depression? | **22.8** | 15.5 | 642 | 98 | 1.47 |
| GSS 1996 | Have you ever felt you were "going to have a nervous breakdown"? | **25.6** | 20.4 | 869 | 93 marg | 1.25 |

*RP is relative proportion, which is the Democratic % divided by the Republican %.

13 Marc A. Levin, "Off Their Rockers for Kerry," in *The Austin Review* (August, 2004), Retrieved April 2, 2004, from: http://www.austinreview.com/archives/2004/08/off_their_rocke_1. html.

*Why are there differences in happiness?*

> One of the indictments of civilizations is that happiness and intel-
> ligence are so rarely found in the same person.
>
> — William Feather, American author and publisher[14]

Survey evidence, by itself, can not determine what causes happiness (or anything else); however, it can be used to identify correlating factors. The factors
that seem to correlate with happiness are identified below.

### Money

Republicans are likely to have higher income, and that variable correlates
positively with happiness. Gallup acknowledges the relationship, but dismisses
the notion that it explains the entire happiness differential:

> Even when accounting for partisan differences in ... household income,
> Republicans are significantly more likely than Democrats and indepen-
> dents to be very happy.

We can test Gallup's assertion by analyzing 34 years of GSS survey data,
grouped by income level (expressed in 2006 dollars). In Figure 183, below, we see
the percentages of happy Democrats and Republicans in each of 6 income ranges.

*Figure 183. "Would you say that you are very happy...?" (26 GSS surveys taken from 1972
through 2006, based on, left to right, 5805, 6358, 5195, 3633, 2040, and 3652 cases, with confidence
level of 99% for all differences, with relative proportions of, left to right, .76, .80, .91, .86, .86, and .85)*

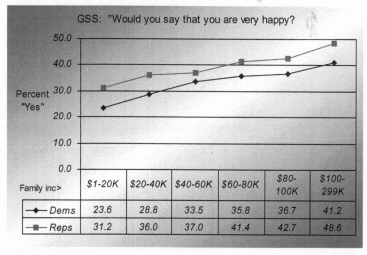

GSS: "Would you say that you are very happy?

| Family inc> | $1-20K | $20-40K | $40-60K | $60-80K | $80-100K | $100-299K |
|---|---|---|---|---|---|---|
| Dems | 23.6 | 28.8 | 33.5 | 35.8 | 36.7 | 41.2 |
| Reps | 31.2 | 36.0 | 37.0 | 41.4 | 42.7 | 48.6 |

We learn two things by analyzing Figure 183: More money does mean more
happiness, and, at any given income level, Republicans seem to be happier than
Democrats.

---

14 William Feather (attributed), "The Quotations Page."

> Having more money does not insure happiness. People with ten million dollars are no happier than people with nine million dollars.
> — Hobart Brown, American sculptor[15]

*Reality check — Does happiness continue to rise as income goes up?*

If we were to extend our analysis into even higher income levels (beyond $299,000), would overall happiness continue to increase? The experts would have us believe that it would not. Psychologists seem to feel that the positive correlation between income and happiness gets smaller — not larger — as we get into higher income ranges. This is stated succinctly by F. Heylighen, co-director of the Center "Leo Apostel" for transdisciplinary research:

> It is interesting to note that the correlation between purchasing power and happiness becomes less important for more wealthy societies, implying that once the basic material needs of nutrition and shelter are satisfied, further prosperity adds little to happiness.[16]

## Marriage

> All marriages are happy. It's the living together afterward that causes all the trouble.
> — Author Raymond Hull[17]

*Figure 184. "Would you say that you are very happy...?" (married only) (combined results of 25 General Social Surveys taken from 1972 through 2004, based on, left to right, 7405, 8368, and 15773 cases, with confidence level of 99% for all differences, and with relative proportions of, from left to right, .88, .83, and .85)*

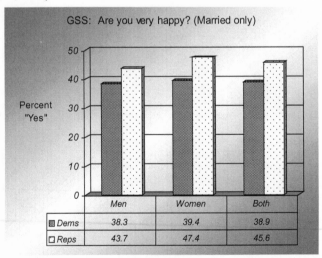

| GSS: Are you very happy? (Married only) | | |
| --- | --- | --- |
| | Men | Women | Both |
| Dems | 38.3 | 39.4 | 38.9 |
| Reps | 43.7 | 47.4 | 45.6 |

15 Hobart Brown (attributed), "The Quotations Page."

16 F. Heylighten. (July 29, 1999), "Happiness", Retrieved April 2, 2007, from Principia Cybernetica Web: http://pcp.lanl.gov/HAPPINES.html.

17 Raymond Hull (attributed), "The Quote Garden," Retrieved April 2, 2007, from: http://www.quotegarden.com/marriage.html.

Marriage is another factor that positively correlates with happiness, according to Gallup and other survey organizations. Like income, however, it explains only a small part of the happiness divide.

As we did for income, we can use GSS data to test the impact of marriage on the happiness gap. In Figure 184, above, we see the combined GSS results for all 25 surveys conducted in 1972 through 2004, limited to Democrats and Republicans who are married.

Note that, even when marital status is controlled, Republican men and women seem to be significantly happier than Democratic men and women.

### Other Factors Correlating With Happiness

Happiness is good health and a bad memory.
— Actress Ingrid Bergman[18]

The Pew report, "Are We Happy Yet" (previously referenced), identified several additional correlating factors. These are listed in Table 44, below.

*Table 44. Miscellaneous factors that correlate with happiness, according to Pew.*

| More happy | Less happy |
|---|---|
| Healthy | Unhealthy |
| Conservative | Liberal |
| Middle aged or older | Young* |
| Better educated | Poorly educated |
| Religious | Not religious |
| White or Hispanic | Black |
| Sunbelt resident | Northern resident |

*No, this is not a mistake. Younger people, especially younger men, tend to be less happy, according to Pew.

Just about every happiness trait shown in Table 44 is a factor typically associated with Republicans rather than Democrats. This caused Pew to broach the question: "[I]s being a Republican really a predictor of happiness, independent of all other factors?" Using multiple regression analysis, Pew concluded that it is. In other words, even if we were to equalize all the correlating factors mentioned heretofore, Republicans would probably still be happier than Democrats to a statistically significant degree.[19] Perhaps the GOP should consider the campaign slogan, "Vote Republican — it will make you happy!"

> [O]f course Republicans are happier — that's what happens when you refuse to face reality and only want to hear "the good news" and your head is stuck up your ass.
> — Blogger named "ImpeachW," posted on the Majority Report Radio show blog[20]

18 Ingrid Bergman (attributed), "Brainyquote.Com."

19 Multiple regression analysis is a statistical technique that can be used to test the relationship between a dependent variable and several independent variables.

20 ImpeachW (pseudonym), "Majority Report," March 15, 2006, Bluestateblogs.com, Retrieved April 3, 2007, 2007, from http://www.bluestateblogs.com/majorityreport/archives/2006/03/

*Does cynicism lead to sadness? (a theory)*

We have established that Republicans are happier than Democrats, and listed several factors correlating with that happiness. Yet, even after Pew controlled for every known factor, a happiness gap remained. What is the missing "X" factor?

Surveys show that Democrats are more likely to have the following three traits, and I would argue that each of these correlates negatively with happiness:

- A lack of trust in others
- A sense that one can not control his or her own destiny
- A feeling that the capitalist economic system is unjust.

These three traits, comprising what I call "Democratic cynicism," warrant detailed analysis.

### Lack of Trust

It's still trust but verify. It's still play — but cut the cards. It's still watch closely. And don't be afraid to see what you see.

— Ronald Reagan, President, in his formal farewell address after two terms in office[21]

*Figure 185. "Generally speaking, would you say that most people can be trusted or that you can't be too careful in life?" (several GSS surveys conducted in 1972 through 2006, based on, left to right, 3915, 1853, 2378, 3916, 3099, 2464, and 3348 cases, with confidence level of at least 99% for all differences, and with relative proportions of, left to right, 1.32, 1.19, 1.27, 1.24, 1.08, 1.15, and 1.19)*

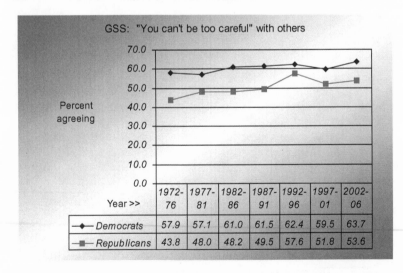

GSS: "You can't be too careful" with others

| Year >> | 1972-76 | 1977-81 | 1982-86 | 1987-91 | 1992-96 | 1997-01 | 2002-06 |
|---|---|---|---|---|---|---|---|
| Democrats | 57.9 | 57.1 | 61.0 | 61.5 | 62.4 | 59.5 | 63.7 |
| Republicans | 43.8 | 48.0 | 48.2 | 49.5 | 57.6 | 51.8 | 53.6 |

*Percent agreeing*

hour_one_wednes_66.php.

21 President Ronald Reagan, "Farewell Address to the Nation," (Ronald Reagan Presidential Foundation, January 11, 1989), Retrieved September 16, 2006, from: http://www.reagan.utexas.edu/archives/speeches/1989/011189i.htm.

I was very surprised to find that, year-in and year-out, Democrats seem to be far less trusting of their fellow citizens than are Republicans. In Figure 185, we see this pattern for the 35-year period from 1972 through 2006, based on GSS surveys. (1972 was the first year GSS conducted surveys.) Respondents were asked whether most people can be trusted or "you can't be too careful in life." In each case, Democrats were much more likely to reject the notion that most people can be trusted.

Figure 186, below, also shows a 30-year trend, based on GSS surveys. This time, the question was slightly different: "Do you think most people would try to take advantage of you if they got the chance ...?" Again, Democrats leaned towards the more cynical response.

*Figure 186. "Do you think most people would try to take advantage of you if they got a chance, or would they try to be fair?" (several GSS surveys conducted in 1975 through 2004, based on, left to right, 2803, 2822, 3557, 3228, 2260, and 2165 cases, with confidence level of at least 99% for all differences, and with relative proportions of, left to right, 1.44, 1.34, 1.33, 1.26, 1.27, and 1.16)*

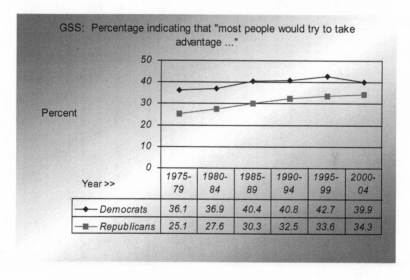

Love all, trust a few.

— Shakespeare[22]

Other surveys pertaining to trust are identified in Table 45, below, and each shows a similar result.

We should not assume that Democrats have innate psychological characteristics that distinguish them from Republicans. Perhaps they live and work among less trustworthy people, which would make their lack of trust understandable and appropriate. Whatever the cause, however, this lack of trust probably correlates negatively with happiness.

---

22 William Shakespeare, *All's Well that Ends Well*, Act 1 Scene 1.

Table 45. *Other surveys addressing the issue of trust*

| Survey and Issue | Dems | Reps | No. of cases | Conf % | *RP |
|---|---|---|---|---|---|
| GSS survey conducted in 2006: Percentage strongly agreeing that "If you are not careful, other people will take advantage of you." | 39.5 | 32.7 | 820 | 96 | 1.21 |
| Harris Interactive conducted in 2002: Do you trust "the ordinary man or woman to tell the truth, or not"? (percentage "yes") | 64.0 | 80.5 | 290 | +99 | .80 |
| NES cumulative surveys from 1996 through 2004: Percentage indicating that most people can not be trusted, so "you can't be too careful." | 58.0 | 50.5 | 4394 | +99 | 1.15 |
| NES cumulative surveys from 1996 through 2004: Percentage indicating that "most people would take advantage you if they got a chance." | 39.3 | 31.5 | 3950 | +99 | 1.25 |
| NES cumulative surveys from 2000 through 2004: Percentage indicating that people are "mostly just looking out for themselves." | 37.5 | 31.4 | 2021 | +99 | 1.19 |
| Several GSS surveys conducted in 1972 through 2006 (combined results): "Would you say that most of the time people ... are mostly just looking out for themselves?" (percentage "yes") | 47.0 | 39.0 | 20068 | +99 | 1.21 |
| GSS survey conducted in 2004: During the last 12 months how often did "other people take credit for [your] work or ideas"? (Percentage responding "often" or "sometimes") | 29.5 | 21.2 | 1142 | +99 | 1.39 |
| GSS 2004: During the last 12 months at work how often did people "put [you] down ..."? | 16.8 | 11.7 | 1144 | 99 | 1.44 |

*RP is relative proportion, which is the Democratic % divided by the Republican %.

> Someone who thinks the world is always cheating him is right. He is missing that wonderful feeling of trust in someone or something.

— Social Writer Eric Hoffer[23]

The link between trust and happiness has been described by researchers comparing the happiness of citizens of different countries. These findings were summarized by Economist Richard Layard in his book about happiness:

23 Eric Hoffer (attributed), "Brainyquote.Com."

As social beings, we want to trust each other. The average happiness in one country compared with another can be largely explained by six key factors ... [the first of which is] the proportion of people who say that other people can be trusted...[24]

Trust and happiness have also been linked to each other by studying the chemical, oxytocin (not to be confused with the addictive pain-killer, "oxycontin"). Scientists have observed that oxytocin seems to promote trust which, in turn, leads to happiness. As one neuroscientist put it: "So, oxytocin is not a happiness chemical, but a brain tool for building trust ... and we feel happiest in learning to trust each other."[25] From this we might speculate that Democrats are less happy because they are less trusting.

### Trust in a bottle?

In Nature Journal, it was reported that a Swiss-led research team produced "a potion that, when sniffed, makes people more likely to give their cash to someone to look after." The potion was tested by a Swiss-led research team on volunteers playing an investment game for real money. Of 29 subjects given the potion, 13 handed over all of their money during the "game." Of the 29 volunteers given a placebo, only 6 gave up their money.

What was the potion's magic ingredient? Oxytocin.[26]

## The Inability to Control One's Destiny

You got to control your own destiny. You got to keep writin' different stuff. Keep switchin' up and never do the same thin' too many times.

— Chris Tucker, American actor and comedian[27]

A GSS survey conducted in 2000 indicates that Democrats are less likely to feel that they have "a great deal" of "control over the way their lives turn out ..." (Figure 187, below). Although the results are for both men and women, most of the difference is attributable to men.

Let's analyze this "control" issue in much more detail. Common sense tells us that insecurities about control can be indirectly revealed, in the following forms:

- A general lack of optimism
- A belief that much of success in life is due to luck
- A belief that you need "connections" to get ahead in life
- A lack of confidence in one's own abilities and worth

24 Richard Layard, *Happiness: Lessons from a New Science* (New York: Penquin Press, 2005), 226.

25 Walter J. Freeman, "Happiness Doesn't Come in Bottles," *Journal of Consciousness Studies* 4 (May 24, 1996): 67-71.

26 Michael Hopkin, "Trust in a Bottle," in *Nature* (June 1, 2005), Retrieved October 6, 2007, from: http://www.nature.com/news/2005/050531/full/news050531-4.html.

27 Chris Tucker (attributed), "Brainyquote.Com."

*Figure 187. Do you have a "great deal" of "freedom of choice and control ... over the way your life turns out? (GSS survey conducted in 2000, based on 801 cases, with confidence level of 97%, and with a relative proportion of .80)*

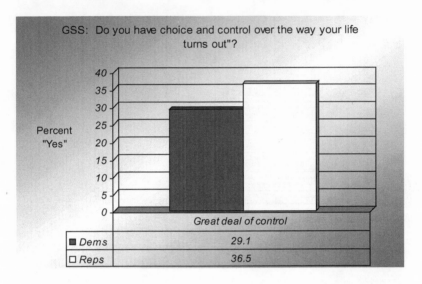

In aggregate, these traits and beliefs effectively constitute a sense of fatalism that could cause one to doubt his or her ability to control destiny. Survey evidence shows significant differences between Democrats and Republicans with regard to each of these four "control" factors, which are separately addressed below.

### A General Lack of Optimism Leads to a Lack of Control

> There's so much to enjoy, so much to learn, so much to experience. ... To sit around and be enmeshed in a whole bunch of suffering, self-imposed and self-created ... that's where the American left is. When you get in that cycle, there's nothing optimistic. ...
>
> — Rush Limbaugh, Author and radio talk show host[28]

Democratic men and women are less likely than Republicans to feel optimistic, according to GSS survey results. Some of these are displayed in Figure 188, below.

*Figure 188. I am not always optimistic about my future (GSS survey taken in 2004, based on, left to right, 670, 837, and 1507 cases, with confidence level of, left to right, 99+%, 98%, and 99+%, and with relative proportions of, left to right, 1.97, 1.46, and 1.68)*

---

28 Rush Limbaugh as cited in, "Rush Limbaugh Radio Show," (transcript: August 31, 2006), Retrieved September 1, 2006, from: http://www.rushlimbaugh.com.

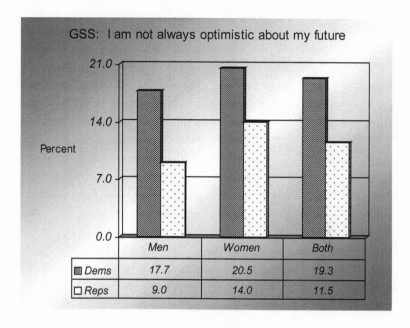

Other surveys showing an optimism gap are displayed in Table 46, below.

Table 46. Surveys addressing the issue of optimism

| Survey and Issue | Dems | Reps | No. of cases | Conf % | *RP |
|---|---|---|---|---|---|
| NES Pilot Survey, 2006: Percentage indicating they are "very optimistic" about their futures. | 36.8 | **52.3** | 240 | 97 | .70 |
| GSS survey conducted in 2004: Percentage indicating that "I hardly ever expect things to go my way." | **24.7** | 13.7 | 685 | +99 | 1.80 |
| GSS survey conducted in 2004: Percentage indicating that "I rarely count on good things happening to me." | **32.0** | 20.4 | 683 | +99 | 1.57 |

*RP is relative proportion, which is the Democratic % divided by the Republican %.

## Luck

Success is simply a matter of luck. Ask any failure.

— Earl Wilson, Major-league ball player[29]

29 Earl Wilson (attributed), "Thinkexist.Com."

The second control indicator is one's belief in the importance of luck. Democrats are much more likely than Republicans to ascribe success in life to chance, good fortune, and/or accident. By implication, some Democrats may be discounting the role that hard work, intelligence, and determination play in getting ahead.

Figure 189, below, shows the aggregate results of several Pew surveys conducted in 1987 through 2003, and these show a large difference between Democrats and Republicans with regard to attitudes about luck.

*Figure 189. Percentage agreeing that "success in life is pretty much determined by forces outside of our control" (Pew surveys conducted in 1987 through 2003, based on 14192 cases, with confidence level of 99+%, and with a relative proportion of 1.43)*

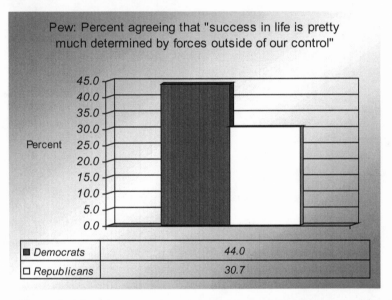

The results of similar survey questions are shown in Table 47, below. All of the surveys support the notion that Democrats are more likely to see their fortunes tied to luck (and bad luck at that).

*Table 47. Other surveys results related to the issue of luck*

| Survey and Issue (percentage agreeing) | Dems | Reps | No. of cases | Conf % | *RP |
|---|---|---|---|---|---|
| GSS — 2006: "The most important reason why people get ahead" is "lucky breaks and help from other people" | 26.5 | 10.3 | 416 | +99 | 2.57 |
| Pew 1987 through 2003 Combined Values Surveys: "Hard work offers little guarantee of success." | 38.2 | 27.4 | 16115 | +99 | 1.39 |

| | | | | | |
|---|---|---|---|---|---|
| GSS — 1996: "Most of my problems are due to bad breaks." (agree or not sure) | 31.3 | 16.2 | 901 | +99 | 1.93 |
| GSS — 1993: "How somebody's life turns out … it's just a matter of chance." | 23.7 | 15.9 | 1004 | +99 | 1.49 |

*RP is relative proportion, which is the Democratic % divided by the Republican %.

### "Connections"

Only in an election year ruled by fiction could a sissy who used Daddy's connections to escape Vietnam turn an actual war hero into a girlie-man

— Frank Rich, Columnist (referring to President Bush and Senator Kerry during the 2004 election campaign) [30]

There is a third reason why people may not feel in control of their destinies: The belief that "connections" are necessary for getting ahead in life. Democrats are more apt to feel it is "very important" or "essential" to "know the right people," has shown in Figure 190, below.

*Figure 190. Percentage indicating that "knowing the right people" is "very important" or "essential … for getting ahead in life." (combined results of GSS surveys conducted in 1987 and 2000, based on 1741 cases, with confidence level of 99+%, and with a relative proportion of 1.33)*

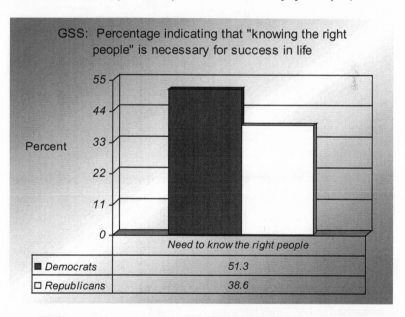

In addition, Democrats are more likely to believe that it is "very important" or "essential" to come from a wealthy background in order to succeed.

---

30 Frank Rich, "How Kerry Became a Girlie-Man," *New York Times*, September 5, 2004, 1.

*Figure 191. Percentage indicating that it is very important or essential to come "from a wealthy family" for "getting ahead in life" (combined results of GSS surveys conducted in 1987 and 2000, based on 1697 cases, with confidence level of 99+%, and with a relative proportion of 1.69)*

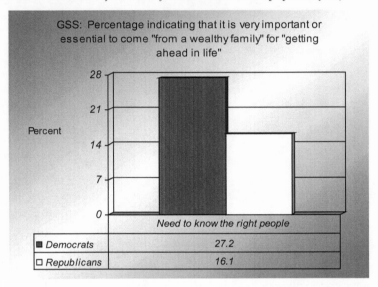

## Confidence In One's Own Abilities

No one can make you feel inferior without your consent. Never give it.

— Eleanor Roosevelt[31]

The fourth and final factor related to the issue of control may be a lack of self-confidence. Both male and female Democrats are less likely than Republicans to say they are satisfied with themselves. See Figure 192.

Democratic males, in particular, seem to suffer from a serious lack of self-assurance. See Table 48, below.

*Table 48. Surveys addressing the issue of self-esteem (Men only)*

| Survey and Issue (Men only) | Dem % | Rep % | No. of cases | Conf % | *RP |
|---|---|---|---|---|---|
| GSS survey conducted in 2004: "At times I think I am no good at all." (percentage agreeing) | 22.6 | 11.0 | 668 | +99 | 2.05 |
| GSS survey conducted in 2004: "I wish I could have more respect for myself." (percentage agreeing) | 27.8 | 21.4 | 667 | 95 | 1.30 |

*RP is relative proportion, which is the Democratic % divided by the Republican %.

---

31 Knowles, ed., *Oxford Dictionary of Twentieth Century Quotations*, 267.

---

*Figure 192. Do you agree with the statement, "On the whole I am satisfied with myself"? (GSS survey taken in 2004, based on survey of 670 Democrats and Republicans, with confidence levels of at least 99%, and with relative proportions of, left to right, 2.41, 1.79, and 2.06)*

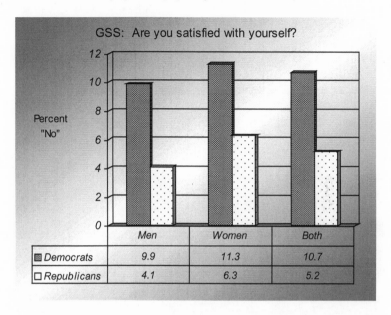

For all four reasons — the general lack of optimism, the feeling that life is heavily subject to luck, the belief that connections are needed to succeed in life, and the lack of self confidence — the average Democrat is more likely to feel that he can not control his own destiny. How does that relate to happiness?

Most psychologists believe that a feeling of control is an essential ingredient of happiness. Psychologist Daniel Gilbert put it this way:

> The fact is that human beings come into the world with a passion for control, they go out of the world the same way, and research suggests that if they lose their ability to control things at any point between their entrance and their exit, they become unhappy, helpless, hopeless, and depressed.[32]

### "Capitalism Is Unjust"

The Democratic Party has so successfully exploited class envy that people hold the wealthy and successful in contempt. The Democrats are breeding resentment. They have many people believing that anybody who is doing well is a cheater, a crook, selfish, and/or doing something unfair and unjust.

— Rush Limbaugh, Author and radio talk show host[33]

---

32 Daniel Gilbert, *Stumbling on Happiness* (New York: Alfred A. Knopf, 2006), 21.
33 Limbaugh, *See, I Told You So*, 16.

We have discussed two of the three elements related to my hypothesis of Democratic cynicism: lack of trust and feeling out of control. There may be a third factor: the belief that the American socio-economic system is unjust.

Democrats are much more likely than Republicans to see a society that is divided into "haves" and "have-nots." A Pew 2005 survey asked:

> Some people think of American society as divided into two groups, the "haves" and the "have-nots," while others think it is incorrect to think of America that way. Do you, yourself, think of America as divided into haves and have-nots, or don't you.

The survey results, shown in Figure 193, below, indicate that far more Democrats than Republicans see an America that comprises two distinct classes.

*Figure 193. "Do you, yourself, think of America as divided into haves and have-nots ...?" (Pew survey conducted in 2005, based on 708 cases, with confidence level of 99+%, and with a relative proportion of 2.71)*

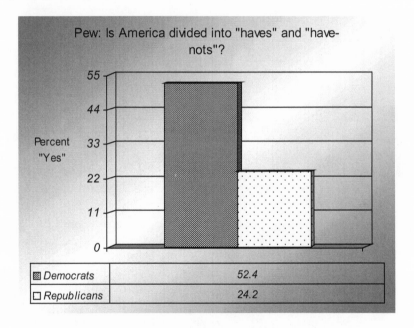

Today, under George W. Bush, there are two Americas, not one: One America that does the work, another that reaps the reward.

— Democratic Senator John Edwards[34]

In addition, Democrats are much more likely than Republicans to be concerned with the income gaps that occur in capitalist societies, and to believe that

---

34 Senator John Edwards, "Two Americas Speech Delivered in Des Moines, Iowa," December 29, 2003, Campaign Web site, from http://www.johnedwards2004.com/page.aspid?+481.

the government should reduce those disparities. A review of Figure 194 shows this to be true, even when we control for income level.[35]

*Figure 194. The "government in Washington ought to reduce the income differences between the rich and the poor ..." (several GSS surveys conducted in 1998 through 2004, based on, left to right, 768, 815, and 184 cases, with confidence level of at least 99% for all differences, and with relative proportions of, left to right, 1.77, 1.92, and 2.68)*

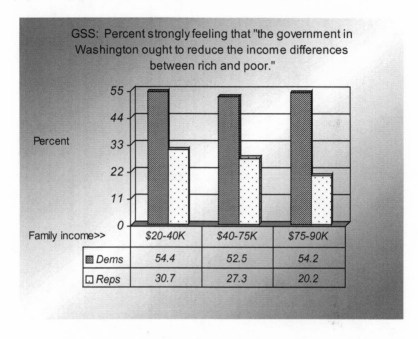

The left wants control. They want to decide the allocation of re-sources, instead of living with the mess made by capitalism and the open market, with its arbitrary and unfair winners and losers.

— Ben Stein and Phil DeMuth, *Can America Survive?* (New Beginnings Press, 2004)[36]

The Democratic dislike of income gaps has existed for many years, and persists despite a dramatic overall increase in per capita prosperity. This is evident from a review of Figure 195, below. Here, we see the percentages of Democrats and Republicans who indicated strong support for having the federal government reduce the income gap. Among Democrats the support is especially high, and reaches 60 percent in years 2002-2006 — despite the fact that per capita

---

35 People were asked to indicate the strength of their feelings on a scale of 1 to 7, with 1 meaning that they strongly believed that government should reduce differences between rich and poor, and 7 meaning that they did not. Figure 194 shows those assigning a 1, 2, or 3 to the issue.

36 Ben Stein and Phil DeMuth, *Can America Survive?* (Carlsbad: New Beginnings Press, 2004), 142.

income rose by 50 percent between 1977 (shown at the left side of the graph) and 2006 (shown at the right side).[37]

*Figure 195. Do you support the idea that the "government in Washington ought to reduce the income differences between the rich and the poor"? (GSS surveys conducted between 1977 and 2006, based on, left to right, 1339, 2855, 3840, 3053, 2162, and 2213 cases, with confidence level of 99+% for all differences, and with relative proportions of, left to right, .1.61, 1.66, 1.55, 1.94, 1.77, and 2.03)*

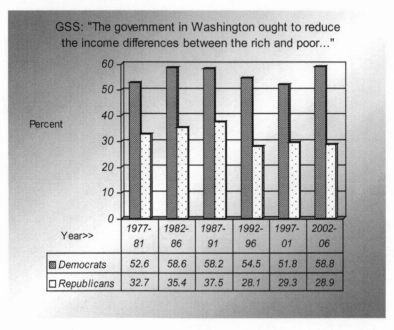

GSS: "The government in Washington ought to reduce the income differences between the rich and poor..."

| Year>> | 1977-81 | 1982-86 | 1987-91 | 1992-96 | 1997-01 | 2002-06 |
|---|---|---|---|---|---|---|
| Democrats | 52.6 | 58.6 | 58.2 | 54.5 | 51.8 | 58.8 |
| Republicans | 32.7 | 35.4 | 37.5 | 28.1 | 29.3 | 28.9 |

Pew identified a similar phenomenon in its report on happiness. It noted that, during recent decades, "average annual per capita income in this country has more than doubled in inflation adjusted dollars ... But in the aggregate, we're no happier." This led Pew to conclude that "What matters on the happiness front is not how much money you have, but whether you have more (or less) at any given time than everyone else."[38]

If the Democratic concern about income gaps is based solely on humanitarian, economic, or academic beliefs (and it often is, no doubt), it is not a "happiness" issue. However, if the concern relates to personal comparisons with the income of peers and colleagues (E.g., my neighbor earns more they I do, and it bothers me.), it can be a very significant problem, leading to unhappiness.

---

37 People were asked to indicate the strength of their feelings on a scale of 1 to 7, with 1 meaning that they strongly believed that government should reduce differences between rich and poor, and 7 meaning that they did not. Figure 195 shows those assigning a 1, 2, or 3 to the issue.

38 Pew, "Are We Happy Yet?," 4.

> What is a Communist? One who has yearnings for equal division
> of unequal earnings.
>
> — Ebenezer Elliot, English poet[39]

Excessive concern with the achievements of others can be destructive and
even pathological. Lyubomirsky observes that some "unhappy people actually
feel better if they do poorly on a test but someone else did worse than if they performed excellently but another person did better." This same phenomenon has
been observed in relation to income levels. Psychologists Hill and Buss describe
this tendency, which is known as "relative poverty:"

> People who earn $40,000 a year may be happy or sad. But they are
> far more likely to be satisfied with their income if their co-workers earn
> $35,000 than if they earned $60,000 a year (Frank, 1999). Individuals ap-
> pear to be satisfied with their incomes only if they are better off than those
> with whom they compare themselves. So pervasive is this effect that econo-
> mists have given it its own name. *Relative poverty* describes individuals who
> are not objectively poor, but feel poor compared to everyone else.[40]

Hill and Buss note that "relative poverty" can lead to "negative feelings,"
which interfere with happiness. Psychologists state that happy people are more
concerned with their own performance, and less concerned with how they "stack
up" to others. Psychologist Sonja Lyubomirsky notes: "Happy people don't rumi-
nate. They concentrate on inner personal standards. If they think much about a
better performance of another person, it is typically to learn something from it
to make themselves better."[41] Her advice: Avoid comparisons that can sap your
energy and happiness.

Like it or not, income gaps are inherent in the capitalist economic system.
Possibly, Democrats put their happiness at risk by focusing on "gaps" rather than
on the growth of their resources and accomplishments, in absolute terms.

> It's not enough to succeed. One's friends must fail.
>
> — Gore Vidal, American novelist[42]

## CONCLUSIONS

The evidence is overwhelming: Republicans are more likely to state that they
are very happy, and the Republican happiness advantage extends to work, finances, and various aspects of personal life. Republicans are also less depressed,
and less likely to let emotions negatively affect their lives.

---

39 Knowles, ed., *Oxford Dictionary of Quotations*, 298.

40 Sarah E. Hill and David M. Buss, "Envy and Positional Bias in the Evolutionary Psychology
of Management," *Managerial and Decision Economics* 27 (2006): 131-43.

41 Sonja Lyubomirsky cited by Bob Condor, "In Pursuit of Happiness," in *Chicago Tribune*
(December 9, 1998).

42 Gore Vidal as cited in, "Why You Think You'll Never Stack Up," ed. Carlin Flora (Psychology
Today, 2005).

Being Republican is associated with several "intervening variables" that are known to correlate with happiness. For example, being Republican correlates with higher income and the increased likelihood of marriage and good health — factors associated with happiness. No doubt, these variables explain a lot of the happiness gap; however, there is evidence suggesting that Republicans are significantly happier — even when all obvious correlating factors are controlled.

We considered an additional factor that may relate to Democratic unhappiness — what I term, "cynicism." Surveys indicate that Democrats are more cynical than Republicans in three ways: They tend to be less trusting of other people, they feel less control over their destinies, and they seem more concerned with the income disparities generally associated with the capitalist economic system. It was postulated that each of the three traits could contribute to the happiness disparity.

# CHAPTER 10: WHO GROWS UP TO BE A DEMOCRAT, AND WHO GROWS UP TO BE A REPUBLICAN?

## INTRODUCTION

*Crossing Over*

> I have gone from a Barry Goldwater Republican to a New Democrat, but I think my underlying values have remained pretty constant: individual responsibility and community.
>
> — Democratic Senator Hillary Clinton[1]

> I became a Republican to make come to life the ideals I had as a Democrat. I believe in equality and social justice. The key to justice and equality is for mom and dad to have a job.
>
> — Republican Senator Norm Coleman[2]

What causes a person to identify with a particular political party, or to change his allegiance from one party to another? In this chapter we examine some of the leading theories offered by political scientists, and identify the constituency that is more likely to change its "political stripes." We also compare and contrast the early childhoods of Democrats and Republicans, with particular focus on the parents who raised them. Some of the factors considered include childhood economics and happiness, and parental education, occupational prestige, and political viewpoints.

---

1 "Hillary Clinton's Education,"  Hillary Rodham Clinton Web page, Retrieved April 7, 2007, from http://www.hillary-rodham-clinton.org/education.html.

2 Senator Norm Coleman as quoted in, "GOP Senator Works to Rally Jewish Support for Bush," *Associated Press via Freerepublic.com* (June 13, 2003), Retrieved October 27, 2006, from http://www.freerepublic.com/focus/f-news/928866/posts.

The survey evidence suggests that the distinguishing values and character-istics of Democrats and Republicans, such as income levels, job prestige, educa-tional attainment, and marriage stability, were also discernable in their parents.

DETAILS

*How political viewpoints develop*

> Rush Limbaugh will "lose his fortune and become destitute. Forced on welfare, Rush will become a Democrat."

> — News reporter Eugene Emery, quoting a 1995 National Examiner prediction[3]

## As Children

Most children have already developed partisan inclinations. According to political scientist Donald R. Kinder:

> Children may be naïve and poorly informed when it comes to politics, but they are far from innocent. They express strong attachment to the na-tion. They think of themselves, proudly, as partisans of one party or the other. They believe that their country and its way of life are best.[4]

Political scientists state that the initial development of our political identi-ties is almost always tied to the political leanings of our parents.

> Though expressed partisanship is not always meaningful among the very young ... by adolescence, most children have a partisan identification connected to political preferences in the same manner as adults, though not always as strongly. Among those children who have a partisan preference, nearly all share it with their parents.[5]

This link between the political views of parents and children exists for two obvious reasons: Parents are usually the most salient initial influences on the development of their children and the "parent and child will often occupy simi-lar positions in the social structure and thus parental experience is likely to be relevant to the child's future adult life."[6]

> The first election campaign that I remember took place in 1956, with my mother patiently explaining that Adlai Stevenson de-

---

3 Eugene Emery, "Psychics Strikes out (Again) in 1995," December 1995, Committee for Skeptical Inquiry, Retrieved October 22, 2006, from http://www.csicop.org/articles/psy-chic-predictions/1995.html.

4 Donald R. Kinder, "Politics and the Life Cycle," *Science* 312 (June 30, 2006): 1905.

5 Christopher H. Achen, "Parental Socialization and Rational Party Identification," *Political Behavior* 24, no. 2 (June, 2002): 152.

6 Ibid.: 155.

served to be president because he was an intellectual and Ike was a dummy.

— Michael Medved, Author and radio talk show host[7]

Recently, a third and more controversial factor — genetics — has been offered to explain the correlation between the political perspectives of parents and children. Kinder summarizes the preliminary findings:

> A number of studies have compared the political views expressed by monozygotic twins (who share an identical genetic inheritance) to the views expressed by dizygotic twins (who develop from two separate eggs fertilized by two separate sperm). ... The results suggest that adult political beliefs — on the death penalty, say, or on school prayer — have a sizable genetic component.[8]

In one of those gene-related studies, researchers studied data pertaining to 8,000 sets of twins, including their opinions regarding 28 "political" issues. They concluded that, in each case, genetics appeared to be a statistically significant factor. This was particularly true with regard to views on property taxes and school prayer.[9]

### Why they became Democrats

> Not so many years back, I was a rather close-minded (is there another type?) conservative Republican. Then, the light came on, and I realized, "This is bulls***. Why did I buy into this philosophy all these years?" ... Every time they said they stood for a principle — they did the exact opposite.
>
> — Blogger Mark in LA

> I was a Republican until I got to New York and had to live on $18 a week. It was then that I became a Democrat.
>
> — The late Julia Child, Master Chef and author

> When I began to admit to myself that I had gay tendencies was when I became a Democrat ... My values could no longer align with a group of people that hated me openly.
>
> — Blogger JakeHalsted

> [I] became a Democrat because of this [George W. Bush] Administration and its preference for using military force.
>
> — General Wesley Clark

> Ronald Reagan ... is the primary reason why I became a Democrat. ... I never hated Reagan the man, but I did despise his policies. I never thought he was evil, but I did think he had a major mean streak.
>
> — Blogger Azael

---

7 Medved, *Right Turns*, 41.
8 Kinder, "Politics and the Life Cycle," 1905.
9 Erin O'Donnell, "Twigs Bent Left or Right," *Harvard Magazine* 108, no. 3 (Jan-Feb, 2006).

## As We Approach Adulthood

Although the correlation between the political views of parent and child can remain high for decades, there is usually some divergence beginning in late adolescent and early adulthood. There are at least three reasons for this: the impact of major world events, peer pressure during college years, and a "rational reevaluation" process based on the different needs and views of the child. Some of the major events that have shaped political viewpoints for decades are the Great Depression, World War II, Viet Nam, and the Civil Rights changes that have taken place since the 1960s.

> Vietnam radicalized me. It caused me to awaken.
>
> — Thom Hartmann, Air America radio talk show host, explaining how he changed from a Goldwater Republican to a liberal Democrat.[10]

The most significant of these events was probably the Great Depression, which led to the New Deal, Social Security, and decades of Democratic popularity.[11] Could an event such as the September 11th al Qaeda attack lead to a long-term change in the political landscape? It is doubtful, according to Radcliffe fellow J. Russell Muirhead:

> If an event impoverishes large numbers of the electorate, like the Great Depression, or slaughters large numbers of the electorate, like the Civil War, or introduces lots of new people into the electorate by enfranchising people who had previously been disenfranchised, like the Voting Rights Act, then the event has a lasting impact. Events that affect our moods or our passions may have consequences for policies, but those consequences last only as long as the mood. September 11 affected our mood, but it didn't change the demographic character of the country.[12]

Of course, Muirhead's conclusion is premised on the assumption that the 911 attack has simply created a bad "mood" that will eventually dissipate. If it turns out to be the first battle in a lengthy and costly war against Islamic radicalism, as assumed by many, the political implications could be far-reaching. This would be particularly true if the war necessitated the resumption of a military draft.

As noted, there are two additional factors that lead young adults to politically separate from their parents: peer pressure and "rational reevaluation." These factors were considered by political scientist Alan Abramowitz after he reviewed 521 interviews that had been conducted (in 1983) with undergraduate students at the State University of New York at Stony Brook. Abramowitz noted that "there was a much higher rate of political defection among students from Republican families than among students from Democratic families," and he attributed

---

10 "Thom Hartmann Brings Context to Today's Political Frays," February 7, 2006, Buzz Flash Political Web site, Retrieved October 27, 2006, from http://www.buzzflash.com/.
11 Kinder, "Politics and the Life Cycle," 1906.
12 J. Russell Muirhead as cited by Erin O'Donnell, "Twigs Bent Left or Right," *Harvard Magazine* 108, no. 3 (Jan-Feb, 2006).

the tendency, in part, to a liberal atmosphere at the school. He reasoned that the liberal environment produced a peer pressure that put Republican views on the defensive, and made it difficult for students to maintain allegiance to the GOP.

> At Bowling Green University, a Spanish language professor ... reserves a ritual ten minutes or 20 percent of his class time in every class . This time is devoted to what he calls a "political parenthesis," by which he means a class segment in which he allows himself to indulge in tirades against Republicans, George Bush, the war in Iraq, and conservatives generally.

— Author and political activist David Horowitz[13]

Abramowitz also concluded that some students simply found more relevance in the liberalism espoused by the Democratic Party. For such students, the move away from the Republican Party was attributable to a "rational reevaluation" of their personal needs, desires, and values. [14]

Given these findings by Abramowitz, you may assume that most young adults are less likely than their parents to identify with the Republican Party. However, this has not always been the case. By analyzing data from the American National Election Studies (NES) (as displayed in Appendix A) we see that young adults were least likely to support the GOP prior to 1985, but have been one of the most supportive age groups since that time.

*Figure 196. Party affiliation of different age groups for two time periods: 1952 through 1984, and 1985 through 2004. This information was derived from the NES survey results displayed in Appendix A.*

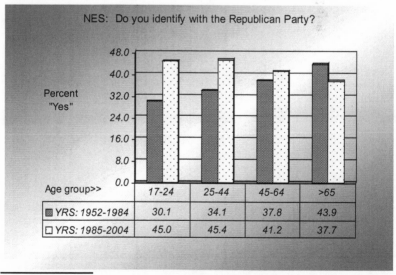

| Age group>> | 17-24 | 25-44 | 45-64 | >65 |
|---|---|---|---|---|
| ■ YRS: 1952-1984 | 30.1 | 34.1 | 37.8 | 43.9 |
| □ YRS: 1985-2004 | 45.0 | 45.4 | 41.2 | 37.7 |

13 David Horowitz, "Bowling Green Barbarians," *Students for Academic Freedom* (April 3, 2005), Retrieved September 14, 2007, from http://cms.studentsforacademicfreedom.org.

14 Alan I. Abramowitz, "Social Determinism, Rationality, and Partisanship among College Students," *Political Behavior* 5, no. 4 (1983): 353, 56-57.

Figure 196 ends with the year, 2004, and since that time, the Republican Party has not been doing well with young voters. A 2006 Pew Survey found:

> Young people today are much more likely to identify or lean Democratic rather than Republican, especially compared with the GenXers and late Baby Boomers who are in their 30s and 40s today. For example, among 18-24 year olds in Pew surveys over the past year and a half, fully 51 percent say they are Democrats ... [but] just 37 percent are Republicans or lean to the GOP.[15]

Thus, the future of the GOP is unclear.

> Young Americans have become so profoundly alienated from Republican ideals on issues including the war in Iraq, global warming, same-sex marriage and illegal immigration that their defections suggest a political setback that could haunt Republicans.

— Columnist Carla Marinucci[16]

## The "Strict Father" And "Nurturing Mother" Metaphors

An interesting explanation for the development of political beliefs has been offered by George Lakoff, a cognitive linguist. He believes that people frequently use metaphors to help them simplify and understand the complexities of life. In the case of politics the metaphors involve parental styles and values. More specifically, people see the nation as the parent and the citizen as the child. According to Lakoff, a Republican is more likely to believe that the nation should govern as a "strict father," who instills discipline in his child (citizen) in order to help her become a responsible adult who makes prudent financial and moral choices. On the other hand, a Democrat is more likely to see that nation as a "nurturing mother," who works to keep an essentially good child (citizen) away from harmful and corrupting factors such as discriminatory employers, greedy retailers, polluting industries, and social injustice. Expressed another way, Lakoff believes that, to a degree, Democrats and Republicans make political choices on the basis of their recollections and appreciation of the parent-child interactions that existed when they were growing up.[17]

> The father is always a Republican toward his son, and his mother's always a Democrat.

— Robert Frost, American poet[18]

---

15 Scott Keeter, "Politics and The "Dotnet" Generation"," *PewResearchCenter Publications* (May 30, 2006), Retrieved September 3, 2007, from http://pewresearch.org/pubs/27/politics-and-the-dotnet-generation.

16 Carla Marinucci, "Poll: Young Voters Disenchanted with Republican Party," *SFGate.com* (August 27, 2007), Retrieved September 3, 2007, from http://sfgate.com/cgi-bin/article.cgi?f=/c/a/2007/08/27/MNMIRNDUK.DTL&tsp=1.

17 George Lakoff. (1995), "Metaphor, Morality, and Politics, Or "Why Conservatives Have Left Liberals in the Dust"", Retrieved September 13, 2007, from George Lakoff: http://www.wwcd.org/issues/Lakoff.html.

18 Robert Frost (attributed), "Simpson's Contemporary Quotations," (Houghlin Mifflin Company, 1988).

## Reality check — Do we have it backwards?

Do our values determine our political identities, or do our political identities determine our values? A political scientist, Paul Goren, compared the stability of our partisan identities with the stability of our beliefs in four core principles: equal opportunity, limited government, traditional family values, and moral tolerance. In essence, he found that we are more likely to adhere to our partisan beliefs than to adhere to our values:

> [P]artisan identities are more stable and resistant to change than abstract beliefs about equal opportunity, limited government, traditional family values, and moral tolerance.... [P]arty identification systematically constrains beliefs about equal opportunity, limited government, and moral tolerance. This influence, while far from overwhelming, is substantively meaningful, and therefore, can produce genuine shifts in value preferences over extended periods of time.[19]

How does this happen? Citing other researchers, Goren states:

> Party identification 'raises a perceptual screen through which the individual tends to see what is favorable to his partisan orientation. The stronger the party bond, the more exaggerated the process of selection and perceptual distortion will be.' Hence, partisan bias 'plays a crucial role in perpetuating and reinforcing sharp differences in opinion between Democrats and Republicans.[20]

This makes sense. We have all seen Democrats and Republicans behave hypocritically — changing their positions when it serves the partisan interest.

### Changes Later In Life

After young adulthood, our political views continue to change, albeit at a slower pace. The changes may be triggered by the transitions we make from student to employee, from child to parent, from tenant to home owner, etc. Some assume that we change our political beliefs as we acquire wealth, but the evidence is murky. According to Harvard professor D. Sunshine Hillygus:

> Researchers have found that even though a lot of people vote on the basis of the economy, they're generally thinking of the economy of the country, rather than their own economic situation. They might think, "If the economy of the country improves, then that's going to have a trickle-down effect and improve my own economic situation." But to say, "I earn $200,000, and if I elect the Republicans, I might get a tax cut"? — that doesn't appear to be part of the decision-making process.[21]

---

19 Paul Goren, "Party Identification and Core Political Values," *American Journal of Political Science* 49, no. 4 (October 2005): 892.

20 Paul Goren citing Angus Campbell et al. and Larry Bartels in "Party Identification and Core Political Values," *American Journal of Political Science* 49, no. 4 (October 2005): 883.

21 D. Sunshine Hillygus as cited by Erin O'Donnell, "Twigs Bent Left or Right," *Harvard Magazine* 108, no. 3 (Jan-Feb, 2006).

Is aging generally accompanied by a move towards the left or right? Donald R. Kinder and other political scientists state that it is not,[22] but the survey data available to me indicate that, until now at least, it is much more likely that a Republican was once a Democrat than vice versa.

This fact is evident from the results of a 2005 PEW survey, shown in Figure 197, below.

*Figure 197. "Has there ever been a time when you have thought of yourself as" [a member of the opposing major political party]? (2005 PEW Political Typology Callback Survey, based on 784 cases, with confidence level of 99+%, and with a relative proportion of .52)*

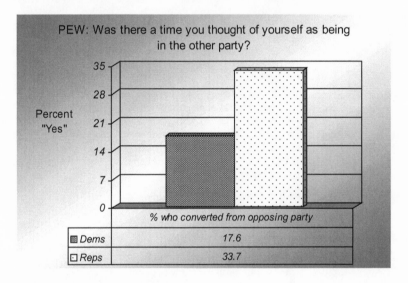

In addition, Republicans are a bit more likely, by 50.6 to 45.7 percent, to be former independents.[23]

> Yes, [I share blame for the recession] because for many years I was a Democrat.
>
> — President Ronald Reagan.[24]

This is not a short-term trend. From 1952 through 1980, the GSS asked respondents if they had always voted for the same political party, or had voted for a different party. The results of these surveys, by political orientation, are shown for 3 different decades in Figure 198, below. Although the results don't identify the "other party," it seems reasonable to assume that more Republicans used to vote as Democrats (the "other party") than vice versa.

---

22 Kinder, "Politics and the Life Cycle," 1906.

23 The results are based on 2005 PEW Political Typology Callback Survey of 603 cases, with overall statistical significance of 99+%.

24 Dan Rather, "Ronald Reagan, Master Storyteller," (CBS News, June 7, 2004), Retrieved April 7, 2007, from: http://www.cbsnews.com/stories/2004/06/07/48hours/main621459. shtml.

*Figure 198. "Have you always voted for the same party ...? (various NES Surveys conducted from 1952 through 1980, based on, left to right, 3899, 4408, and 4394 cases, with confidence level of 99+% for each column, and with relative proportions of, left to right, .86, .77, and .87)*

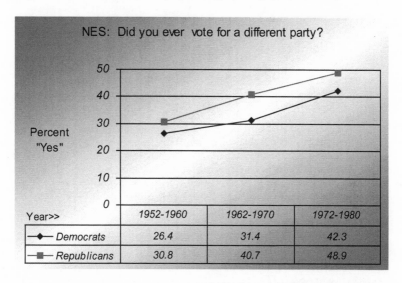

NES: Did you ever vote for a different party?

| Year>> | 1952-1960 | 1962-1970 | 1972-1980 |
|---|---|---|---|
| Democrats | 26.4 | 31.4 | 42.3 |
| Republicans | 30.8 | 40.7 | 48.9 |

Is the movement away from the Democratic Party attributable to the wisdom we acquire as we age (the likely Republican explanation), or because we become corrupted by wealth (the likely Democratic explanation)? More likely, it is due to the fact that, prior to 1985, a very high percentage of young adults started off as Democrats, so there was really only one directional change they could make. In addition, many southern Democrats became Republicans during the 1960s and 70s. Undoubtedly, that was also a factor.

### Why they became Republicans

As a small business owner, I remember coming home from work exhausted after a 10-plus-hour, hot-as-hell, July 1979 day at my then-struggling manufacturing business, arriving just in time for the 6:00 PM ... lecture from a stern-faced Jimmy Carter — the one where he told us that everything was our fault because we had a bad attitude. At that moment I became a Republican. — Joe Sherlock, Mechanical Engineer and consultant

I became a Republican when a very wise young lady asked me how I could remain a Democrat when I didn't agree with what they stood for and did agree with what the Republicans supported. — Republican Senator Jesse Helms[25]

[H]umphrey was talking about more government is the solution, protectionism, and everything he said about government involvement sounded to me more like Austrian Socialism. Then when I heard Nixon talk about it, he said open up the borders, the consumers should be represented there ul-

---

25 Senator Jesse Helms (attributed), "Brainyquote.Com."

timately and strengthen the military and get the government off our backs....
That's how I became a Republican. — Governor Arnold Schwarzenegger

> The more I listened to Rush [Limbaugh], the more he made sense to me.
> I can't say I agree with everything Rush says, but I love the way he frames
> an issue. I have been listening to him since '92 or '93, and the only "preach-
> ing" I remember was for self-reliance and the 3 "Fs" (Family, Friends, and
> Faith), as opposed to reliance on government! The logical extension of this
> is to defeat the Democrats, and this is how I became a Republican, thanks
> to Rush Limbaugh. — Blogger Chris Leavitt

> [M]y final and emotional break with my remaining Left-wing friends
> didn't come until the fall of Saigon and the bloody denouement in Cam-
> bodia. ... I felt that those of us who had participated in the anti-war move-
> ment had a moral obligation to admit that we had been profoundly wrong
> concerning the postwar future of Southeast Asia and the nature of the Viet-
> namese and Cambodian Communists. ... After that, it was as though a spell
> had been broken. I began to view things in a wholly different light. — Mi-
> chael Medved, Author and radio talk show host[26]

### The parents of Democrats and Republicans

> When you have a good mother and no father, God kind of sits in.
> It's not enough, but it helps.
>
> — Dick Gregory, Civil rights leader and comedian[27]

Some of the major sociological surveys have asked thousands of people questions regarding the education, occupations, and political leanings of their parents. When we analyze these data, we find that many of the differences between
today's Democrats and Republicans were the same differences that distinguished
their parents.

### Was Dad in the Home?

In Figure 15 on page 17, we saw that unmarried Democrats are more likely
to have children in the household. This tendency was also found in the previous
generation. In Figure 199, below, we see that more than one in every five Democrats surveyed in 1997 through 2006 was raised in a fatherless home.

The relatively high number of Democratic homes with absent fathers could
be a confirmation of Lakoff's "strict father" and "nurturing mother" metaphors,
discussed earlier. Is it possible that the absence of a father leaves children in
the more "nurturing" care of the mother, and that leads to a creation of a future
Democrat? In other words, does a fatherless home cause people to become Democrats? Or, is the fatherless home simply a reflection of the high value Democrats
place on independent conduct by women?

---

26 Michael Medved, *Second Thoughts: Former Radicals Look Back at the Sixties*, ed. Peter Collier and
David Horowitz, 1st ed. (Lanham: Madison Books, 1989).

27 Dick Gregory cited in, "God Bless the Children - Quotes from 18 Wisdom Speakers," *Essence
Magazine*, May, 1995.

*Figure 199. At age 16, father was absent from home (GSS surveys conducted in 1977 through 2006, based on, left to right, 8038 cases, 9932 cases, and 8506 cases, with confidence level of 99+% for all categories, and with relative proportions of, left to right, 1.39, 1.55, and 1.62)*

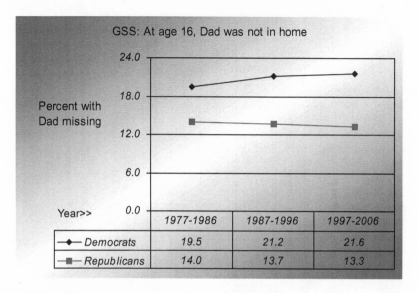

| GSS: At age 16, Dad was not in home | | | |
| --- | --- | --- | --- |
| Year>> | 1977-1986 | 1987-1996 | 1997-2006 |
| Democrats | 19.5 | 21.2 | 21.6 |
| Republicans | 14.0 | 13.7 | 13.3 |

*Figure 200. Did your parents have serious marital problems? Did they divorce before you were age 18? (1999 Michigan SOSS, based on, left to right, 622 and 637 cases, with confidence level of 99% and relative proportions of, left to right, 1.53 and 1.62)*

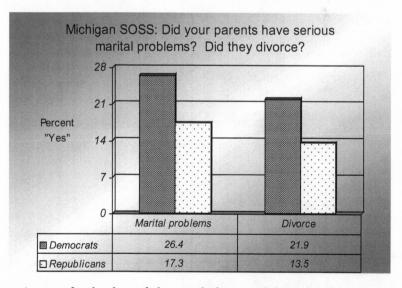

| Michigan SOSS: Did your parents have serious marital problems? Did they divorce? | | |
| --- | --- | --- |
| | Marital problems | Divorce |
| Democrats | 26.4 | 21.9 |
| Republicans | 17.3 | 13.5 |

A reason for the absent fathers might be marital discord or divorce. It appears, based on a 1999 Michigan State of the State (SOSS) survey, that the parents of Democrats are less likely to have had successful marriages (Figure 200). Of course, we saw this same tendency in the current generation of Democrats. (See Figure 11 on page 14.)

> My wife and I were happy for twenty years. — Then we met.
>
> — The late Rodney Dangerfield, Comedian[28]

### How Much Education Did The Parents Have?

The education gap we see in today's generation of Democrats and Republicans existed between their parents. Figure 201 shows the disparity and trend with respect to the fathers of Democrats and Republicans, based on results from the General Social Survey (GSS). The percentage with high school diplomas is compared.

*Figure 201. Did Dad have a high school diploma (or higher degree)? (GSS surveys, conducted from 1972 through 2006, based on, left to right, 3712, 2205, 4011, 4156, 3636, 2505, and 4147 cases, with confidence level of 99+% for all differences, and with relative proportions of, left to right, .62, .76, .69, .67, .80, .81, and .89)*

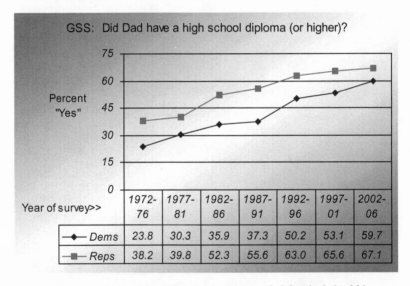

GSS: Did Dad have a high school diploma (or higher)?

| Year of survey>> | 1972-76 | 1977-81 | 1982-86 | 1987-91 | 1992-96 | 1997-01 | 2002-06 |
|---|---|---|---|---|---|---|---|
| Dems | 23.8 | 30.3 | 35.9 | 37.3 | 50.2 | 53.1 | 59.7 |
| Reps | 38.2 | 39.8 | 52.3 | 55.6 | 63.0 | 65.6 | 67.1 |

I've never been jealous. Not even when my dad finished the fifth grade a year before I did.

— Comedian Jeff Foxworthy[29]

Figure 202, below, shows the same information with respect to mothers. Again, there is a significant gap, with the mothers of Republicans likely to have more education. Interestingly, the mothers of both Democrats and Republicans were more likely to have high school diplomas than were the fathers.

---

28 Rodney Dangerfield (attributed), "The Quotations Page."
29 Jeff Foxworthy as cited in, *Squeaky Clean Comedy* (New Jersey: Andrews McMeel, 2005).

*Figure 202. Did Mom have a high school diploma (or higher degree)? (GSS surveys, conducted from 1972 through 2006, based on, left to right, 4125, 2512, 4643, 4724, 4214, 2943, and 4751, with confidence level of 99+% for all differences, and with relative proportions of, left to right, .72, .80, .70, .70, .80, .79, and .88)*

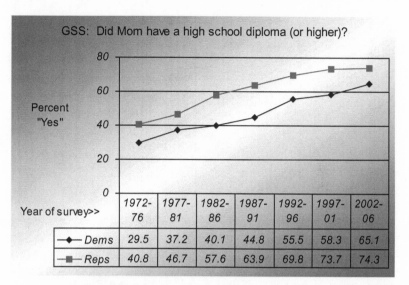

| Year of survey>> | 1972-76 | 1977-81 | 1982-86 | 1987-91 | 1992-96 | 1997-01 | 2002-06 |
|---|---|---|---|---|---|---|---|
| Dems | 29.5 | 37.2 | 40.1 | 44.8 | 55.5 | 58.3 | 65.1 |
| Reps | 40.8 | 46.7 | 57.6 | 63.9 | 69.8 | 73.7 | 74.3 |

## Employment Of The Parents

I grew up in a home where my father was a janitor. I'm used to having bills last till Friday when the paycheck only lasted till Thursday

— Gary Bauer, former Republican presidential aspirant[30]

Republicans are more likely to have dads who held management, professional, technical/sales jobs while they were growing up. In particular, the dads of Republicans are more likely to have worked in the areas of administration, personnel, training, labor relations, engineering, and sales. Democratic dads are more likely to have worked in farming and labor occupations as machine operators, assemblers, truck drivers, construction workers, and farm hands. In the service and trade craft occupations, the overall percentages are about equal. The major categories, and the percentages of Democratic and Republican dads who worked in each, are shown in Figure 203, below. (The service and trade craft occupations are not depicted due to a lack of confidence level.) Of course, these same occupational distinctions were found in the current generation of Democrats and Republicans.

*Figure 203. When you were growing up, what was Dad's occupation? (various GSS surveys conducted in 1988 through 2004, based on 12675 cases, with overall confidence level of 99+%, and a Phi association of .14 for the entire sequence)*

---

30 Gary Bauer, "Online Newshour," (Transcript: PBS, October 29, 1999), Retrieved September 4, 2006, from: http://www.pbs.org/newshour/bb/politics/gop_debate_10-29.html.

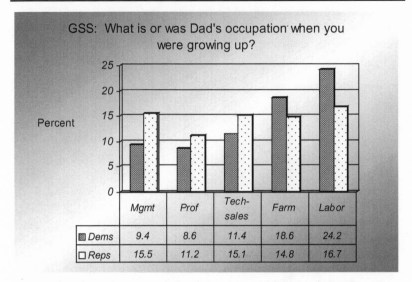

GSS: What is or was Dad's occupation when you were growing up?

| | Mgmt | Prof | Tech-sales | Farm | Labor |
|---|---|---|---|---|---|
| Dems | 9.4 | 8.6 | 11.4 | 18.6 | 24.2 |
| Reps | 15.5 | 11.2 | 15.1 | 14.8 | 16.7 |

With regard to working mothers, there are only 2 occupational categories with significant differences. The moms of Republicans are more likely to have worked in technical/sales jobs — particularly in the fields of bookkeeping and secretarial services. The mothers of Democrats are liable to have worked in the service sector — especially in nursing and cleaning jobs. The percentages of women who work in those two general fields is shown in Figure 204.

*Figure 204. What was Mom's occupation when you were growing up? (various GSS surveys conducted in 1988 through 2004, based on 5954 cases, with overall confidence level of 99+%, and a Phi association of .13 for the sequence)*

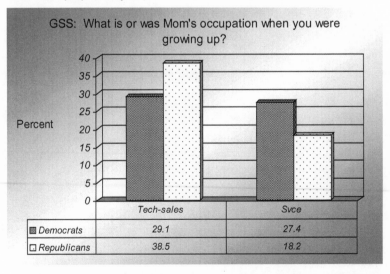

GSS: What is or was Mom's occupation when you were growing up?

| | Tech-sales | Svce |
|---|---|---|
| Democrats | 29.1 | 27.4 |
| Republicans | 38.5 | 18.2 |

I just knew then that I had been a lazy Democrat and I never looked back. I became a Republican.

— Winsome Earle Sears, Republican member of the Virginia House of Delegate, describing her reaction to the Dukakis presidential campaign[31]

Mothers of Democrats and Republicans are about equally likely to have been self-employed. For fathers, however, there is a small difference that is statistically significant. By 34.5 to 29.7 percent, the fathers of Republicans are a little more likely to have owned their own businesses.[32] This disparity has been fairly consistent over the last 30 years or more.

### Mom Worked With Preschooler

Some survey evidence suggests that the mothers of Democrats are more likely to have worked outside of the home before their children reached school age.

According to 4 GSS surveys taken in the early 1990s, Democrats are more likely to recall that, prior to beginning first grade, their mothers worked outside of the home.

*Figure 205. After I was born, and before I started 1st grade, Mom worked for at least 1 year outside of home. (4 GSS surveys, conducted in 1990 through 1994, based on 1903 cases, with confidence level of 99+%, and with a relative proportion of 1.22)*

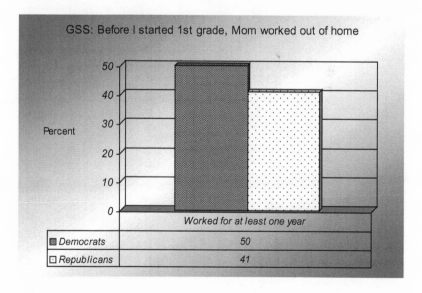

GSS: Before I started 1st grade, Mom worked out of home

| | Worked for at least one year |
|---|---|
| Democrats | 50 |
| Republicans | 41 |

---

31 John H. Fund, "A Winsome Politician," *Wall Street Journal*, November 8, 2001.

32 GSS surveys conducted between 1972 and 2004, based on 24,897 cases, with confidence level of 99+ percent and with a relative proportion of 1.16.

## Parents' Occupational "Prestige"

> Prestige is the shadow of money and power. Where these are, there it is.

— C. Wright Mills, American sociologist[33]

As noted in an earlier chapter, the National Opinion Research Center (NORC), a research organization based at the University of Chicago, developed a system for rating the "prestige" of various occupations. The scores, which range from a low of 17 to a high of 86, were averaged and summarized in a table of "prestige" scores.

GSS uses this rating system to assign a prestige score to the each of the oc-cupations identified in its surveys. Figure 206, below, shows the mean prestige scores for the dads of Democrats and Republicans. There has been a small, but significant difference since 1988, when the most recent index was developed. Like their children, the parents of Republicans generally had more prestigious jobs than their Democratic contemporaries.

*Figure 206. Average occupational prestige scores for the fathers of Democrats and Republicans (GSS surveys conducted in 1988 through 2004, based on, left to right, 4231, 4356, and 4088 cases, with confidence level of 99+%)*

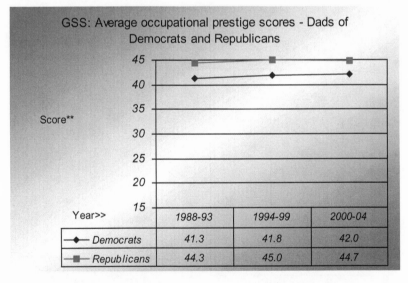

| Year>> | 1988-93 | 1994-99 | 2000-04 |
|---|---|---|---|
| ◆ Democrats | 41.3 | 41.8 | 42.0 |
| ■ Republicans | 44.3 | 45.0 | 44.7 |

**The minimum possible score is 17 and the maximum is 86.

In 1994, GSS began accumulating information regarding the occupations of the mothers of its respondents. In Figure 207 we see that the mothers of Repub-licans generally worked in slightly more prestigious jobs than did the mothers of Democrats.

---

33 C. Wright Mills (attributed), "Quotationz.Com."

*Figure 207. Average occupational prestige scores for the mothers of Democrats and Republicans (GSS surveys conducted in 1988 through 2004, based on, left to right, 2992 and 2962 cases, with confidence level of 99+%)*

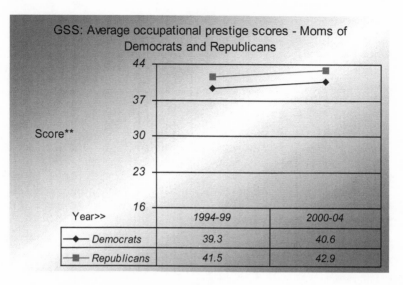

| Year>> | 1994-99 | 2000-04 |
|---|---|---|
| Democrats | 39.3 | 40.6 |
| Republicans | 41.5 | 42.9 |

\*\*The minimum possible score is 17 and the maximum is 86.

## Country of Birth

*Figure 208. "Were both your parents born in this country? (various NES surveys conducted in 1952 through 2004, based on, left to right, 1327, 2610, 6245, 6578, 6572, and 2877 cases, with no statistically significant difference for the 4 differences on the left, and significance of 99% for the 2 differences on the right side, and relative proportions of 1.24 and 1.38 for the 2 right-side differences)*

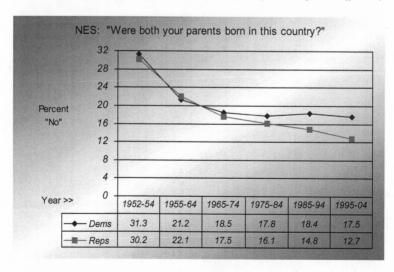

| Year >> | 1952-54 | 1955-64 | 1965-74 | 1975-84 | 1985-94 | 1995-04 |
|---|---|---|---|---|---|---|
| Dems | 31.3 | 21.2 | 18.5 | 17.8 | 18.4 | 17.5 |
| Reps | 30.2 | 22.1 | 17.5 | 16.1 | 14.8 | 12.7 |

It's unclear. And I've looked at this issue, I've talked to my parents about it, and it's just not clear.

— Former Attorney General Alberto Gonzales, describing the citizenship status of his grandparents[34]

It appears that Democrats are a little more likely to have parents who were born in a country other than the U.S. or Canada, as indicated in Figure 208. This disparity has developed during the last 20 to 30 years. Overall, however, there has been a sharp decline in foreign-born parents for constituents of either political party.

## Politics of the Parents

During a 40 year period from 1952 through 1992, NES queried respondents 11 times regarding the political leanings of their fathers. As can be seen in Figure 209, below, a minority of children changed from the party of their fathers; however, those who did were more likely to be Republicans than Democrats. The significance of this pattern is hard to assess. It may simply indicate that the Democratic Party was so popular during the depression and World War II era that most people's parents were Democrats.

*Figure 209. Democrats with Republican fathers, and Republicans with Democratic fathers (various NES surveys conducted in 1952 through 1992, based on, left to right, 2714, 2263, 4542, 2387, and 2774 cases, with a 99+% statistically significant difference for all differences, and with relative proportions of, left to right, .67, .51, .42, .40, and .37)*

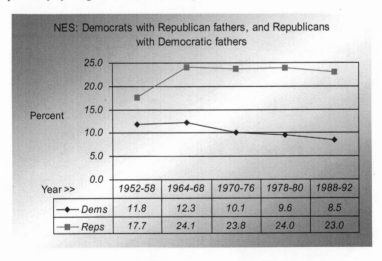

| Year >> | 1952-58 | 1964-68 | 1970-76 | 1978-80 | 1988-92 |
|---|---|---|---|---|---|
| Dems | 11.8 | 12.3 | 10.1 | 9.6 | 8.5 |
| Reps | 17.7 | 24.1 | 23.8 | 24.0 | 23.0 |

I will f---ing find you and I will f---ing hurt you.

— Tim Robbins, who was angry when a reporter wrote that his mother-in-law is a Republican[35]

34 Attorney General Alberto Gonzales, "The Situation Room with Wolf Blitzer," (Transcript: Newsmax.com, May 17, 2006), Retrieved October 27, 2006, from: http://www.newsmax.com/archives/ic/2006/5/17/91751.shtml.

35 Lloyd Grove, "Verbatim," *Washington Life Magazine* 2003.

A similar pattern is seen in a 1999 Pew survey, where 26 percent of Republicans had parents who were Democrats, and only 12 percent of Democrats had parents who were Republicans.[36]

> You have to have been a Republican to know how good it is to be a Democrat.
>
> — Former First Lady Jacqueline Kennedy Onassis[37]

Many sociologists believe that the mother has more influence on the child's eventual political orientation:

> [R]esearch performed in America, Jamaica and Japan shows that ... the mother is more effective in the child's political socialization. (Yesilorman, 2005)[38]

Nevertheless, survey evidence suggests that children are just as likely to shun the mother's political party as they are to shun their dad's political party. This is evident when one compares Figure 210, below, to Figure 209, above. The amounts and patterns are similar. Again, more recent data are unavailable.

*Figure 210. Democrats with Republican mothers, and Republicans with Democratic mothers (various surveys of the American National Election Studies conducted in 1952 through 1992, based on, left to right, 2714, 2263, 4543, 2387, and 2775 cases, with 99+% statistical significance for all differences, and with relative proportions of, left to right, .60, .60, .41, .38, and .36)*

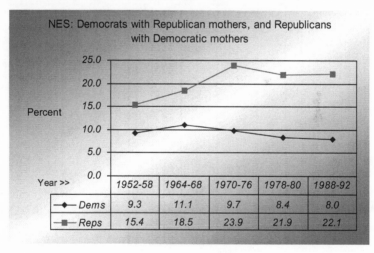

| Year >> | 1952-58 | 1964-68 | 1970-76 | 1978-80 | 1988-92 |
|---|---|---|---|---|---|
| Dems | 9.3 | 11.1 | 9.7 | 8.4 | 8.0 |
| Reps | 15.4 | 18.5 | 23.9 | 21.9 | 22.1 |

*Childhood life*

> The four stages of man are infancy, childhood, adolescence, and obsolescence.
>
> — Art Linkletter, TV performer and motivational speaker[39]

36 Pew July 1999 Typology survey, based upon 2301 cases.

37 "Why I Am a Democrat," San Diego County Democratic Party, Retrieved October 27, 2006, from http://www.sddemocrats.org/why_demo.html.

38 Mehtap Yesilorman, "Do Families Lose Their Political Efficacy or Not?," *Bilig*, no. 32 (Winter 2005): 110.

39 Knowles, ed., *Oxford Dictionary of Quotations*, 469.

### Siblings

So far, we have seen that tendencies in the current generation of Democrats and Republicans were also evident in the generation of their parents. Here is an exception. As noted in Figure 211, Democratic families used to be larger than Republican families — at least with respect to children. Today, however, Democrats and Republicans are averaging about the same number of children (See page 16 for information regarding the family size of the current generation of Democrats and Republicans.)

*Figure 211. How many brothers and sisters did you have when you were a child? (25 GSS surveys, conducted from 1972 through 2004, based on, left to right, 3013, 3834, 4045, 5276, 4853, 3459, 5062, and 29542 cases, with confidence level of 99+%)*

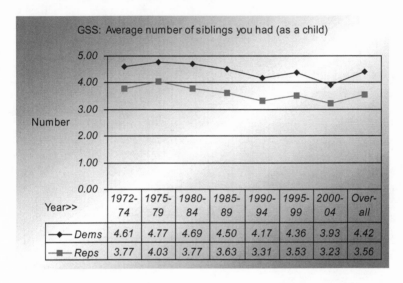

GSS: Average number of siblings you had (as a child)

| Year>> | 1972-74 | 1975-79 | 1980-84 | 1985-89 | 1990-94 | 1995-99 | 2000-04 | Over-all |
|---|---|---|---|---|---|---|---|---|
| Dems | 4.61 | 4.77 | 4.69 | 4.50 | 4.17 | 4.36 | 3.93 | 4.42 |
| Reps | 3.77 | 4.03 | 3.77 | 3.63 | 3.31 | 3.53 | 3.23 | 3.56 |

### Religious Life

As youngsters, Republicans were a bit more likely to be raised as Protestants (65% to 56%), while Democrats were more likely to be raised as Catholics and Jews (31% to 27% and 3.5% to 1%, respectively).[40]

### Family Income During Childhood

> My family got all over me because they said Bush is only for the rich people. Then I reminded them, "Hey, I'm rich."
>
> — Charles Barclay, Professional basketball star[41]

Income level is another attribute passed from one generation to another. Although approximately equal numbers of Democrats and Republicans recall having "average" income when they were aged 16 years (about 50%), Democrats are more likely to report sub-average income.

---

40 The results are based on GSS surveys in 1995-2004 of 8511 cases, with 99+% statistical significance for all differences, and relative proportions of 1.16, 1.15, and 3.5.
41 Charles Barkley (attributed), "Brainyquote.Com."

---

*Figure 212. "Thinking about the time when you were 16 years old, compared with American families in general then, would you say your family income was below average?" (various GSS surveys conducted in 1992 through 2004, based on, left to right, 7825, 9153, and 2718 cases, with confidence level of 99+% for each difference, and with relative proportions of, left to right, .1.38, 1.47, and 1.19)*

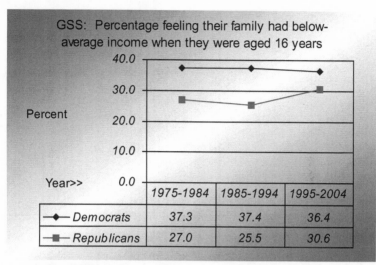

| Year>> | 1975-1984 | 1985-1994 | 1995-2004 |
|---|---|---|---|
| Democrats | 37.3 | 37.4 | 36.4 |
| Republicans | 27.0 | 25.5 | 30.6 |

Conversely, relatively few Democrats state that their family income (at age 16) was above average. The figures are shown in Figure 213, below.

*Figure 213. "Thinking about the time when you were 16 years old, compared with American families in general then, would you say your family income was above average?" (various GSS surveys conducted in 1992 through 2004, based on, left to right, 7825, 9153, and 2718 cases, with confidence level of 99+% for each difference, and with relative proportions of, left to right, .58, .61, and .71)*

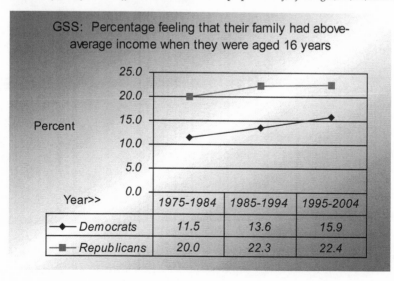

| Year>> | 1975-1984 | 1985-1994 | 1995-2004 |
|---|---|---|---|
| Democrats | 11.5 | 13.6 | 15.9 |
| Republicans | 20.0 | 22.3 | 22.4 |

### Where They Lived

> When I was a kid my parents moved a lot, but I always found them.
>
> — The late Rodney Dangerfield, Comedian[42]

Republicans are more likely to have moved from their childhood cities of residence. The reasons for this disparity are not clear. It is probably partly due to the higher college attendance rates among Republicans, which could have led to post-graduate relocations.

*Figure 214. "When you were 16 years old, were you living in this same city?" (combined results of 25 GSS surveys, conducted from 1972 through 2004, based, left to right, on 4731, 2801, 5122, 5164, 4700, 3279, 3467, and 29264 cases, with confidence level of 99+% in all cases, and with relative proportions of, left to right, 1.14, 1.06, 1.23, 1.17, 1.11, 1.13, 1.19, and 1.16)*

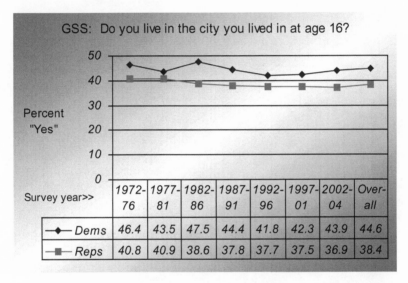

| GSS: Do you live in the city you lived in at age 16? | | | | | | | |
| --- | --- | --- | --- | --- | --- | --- | --- |
| Survey year>> | 1972-76 | 1977-81 | 1982-86 | 1987-91 | 1992-96 | 1997-01 | 2002-04 | Over-all |
| Dems | 46.4 | 43.5 | 47.5 | 44.4 | 41.8 | 42.3 | 43.9 | 44.6 |
| Reps | 40.8 | 40.9 | 38.6 | 37.8 | 37.7 | 37.5 | 36.9 | 38.4 |

Predictably, Democrats were, as 16-year-olds, more likely to live in the large cities, with populations of 250,000 or more. Democrats and Republicans were equally likely to live in small cities, and Republicans were a little more likely to live in towns, on farms, and in the country.

### Childhood Happiness

> Those who seek happiness miss it, and those who discuss it, lack it.
>
> — Holbrook Jackson, British journalist[43]

---

42 Dangerfield (attributed), "The Quotations Page."

43 Holbrook Jackson (attributed), "Happiness Quotes," (Josephson Institute of Ethics), Retrieved April 7, 2007, from: http://www.josephsoninstitute.org/quotes/quotehappiness.htm.

In response to a question on the 1992 Economic Values Survey, Republicans were slightly more likely to indicate that they had very happy childhoods.

*Figure 215. "Thinking back to your childhood, how happy were you then? Would you say very happy...?" (1992 Economic Values Survey, based on 1340 cases, with confidence level of 97%, and with a relative proportion of .89)*

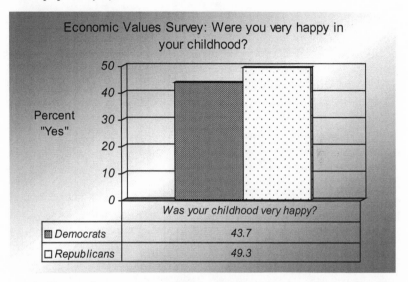

In addition, there is some evidence suggesting that, among young adults, Republicans tend to be happier than Democrats. A 2007 unpublished Northern Kentucky University study of about 60 students, aged 19 to 21 years, reported: "Our research is perhaps the first to show that the higher level of well-being of Republicans can be observed as early as the first few years of college."[44]

### Childhood Miscellaneous

*Table 49. Other*

| Question | Survey | Dem % "yes" | Rep % "yes" | No. of cases | Conf % | *RP |
|---|---|---|---|---|---|---|
| When you were a child, did you and your family have dinner together regularly? | Eagleton New Jersey Poll, 2004 | 77 | 89 | 469 | +99 | .87 |
| When you were a child, did you and your family have regular vacations together? | Eagleton New Jersey Poll, 2004 | 37 | 56 | 469 | +99 | .66 |

*RP is relative proportion, which is the Democratic % divided by the Republican %.

---

44 Alyssa Rowland and David E. Hogan, "A Comparison of Well-Being in Republicans, Democrats and Independents," (Northern Kentucky University, 2007).

## CONCLUSIONS

Most children have rudimentary political beliefs, loosely based upon the views of their parents. They have similar views because their parents are salient initial influences, and because they share common positions within the social structure. Some political scientists believe that genetics may also be a factor, based upon studies of identical twins.

As children approach young adulthood, a divergence of political perspectives often takes place due to the impact of major world events (such as the Great Depression or Viet Nam), peer pressure in college, and a "rational reevaluation" based upon the unique perspectives of the child versus the parent.

Until 1985, young adults were much less likely than other age groups to identify with the Republican Party. However, the opposite was the case between 1985 and 2004. More recent surveys (2006 and 2007) suggest that young people are avoiding the GOP once again.

Survey evidence suggests that Republicans are more likely to be ex-Democrats than vice versa. The reasons are not clear.

Many of the characteristics distinguishing the current generation of Democrats and Republicans were also evident in their childhood homes and among their parents. Republicans may be slightly more likely than Democrats to state that they had happy childhoods, that their fathers lived in the household, and that their mothers did not work outside of the home when they were young.[45] The parents of a Republican child are more likely to have been affluent and well-educated, and more likely to have avoided divorce or other marital discord.

Republican fathers are more likely than their Democratic counterparts to have worked in relatively "prestigious" occupations in professional, managerial, or technical fields. The mothers of Republicans are more likely to have worked in sales or technical jobs.

A change from the previous generation concerns family size. Whereas Democratic families used to have more children than Republican families, in recent years the number of children is likely to be about the same.

---

45 The survey regarding happiness was conducted in 1992, and may not be representative of the feelings of Democrats and Republicans of other eras.

# Chapter 11: Do Deviants Grow Up to be Republicans?

## Introduction

### Ruminative 3-year-olds

Remember the whiny, insecure kid in nursery school, the one who always thought everyone was out to get him, and was always running to the teacher with complaints? Chances are he grew up to be a conservative.

— Columnist Kurt Kleiner, commenting on report in Journal of Research into Personality.[1]

In 2006, some Berkeley psychology professors reported the results of a 20-year longitudinal study of 95 "conservatives" and "liberals," which commenced when the subjects were just 3 years old. Professor Jack Block and his associates concluded that the 3-year-olds who eventually became liberals were:

> ... resourceful and initializing, autonomous, proud of their blossoming accomplishments, confident and self-involving ... bright, competitive, and as having high standards [and exhibited] self-assertiveness, talkativeness, curiosity, openness in expressing negative feelings and in teasing ...[2]

On the other hand, the researchers judged the future conservatives to be:

> ... visibly deviant, feeling unworthy and therefore ready to feel guilty, easily offended, anxious when confronted by uncertainties, distrustful of others, ruminative, and rigidifying when under stress ... indecisive and vac-

---

[1] Kurt Kleiner, "How to Spot a Baby Conservative," *Toronto Star*, March 19, 2006.
[2] Jack Block and Jeanne H. Block, "Nursery School Personality and Political Orientation Two Decades Later," *Journal of Research in Personality* 40, no. 5 (2006): 6.

illating, easily victimized, inhibited, fearful, self-unrevealing, adult-seeking, shy, neat, compliant, [and] anxious when confronted by ambiguity ...[3]

It's worth noting that these kids were practically toddlers when they were assessed to have these psychological traits. At that young age, some of us had different priorities — such as talking and potty training.

What happened to the little kids when they became 23-year-old adults? In some respects, the liberal-conservative chasm grew even larger. Whereas the conservatives were "uncomfortable with uncertainty" and "emotionally bland," the liberals were judged to be "introspective, life contemplative, esthetically responsive ... vital, motivationally aware, perceptive, fluent," and god-like. (OK, I added the last trait.) In addition, the psychologists found that being liberal "correlates positively with intelligence," and the liberal men and women, at age 23, had significantly higher IQs.[4] Professor Block will not be asked to speak to the Heritage Foundation any time soon.

> The more they talk, the more being called a Liberal sounds like a compliment.
>
> — Douglas Giles, ProgressiveThought.net, 1997

### Why analyze the Berkeley study?

In this odd-ball chapter, which doesn't fit the format of any other, we simply analyze one academic study and its many defects. It may seem that we are straying from our topic since the academic study does not directly concern Democrats and Republicans. However, there are good reasons to go through this analytical exercise:

• It demonstrates why this book is based upon Democrat-Republican comparisons rather than the oft-used, but less meaningful, liberal-conservative paradigm.

• It shows that Democratic conservatives are the polar opposites of Republican conservatives. Democratic conservatives generally have the least amount of education, while Republican conservatives tend to have the most.

• It helps us reconcile the findings in this book (concerning Democrats and Republicans) to the dissimilar findings in the study (concerning liberals and conservatives).

• It reminds us to beware of academic studies that are light on data and heavy on interpretations, assumptions, and analysis.

If you've been reading this book in the normal order, you know that Republicans are just as (or more) politically well-informed, educated, happy, and successful in business and personal life as are Democrats. In addition, there are survey data suggesting that Republicans were, as adolescents, at least as happy Democrats, as adolescents. (See page 281.)

---

3 Ibid.: 8.
4 Ibid.: 9-10.

Why are the findings of this book in conflict with the Berkeley results? There are two reasons. First, generalities about liberals and conservatives are never fully applicable to Democrats and Republicans. Second, the Berkeley study was so severely flawed that its conclusions are not applicable, for any purpose and to any degree. The truth of these statements will become apparent as we diagnose each aspect of this classic example of academic "smoke and mirrors."

### Flawed research and reporting

> Experiments with laboratory rats have shown that, if one psychologist in the room laughs at something a rat does, all of the other psychologists in the room will laugh equally. Nobody wants to be left holding the joke.

— Garrison Keillor, American humorist and author[5]

The Berkeley study was flawed in regard to design, execution, and reporting:

1.  In part, the study relied on the self-identifications of the participating subjects. Self-identifications are fine when everyone agrees on the definitions used. However, for the liberal-conservative paradigm self-identifications are not useful because the terms "conservative" and "liberal" (as used in the United States) are vague and subjective, and convey different meanings to different people.

2.  Recognizing the problem identified in item 1, above, the Berkeley researchers supplemented the self-identifications with their own assessments of each participant's degree of liberalism and conservatism. That was a huge mistake that added circularity to the study. The final results of the study were preordained by the assessments made by the Berkeley crew.

3.  The study failed to recognize and report that it included a disproportionally high percentage of Democratic conservatives versus Republican conservatives. These two categories of conservatives are not interchangeable. In addition, the study incorrectly assumed a linear relationship between the personality traits of the participants and their degree of liberalism or conservatism. More likely, there is a U-shaped relationship. These mistakes led to false conclusions.

4.  Researcher bias may have skewed the jargon used to describe psychological and social traits of liberals and conservatives. In addition, important traits were selectively included in and excluded from the study's final summary, giving a false impression of study results.

A full discussion of each deficiency follows:

---

5 Garrison Keillor, *We Are Still Married: Stories and Letters* (New York: Penquin, 1990), Introduction.

## DETAILS OF A SERIOUSLY FLAWED STUDY

*The terms "liberal" and "conservative" are too vague.*

> Have the adjectives — and nouns — "liberal" and "conservative" become meaningless? Not quite. But almost. Inflation first weakened, then liquefied much of their meaning.

— John Lucas, Author[6]

In America few people vote for candidates of the Conservative Party or Liberal Party, so there are no widely-held, institution-related definitions of the terms. Unlike the terms "Democrat" and "Republican," we can't link the meanings of "liberal" and "conservative" to party platforms or political candidates (with rare exceptions). That forces us to use our own, individual definitions.

A huge number of Democrats describe themselves as "conservative." Figure 216, below, shows General Social Survey (GSS) results for Democrats. They were asked if they thought of themselves as liberal, moderate, or conservative. (The results for moderates are not shown.)

*Figure 216. Do you think of yourself as liberal or conservative? (Democrats surveyed by various GSS surveys conducted in 1972 through 2006, based on, left to right, 2952, 5112, 4417, 3170, and 15476 cases)*

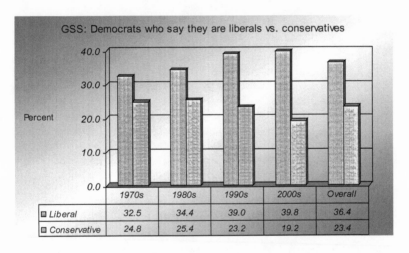

| | 1970s | 1980s | 1990s | 2000s | Overall |
|---|---|---|---|---|---|
| ▣ Liberal | 32.5 | 34.4 | 39.0 | 39.8 | 36.4 |
| ▣ Conservative | 24.8 | 25.4 | 23.2 | 19.2 | 23.4 |

In the "Overall" column, on the right side of the chart, we see that, during the last 30 years, for every 3 Democrats identifying as liberal there were about 2 who felt they were conservative. Do these Democrats really reflect the typical image of a conservative? Do they reflect your vision of a conservative?

---

6 John Lucas, "What Is Left? What Is Right? Does It Matter?," *The American Conservative* (August 28, 2006), Retrieved October 19, 2006, from http://www.amconmag.com/2006/2006_08_28/index1.html.

Before answering, consider a couple of surveys involving recent presidential elections. In 1988, NES asked Democrats to classify themselves as "liberal," "moderate," or "conservative." In that particular survey, more Democrats said they were conservative than liberal or moderate (45% conservative, 17% moderate, and 34% liberal). However, the overwhelming majority of Democrats (83%) said they would be voting for Michael Dukakis rather than George H. Bush. Of those describing themselves as conservative, 77 percent said they would be voting for Dukakis.

The same pattern held in 1996 with regard to the Clinton-Dole race. Far more Democrats claimed to be conservative than liberal or moderate, but nearly all Democrats (about 94%) said they would be voting for Clinton, rather than Dole. This included 96 percent of the Democrats claiming to be "conservative." These results are revealing because most people would probably say that Bush (the elder) was more conservative than Dukakis, and Dole was more "conservative" than Clinton.

> What is a "Conservative"...? It all depends on what you're conserving. A true revolutionary in a truly decent and humane society is almost surely going to be a fool, an ass, a tyrant, or, most likely, all three. A conservative in a truly evil regime is even more likely to be the same.

— Jonah Goldberg, Columnist[7]

This doesn't mean there is a "correct" definition or an "incorrect" definition of conservative, and it doesn't mean that a Democrat can't be one. Rather, it means that we each have our own definition, and this fact can undermine the validity of conclusions about self-identified conservatives. For example, a person might think of himself as conservative because he is easily embarrassed by nudity or likes old-fashioned movies. Yet, that same individual might believe in socialized medicine, unilateral disarmament, and redistribution of wealth via the tax code.[8]

The term "liberal" is also subject to varying interpretations. The proportion of Republicans saying they are liberal is shown in Figure 217, below. Although it is substantially less than the proportion of Democrats claiming to be conservative, it is significant.

*Figure 217. Do you think of yourself as liberal, moderate, or conservative? (Moderates are not shown.) (Republicans surveyed by various GSS surveys conducted from 1972 through 2006, based on, left to right, 1582, 3338, 3670, 2537, and 11127 cases)*

---

7 Goldberg, "What Is a 'Conservative'?."

8 Many Democrats see themselves as "conservatives," and many also regard their political leadership to be conservative. In a 1998-1999 Multi Investigator Study, 661 Democrats and Republicans were asked: "In general, thinking about the political parties in Washington, would you say Democrats are more conservative than Republicans, or Republicans are more conservative than Democrats?" By 52.4 to 47.6 percent, Democrats perceived the Democratic Party to be more conservative than the Republican party. Only 16.1 percent of Republicans shared that view.

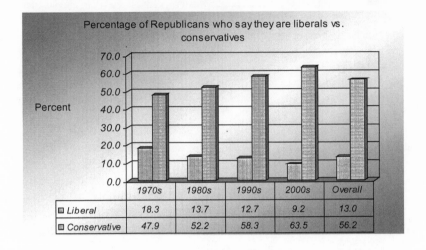

| | 1970s | 1980s | 1990s | 2000s | Overall |
|---|---|---|---|---|---|
| Liberal | 18.3 | 13.7 | 12.7 | 9.2 | 13.0 |
| Conservative | 47.9 | 52.2 | 58.3 | 63.5 | 56.2 |

We don't know why some Republicans think they are liberals. Perhaps they feel liberal because they are friendly, caring, flexible, and "people-oriented." Yet, those same Republicans might advocate repeal of the estate tax, welfare cuts, and an aggressive and militaristic foreign policy.

The bottom line is this: Although the terms "liberal" and "conservative" are a pervasive and indispensable part of our language, we must be cautious when making broad generalizations on the basis of those terms.

> [T]he terms conservative and liberal will continue to be used and misused as we, who doubt we are a part of either, stumble in the swamp, looking for a solid place to put our feet.
>
> — Nicholas von Hoffman, Newspaper columnist and author[9]

As discussed below, the Berkeley researchers tried to supplement the self-identifications with their own standardized definitions of "liberal" and "conservative." Unfortunately, this just made matters worse.

*Researcher assessments added circularity.*

Many sociologists, political scientists, and psychologists know that there is a problem with having people self-identify as liberals or conservatives, and the authors of the Berkeley study were not exceptions. Unfortunately, their attempt to remedy the problem made matters much worse.

Although participants in the Berkeley study were classified as liberals or conservatives based upon self-identifications, they were also classified by the researchers on the basis of their responses to standard measurement devices, such

---

9 Nicholas von Hoffman, "What Is Left? What Is Right? Does It Matter?," *The American Conservative* (August 28, 2006), Retrieved October 19, 2006, from http://www.amconmag.com/2006/2006_08_28/index1.html.

as the Kerlinger Liberalism Scale, the Kerlinger Conservatism Scale, and Mc-Closky's "Dimensions of Political Tolerance. By examining these measurement devices we can readily see the pitfalls inherent in their usage.

Kerlinger, for example, created lists of words or phrases designed to elicit positive or negative reactions, depending upon one's political ideology.[10] One Kerlinger phrase is "government price controls." Presumably, a liberal would re-spond positively to that phrase, and a conservative would not.

Another phrase is "law and order" — designed to get a positive reaction from conservatives. Some of the other Kerlinger words and phrases, used in the Berke-ley research, are shown in Table 50.

*Table 50. Phrases from Kerlinger's "Referent Scale" (REF-IX, 1984)*

| Kerlinger's exact word or phrase | Feeling positive about the phrase suggests you are a: |
| --- | --- |
| "Moral standards" | Conservative |
| "Social stability" | Conservative |
| "Authority" | Conservative |
| "Freedom" | Liberal |
| "Law and order" | Conservative |
| "Social Status" | Conservative |
| "Social Change" | Liberal |
| "Sexual freedom" | Liberal |

There is a problem with using such listings (as in Table 50): The ultimate conclusions about conservatives and liberals are pre-ordained at the moment participants are categorized by the researchers.

> Circularity: The reason I keep insisting that there was a relation-ship between Iraq and Saddam and al Qaeda [is] because there was a relationship between Iraq and al Qaeda.
>
> — President George W. Bush[11]

In Table 51, below, we see the same Kerlinger words and phrases used to classify subjects as being either liberal or conservative. However, there is an ad-ditional column showing some of the conclusions reached in the Berkeley study. Aren't they a surprise?!

---

10 Fred N. Kerlinger, *Liberalism and Conservatism* (New Jersey: Lawrence Erlbaum Associates, 1984).

11 David E. Sanger and Robin Toner, "Bush and Cheney Talk Strongly of Qaeda Links with Hussein," *The New York Times*, June 18 2004.

*Table 51. The connection between the Kerlinger phrases used to classify participants as "conservative" or "liberal," and the final conclusions of the Berkeley study*

| What goes in »»»» | | Dictates what comes out |
|---|---|---|
| If you liked this phrase ... | You were classified by Berkeley researchers as a: | Which led the researchers to this astonishing conclusion: |
| Moral standards | Conservative | A conservative: "Is moralistic and self-righteous;" "Judges self, others in conventional terms;" "Makes moral judgments" |
| Social stability | Conservative | A conservative: "Is uncomfortable with uncertainty" |
| Authority | Conservative | A conservative: "Is power oriented" |
| Freedom | Liberal | A liberal: "Tends to be rebellious, nonconforming" |
| Law and order | Conservative | A conservative: "Behaves in an ethically consistent manner" |
| Social Status | Conservative | A conservative: "Compares self to others" |
| Social Change | Liberal | A liberal: "Tends to be rebellious, nonconforming" |
| Sexual freedom | Liberal | A liberal: "Enjoys sensuous experiences" |

The conclusions shown on the right side of the table could be predicted by the words and phrases used in the classification process (left 2 columns of the table). For example, if we classify, as "conservative," participants who feel favorably about "Moral standards," we should not be surprised to find that these conservatives (as we just defined and selected them) tend to "make moral judgments." And, if we classify as conservative, those who feel positively towards "Social status," should we not expect to find that these conservatives (as we just defined and selected them) "compare [themselves] to others"? The study simply spits out the very same stereotypes put into it. The circularity of the process is illustrated in Figure 218, below.

In short, the use of these measurement devices added a large degree of circularity to the Berkeley study.

> If goodness is a defining attribute of God, then God cannot be used
> to define goodness. If we do so, we are guilty of circular reasoning.

— Minister Ray Cotton[12]

12 Ray Cotton, "Morality Apart from God: Is It Possible?," *Probe Ministries International* (1997), Retrieved November 30, 2007, from http://www.leaderu.com/orgs/probe/docs/god-ethi.html.

*Figure 218. The circularity inherent in the use of measurement "scales"*

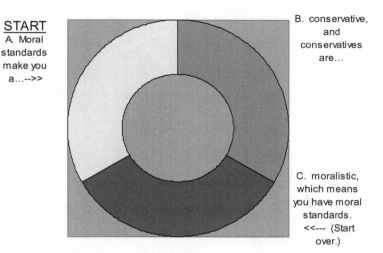

**START**
A. Moral
standards
make you
a...-->>

B. conservative,
and
conservatives
are...

C. moralistic,
which means
you have moral
standards.
<<--- (Start
over.)

*Reality check — What did the Professor say about this?*

Professor Block disagreed that the study suffered from definitional vague-ness. He told me that the tests administered to the 23-year-olds in the study were specifically designed by social scientists to measure "relatively liberal or relatively conservative inclinations." He also noted that the several indices used were standardized and averaged to produce an overall result that was more valid than any single indicator.[13]

Block also disagreed with the circularity criticism. He pointed out that it is important to distinguish between what one says about himself and the opin-ions formed by qualified assessors on the basis of various interactions with that person.

*Did Democrats make the conservatives look bad?*

### A Curious Pattern

In Chapter 2 there is a discussion of political ideology and its correlation with education level achieved. As noted, there is no clear association between political philosophy and educational level, in general; however, there is a curious pattern involving conservative Democrats and liberal Republicans. A chart from page 87 is reproduced below.

*Figure 219, replicating Figure 71: What is your "highest year of school completed"? (GSS sur-veys conducted in 1977 through 2006 of, left to right, 599, 2845, 2998, 8644, 4023, 4095, and 875*

13 Jack Block, e-mail letters to author, 2005 and 2006.

*cases, with confidence level of at least 99+% for all differences except the one designated "Slightly liberal," for which there is 95% confidence level)*

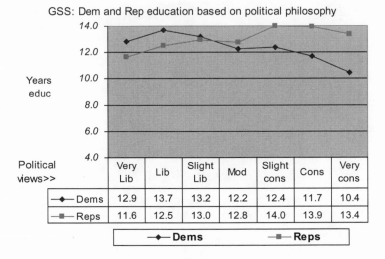

GSS: Dem and Rep education based on political philosophy

| Political views>> | Very Lib | Lib | Slight Lib | Mod | Slight cons | Cons | Very cons |
|---|---|---|---|---|---|---|---|
| —◆—Dems | 12.9 | 13.7 | 13.2 | 12.2 | 12.4 | 11.7 | 10.4 |
| —■—Reps | 11.6 | 12.5 | 13.0 | 12.8 | 14.0 | 13.9 | 13.4 |

| —◆—Dems | —■—Reps |
|---|---|

Look carefully at the chart and you will notice that liberal Democrats tend to have more education than liberal Republicans, while conservative Republicans tend to have more education than conservative Democrats. The gap on the conservative side of the graph (the right side) is particularly large. In fact, Republican conservatives have more education than any other segment, while Democratic conservatives have less education than any other segment.

> Seeing ignorance is the curse of God, Knowledge the wing wherewith we fly to heaven...
>
> — William Shakespeare, King Henry the Sixth, Act 4, Scene 7

The pattern shown above can be found in several other data sources pertaining to education and intelligence. In Figure 220, below, we see percentages of liberals and conservatives with high school diplomas. These ideological groups are further divided by party affiliation. On the left side of the graphic we see the percentages of liberals who have acquired high school diplomas (or higher degrees). Note that Democratic liberals are more educated than Republican liberals. On the right side of the chart, we see similar information for conservatives. We find that Republican conservatives are much more educated than Democratic conservatives. In fact, Democratic conservatives are only 73 percent as likely as the Republican conservatives to have a high school diploma (65.6/89.8 = 73%).

*Figure 220. Percentage of liberals and conservatives with at least a high school diploma, broken out by political party identification (GSS surveys conducted in 1977 through 2006, based on, left to right, 3443 and 4967 cases, with confidence level of at least 99%, and with relative proportions of, left to right, 1.08 and .73)*

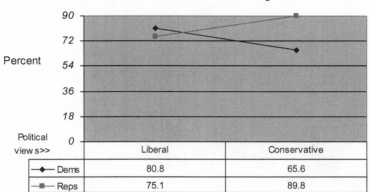

| Political views>> | Liberal | Conservative |
|---|---|---|
| ◆ Dems | 80.8 | 65.6 |
| ■ Reps | 75.1 | 89.8 |

Figure 221, below, also illustrates this phenomenon. We see one of the analytical questions first presented in Chapter 2. This time, however, the results are broken out by political ideology as well as party identification. Liberal Democrats and conservative Republicans were the most likely to correctly answer the question: "How are an egg and seed alike?"

*Figure 221. "How are an egg and seed alike?" (GSS survey conducted in 1994, based on. left to right, 243 and 384 cases, with confidence level of, left to right, 98% and 99+%, and with relative proportions of, left to right, 2.70 and .37)*

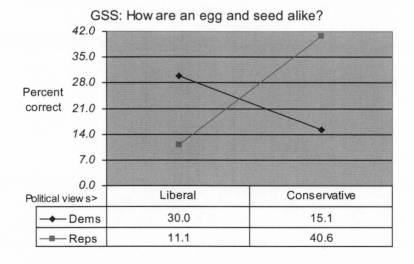

| Political views> | Liberal | Conservative |
|---|---|---|
| ◆ Dems | 30.0 | 15.1 |
| ■ Reps | 11.1 | 40.6 |

> A conservative is a man who sits and thinks, mostly sits.
> — President Woodrow Wilson[14]

A final and very compelling example of this phenomenon is offered. As noted in Chapter 2 (page 78), NES interviewers are usually asked to give an assessment of the "apparent intelligence" of each survey participant. In Figure 222, below, we see a summary of the assessments made in each of the surveys taken in 1996 through 2004. This graphic is limited to Democrats and Republicans who self-identified as "conservatives." (No liberals are included.)

*Figure 222. NES interviewer's assessment of apparent intelligence (NES surveys conducted in 1996 through 2004, based on. left to right, 411, 289, 590, 379, and 272 cases, with confidence level of 99+% for all differences, and with relative proportions of, left to right, .58, .51, .59, .70, and .51)*

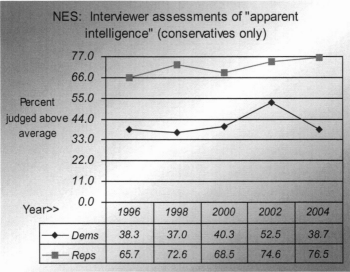

The differences are dramatic. A review of Figure 222 makes it clear that Democratic and Republican conservatives are as different as night and day. Most Republican conservatives were judged to have above-average intelligence, but only a minority of Democratic conservatives was given this rating. Because the "conservatives" analyzed in the Berkeley study all came from a Democratic community, the study's conclusions about conservatives are suspect.[15]

### A U-Shaped Relationship

> The swing voters — I like to refer to them as the idiot voters because they don't have set philosophical principles. You're either a liberal or you're a conservative if you have an IQ above a toaster.
>
> — Author and political activist Ann Coulter[16]

14 President Woodrow Wilson (attributed), "The Quotations Page."

15 A 2005 analysis of Berkeley faculty found a 10 to 1 ratio of registered Democrats to registered Republicans.

16 John Hawkins, "RWN's Favorite Ann Coulter Quotes," (Right Wing News, September 4, 2004), Retrieved April 6, 2007, from: http://www.rightwingnews.com/quotes/coulter.php.

In Figure 220, we compared liberal and conservative educational achievement, and we broke out the results by party affiliation. That chart is reproduced here (as Figure 223), with two changes: The educational achievements of political independents have been added, and the results are all shown on a single line (instead of two lines).

*Figure 223. Percentage of liberals and conservatives with at least a high school diploma, broken out by political party identification and political ideology (GSS surveys conducted in 1975 through 2004, based on, left to right, 2911, 1722, 532, 1523, 1775, and 3444 cases, with overall confidence level of the sequence of 99+%)*

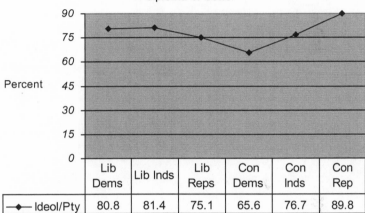

By putting all results on a single line, the "U-shaped" relationship is apparent. If we assume that the most ardent liberals are the Democratic liberals and the least ardent liberals are the Republican liberals, then it appears that education declines as the intensity of the liberal commitment declines. On the other hand, it seems that the level of education increases among those who are increasngly more conservative (i.e., as we move from conservative Democrats to conservative Republicans).[17]

The importance of the U-shaped relationship, shown in Figure 223, can not be overstated. If we didn't see the right side of the chart, we would almost surely reach a false conclusion. For example, if our sample contained only a "few participants tilting towards conservatism" (as was true with the Berkeley study), we would falsely conclude that people who are more conservative are likely to have less education. That conclusion would be ironic, since conservatives are likely to have the most education.

---

17 Credit for recognizing the potential significance of the U-shaped relationship must be given to Jim Lindgren, a law professor at Northwestern University. Posting on The Volokh Conspiracy (www.Volokh.com, March 23, 2006), Lindgren noted that the Berkeley study could be seriously flawed if the liberal-conservative continuum was not linear.

Indeed, this is probably what happened in the Berkeley study, which comprised two groups of unequal size: a huge group of liberals/moderates and a few people leaning towards conservatism.[18]

> To be conservative requires no brains whatsoever. Cabbages, cows and conifers are conservatives, and are so stupid they don't even know it. All that is basically required is acceptance of what exists.

— British journalist Colin Welch[19]

*Reality check — How do we know there were few or no conservatives?*

In their report, the Berkeley researchers concede that most of the 95 participants were either liberal or moderate, with "relatively few participants *tilting toward* conservatism" (emphasis added). And, in recent e-mail correspondence, Professor Block indicated that participants were simply rank-ordered along a liberal/conservative continuum. He added that the researchers did not "breakout" the participants into liberal or conservative categories, so he could not readily identify the number of conservatives who participated (assuming there were any). Given the expansive and controversial claims made by the Berkeley group, it is amazing that no effort was made (apparently) to ascertain that an adequate number of conservatives was included among the participants (or that *any* were included). It is possible that the continuum described by Block merely stretched from liberals to moderates, without extending to conservatives.[20]

In addition, Columnist Michelle Malkin reported, and Professor Block apparently confirmed, that many of the study participants were children of faculty and staff at UC at Berkeley – noted as a liberal university.[21] It seems highly doubtful that the 23-year-old child of a Berkeley professor would be wearing a George W. Bush campaign button.[22]

When the possibility of a U-shaped relationship was raised with Professor Block, he maintained that the analysis was linear; however, he also seemed to concede that he had not tested this belief, stating that the samples were "too small to have enough statistical power to test that U-shape hypothesis." Block

---

18 Block and Block, "Nursery School Personality and Political Orientation Two Decades Later," 4.

19 Colin Welch (attributed), "Columbia World of Quotations," (Columbia University Press, 1996).

20 Block's statements to me are in conflict with a statement he (allegedly) made to online columnist Justin Berton in April, 2006. When Berton asked Block if his conclusions were based upon the experiences of a handful of conservatives, Block responded "absolutely wrong." See *Growing up Right* by Justin Berton in the East Bay Express at http://www.eastbayexpress.com/news/growing_up_right/Content?oid=290796.

21 The Berkeley faculty have a ten to one ratio of Democrats to Republicans according to a voter registration study performed in 2005 by Daniel B. Klein, Associate professor of economics at Santa Clara University (http://lsb.scu.edu/~dklein/)

22 Credit for identifying the venue of the study, the small number of conservatives, and the likely impact of these facts on the study results must be given to Michelle Malkin ("Who are the Whiny Kids?," www.Michellemalkin.com, March 23, 2006).

pointed out that the analysis used "reliable observational data" - both when the subjects were in nursery school and when they were young adults. He also said that comparing the two sets of data produced surprising findings, "which many have over interpreted and apparently found threatening...."[23]

*Researcher bias*

## Skewed Descriptions

> Argument now masquerades as conversation. Spin, the political columnist E.J. Dionne wrote recently, "obliterates the distinction between persuasion and deception."
>
> — Malcolm Gladwell, The New Yorker, July 6, 1998

Is the glass half empty, or half full? It depends upon who is taking the drink. Similarly, the specific findings of the Berkeley study can be viewed as negative or positive, depending upon one's ideological perspective. Table 52, below, shows all of the Berkeley findings for conservative young men aged 23 years. The first finding is obvious, and adds no useful information. The other 7 findings seem to have negative connotations.[24]

*Table 52. Specific findings of the Berkeley study for conservative men*

| Specific findings for conservative men from the Berkeley study (Most have negative connotations.) |
|---|
| "Favors conservative values" |
| "Uncomfortable with uncertainty" |
| "Behaves in sex-typed manner" |
| "Judges self, others in conventional terms" |
| "Tends to proffer advice" |
| "Makes moral judgments" |
| "Compares self to others" |
| "Is power oriented" |

You will find the same 8 findings in Table 53, below; however, this time I have provided my own more positive "spin."

Conversely, the positive study findings for liberal men can be reworded to give them a negative "spin." For example, the finding that liberal men are "introspective, concerned w/self" can be recast as "self-centered." And, the finding that liberal men are "concerned w/philosophical problems" can be re-phrased to indicate that they get "bogged down with impractical considerations." This begs the question: Does the Berkeley study tell us anything at all about liberals

---

23 Block.

24 Block and Block, "Nursery School Personality and Political Orientation Two Decades Later," 9.

and conservatives? Or, does it simply tell us about the ideological biases of a few Berkeley researchers?

*Table 53. Specific findings of the Berkeley study for conservative men, compared to my "more positive" expressions*

| Specific findings for conservative men (verbatim from the Berkeley study) | My more positive expression for the finding |
|---|---|
| "Favors conservative values" | (No comment, since the finding is obvious) |
| "Uncomfortable with uncertainty" | Interested in resolving uncertainties |
| "Behaves in sex-typed manner" | Comfortable with sexual identity |
| "Judges self, others in conventional terms" | Uses established norms to make realistic judgments |
| "Tends to proffer advice" | Willing to give helpful advice |
| "Makes moral judgments" | Strives to be a moral person |
| "Compares self to others" | Displays healthy competitive spirit |
| "Is power oriented" | Respects authority |

## Skewed Summary

There is but one art, to omit.

— Robert Louis Stevenson, Scottish novelist and poet[25]

Notwithstanding, the Berkeley study did report a few positive findings with regard to conservative young women, and it offered a handful of negative findings pertaining to liberal women. For some reason, however, none of those findings made it to the final study summary. For example, the detail indicated that conservative women were "ethically consistent" and liberal women were "self-dramatizing, histrionic," yet those findings did not get into the study summaries. Here is the entire summary for liberal women. Where is the reference to "self-dramatizing, histrionic"?

> At age 23, relatively Liberal young women are assessed independently as: vital, motivationally aware, perceptive, fluent, bright, with extensive and esthetic interests, somewhat non-conforming.

Here is the entire summary for conservative women. Where is the reference to "ethically consistent"?

> Relatively Conservative young women were characterized as: conservative, uneasy with uncertainties, conventional, as sex-typed in their personal behavior and social perceptions, emotionally bland, appearing calm, and candid but also somewhat moralistic.[26]

---

25 Robert Louis Stevenson, *The Letters of Robert Louis Stevenson: Volume One, 1984- April 1874* (London: Yale University Press, 1994).

26 Block and Block, "Nursery School Personality and Political Orientation Two Decades Later," 9.

---

It seems that the researchers had a point to make, and didn't want any inconvenient findings to get in the way of that point.

> Personally, I don't like the terms "liberal" and "conservative." I find them simplistic and largely meaningless.

— Joseph Farah, Editor and CEO, World Net Daily[27]

## CONCLUSIONS

Making generalizations about "liberals" and "conservatives" is fraught with peril. Self-identifications are unreliable and misleading because each of us defines these terms differently. Further, classifying people in accordance with established definitional yardsticks leads to preordained, circular results. For these reasons, I believe that the Democrat-Republican paradigm leads to more meaningful comparisons.

In terms of education and intellectual ability, it appears that Republican liberals are quite different from Democratic liberals, with the Democrats generally being more successful. On the other hand, Republican conservatives tend to have far more education and intellectual ability than their Democratic complements.

The Berkeley study was probably doomed to failure because it overlooked the above factors. In addition:

1.  The researchers incorrectly assumed a linear relationship between the personality traits of the participants and their degree of liberalism or conservatism. In fact, there is probably a U-shaped relationship. In addition, the study's population comprised a large number of liberals and moderates, a small number of conservative "leaners," and few if any strongly conservative participants. These two factors — the U-shaped relationship and the small number of conservatives — probably led to false conclusions.

2.  There was "spin" in the jargon used to describe individual psychological/social factors. Neutral or positive traits were converted to negative traits by the choice of adjectives used.

3.  The study summaries excluded positive conservative traits and negative liberal traits. These omissions raise questions regarding the objectivity of the researchers involved in the study.

---

27 Joseph Farah, "Why Liberal Read More Books," *WorldNetDaily* (2007), Retrieved October 2, 2007, from http://www.worldnetdaily.com/news/article.asp?ARTICLE_ID=57290.

# CHAPTER 12: LESSONS TO BE LEARNED — IN MY OPINION

## INTRODUCTION

### *Lots of Little Differences*

Nothing is particularly hard if you divide it into small jobs. There
are no big problems; there are just a lot of little problems.

— Henry Ford, Industrialist[1]

I'd like to propose a corollary to those wise words of Henry Ford: There are
no big differences distinguishing Democrats from Republicans; there are just a
lot of little differences. But, little differences add up. Although it appears that the
average Republican is happier, more prosperous, and (arguably) more successful
than his Democratic complement; this is not necessarily due to a "big difference"
in lifestyles, abilities, or opportunities.[2] Rather, it may be (partly) attributable
to several small choices made differently by Democrats and Republicans. Some
of these are basic choices that are available to most Americans.

Of course, some people are victimized by forces beyond their control. For example, no woman decides to become a widow (with a few notable exceptions),
and people don't choose to be victimized by discrimination, disability, or illness.
However, it seems that the cumulative effect of decisions regarding marriage,
children, education, work, etc. critically affects the quality of life for Democrats
and Republicans, and their descendants. It may even account for their different
political philosophies.

---

1 Henry Ford (attributed), "The Quotations Page."
2 The argument for Republicans being "more successful" would be based on their attainment
   of higher educational levels, occupations with higher "prestige" scores and more supervisory responsibility, and lower incidents of marital discord and divorce.

In this chapter we revisit each of the preceding chapters to see what lessons can be learned. These are lessons that pertain to Democrats, Republicans, educators and legislators.

Finally, there have been few personal opinions in this book, heretofore (Chapter 9, "Happiness," being a major exception). The goal was to let the numbers "do the talking." However, the muzzle is now gone so be prepared for large doses of hypothesis, conjecture, and righteous opinion.

## DETAILS

*A lesson from Chapter 1: Delay having that first child*

> Clearly, preventing teen pregnancy is a highly effective and efficient way to reduce poverty and improve overall child and family well-being.
>
> — National Campaign to Prevent Teen and Unplanned Pregnancies

One of the most significant lifestyle differences between Democrats and Republicans is the age of procreation. On average, Democrats are about 13 months younger than Republicans when they start having children.[3] In addition, Democratic women are about 60 percent more likely than Republican women, and Democratic men are about twice as likely as Republican men, to have children during their teen years.

At the beginning of this chapter we discussed the many choices that are made differently by Democrats and Republicans — choices which can ultimately result in significant differences in happiness and prosperity. This is one of those choices.

Teenagers who have children put their own educations, careers, and financial futures at risk. In addition, they put their children at great risk. Studies show that those children are more likely to have health problems, to live in poverty, to be abused, to drop out of school, and get into trouble with the law.

Few people are forced to start having children at a young age, regardless of their income level or social standing. The Democratic Party, in particular, should directly help its constituents by forcefully delivering this message to them.

*A lesson from Chapter 2: Make civics education mandatory*

> As long as I live, I will never forget that day 21 years ago when I raised my hand and took the oath of citizenship.... I was so proud that I walked around with an American flag around my shoulders all day long.
>
> — Arnold Schwarzenegger, Actor and Republican Governor of California[4]

---

3 Considering Democratic and Republicans aged 50 years or less at the time of the surveys.

4 "Text of Arnold Schwarzenegger's Speech," in *Associated Press* (Boston.com, 2004), Retrieved August 31,, from: http://www.boston.com/news/politics/conventions/articles/2004/08/31/text_of_arnold_schwarzeneggers_speech/.

---

Many Democrats and Republicans are woefully ill-informed about government, current events and political matters. In Figure 224, below, we see the percentages of Democrats and Republicans who could not correctly answer simple questions about current events and government. In 2004 they were asked to name the terrorist group that attacked the United States on September 11, 2001 (al Qaeda). In 2006 they were asked to identify the Secretary of State (Condoleeza Rice), and in 2007 they were asked to identify the president of Russia (Vladimir Putin).

*Figure 224. Do you know the name of ... (Pew surveys. See Table 17.)*

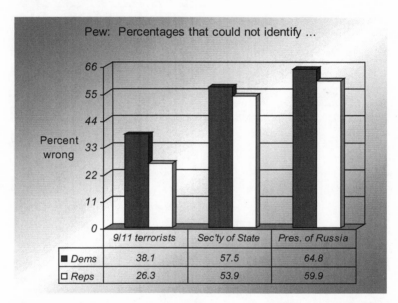

More than one-quarter of Republicans and nearly 40 percent of Democrats did not know the name of the 911 terrorist organization. Over half of Democrats and Republicans could not identify the Secretary of State, and nearly two thirds could not name the president of Russia. These figures suggest that many Americans do not feel it is their civic duty to be informed. Let's just hope that they don't' vote.

### Formal Education Hasn't Helped

Figure 225, below, is a replica of Figure 56. It shows that a woman today is 50 or 60 percent more likely to have a high school diploma than the woman of 50 year ago. A similar trend exists for men.

*Figure 225. Do you have (at least) a high school diploma? (Women) (NES surveys conducted in 1956 through 2004, based on, left to right, 3017, 3332, 3682, 3690, and 2667 cases, with confidence level of 99+% for all differences, and with relative proportions of, left to right, .82, .79, .84, .88, and .90)*

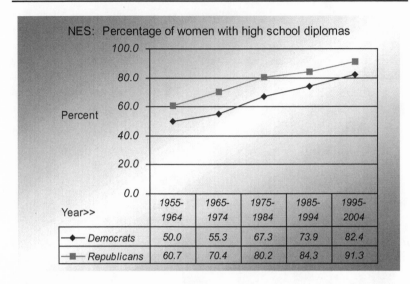

| NES: Percentage of women with high school diplomas | | | | | |
|---|---|---|---|---|---|
| Year>> | 1955-1964 | 1965-1974 | 1975-1984 | 1985-1994 | 1995-2004 |
| Democrats | 50.0 | 55.3 | 67.3 | 73.9 | 82.4 |
| Republicans | 60.7 | 70.4 | 80.2 | 84.3 | 91.3 |

Despite the dramatic increase in the percentage of people with high school diplomas, Democrats and Republicans have not improved their knowledge of civic affairs. For example, in Figure 226, below, we see the percentages of Democrats and Republicans (combined) who could correctly name the political party that held the House majority. In the 2000s, respondents were a little less likely to get the correct answer than in any other decade.

*Figure 226. Do you know who held the House majority prior to the most recent election? (Democrats and Republicans combined in several NES surveys conducted in 1952 through 2004, based on, left to right, 1382, 4281, 4603, 5616, 5529, and 2385 cases)*

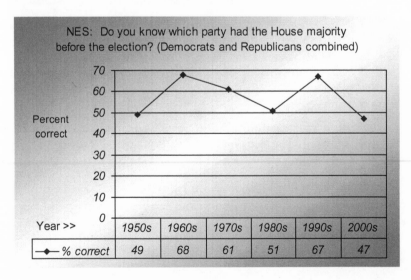

| NES: Do you know which party had the House majority before the election? (Democrats and Republicans combined) | | | | | |
|---|---|---|---|---|---|
| Year >> | 1950s | 1960s | 1970s | 1980s | 1990s | 2000s |
| % correct | 49 | 68 | 61 | 51 | 67 | 47 |

Detailed civics courses should be a mandatory part of the curricula of our nation's elementary and secondary schools, and our colleges. The objectives of such courses should be two-fold: to instill a sense of civic responsibility (to be informed, to vote, etc.), and to give students some of the basic facts needed to carryout those responsibilities. In addition to teaching about the Constitution, the structure of our government, the process of enacting laws, and the role of political parties, these courses should inform students about key societal systems related to the political processes. These include the role of the press and the workings of our economy. Many people are particularly confused by economic concepts. They toss around terms such as "corporations," "revenues," "profits," "write-offs," "loopholes," etc, but they don't know what those terms actually mean. A good citizen must know.

*A lesson from Chapter 3: Work is the key to success*

> In this country, you can succeed if you get educated and work hard. Period. Period.
>
> — Bill O'Reilly, Author and radio talk show host [5]

Between 1977 and 2006, the overall unemployment/laid off rate for Democratic males was 5.4 percent — twice as high as the 2.5 percent rate for Republican males. (See Table 24.) In addition, Democratic men were more likely to miss work due to vacation, illness, strikes, or "keeping house."[6]

The actual work gap was larger because, among men who were employed, Republicans put in 2.0 to 3.8 more hours of work per week (depending on the survey source used). There is a strong and direct correlation between hours worked and total earnings. Thus, the financial impact of the higher rate of employment and the extra hours worked by Republican men is huge. This accounts for much of the prosperity gap between Democrats and Republicans.

It is important for Democratic men to try to close this work gap. Let's assume that Democrats are just as motivated as Republicans in finding jobs, keeping jobs, and working longer hours. If that is the case, Democratic men must be less desirable workers in the eyes of their employers or potential employers. This could be the result of some form of discrimination in the workplace (race, ethic, or age-related), but it also relates, undoubtedly, to the much higher education drop-out rate among Democratic males. And, no employer can be blamed for that.

In Figure 227, below, we see that Democratic men are far less likely than Republican men to have a 4-year college degree.

Part of this gap could be attributable to the high cost of college education; however, there is also a significant gap with respect to high school education — the kind that is free everywhere in this country.

A difference in attitudes could also explain part of the employment gap between Democratic and Republican males. We know, intuitively, that attitudes

5 MediaMatters.org, *Misstating the State of the Union* (New York: Akashic Books, 2004).
6 The source is Table 24 on page 95.

can affect employment success. We also know, on the basis of surveys identified in the "Working Man" chapter (Chapter 3), that Republican men seem to
express attitudes that are more highly-valued by employers. They state that they
are more satisfied with their jobs, more proud of their employers, more willing
to help their employers succeed, and willing to take pay cuts and travel longer
distances to avoid losing their jobs.

*Figure 227. A replica of Figure 55 on page 72*

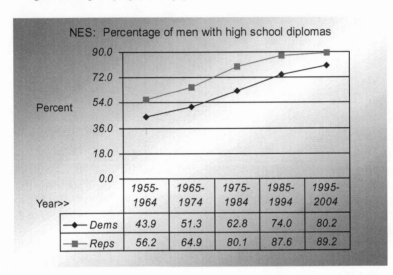

Adopting these attitudes and achieving higher education levels may be
two of the keys that Democratic males need to improve their employment
circumstances.

*Reality check — Is there another factor affecting employment?*

Are Republicans more willing to relocate in order to get a job? In Figure 214
on page 280 we saw that Republican men are significantly more likely to have
relocated from their childhood homes. Although there could be several reasons
for this (e.g., moving due to marriage or college attendance), one reason for the
relocation might be the pursuit of employment. This is mere speculation because
surveys asking about the reasons for relocation could not be located.

*A lesson from Chapter 4: Open the wallet*

> Charity should begin at home, but should not stay there.
>
> — Phillips Brooks, American clergyman[7]

Our federal, state and local governments have useful roles to play in solving many of society's problems. Nevertheless, it is not enough to simply wait for

7 Phillips Brooks (attributed), "Brainyquote.Com."

governmental action. Democrats should consider giving more time and money to charity. If they did, there would be tens of billions of additional dollars, each year, for the specific needs identified by Democrats.

Table 54, below, shows the bottom-line results from 5 of the surveys discussed in Chapter 4. Displayed are the donations made by the average Democrat and Republican who are within the same income bracket. In the right-side columns we see these amounts stated in 2007 amounts (using the change in the Consumer Price Index per the Bureau of Labor Statistics). The dollar difference, based on these 5 surveys, is $785.

*Table 54. The dollar-amount of donations made by Democrats and Republicans who are within the same income brackets*

| Survey and Date | Unadjusted $ | | 2007 $ | |
|---|---|---|---|---|
| | Dems | Reps | Dems | Reps |
| Michigan State of the State (SOSS) 2006 | 1186 | 2227 | 1233 | 2316 |
| Michigan State of the State (SOSS) 2005 | 1140 | 1963 | 1231 | 2120 |
| Michigan State of the State (SOSS) 2003 | 1513 | 2193 | 1725 | 2500 |
| Michigan State of the State (SOSS) 1999 | 942 | 1236 | 1187 | 1557 |
| General Social Survey 1996 | 805 | 1410 | 1079 | 1889 |
| Averages | | | $1291 | $2076 |
| Excess of Rep contributions | | | $785 | |

If each of the estimated 72 million registered Democrats matched Republican gifting rates by donating (on average) another $785 to charity every year, over $56 billion would be raised — each year — for goals and aspirations specifically selected by Democrats. That money could be used for minority lending programs, scholarships, urban renewal loans, research involving stem cells and AIDS, alternative energy sources, and global warming. What's more, the money would not be used to fund government budgets that don't coincide with Democratic objectives (e.g., military conflict spending?)

*A lesson from Chapter 5: Everyone should pay federal income tax*

> I'm proud to pay taxes in the United States; the only thing is, I could be just as proud for half the money.
>
> — The late Arthur Godfrey, TV and radio broadcaster[8]

The following opinion may shock you: Almost everyone in America — even those on welfare — should pay at least some federal income tax. This is essential

---

8 Arthur Godfrey (attributed), "Brainyquote.Com."

if we want people to care about the efficient and effective management of government programs. It is also basic human psychology: If you don't pay for something you don't pay attention to it, and you don't appreciate it. This is precisely why health insurance companies have learned to require that their customers pay, at the minimum, nominal "co-payments."

Important note: I am not advocating a reduction in aid to the poor — only a change in the way we give that aid. Welfare should not be distributed via tax reductions or by means of offsets to federal taxes, such as the Earned Income Tax Credit. Netting benefits against taxes only serves to confuse people about the true cost of federal programs, and the true cost of welfare assistance. It is better to give the full amount of aid directly to those who show need. They, in turn, should be asked to pay back some of those funds to help finance federal programs.[9]

In some cases, the federal income tax levied would have to be nominal, and in other cases we might have to accept the tax in the form of services rendered. This could be the case for unemployed taxpayers. Either way, however, taxpayers would gain a sense of civic concern and pride, and would become keenly interested in controlling government waste. And, here is a side benefit: If everyone paid income tax, everyone would get to participate in subsequent tax rate cuts. Perhaps this would put an end to the old mantra: "Tax cuts are only for the rich."

*Reality check — Don't the poor pay other types of taxes?*

Almost everyone pays some form of sales tax but it is generally used to fund state and local programs. Most workers pay FICA tax, but it is contributed in anticipation of a monthly cash retirement benefit. (And, the Medicare health insurance benefit will greatly exceed any Medicare taxes paid.) We may be overcharging the poor with regard to certain taxes, such as the excise taxes paid on gasoline and alcohol. (And, perhaps these taxes should be reduced.) Nevertheless, federal income taxes should be paid by all, so that everyone participates in the support of our national defense, federal courts, federal highways, disaster relief, EPA, health research, parks, etc.

*A lesson from Chapter 6: Clear up the confusion about free speech*

> It is a paradox that every dictator has climbed to power on the ladder of free speech. Immediately on attaining power each dictator has suppressed all free speech except his own.

— President Herbert Hoover[10]

Survey evidence suggests that Democrats are less tolerant than Republicans with respect to free speech by controversial figures. This may be due to moral

---

9 As a practical matter, the payment of taxes would probably have to be made (largely) via withholding from the welfare check.

10 As cited in Joslyn Pine, *Wit and Wisdom of the American Presidents: A Book of Quotations* (New Jersey: Courier Dover, 2000).

confusion regarding legitimate protest vs. suppression of so-called "hate speech." Columnist John Leo notes that, on many college campuses, free speech has almost become unacceptable. He explains that some college students and faculty feel that conservative ideas are so hateful and so dangerous that it is OK — and even necessary — to prevent those ideas from being expressed:

> Universities tell students they have a right not to be harassed by hostile speech. Well, sure. Nobody should be harassed. But the connection between harassment and speech is made so relentlessly on campus that many students think they have a right not to be offended. Real debate fades as ordinary argument is depicted as a form of assault.[11]

While it is perfectly acceptable, and possibly desirable to express views through protest, that protest should never become a vehicle for the stifling of free speech. This is a lesson that many Democrats, and Republicans, still need to learn.

*A lesson from Chapter 7: Restructure SS and Medicare benefits*

> Social Security is a government program with a constituency made up of the old, the near old and those who hope or fear to grow old. After 215 years of trying, we have finally discovered a special interest that includes 100 percent of the population. Now we can vote ourselves rich.
>
> — P.J. O'Rourke, American political satirist[12]

On the whole, Republicans are probably getting a slightly larger net benefit from Social Security and Medicare than are Democrats. In other words, for every dollar they put into Social Security or Medicare, Republicans get back a little bit more than do Democrats, in the form of benefits. This makes no sense because the Social Security and Medicare systems are supposed to have progressive benefit structures (favoring workers with lower wages), and the average Republican earns substantially more than the average Democrat. Dramatic reform of the core benefit structures of Social Security and Medicare is warranted.

The major problem has to do with spousal and survivor benefits, which tend to make the programs costly and regressive. This is illustrated in Figure 228, below, which compares the net benefits of a single man earning $50,000 to a married man (with a stay-at-home spouse) earning $95,000.

Remember, these are net benefits, and represent the excess of benefits received over payroll taxes paid. In this example, we have effectively taken about $30,000 from the middle-class worker while shifting $165,000 to the upper-class worker. This $195,000 differential is absurd and shameful, and it completely undermines the progressive nature of Social Security. It also explains why higher income Republicans tend to benefit more from Social Security than do Demo-

---

11 Leo, "Ivy League Therapy."
12 O'Rourke, *Parliament of Whores*, 220.

crats, even though the system is supposed to be progressive: Republicans are more likely to get marred and have stay-at-home spouses.

*Figure 228. Net Social Security benefits of a single man earning $50,000 vs. a married worker earning $95,000 (and having a stay-at-home spouse). This graphic, which is based on Figure 167 on page 208, shows that the system is regressively distributing wealth from the middle class worker to the relatively wealthy worker.*

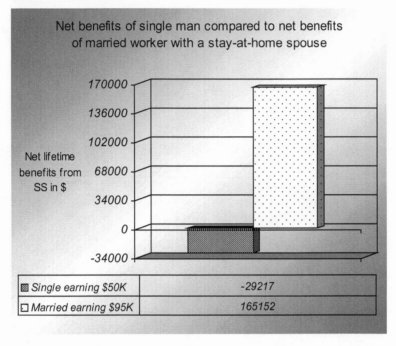

A similar illustration can be made with respect to Medicare. In Figure 229, below, we see that there are two problems with respect to the benefit structure: The net benefits are regressive and the net benefits are, for single and married people, far too high to be sustainable. Future generations are going to be stuck with dramatic increases to the payroll tax unless benefits (and the underlying medical costs) are contained.

The Bush administration may have erred, politically and substantively, by emphasizing private retirement account options while neglecting reform of the core Social Security benefit structure. Spousal and survivor benefits should be eliminated and replaced, in the case of low-income retirees, with an expanded Supplemental Security Income program (SSI). Alternative remedies might include reducing spousal and survivor benefits while increasing the benefits of single workers, or "means testing" spousal and survivor benefits so they are reduced or eliminated for retirees with relatively high incomes.

*Figure 229. Net Medicare benefits of a single working woman vs. a married worker with a stay-at-home spouse (based on Figure 170 on page 215). Note that the wealthier worker derives the greater net benefit.*

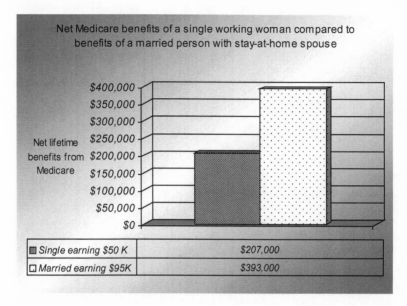

| | |
|---|---|
| ▦ *Single earning $50 K* | $207,000 |
| ☐ *Married earning $95K* | $393,000 |

*A lesson from Chapter 8 : All welfare is not the same*

> Welfare distorts behavior, makes one less personally responsible and reduces the role of private charity. This principle [also] applies to corporate welfare.

> — Larry Elder, Radio talk show host[13]

There is real welfare and there is "public policy" welfare, and it is important to know the difference. Real welfare is the support we give to people so they can eat, stay warm, and stay healthy. Public policy welfare is entirely different. If we give a moderate tax credit to an individual to encourage him to buy an experimental electric car (that he would not otherwise buy), we have not given welfare — provided the tax credit is appropriately designed. Rather, we have compensated someone for taking a risk in an effort to help preserve society's supply of energy.

The same is true with respect to corporate welfare. If we give federal loan guarantees to a business to keep it from closing its doors, that is probably real corporate welfare. On the other hand, if we give tax incentives to businesses that try out perilous new foreign markets or that take a chance on risky inner city investments, that is public policy welfare, designed (we hope) to further some national objective. In those instances, we are simply compensating the businesses for the extra risks and expenses they are undertaking.

---

13 Larry Elder (attributed), "Brainyquote.Com."

Real welfare is often essential — especially for individuals in need. There are also times when a government must encourage behaviors that are in the long-term interests of the nation. This is particularly true with respect to long-term endeavors such as pollution control, resource conservation, and the development of alternative energy supplies.

The line separating real welfare from public policy welfare can get pretty thin, but it is important to keep them separate, and to know when and where each type of "welfare" is appropriately used.

*A lesson from Chapter 9: Be a happy-go-lucky Republican*

> Maybe if I work hard enough at it I can learn to live like a Republican
> for the next few years, say "I got mine" and screw everyone else.

— Actor Alec Baldwin[14]

If Democrats want to lead happier lives, they should consider being more like Republicans. That's because many of the characteristics of Republicans are more likely to correlate with happiness. Some of these traits are included in Table 55, below.

*Table 55. A few of the "happiness" factors discussed in Chapter 9.*

| Row | More happy is being... | Less happy is being... |
|-----|------------------------|------------------------|
| 1 | Wealthier | Poorer |
| 2 | Well-educated | Poorly educated |
| 3 | Married | Single |
| 4 | Healthy | Unhealthy |
| 5 | Concerned with individual achievements | Concerned with social comparisons |
| 6 | Religious | Not religious |
| 7 | Trusting of others | Not trusting of others |

My "let them eat cake" advice may seem Pollyannaish, but further reflection may change your mind. Many of these factors are interrelated and achievable by almost anyone. For example, one of the keys to happiness is wealth (row 1), and one of the keys to building wealth is education (row 2) — itself a factor that correlates with happiness. As noted in Chapter 2, Democrats are significantly more likely to drop out of school before getting a high school diploma. It is likely that in most cases there is no good reason for dropping out of school — especially a free, public high school. That is simply a poor choice that can lead to a less happy life.

Marriage (row 3) is another factor that correlates with happiness and also relates to prosperity. Two people can generally live more inexpensively than one, so people who get married and stay married tend to become wealthier. Marriage

---

14 Ingrid Randoja, "Alec Baldwin," *NOW* 20, no. 16 (December 21-27, 2000).

is, of course, a choice that is available to almost everyone — regardless of socio-economic class.

Another factor relating to happiness is good health (row 4). No one can be guaranteed good health, but we can greatly improve our odds by not smoking tobacco and by not being overweight. Survey evidence indicates that Democrats are significantly more likely to smoke, and may be more overweight than Republicans. Although some may have addictions and metabolic disorders, important decisions regarding smoking and eating can be made by most or all of us.

Row 5 has to do with two different ways people measure their own achievements: by comparison with what they once had, or by comparison with what others have. Psychologists feel that happy people are more concerned with their own progress, while less happy people tend to compare what they have achieved to the accomplishments of others. Possibly, some of the concern regarding income gaps (as opposed to absolute income levels, which are generally increasing) may be hazardous to happiness. If the concern is academic or moral in nature, there should be no "happiness" issue. However, if the concern over income gaps involves personal comparisons, it may be very destructive.

The two factors in rows 6 and 7 are related to happiness and related to each other. Presumably, a person of religious faith is also a trusting person. Psychologists say that trust is a factor that correlates with happiness.

Finally, it should not be assumed that happiness is simply one of the end results of success: It can also be a means for achieving success. After reviewing 225 studies involving 275,000 people, Psychologist Sonja Lyubomirsky concluded:

> Our review provides strong support that happiness, in many cases, leads to successful outcomes, rather than merely following from them, and happy individuals are more likely than their less happy peers to have fulfilling marriages and relationships, high incomes, superior work performance, community involvement, robust health and even a long life.[15]

*A lesson from Chapter 10: Break the inter-generational cycle*

> Children who live in poverty tend to live in a continuous cycle passed on from one generation to the next.
>
> — United States Department of Agriculture[16]

Recently, there was an interesting article in the New York Times regarding the relative affluence of blacks in Queens, New York. It seems that black median incomes have surpassed white median incomes in Queens — something that has not happened in any other county of significant size in the country. How did it happen? One factor was the creation of two-parent black homes, largely by immigrants from the West Indies:

---

15 Sonja Lyubomirsky, "The Benefits of Frequent Positive Affect: Does Happiness Lead to Success?," *Psychological Bulletin* 131, no. 6 (December 2005).

16 "The Impact of Poverty on Learning: Implications for the Classroom," June 22, 2006, United States Department of Agriculture, Retrieved April 8, 2007, from http://www.csrees.usda.gov/nea/family/in_focus/communities_if_poverty.html.

> The gains among blacks in Queens, the city's quintessential middle-class borough, were driven largely by the growth of two-parent families and the successes of immigrants from the West Indies.... They're married-couple families living the American dream in southeast Queens....

> Immigrants helped propel the gains among blacks. The median income of foreign-born black households was $61,151, compared to $45,864 for American-born blacks. The disparity was even more pronounced among black married couple.[17]

The other factor leading to the Queens success story was the great respect and appreciation shown by black immigrants for the American educational system, and for the benefits it could afford. According to a Jamaican immigrant:

> When immigrants come here, they're not accustomed to social programs ... and when they see opportunities they had no access to — tuition or academic or practical training — they are God-sent, and they use those programs to build themselves and move forward.[18]

I would argue that the best part of this story was not even mentioned in the New York Times article: By pulling themselves up, the blacks of Queens have greatly improved the odds that their children will also lead happy, productive, and successful lives.

In Chapter 10 we saw that many of the differences between today's Democrats and Republicans also existed between their respective parents. For example, Democrats are more likely than Republicans to have marital problems, to raise children in 1-parent homes, to have less education, to work in less prestigious jobs, and to earn less income. Likewise, the parents of Democrats were more likely than the parents of Republicans to have the same tendencies.

Clearly, the choices made by one generation have good or bad consequences for the next generation. Even if we don't care about our own happiness and success (and most of us do), as parents we have an obligation to give our children every opportunity to move ahead into happy and successful lives.

Most of the black immigrants in Queens came to the United States recently — in the 80's and 90's. By making wise choices they have already greatly improved their lives, and have greatly improved the chances that their children will lead healthy, happy, and productive lives. As stated at the beginning of this chapter: "[T]he cumulative effect of decisions regarding marriage, children, education, work, etc. critically affects the quality of life for Democrats and Republicans, and their descendants."

---

17 Sam Roberts, "Black Income Surpass Whites in Queens,"
  *The New York Times*, October 1, 2006.
18 Ibid.

*A lesson from Chapter 11: Be careful with the terms "liberal" and "conservative"*

> In this era of a big-spending Republican administration, the differences between conservatives and liberals have shrunk so much, it's hard to tell who's who.

— John Stossel, Author and television commentator[19]

No one is born with an "L" or "C" stamped on his forehead, and few people (in the United States) actively campaign or vote for liberals or conservatives, or take other observable actions on their behalf. To determine who is a liberal and who is a conservative we usually rely on self-identifications, based upon varying individual definitions.

Unfortunately, people do not always say what they really believe, or even know what they really believe. With regard to liberalism and conservatism, everyone seems to have a unique definition. A person may feel conservative because he is prudish, wants lower taxes, opposes abortion, favors recitation of the Pledge of Allegiance in schools, wants to hunt with a shot gun, or because of some combination of the above. A person may feel liberal because he is a "people person," wants national health care, is opposed to war, wants the government to "stay out of the bedroom," or believes in a combination of those ideals.

In an attempt to clarify the definitions of liberal and conservative a researcher could be tempted to ignore self-classifications altogether, opting instead for standardized definitions. This only makes matters worse, however, by interjecting research bias and circularity into the process.

There is another problem with liberal vs. conservative comparisons: In terms of education and intellect, Democratic liberals differ starkly from Republican liberals, and the same is true for Democratic and Republican conservatives.

This author believes that more objective and meaningful comparisons can be made on the basis of political party identification. Please see Appendix E for more discussion of this matter.

---

19 John Stossel, "It's Hard to Tell a Conservative from a Liberal," *RealClearPolitics. com* (September 20, 2006), Retrieved April 8, 2007, from http://www.realclearpolitics.com/articles/2006/09/its_hard_to_tell_a_conservativ.html.

# Appendix A: Demographic Trends over 50 Years

## Part One: Relative Strength of Each Party in the Public

In this section you will find the percentages of the public and key demographic groups who identify as Democrats versus Republicans. Columns add to 100% because other groups, such as independents, are not included.

*In general*

*Figure 230. Party identification — (combined results of several surveys of the American National Election Studies (NES) conducted from 1952 through 2004, based on, left to right, 2168, 5421, 5701, 6201, 6592, and 4724 cases)*

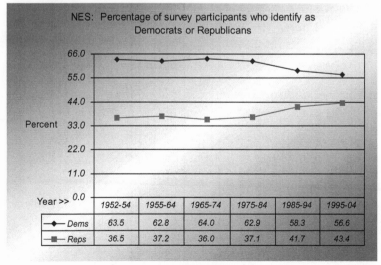

| Year >> | 1952-54 | 1955-64 | 1965-74 | 1975-84 | 1985-94 | 1995-04 |
|---------|---------|---------|---------|---------|---------|---------|
| Dems | 63.5 | 62.8 | 64.0 | 62.9 | 58.3 | 56.6 |
| Reps | 36.5 | 37.2 | 36.0 | 37.1 | 41.7 | 43.4 |

During the last 50 years, there has been a small increase in the percentage of the general public that identifies as Republican, as opposed to Democratic. However, there is still a large disparity, with Democrats having the advantage. Figure 230 ends with the year 2004. Since that time, the Democratic advantage has increased, with nearly 3 self-identified Democrats for every 2 self-identified Republicans, according to Pew surveys taken in early 2007.[1]

*Different age groups*

In Figure 231, below, we see that Democrats generally lost ground with the 17 to 24-year-old age group, until the 1985-94 decade. Since that time, however, it appears that a Democratic "rebound" has been taking place.

*Figure 231. Party identity over years, for the 17-24 age group — (combined results of several NES surveys conducted from 1952 through 2004, based on, left to right, 83, 236, 465, 641, 557, and 314 cases)*

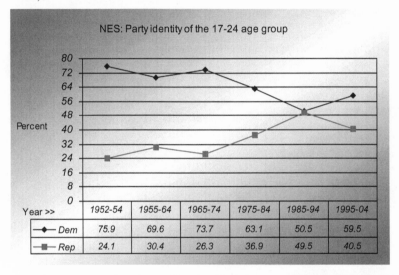

With respect to the 25- to 44-year-old age group, shown in Figure 232, below, the trend has been steadily to the benefit of Republicans. The gains of Republicans with regard to this group exceed the gains of Republicans with respect to the population in general.

*Figure 232. Party identity over years, for the 25-44 age group — (combined results of several NES surveys conducted from 1952 through 2004, based on, left to right, 620, 2333, 1974, 2358, 2860, and 1809 cases)*

---

1 "Trends in Political Values and Core Attitudes: 1987-2007," *Pew Research Center Survey Reports* (March 22, 2007), Retrieved October 27, 2007, from http://people-press.org/reports/pdf/312.pdf.

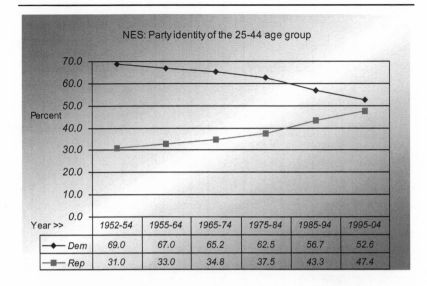

Figure 233 shows the age 45 to 64 year-old-age bracket, where Democrats have maintained a sizable advantage. This includes the all-important "baby boomer" group, which is represented within the 1995-04 column, on the right side of the chart.

*Figure 233. Party identity over years, for the 45-64 age group — (combined results of several NES surveys conducted from 1952 through 2004, based on, left to right, 426, 1950, 2067, 1891, 1714, and 1631 cases)*

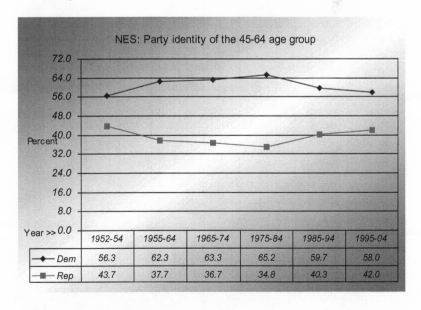

Republicans once had parity with Democrats with respect to the people aged over 65 years. That was in the days of Dwight D. Eisenhower. Since then, Democrats have gained among senior citizens, despite the overall population shift in favor of Republicans (shown in Figure 230). This age group is shown in Figure 234.

*Figure 234. Party identity over years, for the over 65 age group — (combined results of several NES surveys conducted from 1952 through 2004, based on, left to right, 176, 880, 1155, 1278, 1458, and 952 cases)*

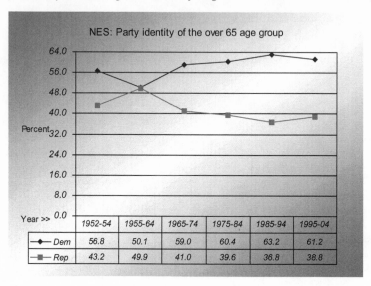

| Year >> | 1952-54 | 1955-64 | 1965-74 | 1975-84 | 1985-94 | 1995-04 |
|---|---|---|---|---|---|---|
| Dem | 56.8 | 50.1 | 59.0 | 60.4 | 63.2 | 61.2 |
| Rep | 43.2 | 49.9 | 41.0 | 39.6 | 36.8 | 38.8 |

*Each gender*

*Figure 235. Percentages of Men who identify as Democrats or Republicans (several NES surveys conducted in 1952 through 2004, based on, left to right, 989, 2386, 2357, 2507, 2841, and 2047 cases)*

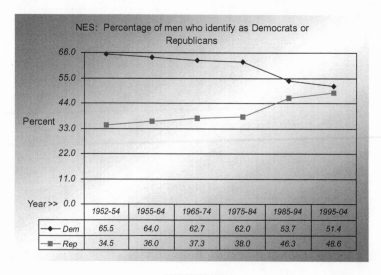

| Year >> | 1952-54 | 1955-64 | 1965-74 | 1975-84 | 1985-94 | 1995-04 |
|---|---|---|---|---|---|---|
| Dem | 65.5 | 64.0 | 62.7 | 62.0 | 53.7 | 51.4 |
| Rep | 34.5 | 36.0 | 37.3 | 38.0 | 46.3 | 48.6 |

Republicans have had steady increases among men for at least 50 years. These gains, which exceed the gains of Republicans in the general population, are shown in Figure 235, above.

With regard to women there has been a gender gap for a long time. It reached its peak during the Viet Nam and feminist days of the late '60s and early '70s.

*Figure 236. Percentages of women who identify as Democrats or Republicans (several NES surveys conducted in 1952 through 2004, based on, left to right, 1179, 3035, 3344, 3694, 3751, and 2677 cases)*

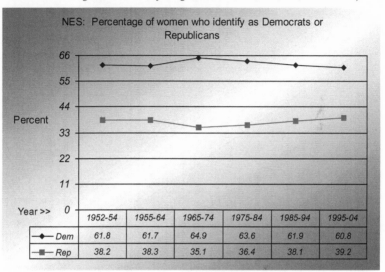

| Year >> | 1952-54 | 1955-64 | 1965-74 | 1975-84 | 1985-94 | 1995-04 |
|---|---|---|---|---|---|---|
| Dem | 61.8 | 61.7 | 64.9 | 63.6 | 61.9 | 60.8 |
| Rep | 38.2 | 38.3 | 35.1 | 36.4 | 38.1 | 39.2 |

*Racial and ethnic groups*

*Figure 237. Percentages of Whites who identify as Democrats or Republicans (several NES surveys conducted in 1952 through 2004, based on, left to right, 1977, 4936, 4944, 5075, 4958, and 3492 cases)*

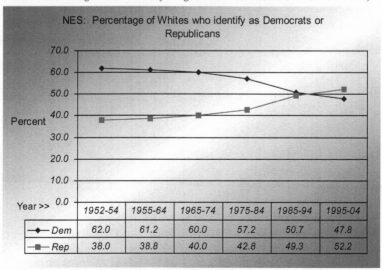

| Year >> | 1952-54 | 1955-64 | 1965-74 | 1975-84 | 1985-94 | 1995-04 |
|---|---|---|---|---|---|---|
| Dem | 62.0 | 61.2 | 60.0 | 57.2 | 50.7 | 47.8 |
| Rep | 38.0 | 38.8 | 40.0 | 42.8 | 49.3 | 52.2 |

As shown in Figure 237, above, most of white America has identified with the Republicans for the last 10 to 20 years.

Black America was solidly Republican until the New Deal days of FDR. Since then, a large majority has been Democratic. That majority grew even larger during the Civil Rights legislative battles of the mid-1960s. See Figure 238, below.

*Figure 238. Percentages of Blacks who identify as Democrats or Republicans (several NES surveys conducted in 1952 through 2004, based on, left to right, 180, 452, 641, 762, 956, and 648 cases)*

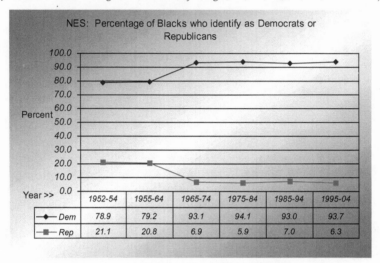

NES didn't keep records with respect to Hispanic preferences until about 30 years ago. At that time 4 out of 5 Hispanics considered themselves to be Democrats. Now the ratio is a little over 2 out of 3. The trend is shown in Figure 239, below.

*Figure 239. Percentages of Hispanics who identify as Democrats or Republicans (several NES surveys conducted in 1975 through 2004, based on, left to right, 189, 381and 309 cases)*

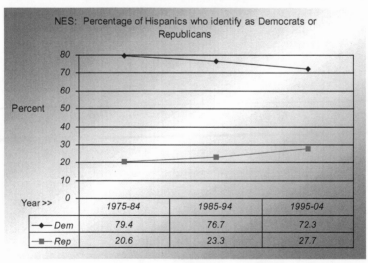

*Religious denominations*

Although more Protestants consider themselves to be Democratic than Republican, the gap has always been a bit smaller than it has been for the population, in general. This can be seen by comparing Figure 240, below, with Figure 230.

*Figure 240. Percentages of Protestants who identify as Democrats or Republicans (several NES surveys conducted in 1952 through 2004, based on, left to right, 1613, 3943, 4062, 4069, 4172, and 2766 cases)*

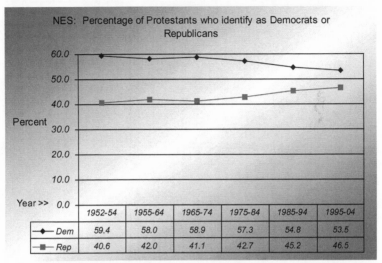

Democrats have lost a lot of ground among Catholics, but they have always held an advantage.

*Figure 241. Percentages of Catholics who identify as Democrats or Republicans (several NES surveys conducted in 1952 through 2004, based on, left to right, 437, 1129, 1258, 1512, 1591, and 1249 cases)*

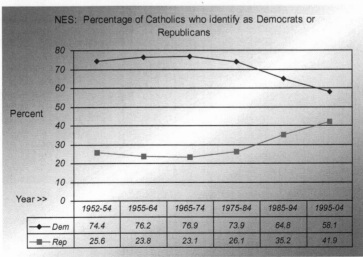

The percentage of Jews who consider themselves to be Democrats is higher than for any other group except Blacks. See Figure 242, below.

*Figure 242. Percentages of Jews who identify as Democrats or Republicans (several NES surveys conducted in 1952 through 2004, based on, left to right, 62, 161, 139, 164, 116, and 123 and 2576 cases)*

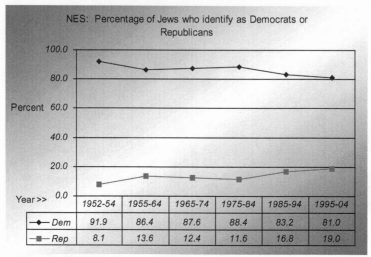

*Married people*

Marriage may effectively serve as a "filter" that separates relatively conservative people from more liberal people. That could explain why married people are more likely to be Republicans than are married and unmarried people, considered as a whole. See Figure 243, below.

*Figure 243. Percentages of married people (living with spouse) who identify as Democrats or Republicans (several NES surveys conducted in 1952 through 2004, based on, left to right, 1034, 4239, 3881, 3756, 3675, and 2590 cases)*

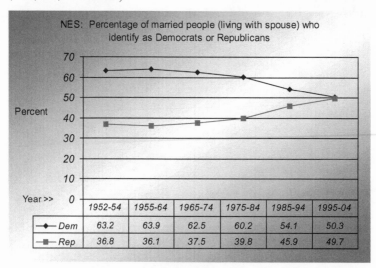

*People in different occupations*

Although more professionals and managers consider themselves to be Democratic, versus Republican, the difference is far less than for the population in general.

*Figure 244. Percentages of professionals and managers who identify as Democrats or Republicans (several NES surveys conducted in 1952 through 2004, based on, left to right, 190, 734, 934, 1414, 1742, and 1012 cases)*

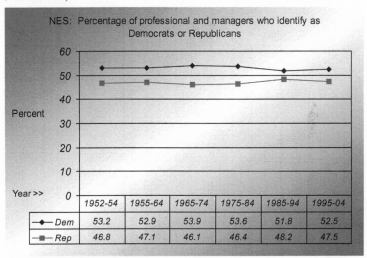

The Democratic advantage with respect to clerical and sales workers is a bit smaller than it is among the population at large.

*Figure 245. Percentages of clerical and sales workers who identify as Democrats or Republicans (several NES surveys conducted in 1952 through 2004, based on, left to right, 139, 531, 660, 1088, 1379, and 860 cases)*

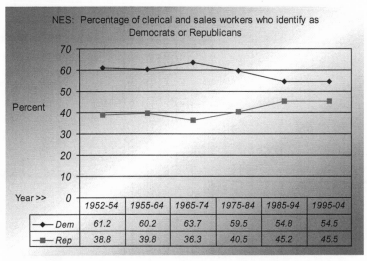

It is not surprising to see a strong Democratic advantage among skilled, semi-skilled, and service workers, since many of these workers are unionized. In the '80s, some of these workers became Republicans because, perhaps, of the popularity of President Ronald Reagan. However, since then, the gap has grown larger again. These trends are shown in Figure 246, below.

*Figure 246. Percentages of skilled, semi-skilled, and service workers who identify as Democrats or Republicans (several NES surveys conducted in 1952 through 2004, based on, left to right, 272, 1215, 1463, 2032, 2133, and 1012 cases)*

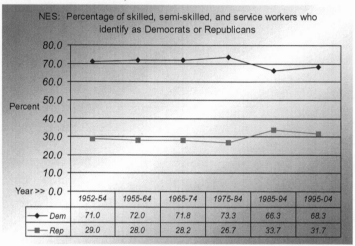

| NES: Percentage of skilled, semi-skilled, and service workers who identify as Democrats or Republicans | | | | | | |
|---|---|---|---|---|---|---|
| Year >> | 1952-54 | 1955-64 | 1965-74 | 1975-84 | 1985-94 | 1995-04 |
| Dem | 71.0 | 72.0 | 71.8 | 73.3 | 66.3 | 68.3 |
| Rep | 29.0 | 28.0 | 28.2 | 26.7 | 33.7 | 31.7 |

Surprisingly, perhaps, Republicans are now doing relatively well with respect to laborers. This is partly due to the inclusion of farmers and farm workers, who tend to be more conservative than city laborers.

*Figure 247. Percentages of laborers, farmers and farm workers who identify as Democrats or Republicans (several NES surveys conducted in 1952 through 2004, based on, left to right, 236, 488, 303, 347, 371, and 135 cases)*

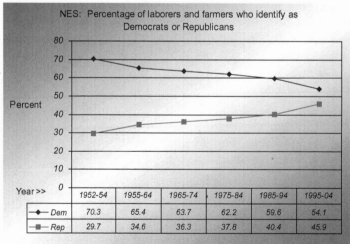

| NES: Percentage of laborers and farmers who identify as Democrats or Republicans | | | | | | |
|---|---|---|---|---|---|---|
| Year >> | 1952-54 | 1955-64 | 1965-74 | 1975-84 | 1985-94 | 1995-04 |
| Dem | 70.3 | 65.4 | 63.7 | 62.2 | 59.6 | 54.1 |
| Rep | 29.7 | 34.6 | 36.3 | 37.8 | 40.4 | 45.9 |

*College graduates*

The Republican advantage among people with college or advanced degrees is very strong when we consider that Democratic advantage among the population in general. Contrast the trends shown in Figure 248, below, with those shown in Figure 230.

*Figure 248. Percentages of people with a college or advanced degree who identify as Democrats or Republicans (several NES surveys conducted in 1952 through 2004, based on, left to right, 118, 547, 685, 1008, 1450, and 1490 cases)*

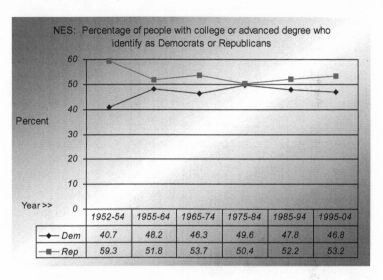

*People in different family income brackets*

NES asks its respondents this question, or a similar question, in each survey:

> Can you give us an estimate of your total family income in 20XX before taxes? This figure should include salaries, wages, pensions, dividends, interest and all other income for every member of your family living in your house in 20XX.

Using this information, respondents are placed within the following income ranges: zero to 16th percentile, 17th to 33rd percentile, 34th to 67th percentile, 68th to 95th percentile, and 96th to 100th percentile. These ranges, and the percentage of Democrats and Republicans in each one, are graphically depicted in the following 5 charts.

The correlation between party identity and family income is strong. By 70 to 30 percent, people with family incomes in the lowest 16 percent of the population favor the Democrats.

*Figure 249. Percentages of people with family incomes in the 0 to 16th percentile who identify as Democrats or Republicans (several NES surveys conducted in 1952 through 2004, based on, left to right, 424, 940, 1013, 882, 1017, and 525 cases)*

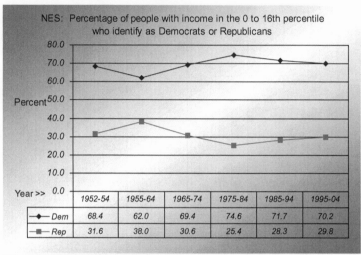

| Year >> | 1952-54 | 1955-64 | 1965-74 | 1975-84 | 1985-94 | 1995-04 |
|---|---|---|---|---|---|---|
| Dem | 68.4 | 62.0 | 69.4 | 74.6 | 71.7 | 70.2 |
| Rep | 31.6 | 38.0 | 30.6 | 25.4 | 28.3 | 29.8 |

The gap is just slightly smaller for those with family incomes in the 17th to 33rd percentiles. See Figure 250, below.

*Figure 250. Percentages of people with family incomes in the 17th to 33rd percentile who identify as Democrats or Republicans (several NES surveys conducted in 1952 through 2004, based on, left to right, 303, 953, 792, 1046, 992, and 655 cases)*

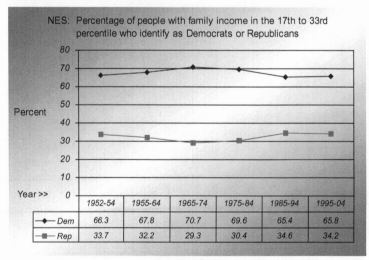

| Year >> | 1952-54 | 1955-64 | 1965-74 | 1975-84 | 1985-94 | 1995-04 |
|---|---|---|---|---|---|---|
| Dem | 66.3 | 67.8 | 70.7 | 69.6 | 65.4 | 65.8 |
| Rep | 33.7 | 32.2 | 29.3 | 30.4 | 34.6 | 34.2 |

We still see a strong Democratic advantage when we consider people with family incomes ranging from the 34th percentile to the 67th percentile. The gap is a bit larger than for the population in general.

*Figure 251. Percentages of people with family incomes in the 34th to 67th percentile who identify as Democrats or Republicans (several NES surveys conducted in 1952 through 2004, based on, left to right, 564, 1580, 1893, 1753, 2022, and 1084 cases)*

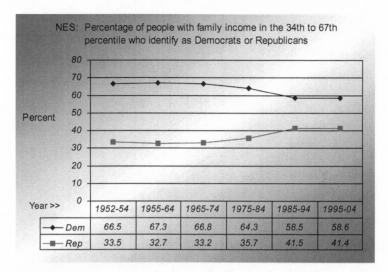

For people with incomes in the 68th percentiles and higher, Republicans have parity or an advantage. This is a fairly recent phenomenon which has taken place during the last 20 years.

*Figure 252. Percentages of people with family incomes in the 68th to 95th percentile who identify as Democrats or Republicans (several NES surveys conducted in 1952 through 2004, based on, left to right, 723, 1457, 1532, 1484, 1747, and 850 cases)*

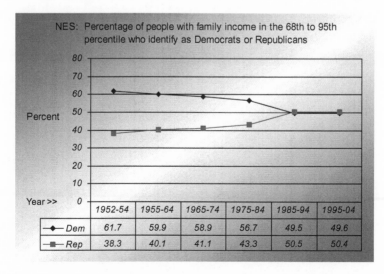

Among those with family incomes in the top 5 percent, the Republican advantage is huge. This may be due to the fact that this small segment of the population pays about 50 percent of the federal income tax, and is attracted to the normal Republican advocacy of lower tax rates.

*Figure 253. Percentages of people with family incomes in the 96th to 100th percentile who identify as Democrats or Republicans (several NES surveys conducted in 1952 through 2004, based on, left to right, 93, 308, 267, 352, 264, and 248 cases)*

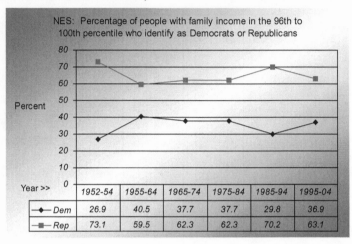

NES: Percentage of people with family income in the 96th to 100th percentile who identify as Democrats or Republicans

| Year >> | 1952-54 | 1955-64 | 1965-74 | 1975-84 | 1985-94 | 1995-04 |
|---|---|---|---|---|---|---|
| Dem | 26.9 | 40.5 | 37.7 | 37.7 | 29.8 | 36.9 |
| Rep | 73.1 | 59.5 | 62.3 | 62.3 | 70.2 | 63.1 |

*People in the "political South"*

Although Democrats still hold a small advantage in the "old South" (the original 11 succession states), the advantage has dramatically decreased during the last 50 years. If the trend continues, Republicans will reach parity in about 10 years.

*Figure 254. Percentages of people living in the "old South" who identify as Democrats or Republicans (several NES surveys conducted in 1952 through 2004, based on, left to right, 324, 1392, 1484, 1804, 2100, and 1618 cases)*

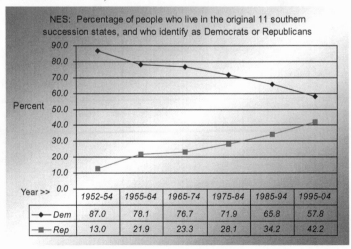

NES: Percentage of people who live in the original 11 southern succession states, and who identify as Democrats or Republicans

| Year >> | 1952-54 | 1955-64 | 1965-74 | 1975-84 | 1985-94 | 1995-04 |
|---|---|---|---|---|---|---|
| Dem | 87.0 | 78.1 | 76.7 | 71.9 | 65.8 | 57.8 |
| Rep | 13.0 | 21.9 | 23.3 | 28.1 | 34.2 | 42.2 |

*People living in different communities*

The final 3 graphs, for this section, address the party identification of people living in different types of communities. Figure 255, below, shows that more than 70 percent of people living in the central cities consider themselves to be Democrats.

*Figure 255. Percentages of people who live in the central city who identify as Democrats or Republicans (several NES surveys conducted in 1952 through 2004, based on, left to right, 694, 1567, 1691, 1828, 1725, and 712 cases)*

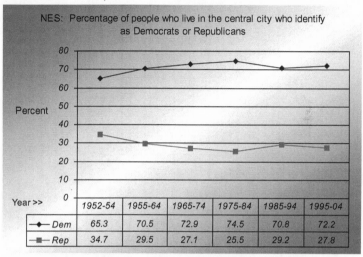

| NES: Percentage of people who live in the central city who identify as Democrats or Republicans | | | | | | |
|---|---|---|---|---|---|---|
| Year >> | 1952-54 | 1955-64 | 1965-74 | 1975-84 | 1985-94 | 1995-04 |
| Dem | 65.3 | 70.5 | 72.9 | 74.5 | 70.8 | 72.2 |
| Rep | 34.7 | 29.5 | 27.1 | 25.5 | 29.2 | 27.8 |

The Democratic advantage is much smaller in the suburbs and rural areas. During the last 10 years, roughly equal numbers of suburbanites have considered themselves to be Republicans and Democrats.

*Figure 256. Percentages of people who live in the suburbs who identify as Democrats or Republicans (several NES surveys conducted in 1952 through 2004, based on, left to right, 661, 1849, 1904, 2404, 2725, and 950 cases)*

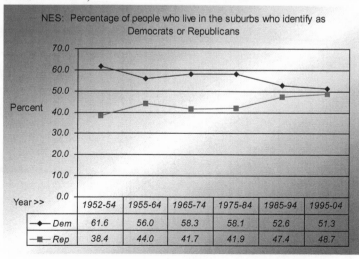

| NES: Percentage of people who live in the suburbs who identify as Democrats or Republicans | | | | | | |
|---|---|---|---|---|---|---|
| Year >> | 1952-54 | 1955-64 | 1965-74 | 1975-84 | 1985-94 | 1995-04 |
| Dem | 61.6 | 56.0 | 58.3 | 58.1 | 52.6 | 51.3 |
| Rep | 38.4 | 44.0 | 41.7 | 41.9 | 47.4 | 48.7 |

For about 4 decades, Republicans gained among people living in small towns and rural areas, however, that trend has reversed during the last 10 years. This may be due to the significant number of big city retirees moving south to smaller retirement communities.

*Figure 257. Percentages of people who live in rural areas and small towns who identify as Democrats or Republicans (several NES surveys conducted in 1952 through 2004, based on, left to right, 813, 2823, 2650, 2346, 2122, and 803 cases)*

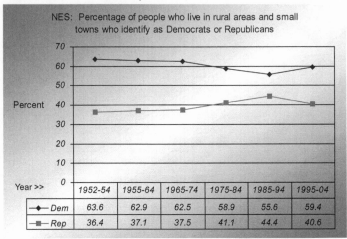

NES: Percentage of people who live in rural areas and small towns who identify as Democrats or Republicans

| Year >> | 1952-54 | 1955-64 | 1965-74 | 1975-84 | 1985-94 | 1995-04 |
|---|---|---|---|---|---|---|
| Dem | 63.6 | 62.9 | 62.5 | 58.9 | 55.6 | 59.4 |
| Rep | 36.4 | 37.1 | 37.5 | 41.1 | 44.4 | 40.6 |

## PART TWO: THE COMPOSITION OF EACH POLITICAL PARTY

In this section, you will find the composition of each party with respect to:

*Age*

*Figure 258. Age breakout of the parties — Democrats (combined results of several NES surveys, conducted from 1952 through 2004, based on, left to right, 1365, 3902, 3970, 4116, 3829, and 2615 cases)*

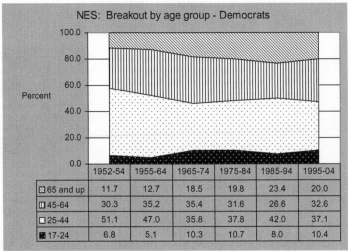

NES: Breakout by age group - Democrats

| | 1952-54 | 1955-64 | 1965-74 | 1975-84 | 1985-94 | 1995-04 |
|---|---|---|---|---|---|---|
| 65 and up | 11.7 | 12.7 | 18.5 | 19.8 | 23.4 | 20.0 |
| 45-64 | 30.3 | 35.2 | 35.4 | 31.6 | 26.6 | 32.6 |
| 25-44 | 51.1 | 47.0 | 35.8 | 37.8 | 42.0 | 37.1 |
| 17-24 | 6.8 | 5.1 | 10.3 | 10.7 | 8.0 | 10.4 |

Each political party is broken out by the proportion of people within 4 different age groups. In Figure 258, above, we see a general increase in the percentage of Democrats who are over age 65, and a general decline in the percentage of Democrats who are ages 25 to 44.[2]

In Figure 259, below, the same information is displayed with regard to Republicans. It is apparent that Republicans have not gained among the elderly, despite the overall aging of the population. In 1952-54 about 16.5 percent of Republicans were over age 65, and the same percentage exists today. Republicans have, however, done well with the 25 to 44 age group, a group that now comprises nearly 44 percent of Republicans (versus just 41% of the general survey population).

*Figure 259. Age breakout of the parties — Republicans (combined results of several NES surveys, conducted from 1952 through 2004, based on, left to right, 776, 2315, 2229, 2424, 2739, and 2005 cases)*

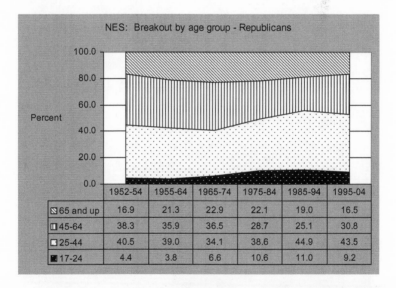

| | 1952-54 | 1955-64 | 1965-74 | 1975-84 | 1985-94 | 1995-04 |
|---|---|---|---|---|---|---|
| ▨65 and up | 16.9 | 21.3 | 22.9 | 22.1 | 19.0 | 16.5 |
| ▥45-64 | 38.3 | 35.9 | 36.5 | 28.7 | 25.1 | 30.8 |
| ☐25-44 | 40.5 | 39.0 | 34.1 | 38.6 | 44.9 | 43.5 |
| ■17-24 | 4.4 | 3.8 | 6.6 | 10.6 | 11.0 | 9.2 |

*Gender*

The modern "gender" gap started in the '60s and '70s, and has become a major political factor for each party during the last 20 to 30 years. In Figure 260, below, we see that, during the last 20 years, men have comprised nearly 50 percent of Republicans, but only 40 percent of Democrats. This might mean that Republicans need to adopt policies and platforms that appeal equally to the genders, while Democrats may find it more advantageous to adopt distaff policies and messages.

---

2 During those same years, the over 65 age group, *as a percentage of the general survey population*, changed from 13 to 16%; and the 25 to 44 age group changed from 48 to 41% of the general survey population.

*Figure 260. The composition of each party with respect to males — (combined results of several NES surveys conducted from 1952 through 2004, based on, left to right, 989, 2748, 2571, 2652, 2848, and 2060 cases)*

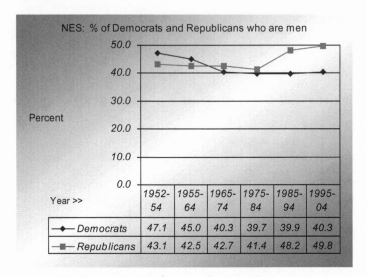

Of course, the gap is reversed with regard to women. In Figure 261, below, we see that about 60 percent of Democrats are women, while only about 50 percent are Republicans.

*Figure 261. The composition of each party with respect to females — (combined results of several NES surveys conducted from 1952 through 2004, based on, left to right, 1179, 3491, 3674, 3925, 3724, and 2576 cases)*

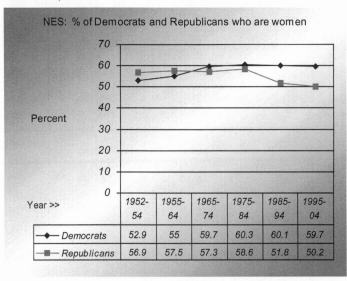

*Race and ethnicity*

Figure 262 shows the percentage of Democratic constituents broken out by race over the last 50 years. Blacks now comprise about one quarter of all Democrats, Hispanics about 10 percent, and other minorities about 5 percent.

*Figure 262. Race breakout — (Democrats) (combined results of several NES surveys, conducted from 1952 through 2004, based on, left to right, 1377, 3915, 3999, 4141, 3831, and 2624 cases)*

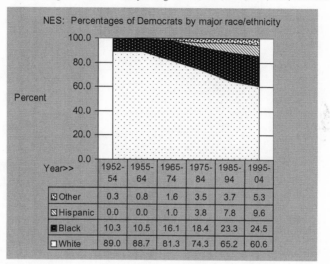

| NES: Percentages of Democrats by major race/ethnicity | | | | | | |
|---|---|---|---|---|---|---|
| Year>> | 1952-54 | 1955-64 | 1965-74 | 1975-84 | 1985-94 | 1995-04 |
| Other | 0.3 | 0.8 | 1.6 | 3.5 | 3.7 | 5.3 |
| Hispanic | 0.0 | 0.0 | 1.0 | 3.8 | 7.8 | 9.6 |
| Black | 10.3 | 10.5 | 16.1 | 18.4 | 23.3 | 24.5 |
| White | 89.0 | 88.7 | 81.3 | 74.3 | 65.2 | 60.6 |

Only about 2 percent of Republicans are Black, a percentage that is less than half that of Hispanics. During the last 10 years, Whites have remained the overwhelming majority of Republicans, comprising about 86 percent. That is far higher than the Democratic percentage, which is only about 61 percent.

*Figure 263. Race breakout — (Republicans) (combined results of several NES surveys, conducted from 1952 through 2004, based on, left to right, 791, 2324, 2246, 2439, 2741, and 2010 cases)*

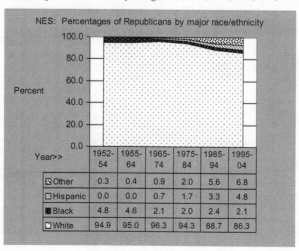

| NES: Percentages of Republicans by major race/ethnicity | | | | | | |
|---|---|---|---|---|---|---|
| Year>> | 1952-54 | 1955-64 | 1965-74 | 1975-84 | 1985-94 | 1995-04 |
| Other | 0.3 | 0.4 | 0.9 | 2.0 | 5.6 | 6.8 |
| Hispanic | 0.0 | 0.0 | 0.7 | 1.7 | 3.3 | 4.8 |
| Black | 4.8 | 4.6 | 2.1 | 2.0 | 2.4 | 2.1 |
| White | 94.9 | 95.0 | 96.3 | 94.3 | 88.7 | 86.3 |

*Religious denominations*

There are some statistically significant differences in religious identification. Protestants comprise a declining percentage of both Democrats and Republicans; however, they remain a larger percentage among Republicans.

*Figure 264. The percentage of each party that is Protestant (combined results of several NES surveys, conducted from 1952 through 2004, based on, left to right, 1613, 4552, 4426, 4319, 4141, and 2694 cases)*

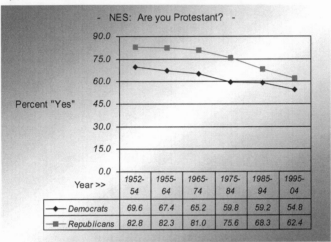

Catholics have grown as a percentage of both Democrats and Republicans; however, the percentage growth has been far larger for Republicans. Now, Catholics comprise nearly equal percentages of each of the two political parties.

*Figure 265. The percentage of each party that is Catholic (combined results of several NES surveys, conducted from 1952 through 2004, based on, left to right, 437, 1279, 1374, 1608, 1598, and 1266 cases)*

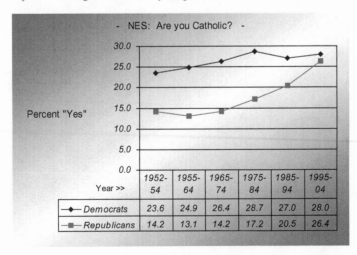

Jews comprise a slightly smaller percentage of Democrats, having dropped from about 4 to 3 percent. The percentage of Republicans who are Jewish has held fairly even at just below 1 percent.

*Figure 266. The percentage of each party that is Jewish (combined results of several NES surveys, conducted from 1952 through 2004, based on, left to right, 62, 177, 161, 173, 113, and 100 cases)*

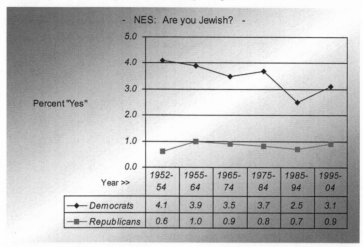

For both political parties there has been a large increase in the percentage of constituents who are either not religious or belong to another religion (e.g., Islam). The percentages for the last decade are 14 and 10 for Democrats and Republicans, respectively.

*Figure 267. The percentage of each party that is another religion, agnostic, or refuses to answer (combined results of several NES surveys, conducted from 1952 through 2004, based on, left to right, 50, 139, 256, 442, 682, and 530 cases)*

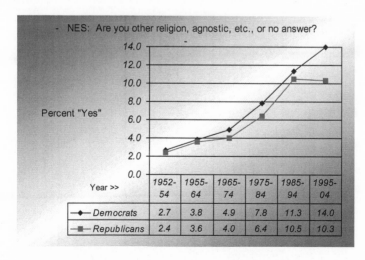

*People who are married*

This topic was covered in "Lifestyles" (Chapter 1). The following chart, showing the percentages of Democrats and Republicans who are married, is a reproduction of Figure 8.

*Figure 268. Are you married? (Men) (various NES surveys conducted in 1952 through 2004, based on, left to right, 592, 2748, 2571, 2653, 2847, and 2059 cases)*

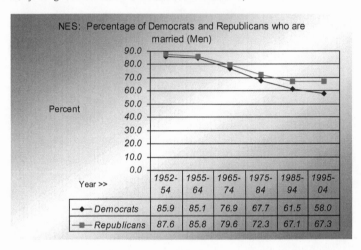

The following chart, pertaining to married women, is a reproduction of Figure 9, shown on page 12. It is interesting to note a "rebound," so to speak in marriage rates among women (but, not among men). Could this be partly due to welfare reform (which was enacted in the mid-90s)?

*Figure 269. Are you married? (Women) (various NES surveys conducted in 1952 through 2004, based on, left to right, 735, 3491, 3674, 3925, 3724, and 2576 cases)*

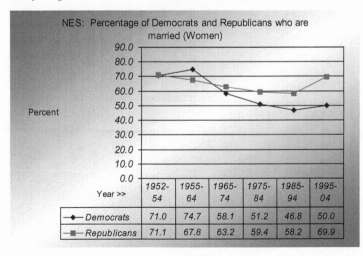

## Occupational categories

The figures below show the percentages of Democrats and Republicans in various occupational categories. The percentages do not add to 100 percent because homemakers and military personnel are not shown. By far, skilled, semi-skilled, and service workers comprise the largest proportion of Democrats (over one third). Professionals and managers come in second at about 27 percent.

*Figure 270. What is your occupational category? (Democrats) (various NES surveys conducted in 1952 through 2004, based on, left to right, 841, 3318, 3415, 4139, 3833, and 2129 cases)*

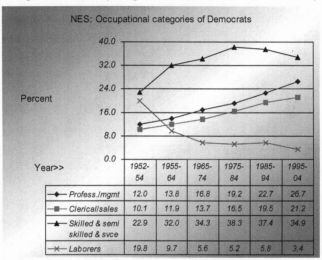

| NES: Occupational categories of Democrats | 1952-54 | 1955-64 | 1965-74 | 1975-84 | 1985-94 | 1995-04 |
|---|---|---|---|---|---|---|
| ◆ Profess./mgmt | 12.0 | 13.8 | 16.8 | 19.2 | 22.7 | 26.7 |
| ■ Clerical/sales | 10.1 | 11.9 | 13.7 | 16.5 | 19.5 | 21.2 |
| ▲ Skilled & semi skilled & svce | 22.9 | 32.0 | 34.3 | 38.3 | 37.4 | 34.9 |
| ✖ Laborers | 19.8 | 9.7 | 5.6 | 5.2 | 5.8 | 3.4 |

For Republicans, professionals and managers are the largest group (about 33%), while clerical and sales workers account for the next largest segment (about 24%).

*Figure 271. What is your occupational category? (Republicans) (various NES surveys conducted in 1952 through 2004, based on, left to right, 486, 1957, 1929, 2439, 2740, and 1562 cases)*

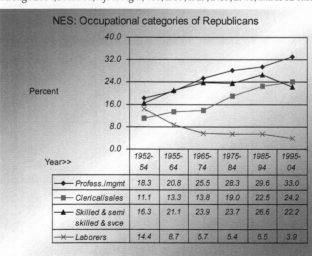

| NES: Occupational categories of Republicans | 1952-54 | 1955-64 | 1965-74 | 1975-84 | 1985-94 | 1995-04 |
|---|---|---|---|---|---|---|
| ◆ Profess./mgmt | 18.3 | 20.8 | 25.5 | 28.3 | 29.6 | 33.0 |
| ■ Clerical/sales | 11.1 | 13.3 | 13.8 | 19.0 | 22.5 | 24.2 |
| ▲ Skilled & semi skilled & svce | 16.3 | 21.1 | 23.9 | 23.7 | 26.6 | 22.2 |
| ✖ Laborers | 14.4 | 8.7 | 5.7 | 5.4 | 5.5 | 3.9 |

*College students and graduates*

Displayed in this section are the 50-year trends for Democrats and Republicans with at least some college education. A review of Figure 272 shows that Republicans have been more likely to have some college training for several decades. However, as noted in Chapter 2, recent trends show a narrowing of the education gap. The amounts depicted here represent Democrats and Republicans of both genders and of all ages. For additional comparison information see Chapter 2.

*Figure 272. Do you have at least some college education?? (various NES surveys from 1952 through 2004, based on, left to right, 2168, 6239, 6245, 6580, 6573, and 4635 cases)*

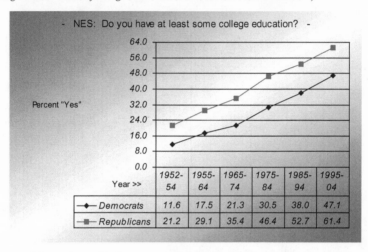

Republicans have also been more likely to have college and advanced degrees. Again, however, this disparity is narrowing in very recent years.

*Figure 273. Do you have a college or advanced degree? (various NES surveys from 1952 through 2004, based on, left to right, 2168, 6239, 6245, 6580, 6573, and 4635 cases)*

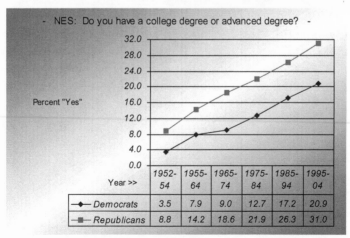

*People in different family income brackets*

Figure 274 shows a direct comparison of those Democrats and Republicans who reported income in the lowest 16 percent of all respondents. In this category, the percentage of Democrats has been fairly constant over the last 50 years, while there has been a steady decline in the percentage of Republicans.

*Figure 274. Democrats and Republicans who place their total family income in the lower 16th percentile (combined results of several NES surveys conducted from 1952 through 2004, based on, left to right, 424, 1075, 1083, 942, 1007, and 484 cases)*

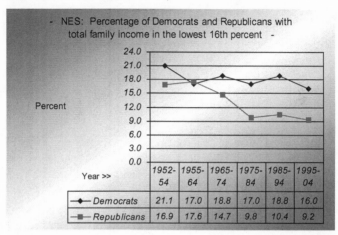

In Figure 275 we see a depiction of people who are not poor but have income that is lower than two thirds of all others. A greater percentage of Democrats are in this category, and that percentage may be increasing slightly.

*Figure 275. Democrats and Republicans who place their total family income in the 17th to 33rd percentile (combined results of several NES surveys conducted from 1952 through 2004, based on, left to right, 303, 1110, 878, 1125, 985, and 652 cases)*

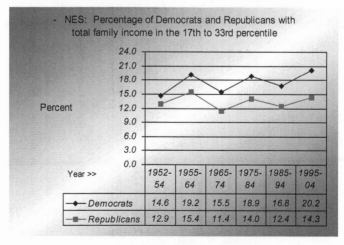

In the middle-income range (34th to 67th percentile) we used to find a higher percentage of Democrats than Republicans; however, in recent years there seems to be no significant difference.

*Figure 276. Democrats and Republicans who place their total family income in the 34th to 67th percentile (combined results of several NES surveys conducted from 1952 through 2004, based on, left to right, 564, 1819, 2093, 1856, 2015, and 1060 cases)*

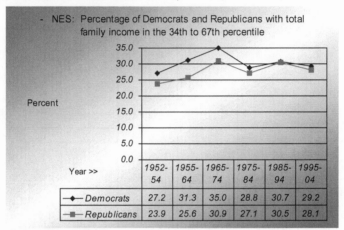

About 32 percent of Democrats used to report that they had total family income in the 68th to 95th percentile; however, this percentage seems to have dropped to just about 20 percent. About 2 percent of those Democrats may have moved up to the top 4 percent of income earners, but (by deduction) most must have moved down, relative to others. Among Republicans there has been a decline of about 8 percent reporting income in this income range. Most of those Republicans must have also moved down in income, relative to others.

*Figure 277. Democrats and Republicans who place their total family income in the 68th to 95th percentile (combined results of several NES surveys conducted from 1952 through 2004, based on, left to right, 723, 1689, 1654, 1574, 1751, and 845 cases)*

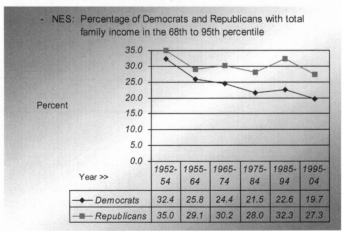

Figure 278 shows the Democrats and Republicans who reported income in the highest 4 percent of all respondents. The percentage of Republicans in this range seems to consistently be at least twice the percentage of Democrats in this range.

*Figure 278. Democrats and Republicans who place their total family income in the 96th to 100th percentile (combined results of several NES surveys conducted from 1952 through 2004, based on, left to right, 93, 341, 289, 366, 265, and 244 cases)*

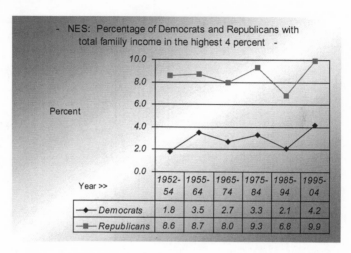

*People in the "political South"*

Fifty years ago, less than 10 percent of Republicans hailed from the Southern secession states. Now such people comprise about one third of all Republicans. They also constitute approximately that percentage of Democrats.

*Figure 279. What is your occupational category? (Democrats) (various NES surveys conducted in 1952 through 2004, based on, left to right, 1327, 6239, 6245, 6578, 6573, and 4634 cases)*

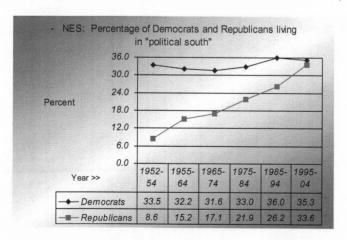

*People in different communities*

Most Democratic and Republican constituents used to live in rural areas and small towns. Today, the Democratic constituents are evenly divided between the central cities, the suburbs, and the rural areas.

*Figure 280. In what type of community do you live? (Democrats) (combined results of several NES surveys, conducted from 1952 through 2004, based on, left to right, 1377, 3915, 3999, 4139, 3832, and 1478 cases)*

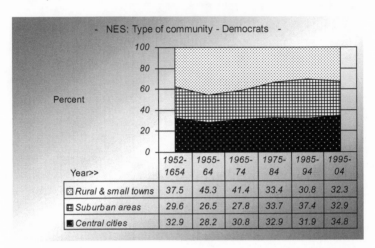

On the other hand, Republicans are not divided evenly among the three major types of communities. Nearly 47 percent of Republicans live in the suburbs, while just 20 percent live in the central cities.

*Figure 281. In what type of community do you live? (Republicans) (combined results of several NES surveys, conducted from 1952 through 2004, based on, left to right, 791, 2324, 2246, 2439, 2740, and 987 cases)*

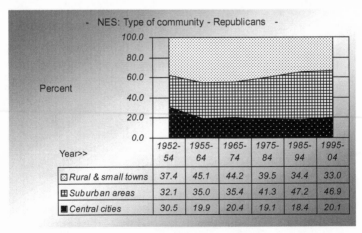

## APPENDIX B: INFORMATION OVERFLOW AND ANALYSIS

*Appendix B 1. GSS Surveys For High School Diploma Rates (relates to page 74)*

Figure 282, below, depicts the percentages of Democrats and Republicans who received (at the least) high school degrees, according to GSS surveys conducted during the last 30 years. The Republican advantage has been clear; however, Democrats have mostly closed the gap.

*Figure 282. Do you have (at the least) a high school diploma (men and women)? (GSS surveys conducted in 1977 through 2006, based on, left to right, 2861, 5170, 5199, 4711, 3279, and 6034 cases, with confidence level of 99+% for all differences, and with relative proportions of, left to right, .88, .81, .86, .93, .91, and .94)*

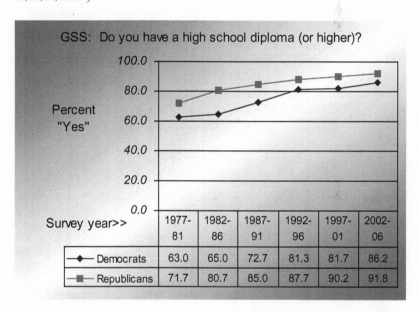

| Survey year>> | 1977-81 | 1982-86 | 1987-91 | 1992-96 | 1997-01 | 2002-06 |
|---|---|---|---|---|---|---|
| Democrats | 63.0 | 65.0 | 72.7 | 81.3 | 81.7 | 86.2 |
| Republicans | 71.7 | 80.7 | 85.0 | 87.7 | 90.2 | 91.8 |

*Appendix B 2. More Surveys For College Graduation Rates (relates to page 75.*

### Pew Surveys

Pew surveys show that, overall, Republicans continue to have the edge with regard to college diplomas. Note that these are statistically "weighted" numbers (designed to make the results more reflective of the overall population), and are somewhat larger than the actual sample sizes (which are not shown).

*Table 56. Pew surveys pertaining to 4-year college graduation rates (men and women combined)*

| Pew Surveys: Percentage of Democrats and Republicans with a 4-year college degree, or advanced graduate degree | Democrats | | Republicans | |
|---|---|---|---|---|
| | With 4-yr. deg. | Total | With 4-yr. deg. | Total |
| Pew February 2007 Political Survey: | 362 | 1311 | 308 | 988 |
| Pew 2006 Biennial Media Consumption survey: | 562 | 2202 | 605 | 1954 |
| Pew 2005 Religion and Public Life: " | 358 | 1392 | 416 | 1390 |
| Pew June 2005 News Interest Index survey: | 329 | 1206 | 338 | 1138 |
| Pew 2005 Political Typology Callback survey: | 221 | 905 | 237 | 797 |
| Pew March 2005 News Interest Index survey: | 181 | 596 | 141 | 512 |
| Pew February 2005 News Interest Index survey: | 264 | 973 | 288 | 920 |
| Pew 2004 Political Typology survey: | 358 | 1421 | 352 | 1282 |
| Pew 2004 Biennial Media Consumption survey | 462 | 1903 | 498 | 1575 |
| Pew 2003 Religion and Public Life survey: | 295 | 1228 | 356 | 1163 |
| Pew 2002 Biennial Media Consumption survey: | 518 | 2089 | 527 | 1888 |
| Totals | 3910 | 15226 | 4066 | 13607 |
| Average percentage | 25.7 | | 29.9 | |
| Overall proportion (Dem % divided by Rep %) | 86.0% | | | |
| Confidence level | 99+% | | | |

## GSS Surveys

*Figure 283. Do you have a 4-year college diploma (or higher degree)? (Men) (GSS surveys conducted in 1977 through 2006, based on, left to right, 3250, 4083, and 3988 cases, with confidence level of 99+% for all differences, and with relative proportions of, left to right, .57, .62, and .71)*

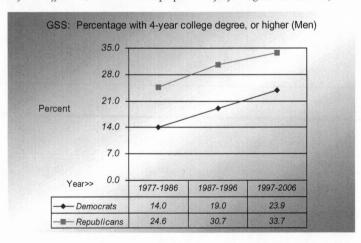

GSS: Percentage with 4-year college degree, or higher (Men)

| Year>> | 1977-1986 | 1987-1996 | 1997-2006 |
|---|---|---|---|
| Democrats | 14.0 | 19.0 | 23.9 |
| Republicans | 24.6 | 30.7 | 33.7 |

GSS surveys for men are similar to those of NES, and show that Republican men are more likely to have 4-year college degrees.

In the case of women, the GSS figures show less of a gap than the NES figures. These results show that Democratic women are now just as likely to have earned a 4-year college degree. See Figure 284.

*Figure 284. Do you have a 4-year college diploma (or higher degree)? (Women) (GSS surveys conducted in 1977 through 2006, based on, left to right, 4776, 5820, and 5322 cases, with confidence level of 99+% for the left and middle differences, and no statistical significance for the right-side column, and with relative proportions of, left to right, .69, .80 and n/a)*

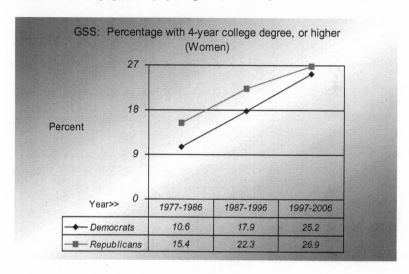

GSS: Percentage with 4-year college degree, or higher (Women)

| Year>> | 1977-1986 | 1987-1996 | 1997-2006 |
|---|---|---|---|
| Democrats | 10.6 | 17.9 | 25.2 |
| Republicans | 15.4 | 22.3 | 26.9 |

*Appendix B 3. Factors That Account For The Education Gap — 30-Year Analysis (relates to page 84)*

Using the multiple regression function of the SDA Web-based statistical program and GSS data for the years 1977 through 2006, I tested the relationship between several independent variables and the dependent variable, years of education (the GSS variable called "EDUC"). The independent variables tested are shown on the left side of Table 57. Each variable is expressed as a range starting at "0" and ending at "1." In the case of the first variable, party identification, being a Democrat is considered to be a "0" and being a Republican is considered to be a "1." (The assignment is arbitrary, and not meant to have hidden meanings!) As we move from the "0" end of the variable towards the "1" end, the strength of the independent variable's correlation with years of education is shown in the "Beta" column. Large, positive beta numbers indicate a strong and positive correlation, while small, negative beta numbers suggest a weak and negative correlation. In Table 57 we see a strong and positive relationship between income and years of education. (The beta number is +.300.) We also find positive relationships between education and good health (beta is .195) and between education and being Republican (beta is .062). On the other hand, being married does not correlate positively with more years of education. Rather, it is moderately associated with less years of education (beta is negative .088).

*Table 57. Independent variables regressed against education — 30 years*

| Variable | Variable details | Beta | T-Stat | Prob. |
|---|---|---|---|---|
| Party identification (PARTYID) | Reps = 1 Dems = 0 | .062 | 7.510 | .000 |
| Income (REALINC) | Over $50K in 2006 dollars = 1 Less than $50K = 0 | .300 | 38.161 | .000 |
| Health (HEALTH) | Good or excellent health = 1 Other = 0 | .195 | 25.858 | .000 |
| Race (RACE) | White = 1 Other race = 0 | .039 | 4.999 | .000 |
| Marital status (MARITAL) | Married = 1 Single = 0 | −.088 | −11.424 | .000 |
| Political views (POLVIEWS) | Conservative = 1 Moderate or liberal = 0 | .018 | 2.299 | .022 |
| Religious strength (RELITEN) | Strongly religious = 1 fairly or weakly religious = 0 | −.010 | −1.394 | * |
| Gender (SEX) | Male = 1 Female = 0 | −.006 | −851 | * |

*Not statistically significant

*Appendix B 4. Factors Correlating With The Education Gap — 9-Year Analysis (relates to page 86)*

Using the multiple regression function of the SDA Web-based statistical program, and GSS data for the years 1998 through 2006, I tested the relationship between several independent variables and the dependent variable, education (the GSS variable called "EDUC"). The independent variables tested are identical to those shown in Table 57, in Appendix B 3. The only element changed is in the number of years tested (9 years instead of 30 years). Please see Appendix B 3 for an explanation of the methodology. The results of the 9-year analysis are shown in Table 58, below. Again, high income and good health are the variables that correlate most strongly with education. Party identification is no longer an important factor. Being (racially) white correlates positively with more years of education, while being married and being male correlate negatively (although only to a minor degree).

*Table 58. Independent variables regressed against education — 9 years*

| Variable | Variable details | Beta | T-Stat | Prob. |
|---|---|---|---|---|
| Party identification (PARTYID) | Reps = 1 Dems = 0 | .012 | .761 | * |
| Income (REALINC) | Over $50K in 2006 dollars = 1 Less than $50K = 0 | .309 | 21.890 | .000 |
| Health (HEALTH) | Good or excellent health = 1 Other = 0 | .176 | 13.311 | .000 |
| Race (RACE) | White = 1 Other race = 0 | .058 | 4.137 | .000 |
| Marital status (MARITAL) | Married = 1 Single = 0 | −.052 | −3.771 | .000 |
| Political views (POLVIEWS) | Conservative = 1 Moderate or liberal = 0 | .016 | 1.064 | * |
| Religious strength (RELITEN) | Strongly religious = 1 fairly or weakly religious = 0 | .003 | .192 | * |
| Gender (SEX) | Male = 1 Female = 0 | −.025 | −1.906 | .057 (marg) |

*Not statistically significant

### Appendix B 5. Calculation Of The Average Male Hourly Wage Rate (relates to page 99)

The average male hourly rate of $21.16 was calculated by putting the gender-neutral rate of $19.29 (per BLS's National Compensation Survey for June, 2006) into the following algebraic formula: .4648W + .5352M = 19.29, where .4648 represents the percentage of women in the labor force, .5352 represents the percentage of men in the labor force, W represents the average hourly rate for women, and M equals the average hourly rate for men. Since we know that the hourly rate for women is about 81 percent of the hourly rate per men (per US Dept. of Labor "Charting the U.S. Labor Market in 2006"), we can substitute .81M for the W in the formula, and solve for M.

### Appendix B 6. Factors That Correlate With Hours Worked (Men) (relates to page 98)

Using the multiple regression function of the SDA Web-based statistical program, and GSS data for the years 1998 through 2004, I tested the relationship between several independent variables and the dependent variable, hours worked ("HR1"). The independent variables tested, and the results, are shown in Table 59, below. Only two of the variables correlated significantly with hours worked: having total family income over $50,000 per year, and being Republican. Note, very similar results were obtained when the income variable was changed to indicate family income over $25,000 per year. (Those results are not shown.)

Table 59. *Independent variables regressed against hours worked (men) (1998-2004). There were a total of 1108 cases.*

| Variable | Variable details | Beta | T-Stat | Prob. |
|---|---|---|---|---|
| Party identification (PARTYID) | Reps = 1; Dems = 0 | .079 | 2.242 | .025 |
| Income (INCOME98) | Over $50K = 1; Less = 0 | .137 | 4.156 | .000 |
| Health (HEALTH) | Good or excellent = 1; Other = 0 | .002 | .062 | * |
| Race (RACE) | White = 1; Other = 0 | 0 | 0 | * |
| Marital status (MARITAL) | Married = 1; Other = 0 | −.002 | −.078 | * |
| Political views (POLVIEWS) | Conservative = 1; Other = 0 | −.012 | −.356 | * |
| Religious strength (RELITEN) | Strong = 1; fair or weak = 0 | −.038 | −1.238 | * |
| Degree (DEGREE) | 2yr deg. or higher = 1; other = 0 | .034 | 1.094 | * |

*Not statistically significant

We see that, even after the income variable is controlled, Republicans are significantly more likely to work longer hours than are Democrats. If those results are accurate, there might be some Republican traits, not yet identified, that explain the remaining differential (i.e., that explain the Beta correlation factor of .079). Of course, it could be the other way around. The practice of working longer hours could cause a person to become a Republican (for some reason unknown to the author).

*Appendix B 7. The Impact Of Education On Wages (Men) (relates to page 101)*

In the third column of Table 60, below, average male earnings are listed by level of educational attainment. The source is the Current Population Survey (CPS) conducted by the Bureau of Labor Statistics and the Bureau of the Census. These are year 2000 amounts, restated to 2007 values using the consumer price index. In the table's middle columns we find the percentages of Democratic and Republican males at each of the educational levels, according to GSS survey results. There were no statistically significant differences between working Democrats and Republicans with respect to the high school, junior college, or post-graduate college levels (shown in rows 2, 3, and 5), so the percentages used in Table 60 for these educational levels are simply the overall averages (i.e., the same regardless of party identification). For rows 1 and 4, however, the percentages are different, and correspond to those in Figure 79, on page 100.

The amounts in the last two columns were derived by multiplying the average earnings amounts in each row by the Democratic and Republican percentages shown in the two middle columns. By totaling the two right-side columns, we can estimate the expected earnings of average Democratic and Republican males, given the levels of their average educational achievement.

*Table 60. Expected earnings of Democratic and Republican men aged 22 to 65 years, based on educational level*

| Row | Educational level | Average earnings per CPS (restated to 2007 values) | Per Figure 79* | | Dem earnings amount ** | Rep earnings amount ** |
|---|---|---|---|---|---|---|
| | | | Dem educ.% | Rep educ. % | | |
| 1 | Less than HS | $26767 | 10.4 | 5.3 | $2784 | $1419 |
| 2 | HS diploma | 39064 | 49.5 | 49.5 | 19337 | 19337 |
| 3 | Jr. college | 51906 | 9.5 | 9.5 | 4931 | 4931 |
| 4 | Bachelor's deg. | 77124 | 15.7 | 23.8 | 12108 | 18356 |
| 5 | Post-grad. deg. | 93135 | 13.2 | 13.2 | 12294 | 12294 |
| 6 | Total expected earnings | | | | $51454 | $56337 |

*Only the "Less than HS" and "Bachelor's degree" rows show statistically significant differences.

**Note: The CPS average earnings have been restated to 2007 amounts.

The bottom line of Table 60 shows that, given the differing educational achievements, we would expect the average Democratic and Republican males to earn about $51,500 and $56,300, respectively.

## Appendix B 8. Description Of Charity Surveys And Wording Of Questions (relates to page 131)

*Table 61. Description of surveys and wording of questions asked.*

| Row No. | Survey/Date | Question asked in survey |
|---|---|---|
| 1 | Michigan State of the State Survey (Michigan SOSS) — 2006 | Respondents were asked if they had "contributed money, property, or both to a charity or non-profit organization last year...." |
| 2 | Harris Interactive survey - 2006 | Respondents were asked if they had "given money to charity ... in the past 30 days." |
| 3 | Michigan State of the State Survey (Michigan SOSS) — 2005 | Respondents were asked if they had "contributed money, property, or both to a charity or non-profit organization last year...." |
| 4 | American National Election Studies (NES) — 2004 | Respondents were asked if they were "able to contribute any money to church or charity in the last 12 months." |
| 5 | General Social Survey (GSS) — 2004 | Respondents were asked: "During the last 12 months, how often have you ... given money to a charity?" |

| | | |
|---|---|---|
| 6 | Michigan State of the State Survey (Michigan SOSS) — 2003 | Respondents were asked if they had "contributed money, property, or both to a charity or non-profit organization this year...." |
| 7 | Community Fdtn Trends Survey (CFTS) — 2002/ 2003 | Respondents were asked: "Did you or other members of your household donate money, assets, goods, or property for charitable purposes?" |
| 8 | American National Election Studies (NES) — 2002 | Respondents were asked if they were able to "contribute any money to church or charity in the last 12 months." |
| 9 | General Social Survey (GSS) — 2002 | Respondents were asked: "During the last 12 months, how often have you ... given money to a charity?" |
| 10 | Michigan State of the State Survey (Michigan SOSS) — 2001 | Respondents were asked if they had "contributed money, property, or both to a charity or non-profit organization this year...." |
| 11 | Individual Philanthropy Patterns Survey — 2000 | Respondents were asked if they had "given financially to charities." |
| 12 | American National Election Studies (NES) — 2000 | Respondents were asked if they were able to "contribute any money to church or charity in the last 12 months." |
| 13 | Michigan State of the State Survey (Michigan SOSS) — 1999 | In the Michigan SOSS no. 19 respondents were given a lengthy list of specific types of nonprofit organizations, and asked if, with respect to any of the organizations, they donated "money or other property for charitable purposes." In Table 28 respondents are classified as having donated if they answered affirmatively with regard to any type of organization. |
| 14 | General Social Survey (GSS) — 1996 | In the GSS 1996 survey respondents were given a list of specific types of organizations, and asked if, with respect to those organizations, they had donated "money or other property for charitable purposes." In Table 28 respondents are classified as having donated if they answered affirmatively with regard to any one or more of those types of charitable entities. NOTE: "work-related organizations," such as unions are included among the listed types of entities. |
| 15 | American National Election Studies (NES) — 1996 | Respondents were asked if they were able to "contribute any money to church or charity in the last 12 months." |
| 16 | Economic Values Survey — 1992 | Respondents were asked: "Do you give to any charitable organizations?" |

*Appendix B 9. Impact of Income on Charitable Donations (relates to page 144)*

Using the dataset from the Michigan State of the State survey number 42, conducted in 2006, "Total Contributions — Dollars" (variable "N9") was co-tabulated with the party identification variable called "PARTYID." The "STATE-WT" variable was selected (to provide state-wide weighting), and the results were sorted by the 8 available income brackets.

The Republican results were then re-weighted so that the Republican number of cases within each income bracket would be identical to the Democratic number of cases in the respective bracket. The Republican grand contributions mean was recalculated using the new case numbers, and the standard error of the grand mean was recalculated using the assumption that one half of the cases were a standard deviation above the mean and the other half of the cases were a standard deviation below the mean. Using the recalculated Republican grand mean, standard error of the mean, and number of cases, as well as the corresponding Democratic amounts, it was a simple matter to run a "T-test" to calculate the P value, which was .0001. This value suggests that the difference in giving is statistically very significant, even after adjusting for income.

*Appendix B 10. Calculation of Federal Income Tax Amounts (relates to page 155)*

Democratic and Republican federal income tax amounts were calculated using two data sources: "Historical Effective Federal Tax Rates," published by the Congressional Budget Office (CBO) in March and December, 2005, and the cumulative General Social Survey (GSS) for 2004. CBO figures are grouped into 5 "comprehensive household income" quintiles "defined by ranking all people by their comprehensive household income adjusted for household size — that is, divided by the square root of the household's size."[3] The following steps were employed to produce the Democratic vs. Republican estimates:

1.    Using an Excel spreadsheet, quintile dollar-amount ranges were created for each size household, based on the 2002 "minimum adjusted income" figures in the March, 2005 release of the CBO publication (Table 1C). For example, the lowest quintile income range for a 1-person household is zero to $15,900, according to the CBO. To get the lowest quintile range for a 4-person family, the $15,900 amount was multiplied times the square root of 4 to get $31,800. This produced a low-end quintile range of zero to $31,800 for a

---

3 According to a footnote in the CBO table, "Comprehensive household income equals pretax cash income plus income from other sources. Pretax cash income is the sum of wages, salaries, self employment income, rents, taxable and nontaxable interest, dividends, realized capital gains, cash transfer payments and retirement benefits plus taxes paid by businesses (corporate income taxes and the employer's share of Social Security, Medicare, and federal unemployment insurance payroll taxes) and employees' contributions to 401(k) retirement plans. Other sources of income include all in-kind benefits (Medicare, Medicaid, employer-paid health insurance premiums, food stamps, school lunches and breakfasts, housing assistance, and energy assistance."

4-person household.[4]

2. GSS frequencies were printed by party identification and by income level for the combined years 1998 through 2004 (variable = "income98"). This was done separately by gender and separately by household population (variable = "hompop"). The GSS income levels did not exactly coincide with the CBO income ranges, so some frequencies had to be prorated between 2 CBO income ranges.

3. Another Excel work paper was created to add up the frequencies within each income quintile by party identification. Again, this was done separately by gender and separately by household population.

4. The percentages of Democrats and Republicans at each income quintile level were multiplied by the income tax rate and average income amounts for each quintile, according to the 2003 amounts released by CBO in December, 2005. This was done separately for men and women.

5. The results for men and women were then combined and averaged, to get a gender-neutral estimated amount.

*Appendix B 11. Estimation Of Median Federal Income Tax Amounts (relates to page 160)*

Median tax amounts were estimated by using extrapolation plus the income quintiles discussed in Appendix B 10. Democratic and Republican men and women were separately sequenced by income level using GSS frequencies for 1998 through 2004, and the medians (midpoints) of the sequences were determined. The location of each median was then identified as a percentage of the distance between the midpoints of the two nearest quintiles. Finally, that percentage was used to estimate the income tax dollar-amount paid by a person with median income.

For example, there were 2,043 Democratic women surveyed and sequenced by income. The midpoint of the sequence (person number 1,022) fell into the second income quintile, and was 21.2 percent of the way between the midpoint of that quintile and the midpoint of the next (higher) quintile. Since the average federal income tax paid by people in those two quintiles is negative $375 and $1,401, 21.2 percent of the way between those two amounts is a tax level of $2.

*Appendix B 12. Calculation Of State And Local Taxes Of Various Types (relates to page 164)*

This complicated calculation was performed in two parts that were then combined. First, the taxes were estimated for people under the age of 65; then they were calculated for people aged 65 or more.

For people under 65 years old, state and local taxes were estimated using information in the Tax Policy Center's publication, "Who pays? A distributional Analysis of the Tax Systems in All 50 States, 2nd Edition." That publication lists average income, excise, sales, and property tax rates, at various income levels for

---

4 The method of adjusting for household size (multiplying by the square root of family size) is prescribed in the footnotes to the CBO report.

2002, for taxpaying units under age 65. Using those results, and the distribution of Democrats and Republicans among those income levels, based upon results from the General Social Surveys (GSS) for 1998 through 2004, it was possible to roughly estimate the average state and local tax amounts paid by Democrats and Republicans — under 65 years old. This was done for men and women separately.

For men and women 65 years old and older, preparing state and local tax estimates was much more difficult. First, income tax estimates were prepared by creating 10 elderly taxpayer profiles, individualized for marital status and the varying types of income most elderly taxpayers have at different income levels. The source for these data was Income of the Population 55 and Older (2002), published by the Social Security Administration. Using 2004 TaxAct software (commercially available tax preparation software), actual income tax amounts were calculated for each of the 10 profiles, and for each of the 43 states that has an income tax — a total of 430 returns. (Yes, that was a lot of work!) A weighted average of the state tax results was created for each of the ten profiles on the basis of the number of elderly people in each state. Using those ten averages and the distribution of Democrats and Republicans subject to those averages (based upon income distributions per GSS surveys), it was possible to roughly estimate the average state income tax amounts for Democrats and Republicans 65 years old or older.

The estimation of tax paid by people aged 65 years or more required one additional step: the addition of sales, excise, and property tax. Those additional amounts were estimated on the basis of data published by TPC, coupled with GSS survey data showing the distribution of Democrats and Republicans among the TPC income and tax brackets. It was assumed that the TPC sales, excise and property tax rates, which applied to people under the age of 65, would be roughly applicable to people aged 65 years or more.

The over age 65 and under age 65 estimates were then combined in proportion to the percentages of the general population in each of those age categories.

*Appendix B 13. Web-Based Social Security And Medicare Calculator (relates to page 209)*

On October 4, 2004, USA Today (online) published a Web-based calculator, designed by C. Eugene Steuerle and Adam Carasso of the Urban Institute. The calculator can be used to estimate the net lifetime value of Social Security and Medicare benefits for men and women in different age cohorts, with different incomes (by $5,000 increments), with different marital status, and with different divisions of income for married couples (i.e., two-earner couples vs. one-earner couples).

The net lifetime value of benefits is the actuarial present value of all expected benefits to the retired worker and his survivors (given gender, age, income, and marital circumstances), less that present cost of all expected costs (i.e., payroll taxes paid by employee and employer).

The Medicare prescription drug program, signed into law by President George W. Bush, has been factored into the calculator; however, the calculator does not include the benefits associated with disability.

Certain simplifying assumptions were made by Steuerle and Carasso: They assumed that workers were employed from ages 22 through 65, with 5 years off from ages 30 to 34. They assumed that husbands and wives were of the same age, and that their children were fully grown (an ineligible for benefits) by the time the parents applied for benefits. For all long-term projections, Steuerle and Carasso used the April, 2004 intermediate economic and demographic assumptions made by the Social Security Trustees. A real (after inflation) interest rate of 2 percent was used for present value/cost calculations.

The calculator can be accessed on the Web site of the Urban Institute at http://www.urban.org/publications/900746.html.

*Appendix B 14. Estimation Of Medicare Lifetime Net Benefits (relates to page 216)*

Medicare lifetime net benefits were estimated in a two-step process. First, the expected net benefits were determined for retirees in each of 5 different beneficiary categories: two-earner couples, men with stay-at-home-wives, women with stay-at-home husbands, single men, and single women. This was done separately for Democrats and Republicans, using their respective earnings within each category, as estimated on the basis of wage information from the GSS surveys conducted from 1991 through 2004, and using the USA Today Web-based calculator (see Appendix B 13) to estimate the appropriate benefit amounts within the categories. The results of step one are shown in Table 62, and all differences are entirely attributable to differences in average income between Democrats and Republicans.

*Table 62. Estimated net Medicare benefits for people with different marital status and different work-sharing arrangements. Differences between Democrats and Republicans are due to different income levels.*

| Average net Medicare benefits for all income brackets and for people reaching age 65 between 2005 and 2045 | Dems in $s | Reps in $s |
|---|---|---|
| Married, with spouse who works full-time (benefit each) | 209,600 | 205,100 |
| Married men, with spouse who works part-time or less | 463,300 | 444,600 |
| Married women, with spouse who works part-time or less | 476,300 | 471,400 |
| Single man | 196,500 | 193,700 |
| Single woman | 241,300 | 241,300 |

The second step was simply to multiply the figures shown in Table 62, above, times the percentages of Democrats and Republicans within each broad category. The results are shown in Table 63.

*Table 63. Estimated net Medicare benefits for people turning 65 in years 2005 through 2045*

| Party » | Democrats | | | Republicans | | |
|---|---|---|---|---|---|---|
| Status | % in the category | $—amt. per Table 62 | % times dollar amt. | % in the category | $—amt. per Table 62 | % times dollar amt. |
| Married and spouse works full-time | 0.41 | 209,600 | 85,936 | 0.50 | 205,100 | 102,550 |
| Married and spouse works part-time or not at all — men | 0.07 | 463,300 | 32,431 | 0.14 | 444,600 | 62,244 |
| Married and spouse works part-time or not at all — women | 0.00 | 476,300 | 0 | 0.01 | 471,400 | 4,714 |
| Single men | 0.19 | 196,500 | 37,335 | 0.19 | 193,700 | 36,803 |
| Single women | 0.33 | 241,300 | 79,629 | 0.16 | 241,300 | 38,608 |
| Total benefits | 1.00 | | 235,331 | 1.00 | | 244,919 |

The bottom line of Table 63 shows us that, during his lifetime, the average Republican will get slightly more in net benefits than his Democratic counterpart. The amount is not statistically significant, and this is the also the case when the calculation is done on a gender-neutral basis, as is evident from Table 64, below:

*Table 64. Estimated net Medicare benefits for people turning 65 in years 2005 through 2045 — gender neutral*

| Gender | Democrats | Republicans |
|---|---|---|
| Males | 235,500 | 251,100 |
| Females | 232,500 | 230,500 |
| Total | 468,000 | 481,600 |
| Gender neutral (average) | $234,000 | $240,800 |

*Appendix B 15. More Survey Results Related To Voting Trends (relates to page 194.)*

Figure 285, below, shows the percentages of Democrats and Republicans voting in presidential elections since 1980, based upon GSS surveys. From these results, it appears that Republican voting has been somewhat steady, while the rate of Democratic voting has fluctuated. Democrats voted at a very low rate in the Dukakis-Bush election, but at a rather high rate in the Clinton elections. However, they have never been as likely as Republicans to vote in presidenti al elections.

*Figure 285. Did you vote in the presidential election? (GSS surveys conducted between 1980 and 2004, based on, left to right, 4964, 4882, 3762, 5984, 4579, 3244, and 2400 cases, with confidence levels of, left to right, 99%, 99%, 99%, n/a, 94% (marginal), 99%, and 99%, and with relative proportions of, left to right, .94, .92, .91, n/a, .98, .97, and .93)*

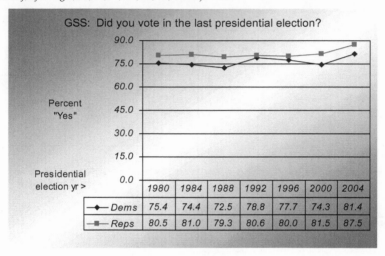

*Appendix B 16. Other Surveys Addressing The Subject Of Happiness (relates to page 233.)*

Table 65. Other surveys addressing the happiness issue

| Survey and Question | Dems | Reps | No. of cases | Conf % | *RP |
|---|---|---|---|---|---|
| Rasmussen 2006: Is your life "good or excellent"? Percentage "Yes" | 66.0 | **80.0** | **1000 | 95 | .83 |
| NES 2000: Is your life completely satisfying? Percentage "Completely satisfying" | 18.0 | 26.3 | 901 | +99 | .68 |
| Multi Investigator Study 1998-1999: "On the whole, how satisfied with your life are you these days?" Percentage "Very satisfied" | 48.8 | 59.4 | 675 | 99 | .82 |
| Economic Values Survey 1992: "On the whole, how happy are you?" Percentage "Very happy" | 43.9 | 54.0 | 1340 | +99 | .81 |

*RP is relative proportion, which is the Democratic % divided by the Republican %.

**Case numbers include independents and others in addition to Democrats and Republicans.

# Appendix C: Interpreting Survey Data

*The "Socially Desirable" Response*

A strange survey result was noted by David Moore, Senior Gallup Poll Editor.

> In a survey on Jan. 3-5, a little over a week after the earthquake in the Indian Ocean, 45 percent of respondents in a Gallup survey indicated they had already contributed money to the relief efforts for Asian countries hit by the resulting tsunami. Only four days later, in a similar survey, the same question about contributing [to] relief efforts showed that just 33 percent said they had contributed money to tsunami relief efforts.[1]

Indeed, this was odd because, after 4 days, the number of people contributing to the relief effort should have *increased* or, at least, stayed the same. Instead, there was a large drop in the percentage who gave (larger than the margin of error).

Mr. Moore identified two possible explanations for this phenomenon: The drop in reported giving was caused by a slight change in the survey question, or it was caused by a change in social pressure. The latter scenario was described by Mr. Moore:

> Perhaps during the time of the first poll, there was such a media frenzy over the disaster that people felt they almost had to say they had done something for the victims.

> Pollsters call this phenomenon a "socially desirable" response. When social norms approve of a certain behavior, some respondents are unwilling to admit that they don't conform.[2]

This "socially desirable" phenomenon could have affected the results of this book if social pressures affect the constituents of one political party more than the constituents of the other party. For example, if Republicans have a greater need to impress survey interviewers by exaggerating their achievements, the results have probably been skewed in their favor. I simply don't know if this is the case.

*The "Politically Desirable" Response*

In addition to the "socially desirable" response, I believe there may be a "politically desirable" response — particularly with respect to certain "hot-button" issues, or questions asked in the heat of a political campaign. A couple of examples were noted in Chapter 2, regarding education and intelligence. In response to a Pew survey, conducted in mid-2005, Democrats were more likely than Republi-

---

1 David W. Moore, "The Elusive Truth," *The Gallup News Service* (January 18, 2005), Retrieved July 4, 2006, from Http://brain.gallup.com.
2 Ibid.

cans to overstate the Iraq War casualty count. On the other hand, Republicans were more likely to assert that Saddam Hussein had weapons of mass destruction, even after many published reports declared that none were found. Are these indications of ignorance, or do they reflect Democratic pessimism about the war, Republican optimism about the war, and/or political posturing by each side? It is hard to tell, so I avoided such controversial questions.

With respect to Chapter 4, concerning charitable donations, there was another type of question that I avoided: those concerning very specific organizations or causes. For example, one survey asked respondents if they volunteered to assist the Boy Scouts organization. I didn't use that survey question because the results would not tell us who is more likely to volunteer for charities. Rather, it would only tell us who feels more favorably towards the Boy Scouts.

# APPENDIX D: A FEW NOTES ABOUT THE STATISTICS USED

There are no complicated statistics in this book. Where the underlying support for a chart or table is a two-column by two-row cross tabulation of dichotomous variables (e.g., the percentages of Democrats and Republicans who answered "yes" or "no" to a survey question) you will usually find the statistical "confidence level" (100% minus the probability value) and the Relative Proportion (RP), which I have defined as the percentage of Democrats responding in a certain way to a survey question divided by the percentage of Republicans responding in the same way to that same question. RP values that are close to one (1) indicate a small difference between Democrats and Republicans, whereas values that are substantially below or above one (1) indicate large differences.

Where the underlying support for a chart or table is a cross tabulation of two columns by three or more rows (e.g., the percentages of Democrats and Republicans that answered "yes," "no," or "maybe" to a survey question) you will usually find a Phi association value, which is a common measure of the statistical strength of a described relationship. When comparing means I give the confidence level based upon the T statistic or F statistic, as appropriate.

In a few cases, multiple regression analyses were prepared to help identify variables that, along with party identification, correlate with certain specific behaviors or achievements. These regressions, and most of the other statistical calculations in this book, were performed using SPSS software or the SDA Web-based statistical program, developed by the Computer-Assisted Survey Methods program at the University of California at Berkeley.

Unless otherwise noted, Democrats and Republicans include only respondents who self-identified as such. (independent "leaners" are not included.)[1]

---

[1] Neither SPSS nor the SDA program of Berkeley are responsible for how I used their programs, or the ideas or assertions in this book.

---

# Appendix E: The Superiority of the Democrat–Republican Paradigm

> In effect, the critic is saying that there are no "entities" liberalism and conservatism. Such labeling of attitudes or constellations of attitudes is scientifically unsound.
>
> — Psychologist Fred N. Kerlinger[1]

For comparisons that are political in nature, I suspect that party identification is a more reliable measurement tool than political ideology. In the United States, ideological terms such as "liberal" and "conservative" are usually self-defined, and cannot be linked to objective and observable standards (such as a party platform), or to individuals who exemplify those standards (such as political candidates). Many people are not even sure how they fit into the ideological spectrum. Gallup notes that Americans often choose multiple ideological labels, when given the opportunity:

> What is of interest is the degree to which Americans — when given a choice — choose multiple ideological labels for themselves. Much as the census bureau has decided that many Americans need to use multiple race and ethnicity labels to describe themselves, these data suggest that Americans may view themselves as fitting into several ideological "boxes" rather than just one.[2]

On the other hand, party identification can be linked to an observable candidate, office holder, and/or political platform. Admittedly, party identity is a changeable demographic, but so are political ideology, income, marital status, family size, and education. And, while it is changeable, party identification is surprisingly stable. This was noted by Rasmussen Reports in April, 2006:

> Party allegiances tend to be quite stable over time. Despite the enormous news and political events of the past 27 months, the gap between Republicans and Democrats has never varied by more than 3.4 percentage points from the highest to the lowest.[3]

It is true that, over longer time-spans, significant numbers of Democrats and Republicans join the opposing party. (See Figure 197.) However, the relative attributes of the parties remain fairly constant — even though the people com-

---

1 Kerlinger, *Liberalism and Conservatism*, 4.

2 Joseph Carroll, "Many Americans Use Multiple Labels to Describe Their Ideology," *The Gallup News Service* (December 6, 2006), Retrieved January 2, 2007, from Http://brain.gallup.com.

3 "37% Democrats, 34% Republicans," *The Gallup News Service* (April 10, 2006), Retrieved December 27, 2006, from http://www.rasmussenreports.com/2006/April%20Dailies/Partisan%20Trends.htm.

prising them change. (If one doubts this, consult many 50-year trend graphs in Appendix A, starting on page 317.)

One might argue that partisanship is simply a collection or running tally of individual political assessments. However, there is evidence suggesting that this is not the case. In 2002, Larry Bartels (Princeton University) analyzed panel survey data in an examination of the impact of long-term partisan loyalties on perceptions of specific political individuals and events. In "Beyond the Running Tally: Partisan Bias in Political Perceptions," he reports:

> Taken as a whole, my analysis provides strong evidence of "the influence of party identification on attitudes toward the perceived elements of politics" (Campbell et al., 1960, p. 135). Far from being a mere summary of more specific political opinions, partisanship is a powerful and pervasive influence on perceptions of political events.[4]

Another political scientist, Paul Goren, examined data from NES surveys and reached a similar conclusion:

> [P]artisan identities are more stable and resistant to change than abstract beliefs about equal opportunity, limited government, traditional family values, and moral tolerance. ... [P]arty identification systematically constrains beliefs about equal opportunity, limited government, and moral tolerance. This influence, while far from overwhelming, is substantively meaningful, and therefore, can produce genuine shifts in value preferences over extended periods of time.[5]

Thus, there is evidence that party identification is strong and stable.

There is another reason I prefer the Democrat-Republican paradigm: It is less misleading. During the last 35 years, 25 to 50 percent of all self-identified "conservatives" have been Democrats, and I simply do not believe most people are aware of that fact. My studies have shown that these Democratic conservatives are quite different, education-wise, from Republican conservatives. (See Chapter 11.) Combining these two distinct types of "conservatives" is a bit misleading, and is best avoided.

For all of these reasons, I believe that comparisons based on political party identification are generally preferable to those based upon political ideology.

---

4 Larry M. Bartels, "Beyond the Running Tally: Partisan Bias in Political Perceptions," *Political Behavior* 24, no. 2 (June, 2002): 120.
5 Goren, "Party Identification and Core Political Values."

## Appendix F: Survey Sources Used

For the most part, this book was produced by extracting and processing data from several large and well-respected surveys. Although I am very grateful for the access I was given to this information, the reader should understand that any opinions, findings and conclusions or recommendations expressed in this book are mine, and do not necessarily reflect the views of the surveying entities or their funding organizations. They bear no responsibility for the analyses or interpretations of the data presented herein.

In particular, I relied heavily upon the following sources:

The 1948-2004 American National Election Studies (NES) [machine readable data file] produced by Stanford University and the University of Michigan in 2005. NES is based on work supported by the National Science Foundation under Grant Numbers: SBR-9707741, SBR-9317631, SES-9209410, SES-9009379, SES-88008361, SES-8341310, SES-8207580, and SOC77-08885.

The 1972-2006 General Social Survey (GSS) [machine readable data file]. Principal Investigator, James A. Davis; Director and Co-Principal Investigator, Tom W. Smith; Co-Principal Investigator, Peter V. Marsden, NORC ed. Chicago: National Opinion Research Center, producer, 2005; Storrs, CT: The Roper Center for Public Opinion Research, University of Connecticut, distributor. 1 data file (51,020 logical records and 1 codebook (2,552 pp).

Several surveys conducted and reported on by The Pew Research Center for the People & the Press, Washington, DC, which is sponsored by The Pew Charitable Trusts. The specific Pew surveys used are cited within the text.

Several surveys conducted and reported on by the Gallup Organization, Washington, DC. The specific Gallup surveys used are cited within the text, and can be found on the Gallup Organization Web site at www.gallup.com.

Several Michigan "State of the State" (SOSS) surveys conducted by the Institute for Public Policy and Social Research (IPPSR), which is a nonprofit entity located on the campus of the Michigan State University. The specific Michigan SOSS surveys used are cited within the text.

Harris Interactive surveys found in the Public Opinion Poll Question Data Base of the Virtual Data Center network of the Odum Institute at the University of North Carolina.

Surveys conducted by Rasmussen Reports, and available from its Web site at RasmussenReports.com.

In addition, I am extremely grateful to the Computer-Assisted Survey Methods Program at the University of California at Berkeley. Its *Survey Documentation & Analysis* Web-based documentation and analysis program (SDA) was used extensively — particularly with respect to retrieval and analysis of *General Social Surveys*.

# APPENDIX G: ACRONYMS AND ABBREVIATIONS

BLS – United States Bureau of Labor Statistics

CBO – Congressional Budget Office

Conf – Confidence level, which is generally considered to be statistically significant if it is 95 percent or higher, and marginally significant if it is between 90 and 95 percent. The confidence level is equal to one (1) minus the probability value (p-value).

EITC – Earned Income Tax Credit, a federal income tax credit aimed at helping low-income wage-earners. In essence, it is a form of welfare distributed via the tax system.

FICA – Federal Insurance Contributions Act (Social Security and Medicare tax)

Gallup – The Gallup Organization, a company conducting various surveys and polls, and issuing public reports on its findings

GSS – General Social Survey of the National Opinion Research Center at the University of Chicago (see NORC)

Harris – Harris Interactive, a company producing the Harris Poll, and other survey tools and reports

IPPSR – Institute for Public Policy and Social Research, an organization "extending scholarly expertise to Michigan's policymaking community" (see SOSS)

Marg – Marginal

NES – American National Election Studies, produced and distributed by Stanford University and the University of Michigan (Also known as ANES)

NORC – National Opinion Research Center at the University of Chicago, which produces the periodic General Social Surveys (GSS)

Pew – Pew Research Center for the People and the Press, which is sponsored by the Pew Charitable Trusts

Phi – Phi coefficient, which is a measure of the degree of association between two variables

RP – Relative proportion, which is (in this book) the percentage of Democrats responding in a certain way to a survey question divided by the percentage of Republicans responding in that same way to that same question

SDA – Survey Documentation & Analysis, a Web-based statistical program developed by the Computer-Assisted Survey Methods program at the University of California at Berkeley

SOSS – State of the State Surveys, which are a series of surveys prepared by the Institute for Public Policy and Social Research for policy makers in the State of Michigan (see IPPSR)

SPSS – Computer software designed to aid researchers in analyzing statistical data, originally known as Statistical Package for the Social Sciences

# Index

Made in the USA
San Bernardino, CA
02 December 2012